Numerical Computation, Data Analysis and Software in Mathematics and Engineering

Numerical Computation, Data Analysis and Software in Mathematics and Engineering

Editor

Yumin Cheng

MDPI • Basel • Beijing • Wuhan • Barcelona • Belgrade • Manchester • Tokyo • Cluj • Tianjin

Editor
Yumin Cheng
Shanghai University
China

Editorial Office
MDPI
St. Alban-Anlage 66
4052 Basel, Switzerland

This is a reprint of articles from the Special Issue published online in the open access journal *Mathematics* (ISSN 2227-7390) (available at: https://www.mdpi.com/journal/mathematics/special_issues/Numerical_Computation_Data_Analysis_Software).

For citation purposes, cite each article independently as indicated on the article page online and as indicated below:

LastName, A.A.; LastName, B.B.; LastName, C.C. Article Title. *Journal Name* **Year**, *Volume Number*, Page Range.

ISBN 978-3-0365-4777-0 (Hbk)
ISBN 978-3-0365-4778-7 (PDF)

© 2022 by the authors. Articles in this book are Open Access and distributed under the Creative Commons Attribution (CC BY) license, which allows users to download, copy and build upon published articles, as long as the author and publisher are properly credited, which ensures maximum dissemination and a wider impact of our publications.

The book as a whole is distributed by MDPI under the terms and conditions of the Creative Commons license CC BY-NC-ND.

Contents

About the Editor . . . . **vii**

Preface to "Numerical Computation, Data Analysis and Software in Mathematics and Engineering" . . . . **ix**

Yumin Cheng
Preface to the Special Issue on "Numerical Computation, Data Analysis and Software in Mathematics and Engineering"
Reprinted from: *Mathematics* **2022**, *10*, 2267, doi:10.3390math10132267 . . . . **1**

Zhijuan Meng, Yanan Fang and Lidong Ma
A Method for Rapid Prediction of Edge Defects in Cold Roll Forming Process
Reprinted from: *Mathematics* **2021**, *9*, 1902, doi:10.3390/math9161902 . . . . **7**

Yajie Deng, Xingkeng Shen, Jixiao Tao and Ying Dai
Analysis of Elastic–Plastic Problems Using the Improved Interpolating Complex Variable Element Free Galerkin Method
Reprinted from: *Mathematics* **2021**, *9*, 1967, doi:10.3390/math9161967 . . . . **19**

Jing Cheng
Mathematical Models and Data Analysis of Residential Land Leasing Behavior of District Governments of Beijing in China
Reprinted from: *Mathematics* **2021**, *9*, 2314, doi:10.3390/math9182314 . . . . **35**

Jufeng Wang, Fengxin Sun and Rongjun Cheng
A Dimension Splitting-Interpolating Moving Least Squares (DS-IMLS) Method with Nonsingular Weight Functions
Reprinted from: *Mathematics* **2021**, *9*, 2424, doi:10.3390/math9192424 . . . . **49**

Huimin Liu, Rongjun Cheng and Tingliu Xu
Analysis of a Novel Two-Dimensional Lattice Hydrodynamic Model Considering Predictive Effect
Reprinted from: *Mathematics* **2021**, *9*, 2464, doi:10.3390/math9192464 . . . . **71**

Xiaona Fan, Yu Guo, Qin Zhao and Yiyun Zhu
Structural Optimization and Application Research of Alkali-Activated Slag Ceramsite Compound Insulation Block Based on Finite Element Method
Reprinted from: *Mathematics* **2021**, *9*, 2488, doi:10.3390/math9192488 . . . . **85**

Fengxin Sun, Jufeng Wang, Xiang Kong and Rongjun Cheng
A Dimension Splitting Generalized Interpolating Element-Free Galerkin Method for the Singularly Perturbed Steady Convection–Diffusion–Reaction Problems
Reprinted from: *Mathematics* **2021**, *9*, 2524, doi:10.3390/math9192524 . . . . **107**

Jing-Ang Zhu, Yetong Jia, Jincheng Lei and Zishun Liu
Deep Learning Approach to Mechanical Property Prediction of Single-Network Hydrogel
Reprinted from: *Mathematics* **2021**, *9*, 2804, doi:10.3390/math9212804 . . . . **123**

Li Li, Jiahui Yu, Hang Cheng and Miaojuan Peng
A Smart Helmet-Based PLS-BPNN Error Compensation Model for Infrared Body Temperature Measurement of Construction Workers during COVID-19
Reprinted from: *Mathematics* **2021**, *9*, 2808, doi:10.3390/math9212808 . . . . **145**

Zili Dai, Jinwei Xie, Zhitang Lu, Shiwei Qin and Lin Wang
Numerical Modeling on Crack Propagation Based on a Multi-Grid Bond-Based Dual-Horizon Peridynamics
Reprinted from: *Mathematics* **2021**, *9*, 2848, doi:10.3390/math9222848 . . . . **165**

Hongxia Ge, Siteng Li and Chunyue Yan
An Extended Car-Following Model Based on Visual Angle and Electronic Throttle Effect
Reprinted from: *Mathematics* **2021**, *9*, 2879, doi:10.3390/math9222879 . . . . **185**

Jinfei Chai
Research on Dynamic Response Characteristics for Basement Structure of Heavy Haul Railway Tunnel with Defects
Reprinted from: *Mathematics* **2021**, *9*, 2893, doi:10.3390/math9222893 . . . . **203**

Huimin Liu and Yuhong Wang
Impact of Strong Wind and Optimal Estimation of Flux Difference Integral in a Lattice Hydrodynamic Model
Reprinted from: *Mathematics* **2021**, *9*, 2897, doi:10.3390/math9222897 . . . . **227**

Heng Cheng and Miaojuan Peng
The Improved Element-Free Galerkin Method for 3D Helmholtz Equations
Reprinted from: *Mathematics* **2022**, *10*, 14, doi:10.3390/math10010014 . . . . **241**

About the Editor

Yumin Cheng

Dr. Yumin Cheng is a Professor at the Shanghai Institute of Applied Mathematics and Mechanics and Shanghai University. His research interests include the meshless method, boundary element method, and scientific and engineering computing. He has published more than 180 journal papers with 5100 citations. His h-index in scopus.com is 47. He has been honored as a Fellow of The International Association of Applied Mechanics (IAAM), Fellow of International Association of Advanced materials and at the VEBLEO Fellow awards. He is an Executive Committee member of IAAM and Chairman of Committee of IAAM Standards and Codes. He has been Lead Guest Editor of the Special Issues of *Mathematical Problems in Engineering* and *CMES-Computer Modeling in Engineering & Sciences*, and he is Associate Editor of the *International Journal of Computers*, Editor and Member of the Editorial Board of the *International Journal of Applied Mechanics*, and Member of the Editorial Board of *Mathematics, International Journal of Computational Materials Science and Engineering, Journal of Computational Engineering, International Journal of Applied & Experimental Mathematics*, and *International Journal of Mathematical Physics and Video Proceedings of Advanced Materials*.

Preface to "Numerical Computation, Data Analysis and Software in Mathematics and Engineering"

In recent years, mathematical models, numerical methods and data analysis have been paid more attention. After the finite-element method, the meshless method is another effective tool for solving science and enginnering problems. Numerical methods, such as the finite-element method, boundary element method and meshless method, have played important roles in numerical simulations of complicated problems in the science, engineering and society fields. Various numerical methods are presented to solve problems in different fields, and their corresponding computational efficiency, accuracy and convergence are also studied. With the development of big data, numerical simulation based on data analysis or big data will be an important direction for science and engineering computation. Deep learning is another new and effective approach to analyzing the properties of new materials.

The present book contains 14 articles that were accepted for publication in the Special Issue "Numerical Computation, Data Analysis and Software in Mathematics and Engineering" of the MDPI journal *Mathematics*. These articles were published in Volumes 9 (2021) and 10 (2022) of the journal. The topics of these articles include the aspects of meshless method, numerical simulation, mathematical model, deep learning and data analysis. Meshless methods, such as the improved element-free Galerkin method, the dimension-splitting, interpolating, moving, least squares method, the dimension-splitting, generalized, interpolating, element-free Galerkin method and the improved interpolating, complex-variable, element-free Galerkin method, are presented for some problems. Some complicated problems, such as the cold roll-forming process, ceramsite compound insulation block, crack propagation and heavy-haul railway tunnel with defects are numerically analyzed. Mathematical models, such as the lattice hydrodynamic model, extended car-following model and smart helmet-based PLS-BPNN Error compensation model, have been proposed. The use of the deep learning approach to predict the mechanical properties of single-network hydrogel is presented, and land-leasing data are analyzed and discussed. As the Guest Editor of this Special Issue, I am grateful to the authors of these articles for their high-quality contributions, to the reviewers for their valuable comments and to the administrative staff of MDPI publications for their support in completing this Special Issue. Special thanks to the Section Managing Editor Ms. Linn Li for her collaboration and valuable assisstance.

Yumin Cheng
Editor

Editorial

Preface to the Special Issue on "Numerical Computation, Data Analysis and Software in Mathematics and Engineering"

Yumin Cheng

Shanghai Key Laboratory of Mechanics in Energy Engineering, Shanghai Institute of Applied Mathematics and Mechanics, School of Mechanics and Engineering Science, Shanghai University, Shanghai 200072, China; ymcheng@shu.edu.cn

In recent years, mathematical models, numerical methods and data analysis have been paid more attention. After the finite element method was introduced, the meshless method became another effective tool for solving scientific and engineering problems. Numerical methods, such as the finite element method, boundary element method and meshless method, have played important roles in the numerical simulations of complicated problems in the fields of science, engineering and society. Various numerical methods have been presented for solving problems in different fields, and the corresponding computational efficiency, accuracy and convergence have been studied as well. With the development of big data, numerical simulations based on data analysis or big data will be an important direction for computation in science and engineering.

The objective of this Special Issue is to summarize the most recent developments of numerical simulations and data analysis within the last five years, especially for new problems. Many papers were submitted to this Special Issue for consideration for publication, and finally, fourteen papers were accepted after undergoing a careful peer-review process based on criteria of quality and novelty. These papers include aspects of the meshless method, numerical simulation, mathematical models, deep learning and data analysis. Meshless methods, such as the improved element-free Galerkin method, the dimension-splitting interpolating moving least-squares method, the dimension-splitting generalized interpolating element-free Galerkin method and the improved interpolating complex variable element-free Galerkin method, are presented for various problems. Some complicated problems, such as the cold roll forming process, ceramsite compound insulation blocks, crack propagation and heavy haul railway tunnels with defects are analyzed numerically. Mathematical models, such as lattice hydrodynamic models, extended car-following models and smart-helmet-based PLS-BPNN error compensation models, are proposed. Of particular note, a deep learning approach to predict the mechanical properties of a single-network hydrogel is presented, and data analysis for land leasing is discussed.

The improved element-free Galerkin (IEFG) method [1], which is based on the improved moving least-squares (IMLS) approximation [2], is an important meshless method. In the paper submitted to this Special Issue by Cheng et al. [3], the IEFG method for solving three-dimensional (3D) Helmholtz equations is proposed. The IMLS approximation is used to form the trial function, the penalty method is used to enforce the essential boundary conditions and Galerkin weak form of 3D Helmholtz equations are used to obtain the final discretized equations. The influences of the node distribution, the weight functions, the scale parameters of the influence domain and the penalty factors on the computational accuracy of the solutions are analyzed. The numerical results show that the proposed method in this paper can not only enhance the computational speed of the element-free Galerkin method but can also eliminate the phenomenon of the singular matrix.

In the paper submitted to this Special Issue by Deng et al. [4], the improved interpolating complex variable element-free Galerkin (IICVEFG) method for solving two-dimensional (2D) nonlinear elastoplasticity problems is proposed. The improved interpolating complex variable moving least-squares method, which is based on the complex variable moving least-squares approximation [5] and improved interpolating moving least-squares method [6], is used to obtain the trial function of the increment in the displacement. The integral weak form of 2D elastoplasticity problem, which is described with the increments in the displacement, stain and stress, is used to obtain the discretized equations. The incremental tangent stiffness matrix method is used to solve the discretized equations. The numerical examples show that the IICVEFG method has good convergence and high computational precision and efficiency.

The dimension-splitting method (DSM) has been introduced into meshless methods, such as the improved element-free Galerkin method [7], the improved complex variable element-free Galerkin method [8,9] and the reproducing kernel particle method [10,11], to improve computational efficiency. In the paper submitted to this Special Issue by Wang et al. [12], the DSM is combined with the improved interpolating moving least-squares (IIMLS) method based on a nonsingular weight function to propose a dimension-splitting–interpolating moving least-squares (DS-IMLS) method with high approximation accuracy. Then, an improved interpolating element-free Galerkin method for 2D potential problems is presented. In the improved interpolating element-free Galerkin method, the DS-IMLS method and the Galerkin weak form are used to obtain the discrete equations of the problem. Numerical examples show that the DS-IMLS and the improved IEFG methods have high accuracy.

In the paper submitted to this Special Issue by Sun et al. [13], by introducing the DSM into the generalized element-free Galerkin (GEFG) method, a dimension splitting generalized interpolating element-free Galerkin (DS-GIEFG) method is presented for analyzing the singularly perturbed steady convection-diffusion-reaction (CDR) problems. By using the DSM, a 2D CDR problem is transformed into a series of lower-dimensional problems. The IIMLS method is combined with the GEFG method to obtain the discrete equations on the subdivision plane. Finally, the IIMLS method is applied to assemble the discrete equations of the entire problem. Some examples are solved to verify the effectiveness of the DS-GIEFG method. The numerical results show that the numerical solution converges to the analytical solution with the decrease in node spacing, and the DS-GIEFG method has high computational efficiency and accuracy.

In recent years, big data and data analysis have been paid more and more attention. In the paper submitted to this Special Issue by Cheng [14], based on city data, the mathematical models of the price and the total area of the leased residential land are presented to analyze the leasing behavior of residential land in Beijing. The variables of the mathematical models are proposed by analyzing the factors influencing the district government's leasing behavior for residential land based on the leasing rights for residential land in Beijing. The regression formulae of the mathematical models are obtained with the ordinary least-squares method. Based on the data of the districts in Beijing from 2004 to 2015, the numerical results of the coefficients in the mathematical models are obtained. The numerical results show the factors influence the leased price and the total leased area of residential land for this large city in China, which is in agreement with the conclusion of the previous publications [15]. Finally, policy implications for the district government regarding residential land leasing in Beijing are proposed. The results of the data analysis can be referenced by the governments to make better policy.

In the paper submitted to this Special Issue by Liu et al. [16], a novel 2D lattice hydrodynamic model considering a driver's predictive effect is proposed. The stability condition of the model is obtained by performing the linear stability analysis method. The kink–antikink of the modified Korteweg–de Vries (mKdV) equation is obtained to describe the propagation characteristics of the traffic density flow waves near the critical point. The numerical results are in agreement with those of the theoretical analysis, which indicates that the predictive effect of drivers can effectively avoid traffic congestion and that the fraction of eastbound cars can also improve the stability of traffic flow to a certain extent.

In another paper submitted to this Special Issue by Liu et al. [17], a modified lattice hydrodynamic model considering the impact of strong wind and the optimal estimation of flux difference integral is proposed. Based on the control theory, the stability condition is acquired through linear analysis. The modified mKdV equation is obtained via a nonlinear analysis to express a description of the evolution of density waves. From the numerical results, it is shown that strong wind can largely influence the stability of traffic flow and that the optimal estimation of the flux difference integral contributes to stabilizing the traffic flow.

In the paper submitted to this Special Issue by Ge et al. [18], based on the visual angle model (VAM), a car-following model considering the electronic throttle angle of the preceding vehicle is proposed. The time-dependent Ginzburg–Landau (TDGL) equation and the modified mKdV equation are obtained. The numerical results are obtained by using MATLAB software to verify the validity of the model. From the numerical simulations, it is shown that the visual angle and electronic throttle can improve traffic stability.

As a kind of soft material, the large deformation of hydrogel is very complicated [19]. With the developments of deep learning and data analysis, complex network has been applied in many fields in science and engineering [20]. In the paper submitted to this Special Issue by Zhu et al. [21], based on the complex network structure of hydrogel with inhomogeneous and random distribution of polymer chains, a deep learning approach to predict the mechanical properties of hydrogels from polymer network structures is presented. The network structural models of hydrogels are constructed from the mesoscopic scale by using the self-avoiding walk method. Then, two deep learning models are proposed to capture the nonlinear mapping from mesoscopic hydrogel network structural model to its macroscale mechanical property. A deep neural network and a 3D convolutional neural network containing the physical information of the network structural model are implemented to predict the nominal stress–stretch curves of hydrogels under uniaxial tension. The results show that the deep learning models are able to capture the internal relationship between complex network structures and mechanical properties.

With the spread of COVID-19 in the world, the implementation of personnel health monitoring in construction sites has become an important problem in construction management. The paper submitted to this Special Issue by Li et al. [22] develops a smart helmet equipped with an infrared temperature sensor and conducts a simulated construction experiment to collect data of temperature and its influencing factors in indoor and outdoor construction operation environments. A partial least-square–back propagation neural network (PLS-BPNN) model is presented to correct the temperature measurement results of the smart helmet. The temperature compensation effects of different models were also compared, and the results show that the PLS-BPNN model has higher accuracy and reliability.

The paper submitted to this Special Issue by Meng et al. [23] proposes a new analytical method to predict the edge defects in the cold roll forming process based on the mean longitudinal strain of the racks. A cubic spline curve with the parameters of the cumulative chord length is applied to fit the corresponding points and center points of different passes. By comparing the mean longitudinal strain between racks and the yield strain of the material, it can be judged whether or not there are defects at the edges. The results of the analytical method are compared with the ones of the non-linear finite element software ABAQUS to show the correctness of the method. This method can predict the roll forming effect quickly and the position where a greater longitudinal strain occurred can be determined.

Peridynamics is a nonlocal theory of continuum mechanics, and it can describe crack formation and propagation without defining any fracture rules in advance. In the paper submitted to this Special Issue by Dai et al. [24], a multi-grid bond-based dual-horizon peridynamics (DH-PD) model is presented, which includes varying horizon sizes and can avoid spurious wave reflections. This model incorporates the volume correction, surface correction, and a technique of nonuniformity discretization to improve calculation accuracy and efficiency. Two benchmark problems are simulated to verify the reliability of the proposed model with the effect of the volume correction and surface correction on the computational accuracy confirmed. In addition, two numerical examples are given to verify the computational accuracy of the corrected DH-PD model and its advantages over some other models, such as the traditional peridynamics model.

In the paper submitted to this Special Issue by Fan et al. [25], the effects of different numbers of the rows and the ratios of holes on the thermal and mechanical performances of an alkali-activated slag ceramsite compound insulation block are analyzed by using the finite element analysis software ANSYS CFX. From the multi-objective optimization analysis, the alkali-activated slag ceramsite compound insulation block with the optimal comprehensive performance is determined. Finally, the improvement effect of the wall of the alkali-activated slag ceramsite compound insulation block on the indoor thermal environment relative to an ordinary block wall is analyzed.

In the paper submitted to this Special Issue by Chai [26], an elastoplastic damage constitutive model of concrete is obtained based on the basic principle of thermodynamics. The dynamic response and damage distribution of the base structure of a heavy-duty railway tunnel with defects are analyzed numerically according to the constitutive model. By analyzing the response characteristics of the tunnel basement structure under different surrounding rock softening degrees, different foundation suspension range and different foundation structure damage degree are determined. The numerical results of post-peak softening are in good agreement with the ones of the test.

As the Guest Editor of the Special Issue, I am grateful to the authors of these articles for their quality contributions, to the reviewers for their valuable comments and to the administrative staff of the MDPI publications for the support to complete this Special Issue. Special thanks to the Section Managing Editor Ms. Linn Li for her excellent collaboration and valuable assistance. I hope that these published papers will be impactful in the fields of numerical method and data analysis and that the methods in these papers will be used for solving complicated science and engineering problems.

Funding: This research received no external funding.

Conflicts of Interest: The author declares no conflict of interest.

References

1. Zheng, G.; Cheng, Y. The Improved Element-Free Galerkin Method for Diffusional Drug Release Problems. *Int. J. Appl. Mech.* **2020**, *12*, 2050096. [CrossRef]
2. Yu, S.; Peng, M.; Cheng, H.; Cheng, Y. The improved element-free Galerkin method for three-dimensional elastoplasticity problems. *Eng. Anal. Bound. Elem.* **2019**, *104*, 215–224. [CrossRef]
3. Cheng, H.; Peng, M. The Improved Element-Free Galerkin Method for 3D Helmholtz Equations. *Mathematics* **2022**, *10*, 14. [CrossRef]
4. Deng, Y.; Shen, X.; Tao, J.; Dai, Y. Analysis of Elastic–Plastic Problems Using the Improved Interpolating Complex Variable Element Free Galerkin Method. *Mathematics* **2021**, *9*, 1967. [CrossRef]
5. Peng, M.; Liu, P.; Cheng, Y. The complex variable element-free galerkin (CVEFG) method for two-dimensional elasticity problems. *Int. J. Appl. Mech.* **2009**, *1*, 367–385. [CrossRef]
6. Ren, H.; Cheng, Y. The interpolating element-free galerkin (IEFG) method for two-dimensional elasticity problems. *Int. J. Appl. Mech.* **2011**, *3*, 735–758. [CrossRef]
7. Meng, Z.J.; Cheng, H.; Ma, L.D.; Cheng, Y.M. The hybrid element-free Galerkin method for three-dimensional wave propagation problems. *Int. J. Numer. Methods Eng.* **2019**, *117*, 15–37. [CrossRef]
8. Cheng, H.; Peng, M.; Cheng, Y. A Fast Complex Variable Element-Free Galerkin Method for Three-Dimensional Wave Propagation Problems. *Int. J. Appl. Mech.* **2017**, *9*, 1750090. [CrossRef]
9. Cheng, H.; Peng, M.; Cheng, Y. The dimension splitting and improved complex variable element-free Galerkin method for 3-dimensional transient heat conduction problems. *Int. J. Numer. Methods Eng.* **2018**, *114*, 321–345. [CrossRef]
10. Peng, P.; Wu, Q.; Cheng, Y. The dimension splitting reproducing kernel particle method for three-dimensional potential problems. *Int. J. Numer. Methods Eng.* **2020**, *121*, 146–164. [CrossRef]
11. Peng, P.; Fu, Y.; Cheng, Y. A Hybrid Reproducing Kernel Particle Method for Three-Dimensional Advection-Diffusion Problems. *Int. J. Appl. Mech.* **2021**, *13*, 2150085. [CrossRef]

12. Wang, J.; Sun, F.; Cheng, R. A Dimension Splitting-Interpolating Moving Least Squares (DS-IMLS) Method with Nonsingular Weight Functions. *Mathematics* **2021**, *9*, 2424. [CrossRef]
13. Sun, F.; Wang, J.; Kong, X.; Cheng, R. A Dimension Splitting Generalized Interpolating Element-Free Galerkin Method for the Singularly Perturbed Steady Convection–Diffusion–Reaction Problems. *Mathematics* **2021**, *9*, 2524. [CrossRef]
14. Cheng, J. Mathematical Models and Data Analysis of Residential Land Leasing Behavior of District Governments of Beijing in China. *Mathematics* **2021**, *9*, 2314. [CrossRef]
15. Cheng, J.; Luo, X. Analyzing the Land Leasing Behavior of the Government of Beijing, China, via the Multinomial Logit Model. *Land* **2022**, *11*, 376. [CrossRef]
16. Liu, H.; Cheng, R.; Xu, T. Analysis of a Novel Two-Dimensional Lattice Hydrodynamic Model Considering Predictive Effect. *Mathematics* **2021**, *9*, 2464. [CrossRef]
17. Liu, H.; Wang, Y. Impact of Strong Wind and Optimal Estimation of Flux Difference Integral in a Lattice Hydrodynamic Model. *Mathematics* **2021**, *9*, 2897. [CrossRef]
18. Ge, H.; Li, S.; Yan, C. An Extended Car-Following Model Based on Visual Angle and Electronic Throttle Effect. *Mathematics* **2021**, *9*, 2879. [CrossRef]
19. Liu, Z.; Toh, W.; Ng, T.Y. Advances in Mechanics of Soft Materials: A Review of Large Deformation Behavior of Hydrogels. *Int. J. Appl. Mech.* **2015**, *7*, 1530001. [CrossRef]
20. Cheng, J.; Xie, Y.; Zhang, J. Industry structure optimization via the complex network of industry space: A case study of Jiangxi Province in China. *J. Clean. Prod.* **2022**, *338*, 130602. [CrossRef]
21. Zhu, J.-A.; Jia, Y.; Lei, J.; Liu, Z. Deep Learning Approach to Mechanical Property Prediction of Single-Network Hydrogel. *Mathematics* **2021**, *9*, 2804. [CrossRef]
22. Li, L.; Yu, J.; Cheng, H.; Peng, M. A Smart Helmet-Based PLS-BPNN Error Compensation Model for Infrared Body Temperature Measurement of Construction Workers during COVID-19. *Mathematics* **2021**, *9*, 2808. [CrossRef]
23. Meng, Z.; Fang, Y.; Ma, L. A Method for Rapid Prediction of Edge Defects in Cold Roll Forming Process. *Mathematics* **2021**, *9*, 1902. [CrossRef]
24. Dai, Z.; Xie, J.; Lu, Z.; Qin, S.; Wang, L. Numerical Modeling on Crack Propagation Based on a Multi-Grid Bond-Based Dual-Horizon Peridynamics. *Mathematics* **2021**, *9*, 2848. [CrossRef]
25. Fan, X.; Guo, Y.; Zhao, Q.; Zhu, Y. Structural Optimization and Application Research of Alkali-Activated Slag Ceramsite Compound Insulation Block Based on Finite Element Method. *Mathematics* **2021**, *9*, 2488. [CrossRef]
26. Chai, J. Research on Dynamic Response Characteristics for Basement Structure of Heavy Haul Railway Tunnel with Defects. *Mathematics* **2021**, *9*, 2893. [CrossRef]

A Method for Rapid Prediction of Edge Defects in Cold Roll Forming Process

Zhijuan Meng [1], Yanan Fang [1] and Lidong Ma [2,3,*]

[1] School of Applied Science, Taiyuan University of Science and Technology, Taiyuan 030024, China; mengzj@tyust.edu.cn (Z.M.); S20201801009@stu.tyust.edu.cn (Y.F.)
[2] School of Mechanical Engineering, Taiyuan University of Science and Technology, Taiyuan 030024, China
[3] Coordinative Innovation Center of Taiyuan Heavy Machinery Equipment, Taiyuan University of Science and Technology, Taiyuan 030024, China
* Correspondence: mald@tyust.edu.cn

Abstract: In order to implement rapid prediction of edge defects in the cold roll forming process, a new analytical method based on the mean longitudinal strain of the racks is presented. A cubic spline curve with the parameters of the cumulative chord length is applied to fit the corresponding points and center points of different passes, and fitting curves are obtained. As the cold roll forming is micro-tension forming, the tensions between racks are ignored. Then the mean longitudinal strains between racks are obtained. By comparing the mean longitudinal strain between racks and the yield strain of the material, we can judge whether there are defects at the edges. Finally, the reasonableness of this method is illustrated and validated by an example. With this method, the roll forming effect can be quickly predicted, and the position where a greater longitudinal strain occurred can be determined. In order to prevent the defects, the deformation angles need to be modified when the result is beyond the yield strain. To further prove the correctness of the theory, the results of the analytical method are compared with the ones of the non-linear finite element software ABAQUS. The analytical results have the same trend as the finite element results. This method can provide useful guidance to the actual design process.

Keywords: cold-roll forming; longitudinal strain; cubic spline function; cumulative chord

1. Introduction

Cold roll forming (CRF) is a continuous bending operation during which a long strip of metal is passed through consecutive sets of rolls, each performing only an incremental part of the bend until the desired cross-section profile is obtained [1]. At present, the main research methods of roll forming are the analytical method, finite element method and finite strip method [2]. In the early days, the main research method used by experts and scholars is the analytical method, and with the rapid development of computer technology, the computing speed has significantly improved, the finite element method and finite strip method have been the mainstream approach to the process of the roll forming. The meshless method is a new numerical method developed after the finite element method [3–6]. Heislita [7] simulated the cold roll forming process with a 3-dimension (3D) finite element method (FEM) code PAM-STAMP. Brunet [8] simulated the process with a combined 2D and 3D FEM code. Han [9–12] studied the cold roll forming process of a channel section, welded pipes, a thick channel section and a channel section with the outer edge with the spline finite strip method (SFSM). Liu [13] used MARC to study the forming of high-strength steel cold forming. However, the finite element method and finite strip method are still faced with the problem of excessive computation time. Cheng [14–19] proposed a fast method for solving 3D problems. For the technology of cold roll forming, the main defects are edge waves, folds and so on, and these types of defects arise mainly due to the large longitudinal strain. Before numerical methods were applied to the rolling in the 1980s, engineers calculated the roll forming parameters relying on experiences and some of the existing glancing analytical methods. The basic idea of these analytical methods is calculating the elongation of longitudinal fiber to predict the forming process. Angel [20] proposed the linear deformation model. Firstly, connect the corresponding points of two adjacent roll passes using straight lines, and then calculate the elongation of the line and the distance of the two racks. Bhattacharyya et al. [21] calculated the length of deformation in a transition zone and used the length of a transition zone to calculate the elongation, but the length of this smooth transition needs the experimental device or experiences to determine, and the actual process is very complicated. Nakajima and Miznutani [22] proposed a model of longitudinal strain and gave an approximate formula to calculate the longitudinal strain. Walker and Pick [23,24] used the cubic B spline function to fit the whole surface, and the longitudinal strain they defined is

$$\varepsilon = \frac{\sqrt{\left(\frac{dx}{dv}\right)^2 + \left(\frac{dy}{dv}\right)^2 + \left(\frac{dz}{dv}\right)^2} - \sqrt{\left(\frac{dx}{dv}\right)^2 + \left(\frac{dy}{dv}\right)^2 + \left(\frac{dz}{dv}\right)^2}datum}{\sqrt{\left(\frac{dx}{dv}\right)^2 + \left(\frac{dy}{dv}\right)^2 + \left(\frac{dz}{dv}\right)^2}datum}. \quad (1)$$

Zhang [25] utilized the updated Lagrangian method of elastic-plastic large-deformation spline finite strip method to analyze cold-rolled forming and deal with boundary conditions, and Zhang [26] combined theoretical formulas and new analytical models on the previous basis to simulate the pipe forming process.

In recent years, roll forming technology has been developed rapidly and widely used in the manufacturing field. Therefore, the defects caused by the longitudinal strain in the roll forming process have become a research hotspot. JOO et al. [27] studied the flexible roll forming process of variable cross-section profiles and analyzed the effect of geometrical parameters such as base section width, side wall height and flange width on the longitudinal strain. Woo et al. [28] used FEM simulation and experiment to study the influence of profile flange length on the transverse distribution of longitudinal strain in flexible roll forming, and the result showed that the longitudinal strain and longitudinal bow decrease with increasing flange length for a trapezoid and a concave blank. Abeyrathna et al. [29] researched the effect of process and part shape parameters on the peak longitudinal edge strain, longitudinal bow and spring back for three different advanced high-strength steel (AHSS) and Ultra High Strength Steel (UHSS) commonly used in automotive manufacturing. Liu et al. [30] proposed a mathematical model to predict the bend angle distribution and longitudinal strain development in the deformation process. Sun et al. [31] took the chain-die forming as the research object, studied permanent longitudinal strain and the web-warping in the forming process. Rezaei [32] used Abaqus software to perform finite element simulation, obtained longitudinal edge strain and web warpage in the transition zone, and calculated the edge longitudinal strain in this zone. Wang [33] showed that the necessary condition for longitudinal bending deformation is the linear distribution of longitudinal fibers. Su [34,35] studied the roll forming process and springback based on a five-boundary condition-forming angle distribution function and analyzed the effects of plate thickness, forming angle and material yield strength on stress, strain and springback angle.

The above analytical methods have played a very important role in calculating the roll forming parameters, but there are some problems to solve. One of the problems is that the track of the formation between corresponding points cannot be scientifically fitted. The parameters of cold roll forming cannot be well designed. The spline function works well when it stimulates the small deflection curve. For the large deflection curve, the result is poor, and for the multi-valued curve, it cannot be applied. In this paper, a new cubic spline function with the parameters of cumulative chords is presented. This function is selected as the fitting function to fit the track of the formation. This method can calculate the mean longitudinal strain of strip steel more accurately. The analytical method based on the mean longitudinal strain proposed can give fast analysis for different deformation angles and different rack spacing, which can be used as an important reference before numerical simulation to speed up the optimization of numerical simulation parameters.

2. Problem Statement

Roll forming is a process in which the strip steel is gradually bent into a product with a certain cross-section shape through the action of multi-pass rolls. As shown in Figure 1, when the strip steel passes through A_1–A_5, B_1–B_5 and C_1–C_5 passes, the stress state of each longitudinal fiber on the strip steel is inconsistent. Some fibers are stretched, such as edge fiber A_5-B_5-C_5, and some fibers are compressed, such as intermediate fiber A_3-B_3-C_3. After the final forming of the product, the fiber length of each layer will become the same. If the tensile or compressive strain exceeds the ultimate elastic strain during the forming process, the material will undergo plastic deformation, which will lead to wrinkles at the edge or local waves during the final forming.

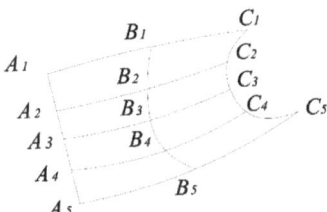

Figure 1. Schematic diagram of fiber deformation of roll forming process.

Therefore, the rapid prediction of the longitudinal strain state of each fiber in the forming process has become an effective method to predict the occurrence of defects. In the forming process, each fiber is regarded as a curve, and the defects are predicted by calculating the longitudinal strain of the curve.

It is necessary to study an analytical method to accurately and quickly fit each fiber curve. After obtaining the curve, the forming process can be predicted to a certain extent by calculating the average longitudinal strain of each curve between frames.

In this paper, a method of fitting the fiber curve by the cubic spline function with the cumulative chord length as a parameter is proposed, which can quickly predict the forming process.

3. Theoretical Derivation

The parametric equation is used to represent the fiber curve, and then the cubic spline function is used to interpolate each coordinate function. Taking these interpolation cubic spline functions as coordinate functions, it is a new curve, and this curve is regarded as the interpolation curve of the original fiber curve.

If a curve takes its own arc length as a parameter, it has the following characteristics. $p_0, p_1, \cdots, p_n$ for the two groups of value, we can determine the two single-variable spline functions $X(s)$ and $Y(s)$ in the appropriate conditions. $X(s)$ is the interpolation function of $x(s)$, and $Y(s)$ is the interpolation function of $y(s)$. If we use the curve

$$\begin{cases} x = X(s) \\ y = Y(s) \end{cases} (s_0 \leq s \leq s_n) \tag{2}$$

to fit the original curve since

$$\begin{cases} X(s_i) = x_i = x(s_i) \\ Y(s_i) = y_i = y(s_i) \end{cases} (i = 0, 1, 2, \cdots, n) \tag{3}$$

we know that the new parametric curve also drills through $p_0, p_1, \cdots, p_n$. These $n + 1$ points are the intersection of old and new curves. $X(s)$ and $Y(s)$ are the cubic spline function, so $X(s)$, $Y(s)$, $X''(s)$ and $Y''(s)$ are continuous in $[s_0, s_n]$. We can obtain that the new curve has a continuous slope and curvature.

For the original curve, S is the arc length, so $\left(\frac{dx}{ds}\right)^2 + \left(\frac{dy}{ds}\right)^2 \equiv 1$, and the following inequality for all S is tenable.

$$\left|\frac{dx}{ds}\right| \leq 1 \quad \left|\frac{dy}{ds}\right| \leq 1 \tag{4}$$

Thus, for $x(s)$ and $y(s)$, a large slope will never occur. Actually, we use the parametric spline curve to fit a group of organized points $p_0, p_1, \cdots, p_n$, which are in the same plane. In order to realize parameterization, the cumulative chord length is used to replace the arc length. Let

$$L_i = \overline{P_{i-1}P_i} \tag{5}$$

$$\begin{cases} S_0 = 0 \\ S_1 = L_1 \\ S_2 = L_1 + L_2 \\ \cdots \\ S_n = L_1 + L_2 + \ldots + L_n \end{cases} \tag{6}$$

we get interpolation curves that have the same properties as the interpolation curve with the arc length as a parameter.

The following is the detailed course to obtain the mean longitudinal strain of the racks. As shown in Figure 2, if we want to verify the process of forming a channel steel with 7 roll passes, the forming angles are $0°$, $15°$, $30°$, $45°$, $60°$, $75°$ and $90°$. Thus, 7 roll pass curves are formed. These 7 pass curves will divide the plate into 6 parts. Each roll pass curve is divided into $n - 1$ segments and get n points (the curve in Figure 2).

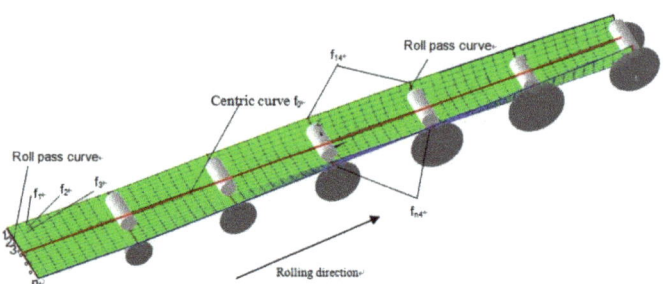

Figure 2. A schematic diagram of surface segmentation.

According to the assumption of straight normal, the points on the normal of the middle surface before deformation are still on the same normal of the surface after deformation, and the distance between the points on the normal is constant. We think the pass curve is coplanar. Apply the spline function with the cumulative chord length parameter to fit the corresponding point on each roll pass curve and form n curves $f_1, f_2, f_3, \cdots, f_n$.

Calculate the centric point for each roll pass and apply the spline function with a cumulative chord length parameter to fit each coordinate and form the curve function f_0. Divide $f_1, f_2, f_3, \cdots, f_n$ and f_0 into several parts by the racks, and define the parts as $f_{ij}(i = 1, 2, \cdots, n; j = 1, 2, \cdots, 6)$, where i represents the i-th point among n points, and j represents j-th segment in the pass that was divided into 6 segments. Each f_{ij} is divided into equidistant m points. It is better to take a big value for m, e.g., 30. The m points are connected by straight lines and calculate the length of each line segment to finally obtain the total length of the m points. In order to facilitate the description, we choose the part between the first and second rack and, respectively, record it as $L_1, L_2, L_3, \cdots, L_n$ and centric line L. Calculate the longitudinal strain of the f_{11} curve segment as $\varepsilon_1 = \ln(L_1/L)$. If the longitudinal strain is too small, ε_1 could be expressed approximately as

$$\varepsilon_1 = \frac{(L-L_1)}{L} \tag{7}$$

In the same way,

$$\begin{cases} \varepsilon_2 = \frac{(L-L_2)}{L} \\ \varepsilon_3 = \frac{(L-L_3)}{L} \\ \cdots \\ \varepsilon_n = \frac{(L-L_n)}{L} \end{cases} \tag{8}$$

where ε_n represents the nth strain between the first and the second rack. The above is only the approximate longitudinal strain; to make it more accurate, taking it into account that the cold roll forming is a micro-tension course, the tension is approximately equal to 0. Likewise, we study the part between the first and the second rack frame. The initial roll pass segment of the blank is shown in Figure 3, which is divided into $n-1$ parts corresponding to n points, which corresponds to the n strains. In order to make the results more accurate, we take the $S/2$ length of both sides (ε_1 and ε_n excluded) with each strain as the center.

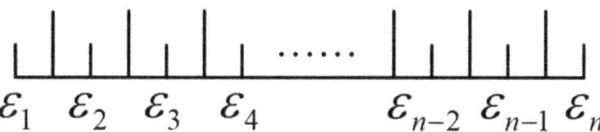

Figure 3. Partition of the cross-section.

As cold roll forming is micro-tension forming, the tensions between racks are ignored. Therefore, section tension $F = 0$. According to the basic principles of mechanics, we have

$$F = \frac{SEt\varepsilon_1}{2} + SEt\varepsilon_2 + SEt\varepsilon_3 + \ldots + \frac{SEt\varepsilon_n}{2} = 0 \tag{9}$$

Here, S is the segment length after the roll pass is equal divided into $n-1$ parts, t is the thickness, and E is the modulus of elasticity, so

$$\frac{\varepsilon_1}{2} + \varepsilon_2 + \varepsilon_3 + \ldots + \frac{\varepsilon_n}{2} = 0 \tag{10}$$

From Equations (5) and (6), we obtain

$$\frac{\varepsilon_1}{2} + \varepsilon_2 + \varepsilon_3 + \ldots + \frac{\varepsilon_n}{2} \neq 0 \tag{11}$$

Assume

$$\frac{\varepsilon_1}{2} + \varepsilon_2 + \varepsilon_3 + \ldots + \frac{\varepsilon_n}{2} = V \tag{12}$$

V is evenly divided into $n-1$ components, let $\overline{V} = V/(n-1)$

$$\varepsilon_i = \varepsilon_i - \overline{V} \ (i = 1, 2, \cdots, n) \tag{13}$$

Finally, we acquire $\varepsilon_1, \varepsilon_2, \varepsilon_3, \ldots \varepsilon_n$.

In the same way, we can obtain the strain from the 2nd rack to the 7th rack, and then we obtain the mean longitudinal strain between two adjacent racks. Define the strain as ε_{nj}, where n is the number of the roll pass points, and j is the jth segment of f_n divided by the rack.

Yield strain is the strain value when the material yields. We are usually given material yield stress σ_s since

$$\varepsilon_s = \frac{\sigma_s}{E} \tag{14}$$

we get the yield strain ε_s. Each material has a corresponding yield strain, and the yield strain is only an approximate value. However, we can use it as a criterion to determine whether the material has undergone plastic deformation.

According to this theory, the corresponding module, which is used to calculate the mean longitudinal strain, is programmed.

4. An Example of Forming Channel Steel with the Outer Edge

To verify the rationality of this theory, we select channel steel with an outer edge from Shijiazhuang Bearing Equipment Factory. Figure 4 shows the section diagram of the channel steel with an outer edge, and Figure 5 shows the schematic diagram of the blank width calculation of the channel steel with an outer edge. In Figure 5A–D are invariant points on the strip, and B and C are the midpoints of the arc. R is the fillet radius of B and C. Finally, the blank width is 1160 mm.

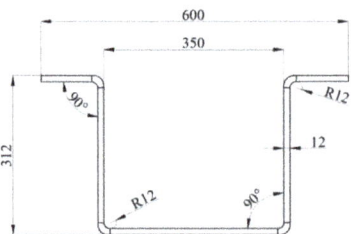

Figure 4. A section diagram of the channel steel with an outer edge.

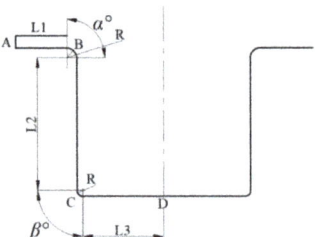

Figure 5. A schematic diagram of the calculation of the channel steel with an outer edge.

The section size of the product is 600 mm × 312 mm × 12 mm. The material is weathering steel Q450. The yield stress of Q450 is 450 MPa, and the elastic modulus is 210,000 MPa. The forming style is Listenfcontinuous roll bend forming. The whole forming unit has nine flat roller machines, two vertical roller machines, three universal roller machines and two straightening machines. Flat rollers are initiative, and vertical rollers are passive. In the computing process, we only consider the nine flat roller machines and three universal roller machines. Two sets of forming parameters are used. The flower diagrams of the two sets of parameters are shown in Figures 6 and 7. The distance between adjacent racks is 1200 mm. The first group is proven to produce qualified products effectively, while the second group is not able to produce qualified products. The difference between the two sets of parameters is the bending angle β in the second rack. In the first set, the bending angle is 15 degrees, while in the second set, the bending angle is 30 degrees.

Figure 6. A reasonable flower diagram.

Figure 7. An inappropriate flower diagram.

According to the above theory, we calculate the mean longitudinal strain with the first set of parameters. In order to conveniently show the results, the post-processing program of Marc finite element software is applied to show the cloud diagram and contour diagram of the mean longitudinal strain from the 1st to 12th rack. Figure 8 is the cloud diagram of the mean longitudinal strain from the 1st to 12th rack, and Figure 9 is the contour diagram. During the forming process, the edge is stretched, the middle part is compressed, and the edge is stretched to a greater extent, as shown in Figures 8 and 9.

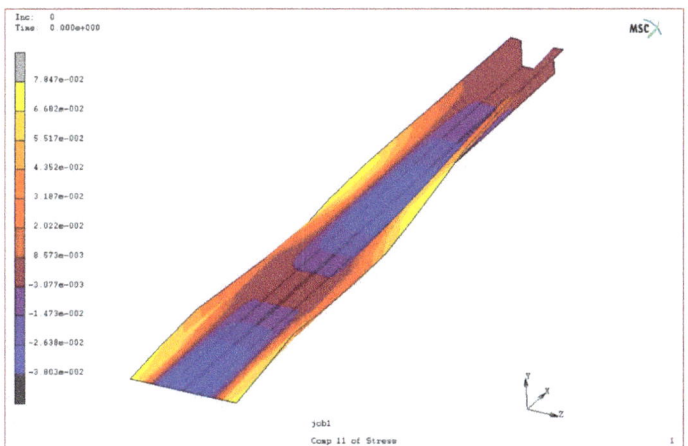

Figure 8. A cloud diagram of the mean longitudinal strain from the 1st to 12th rack.

According to the calculations, the maximum longitudinal tensile strain of the slab is 0.183895%, and the maximum compressive strain is 0.085467%. The material yield strain $\varepsilon_s = \frac{\sigma_s}{E} = 450/210{,}000 = 0.002143$. The longitudinal strain is in the range, so the parameters are reasonable. The biggest mean longitudinal strain of the second group of parameters is 4.00537e-3, which occurred between the first two racks. The value is larger than the yield strain 0.002143, so this group of parameters is not suitable, and the second forming angle has to be changed.

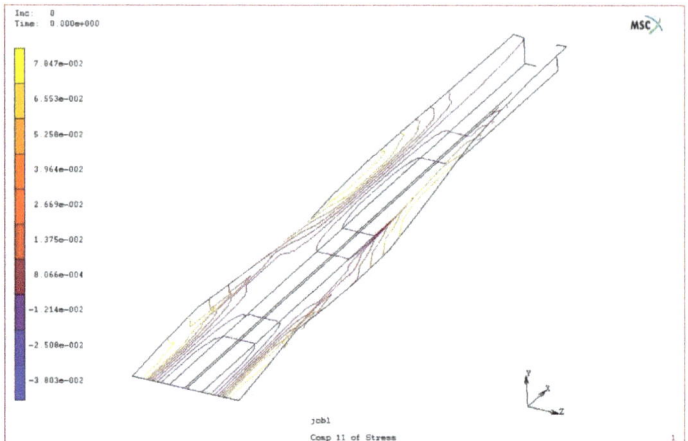

Figure 9. A contour diagram of the mean longitudinal strain from the 1st to 12th rack.

To further prove the correctness of the theory, this paper compares the reasonable analytical results with the results of the non-linear finite element software ABAQUS (6.14). In order to reduce the calculation scale, a half part is selected for finite element modeling as the symmetry of the product. The geometric model in ABAQUS is shown in Figure 10. The parameters of the finite element geometric model are consistent with those of the analytical method. Because the first frame is a pinch roll, its influence is not considered in the simulation.

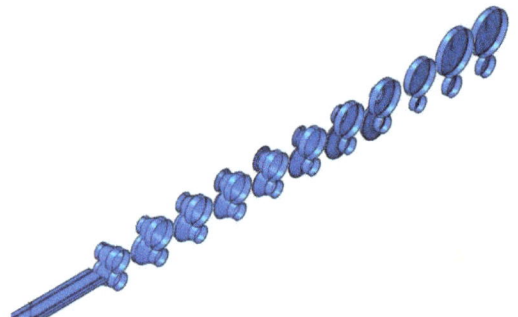

Figure 10. The geometric model of ABAQUS.

In order to reflect the actual rolling process, a series of boundary conditions are set for the simulation process. For each roll, only rotation is allowed. All the lower rolls are active rolls, and all the upper rolls are passive rolls. The linear speed of the lower roller is 200 mm/s. Because the rolls are analytic rigid bodies, only the strip blank needs to be meshed. For cold roll forming, the strip changes greatly at the corner, and the stress is also the largest. Therefore, we subdivide the grid at the corner when meshing, which not only improves the accuracy of calculation but also does not affect the speed. The element type is quadrilateral shell element S4R. Figure 11 shows the meshing status.

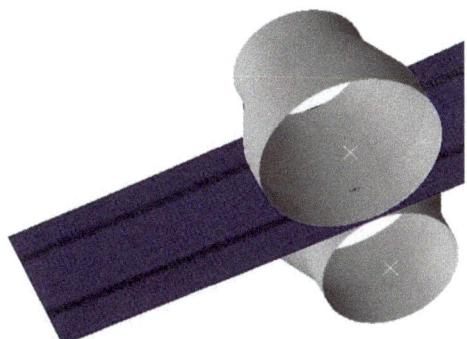

Figure 11. Meshing status.

In ABAQUS post-processing, we get the coordinates of each node by analyzing the results after the slab has been formed and calculate the length changes of the edge and symmetrical lines before and after forming between two adjacent racks. The mean longitudinal strain of ABAQUS results can be obtained by these length changes. Compared to the mean longitudinal strain of the edge and symmetrical lines of the ABAQUS results obtained by the above theory, as shown in Figure 12, the results obtained by the finite element method are more volatile, which is consistent with the actual situation. In the actual rolling process, the material changes are more complex, while the mean longitudinal strain obtained by the analytical method is relatively stable. According to the changes of the curves, the changing trend is accordant. The Pearson correlation coefficient of analytical results and FEM results on the edge line reaches 87%.

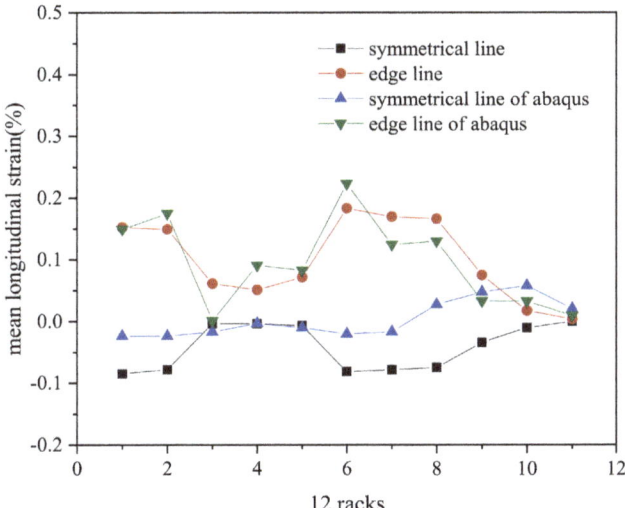

Figure 12. The comparison of the longitudinal strain between the finite element method and analytical method.

5. Conclusions

This paper gives a fast prediction method of edge defects based on the mean longitudinal strain of the roll forming process in detail. The cubic spline curve with the parameters of the cumulative chord length is applied to fit the corresponding points and center points of different passes, and since the cold roll forming is micro-tension forming, the tensions between racks are ignored. Then, the mean longitudinal strains between racks are obtained. The reasonableness of this method is illustrated and validated by an example. With this method, the roll forming effect can be quickly predicted, and the position where a greater longitudinal strain occurred can be determined. In order to prevent the defects, the deformation angles need to be modified when the result is beyond the yield strain. To further prove the correctness of the theory, the results of the analytical method are compared with the ones of the non-linear finite element software ABAQUS. The analytical results have the same trend as the finite element results. This method can provide useful guidance to the actual design process.

Author Contributions: Conceptualization, Z.M. and L.M.; methodology, Z.M. and L.M.; software, Y.F.; writing—original draft preparation, Y.F.; writing—review and editing, Z.M. and Y.F. All authors have read and agreed to the published version of the manuscript.

Funding: This research was funded by the National Natural Science Foundation of China (Grant No. 52004169), the Natural Science Foundation of Shanxi Province (Grant No. 201901D211311, 201901D111244), the Science and Technology Innovation Foundation of Higher Education of Shanxi Province (Grant No. 2020L0337) and Doctoral research initiation fund of Taiyuan University of science and technology (Grant No. 20192058).

Conflicts of Interest: The authors declare no conflict of interest.

Abbreviations

FEM	Finite Element Method
SFSM	Spline Finite Strip Method
3D	3-Dimension
2D	2-Dimension
AHSS	Advanced High-Strength Steel
UHSS	Ultra High Strength Steel

References

1. Drozda, T.; Wick, C. Material and Part Handling in Manufacturing. In *Tool and Manufacturing Engineer's Handbook*; Society of Manufacturing Engineers: Dearborn, MI, USA, 1998; Volume 9.
2. Li, D.; Luo, Y.; Zhang, S.; Peng, Y. Review of numerical research on roll forming and key problems in whole process simulation. *J. Mech. Sci. Technol.* **2004**, *23*, 1466–1469.
3. Liu, F.; Wu, Q.; Cheng, Y. A Meshless Method Based on the Nonsingular Weight Functions for Elastoplastic Large Deformation Problems. *Int. J. Appl. Mech.* **2019**, *11*, 1950006. [CrossRef]
4. Liu, F.; Cheng, Y. The Improved Element-Free Galerkin Method Based on the Nonsingular Weight Functions for Inhomogeneous Swelling of Polymer Gels. *Int. J. Appl. Mech.* **2018**, *10*, 1850047. [CrossRef]
5. Cheng, J. Analyzing the factors influencing the choice of the government onleasing different types of land uses: Evidence from Shanghai of China. *Land Use Policy* **2020**, *90*, 104303. [CrossRef]
6. Cheng, J. Data Analysis of the Factors Influencing the Industrial Land Leasing in Shanghai Based on Mathematical Models. *Math. Probl. Eng.* **2020**, *2020*, 1–11. [CrossRef]
7. Heislita, F.; Livatyail, H.; Ahmetoglu, M.A. Simlulation of roll forming process with the 3-D FEM code PAM-STAMP. *J. Mater. Process. Technol.* **1996**, *59*, 59–67. [CrossRef]
8. Brunet, M.; Mguil, S.; Pol, P. Modelling of a roll-forming process with a combined 2D and 3D FEM code. *J. Mater. Process. Technol.* **1998**, *80–81*, 213–219. [CrossRef]
9. Han, Z.-W.; Liu, C.; Lu, W.-P.; Ren, L.-Q.; Tong, J. Spline finite strip analysis of forming parameters in roll forming a channel section. *J. Mater. Process. Technol.* **2005**, *159*, 383–388. [CrossRef]
10. Han, Z.-W.; Liu, C.; Lu, W.-P.; Ren, L.-Q.; Tong, J. Experimental investigation and theoretical analysis of roll forming of electrical resistance welded pipes. *J. Mater. Process. Technol.* **2004**, *145*, 311–316. [CrossRef]
11. Han, Z.-W.; Liu, C.; Lu, W.-P.; Ren, L.-Q. Simulation of a multi-stand roll-forming process for thick channel section. *J. Mater. Process. Technol.* **2002**, *127*, 382–387. [CrossRef]
12. Han, Z.-W.; Liu, C.; Lu, W.-P.; Ren, L.-Q. The effects of forming parameters in the roll-forming of a channel section with an outer edge. *J. Mater. Process. Technol.* **2001**, *116*, 205–210. [CrossRef]
13. Shi, Y.; Liu, J. Simulation study on the bending process of advanced high strength steel. *Welded. Pipe.* **2007**, *30*, 59–62.
14. Ma, L.D.; Meng, Z.J.; Chai, J.F.; Cheng, Y.M. Analyzing 3D advection-diffusion problems by using the dimension splitting ele-ment-free Galerkin method. *Eng. Anal. Bound. Elem.* **2020**, *111*, 167–177. [CrossRef]

15. Meng, Z.; Cheng, H.; Ma, L.; Cheng, Y. The dimension splitting element-free Galerkin method for 3D transient heat conduction problems. *Sci. China Ser. G Physics Mech. Astron.* **2018**, *62*, 40711. [CrossRef]
16. Meng, Z.J.; Cheng, H.; Ma, L.D.; Cheng, Y.M. The hybrid element-free Galerkin method for three-dimensional wave propagation problems. *Int. J. Numer. Methods Eng.* **2019**, *117*, 15–37. [CrossRef]
17. Meng, Z.J.; Cheng, H.; Ma, L.D.; Cheng, Y.M. The dimension split element-free Galerkin method for three-dimensional potential problems. *Acta Mech. Sin.* **2018**, *34*, 462–474. [CrossRef]
18. Cheng, H.; Peng, M.; Cheng, Y. The dimension splitting and improved complex variable element-free Galerkin method for 3-dimensional transient heat conduction problems. *Int. J. Numer. Methods Eng.* **2018**, *114*, 321–345. [CrossRef]
19. Cheng, H.; Peng, M.; Cheng, Y. A hybrid improved complex variable element-free Galerkin method for three-dimensional advection-diffusion problems. *Eng. Anal. Bound. Elem.* **2018**, *97*, 39–54. [CrossRef]
20. Angel, R.T. Iron Age. *J. Jpn. Soc. Mech. Eng.* **1949**, *3*, 83.
21. Bhattacharyya, D.; Smith, P.; Yee, C.; Collins, I. The prediction of deformation length in cold roll-forming. *J. Mech. Work. Technol.* **1984**, *9*, 181–191. [CrossRef]
22. Nakajima, K.; Miznutani, W. Development of new vertical roll forming process for ERW pipe. *Nippon. Steel. Tech. Rep.* **1980**, *15*, 127–144.
23. Walker, T.R.; Pick, R.J. Approximation of the axial strains developed during the roll forming of ERW pipe. *J. Mater. Process. Technol.* **1990**, *22*, 29–44. [CrossRef]
24. Walker, T.; Pick, R. Developments in the geometric modelling of an ERW pipe skelp. *J. Mater. Process. Technol.* **1991**, *25*, 35–54. [CrossRef]
25. Zhang, L.; Tan, N.; Liu, C. Simulation and application of spline method for cold roll-forming process. *J. Syst. Simul.* **2008**, *20*, 1703–1706.
26. Zhang, L.; Tan, N.; Liu, C. A New Model for Simulation of Cold Roll-Forming of Tubes by Using Spline Finite Strip Method. *J. Shanghai Jiaotong Univ.* **2010**, *15*, 70–75. [CrossRef]
27. Joo, B.D.; Han, S.W.; Shin, S.G.R.; Moon, Y.H. Flexible roll forming process design for variable cross-section profile. *Int. J. Automot. Technol.* **2015**, *16*, 83–88. [CrossRef]
28. Woo, Y.Y.; Kang, P.G.; Oh, I.Y.; Moon, Y.H. The Effect of Flange Length on the Distribution of Longitudinal Strain during the Flexible Roll Forming Process. *Mater. Sci. Forum* **2018**, *920*, 46–51. [CrossRef]
29. Abeyrathna, B.; Rolfe, B.; Weiss, M. The effect of process and geometric parameters on longitudinal edge strain and product defects in cold roll forming. *Int. J. Adv. Manuf. Technol.* **2017**, *92*, 743–754. [CrossRef]
30. Liu, C.-F.; Zhou, W.-L.; Fu, X.-S.; Chen, G.-Q. A new mathematical model for determining the longitudinal strain in cold roll forming process. *Int. J. Adv. Manuf. Technol.* **2015**, *79*, 1055–1061. [CrossRef]
31. Sun, Y.; Qian, Z.; Shi, L.; Meehan, P.A.; Ding, S.; Daniel, J.T. Numerical Investigation of the Permanent Longitudinal Strain and Web-warping in Chain-die Formed AHSS Variable Width Sections. In Proceedings of the 3rd International Conference on High Manganese Steels (HMnS2016), Chengdu, Sichuan, China, 16 November 2016; pp. 581–585.
32. Rezaei, R.; Naeini, H.M.; Tafti, R.A.; Kasaei, M.M.; Mohammadi, M.; Abbaszadeh, B. Effect of bend curve on web warping in flexible roll formed profiles. *Int. J. Adv. Manuf. Technol.* **2017**, *93*, 3625–3636. [CrossRef]
33. Wang, M.; Lu, G.L.; Cai, Z.Y.; Yang, S.C.; Li, M.Z. Linear Distribution Principle for Sheet Forming Using Continuous Roll Forming Process. *Int. J. Pract. Eng. Man-Gt.* **2020**, *21*, 557–564. [CrossRef]
34. Chun-Jian, S.; Long-Yun, Y.; Shu-Mei, L.; Wang, Q.; Wang, R. Research on roll forming process based on five-boundary condition forming angle distribution function. *Int. J. Adv. Manuf. Tech.* **2019**, *102*, 3767–3779.
35. Su, C.; Liu, J.; Zhao, Z.; Lou, S.; Wang, R.; Yang, L. Research on roll forming process and springback based on five-boundary condition forming angle distribution function. *J. Mech. Sci. Technol.* **2020**, *34*, 9–12. [CrossRef]

Article

Analysis of Elastic–Plastic Problems Using the Improved Interpolating Complex Variable Element Free Galerkin Method

Yajie Deng [1], Xingkeng Shen [1], Jixiao Tao [2] and Ying Dai [1,*]

[1] School of Aerospace Engineering and Applied Mechanics, Tongji University, Shanghai 200092, China; yjdeng@tongji.edu.cn (Y.D.); shenxingkeng@tongji.edu.cn (X.S.)
[2] Department of Mechanics and Aerospace Engineering, Southern University of Science and Technology, Shenzhen 518055, China; taojx@sustech.edu.cn
* Correspondence: ydai@tongji.edu.cn

Abstract: A numerical model for the two-dimensional nonlinear elastic–plastic problem is proposed based on the improved interpolating complex variable element free Galerkin (IICVEFG) method and the incremental tangent stiffness matrix method. The viability of the proposed model is verified through three elastic–plastic examples. The numerical analyses show that the IICVEFG method has good convergence. The solutions using the IICVEFG method are consistent with the solutions obtained from the finite element method using the ABAQUS program. Moreover, the IICVEFG method shows greater computing precision and efficiency than the non-interpolating meshless methods.

Keywords: elastic–plastic problem; complex variable meshless method; interpolating shape function; singular weight function; complete basis function

1. Introduction

In the science and engineering fields, nonlinear elastic–plastic problems are very common, and are complicated due to the nonlinearity of the plastic state. In addition, the corresponding analytical solutions are difficult to be obtain [1–3]. Thus, it is important to study efficient and accurate computational models for solving nonlinear elastic–plastic problems, particularly those problems characterised by geometric [4–6] and material nonlinearities [7–9]. In recent years, the meshless method has played a great role in numerical simulation. Unlike conventional mesh-based numerical methods [10,11], the meshless method is built on discrete nodes, which does not cause mesh distortion. Therefore, the meshless method is more suitable for nonlinear large deformation and fracture problems, as well as complicated porous structures [12–17].

As a popular numerical computing method, the meshless method has developed various branches, such as the smoothed particle hydrodynamics method [18], the famous moving least squares (MLS) approximation [11], the reproducing kernel particle method [19], and so on. In this paper, we mainly study methods that improve upon the original MLS approximation in order to overcome shortcomings which lead to low efficiency and low accuracy [20–22]. The shortcomings include relying on numerous nodes, possessing a non-interpolating shape function, and possibly producing an ill-conditioned final discrete system.

To overcome inefficiency, complex variables were introduced into the MLS approximation, and the complex variable moving least squares (CVMLS) approximation was proposed [20]. Since the CVMLS approximation can use a complex variable to express the two directional variables, the CVMLS approximation has a higher computing efficiency [21,22]. However, this approximation lacks specific mathematical implications. Thus, the improved complex variable moving least squares (ICVMLS) approximation was proposed, which brings in a conjugated basis function and a new functional [23–25].

Identically to the MLS approximation, there are no interpolating features for the shape functions in the CVMLS and ICVMLS approximations [26–29]. Thus, on the foundation of the ICVMLS approximation, the interpolating property of the shape function was improved according to the following steps. First, to guarantee computing accuracy, a complete basis function is applied [30]. Second, the basis function is orthogonalized to obtain a set of new basis functions with a singular weight function [31]. Finally, based on these novel basis functions, a new interpolating shape function and interpolating trial function are derived. This new method was named the improved interpolating complex variable moving least squares (IICVMLS) method [30].

Combining the IICVMLS method with the integral weak forms of diverse problems, the corresponding improved interpolating complex variable element free Galerkin (IICVEFG) methods were presented. By virtue of the interpolating shape function in the IICVMLS method, the above meshless method is able to directly exert the essential boundary conditions, similarly to the finite element method. Thus, the derived final discrete system is more concise, which leads to greater computing efficiency and accuracy, in contrast to other non-interpolating complex variable meshless methods. Because of the above merits, the IICVEFG method has been widely applied to many potential problems, including the bending problems of Kirchhoff plates and even the pattern transformation of hydrogels, in which has displayed great computational advantages [30,32,33].

The intention of this paper is to build a more efficient and accurate numerical model for the two-dimensional nonlinear elastic–plastic problem based on the IICVEFG method, and to verify the viability of the proposed model. The detailed modelling process of the IICVEFG method is described, and the implementation process for solving the final discrete system is also presented. Through three numerical examples, the computational advantages of the IICVEFG method are demonstrated, in comparison with the ABAQUS program and other non-interpolating meshless methods.

2. Implementation of the Elastic–Plastic Problem Based on the IICVEFG Method

2.1. Brief Descriptions of the Two-Dimensional Elastic–Plastic Problem

Within the problem domain Ω, the classic equilibrium equation of a two-dimensional elastic–plastic problem is [34]

$$\mathbf{L}^T \dot{\boldsymbol{\sigma}} + \dot{\boldsymbol{b}} = 0. \tag{1}$$

For an arbitrary point $z = x_1 + ix_2 \in \Omega$, $\dot{\boldsymbol{\sigma}}^T = (\dot{\sigma}_{11}, \dot{\sigma}_{22}, \dot{\sigma}_{12})$ is the stress rate field, $\dot{\boldsymbol{b}}^T = (\dot{b}_1, \dot{b}_2)$ is the body force rate field, and $\mathbf{L}$ is the differential operator matrix,

$$\mathbf{L}^T(\cdot) = \begin{bmatrix} \frac{\partial}{\partial x_1} & 0 & \frac{\partial}{\partial x_2} \\ 0 & \frac{\partial}{\partial x_2} & \frac{\partial}{\partial x_1} \end{bmatrix} (\cdot). \tag{2}$$

The relationship between the strain rate field $\dot{\boldsymbol{\varepsilon}}^T = (\dot{\varepsilon}_{11}, \dot{\varepsilon}_{22}, \dot{\varepsilon}_{12})$ and the velocity field $\dot{\boldsymbol{u}}^T = (\dot{u}_1, \dot{u}_2)$ is described as

$$\dot{\boldsymbol{\varepsilon}} = \mathbf{L}(\dot{\boldsymbol{u}}), \tag{3}$$

and the stress-strain relationship is

$$\dot{\boldsymbol{\sigma}} = \mathbf{D}\dot{\boldsymbol{\varepsilon}}. \tag{4}$$

Considering that this problem is a plane stress problem, the constitutive matrices $\mathbf{D}$ are different in the elastic and plastic state, which are shown in the following, respectively [35].

$$\mathbf{D}_e = \frac{E}{1-v^2} \begin{bmatrix} 1 & v & 0 \\ v & 1 & 0 \\ 0 & 0 & \frac{1-v}{2} \end{bmatrix}, \tag{5}$$

$$\boldsymbol{D}_{ep} = \frac{E}{Q} \begin{bmatrix} \sigma'^2_{22} + 2P & -\sigma'_{11}\sigma'_{22} + 2\nu P & -\frac{\sigma'_{11}+\nu\sigma'_{22}}{1+\nu}\sigma_{12} \\ -\sigma'_{11}\sigma'_{22} + 2\nu P & \sigma'^2_{11} + 2P & -\frac{\sigma'_{22}+\nu\sigma'_{11}}{1+\nu}\sigma_{12} \\ -\frac{\sigma'_{11}+\nu\sigma'_{22}}{1+\nu}\sigma_{12} & -\frac{\sigma'_{22}+\nu\sigma'_{11}}{1+\nu}\sigma_{12} & \frac{R}{2(1+\nu)} + \frac{2H'}{9E}(1-\nu)\overline{\sigma}^2 \end{bmatrix}, \quad (6)$$

where E is the elastic modulus, ν is the Poisson's ratio, and $\overline{\sigma}$ is the equivalent stress

$$\overline{\sigma} = \sqrt{\sigma_{11}^2 + \sigma_{22}^2 - \sigma_{11}\sigma_{22} + 3\sigma_{12}^2}, \quad (7)$$

$$P = \frac{2H'}{9E}\overline{\sigma}^2 + \frac{\sigma_{12}^2}{1+\nu}, \quad (8)$$

$$R = \sigma'^2_{11} + 2\nu\sigma'_{11}\sigma'_{22} + \sigma'^2_{22}, \quad (9)$$

$$Q = R + 2(1-\nu^2)P. \quad (10)$$

Assume that the stress-strain relationship in the plastic state satisfies the linear hardening model, the plastic modulus for hardening H' is expressed as

$$H' = \frac{EE'}{E - E'}, \quad (11)$$

where E' is the tangent modulus. In addition, σ'_{ij} is the stress deviation which can be written as

$$\sigma'_{ij} = \sigma_{ij} - \frac{\sigma_{11}+\sigma_{22}}{3}\delta_{ij}, \quad (i,j=1,2). \quad (12)$$

The velocity and natural boundary conditions are

$$\dot{u} = \overline{\dot{u}}, \quad (z \in \Gamma_u), \quad (13)$$

$$\boldsymbol{n}\dot{\sigma} = \overline{\dot{t}}, \quad (z \in \Gamma_t), \quad (14)$$

where $\overline{\dot{u}}^{\mathrm{T}} = (\overline{\dot{u}}_1, \overline{\dot{u}}_2)$ is the prescribed velocity vector on the velocity boundary Γ_u, $\overline{\dot{t}}^{\mathrm{T}} = (\overline{\dot{t}}_1, \overline{\dot{t}}_2)$ is the given traction rate, and $\boldsymbol{n}$ is the unit vector of the outer normal direction on the natural boundary Γ_t.

2.2. The IICVEFG Method for the Elastic–Plastic Problem

In this paper, the IICVMLS method is applied to disperse the integral weak form of the elastic–plastic problem, and then the corresponding IICVEFG method is presented [30]. According to Equations (1) and (14), the integral weak form is expressed as

$$\int_\Omega \delta\dot{\boldsymbol{\varepsilon}}^{\mathrm{T}}\dot{\boldsymbol{\sigma}}\mathrm{d}\Omega - \int_\Omega \delta\dot{\boldsymbol{u}}^{\mathrm{T}}\dot{\boldsymbol{b}}\mathrm{d}\Omega - \int_{\Gamma_t} \delta\dot{\boldsymbol{u}}^{\mathrm{T}}\overline{\dot{\boldsymbol{t}}}\mathrm{d}\Gamma = 0. \quad (15)$$

In the IICVMLS method, the trial function of velocity $\dot{u}^h(z)$ is expressed as

$$\dot{u}^h(z) = \dot{u}_1^h(z) + i\dot{u}_2^h(z) = \boldsymbol{\Phi}(z)\dot{\boldsymbol{u}}_* = \sum_{I=1}^n \Phi_I(z)\dot{u}(z_I), \quad (16)$$

where

$$\boldsymbol{\Phi}(z) = (\Phi_1(z), \Phi_2(z), \ldots, \Phi_n(z)) = \boldsymbol{v}^{\mathrm{T}}(z) + \boldsymbol{b}^{\mathrm{T}}(z)\boldsymbol{A}_z^{-1}(z)\boldsymbol{B}_z(z), \quad (17)$$

$$\dot{\boldsymbol{u}}_* = (\dot{u}(z_1), \dot{u}(z_2), \ldots, \dot{u}(z_n))^{\mathrm{T}}, \quad (18)$$

$$\boldsymbol{v}(z) = (v(z-z_1), v(z-z_2), \ldots, v(z-z_n))^{\mathrm{T}}, \quad (19)$$

$$\boldsymbol{b}(z) = (b_z^{(2)}(z), b_z^{(3)}(z), \ldots, b_z^{(m)}(z))^{\mathrm{T}}, \quad (20)$$

$$A_z(z) = \overline{C}_z^T W(z) C_z, \tag{21}$$

$$B_z(z) = \overline{C}_z^T W(z), \tag{22}$$

$$C_z = \begin{bmatrix} b_z^{(2)}(z_1) & b_z^{(3)}(z_1) & \cdots & b_z^{(m)}(z_1) \\ b_z^{(2)}(z_2) & b_z^{(3)}(z_2) & \cdots & b_z^{(m)}(z_2) \\ \vdots & \vdots & \ddots & \vdots \\ b_z^{(2)}(z_n) & b_z^{(3)}(z_n) & \cdots & b_z^{(m)}(z_n) \end{bmatrix}, \tag{23}$$

$$W(z) = \begin{bmatrix} w(z-z_1) & 0 & \cdots & 0 \\ 0 & w(z-z_2) & \cdots & 0 \\ \vdots & \vdots & \ddots & \vdots \\ 0 & 0 & \cdots & w(z-z_n) \end{bmatrix}, \tag{24}$$

$$\dot{u}_1^h(z) = \text{Re}[\boldsymbol{\Phi}(z)\dot{u}*] = \text{Re}[\sum_{I=1}^n \Phi_I(z)\dot{u}(z_I)], \tag{25}$$

$$\dot{u}_2^h(z) = \text{Im}[\boldsymbol{\Phi}(z)\dot{u}*] = \text{Im}[\sum_{I=1}^n \Phi_I(z)\dot{u}(z_I)]. \tag{26}$$

Then the velocity matrix $\dot{u}(z)$ in Equation (15) can be written as

$$\dot{u}(z) = \begin{bmatrix} \dot{u}_1(z) \\ \dot{u}_2(z) \end{bmatrix} = \sum_{I=1}^n \begin{bmatrix} \text{Re}[\Phi_I(z)] & -\text{Im}[\Phi_I(z)] \\ \text{Im}[\Phi_I(z)] & \text{Re}[\Phi_I(z)] \end{bmatrix} \begin{bmatrix} \dot{u}_1(z_I) \\ \dot{u}_2(z_I) \end{bmatrix} \\ = \widetilde{\boldsymbol{\Phi}}(z)\dot{U}(z) = \sum_{I=1}^n \widetilde{\boldsymbol{\Phi}}_I(z)\dot{U}(z_I), \tag{27}$$

where

$$\widetilde{\boldsymbol{\Phi}}(z) = (\widetilde{\boldsymbol{\Phi}}_1(z), \widetilde{\boldsymbol{\Phi}}_2(z), \ldots, \widetilde{\boldsymbol{\Phi}}_n(z)), \tag{28}$$

$$\widetilde{\boldsymbol{\Phi}}_I(z) = \begin{bmatrix} \text{Re}[\Phi_I(z)] & -\text{Im}[\Phi_I(z)] \\ \text{Im}[\Phi_I(z)] & \text{Re}[\Phi_I(z)] \end{bmatrix}, \tag{29}$$

$$\dot{U}(z) = (\dot{U}(z_1), \dot{U}(z_2), \ldots, \dot{U}(z_n))^T, \tag{30}$$

$$\dot{U}(z_I) = \begin{bmatrix} \dot{u}_1(z_I) \\ \dot{u}_2(z_I) \end{bmatrix}. \tag{31}$$

According to Equation (27), the strain rate of point z in Equation (3) can be rewritten and simplified as

$$\dot{\varepsilon}(z) = L(\dot{u}(z)) = L(\widetilde{\boldsymbol{\Phi}}(z)\dot{U}(z)) = B(z)\dot{U}(z), \tag{32}$$

where

$$B(z) = (B_1(z), B_2(z), \ldots, B_n(z)), \tag{33}$$

$$B_I(z) = \begin{bmatrix} \text{Re}[\Phi_{I,1}(z)] & -\text{Im}[\Phi_{I,1}(z)] \\ \text{Im}[\Phi_{I,2}(z)] & \text{Re}[\Phi_{I,2}(z)] \\ \text{Re}[\Phi_{I,2}(z)] + \text{Im}[\Phi_{I,1}(z)] & -\text{Im}[\Phi_{I,2}(z)] + \text{Re}[\Phi_{I,1}(z)] \end{bmatrix}. \tag{34}$$

Then the stress rate of point z in Equation (4) is expressed as

$$\dot{\sigma}(z) = D\dot{\varepsilon}(z) = DB(z)\dot{U}(z). \tag{35}$$

Substitute Equations (27), (32) and (35) into Equation (15), then consider the arbitrary of $\delta \dot{U}(z)^T$. Finally, we obtain the discrete matrix equation

$$K\dot{U}(z) = F, \tag{36}$$

where

$$K = \int_\Omega B(z)^T DB(z) d\Omega, \qquad (37)$$

$$F = \int_\Omega \tilde{\Phi}(z)^T \dot{b}(z) d\Omega + \int_{\Gamma_t} \tilde{\Phi}(z)^T \dot{\bar{t}}(z) d\Gamma. \qquad (38)$$

The shape function of Equation (17) in the IICVMLS method has the interpolating feature, which results in the fact that Equation (13) can be enforced into Equation (36) directly. Therefore, the final matrix Equation (36) is more succinct than that in the non-interpolating complex variable meshless method. Thus, the IICVEFG method can, theoretically, solve the problem with greater precision and efficiency.

2.3. Incremental Tangent Stiffness Matrix Method

In this part, the incremental tangent stiffness matrix method is applied to solve the nonlinear Equation (36) in the plastic state, due to the nonlinearity of the constitutive relationship in Equation (6) [36,37]. In this method, the total load is divided into sufficiently small loads, which are applied step by step. Then, the nonlinear process is decomposed into a sequence of approximately linear processes.

In each approximately linear process, the relation between the stress increment tensor $\Delta\sigma$ and strain increment tensor $\Delta\varepsilon$ is

$$\Delta\sigma = D_{ep}\Delta\varepsilon, \qquad (39)$$

which is linear, and D_{ep} is only connected with the known stress and strain.

To solve this problem, first, we must determine whether the structure produces plastic deformation when applying the total external force. Under this circumstance, assume that the structure is completely in the elastic state; then the displacement, strain, stress, equivalent stress, and the maximum equivalent stress $\bar{\sigma}_{max}$ of all nodes and Gauss points are obtained by using the elastic constitutive relationship in Equation (5). Denote the material yield stress as σ_s.

If $\bar{\sigma}_{max} \leq \sigma_s$, the structure is still in the elastic state, and the above solutions are the final solutions of this problem. If $\bar{\sigma}_{max} > \sigma_s$, the structure has produced plastic deformation, and the external force should be applied using the incremental method. Define the elastic limit load $F_0 = \frac{\sigma_s}{\bar{\sigma}_{max}} F$; then the displacement, stress, and strain in the elastic state can be obtained. Behind the elastic state, we use the incremental method to apply the rest of the external force,

$$\Delta F_i = \frac{1}{N}(1 - \frac{\sigma_s}{\bar{\sigma}_{max}})F, \qquad (40)$$

where N is the total number of load steps. In the $i-th$ load step, ΔF_i is the incremental force. Then, the solving equation is obtained,

$$K(\sigma_{i-1})\Delta U_i = \Delta F_i, \qquad (41)$$

where the matrix K is related to the known stress σ_{i-1} in the previous load step, and ΔU_i is the displacement increment in the $i-th$ load step. Then, depending on ΔU_i, we can obtain the strain increment $\Delta\varepsilon_i$ and the stress increment $\Delta\sigma_i$ in the current load step.

Then the stress in the $i-th$ load step can be obtained as,

$$\sigma_i = \sigma_{i-1} + \Delta\sigma_i. \qquad (42)$$

In each load step, it is still necessary to choose the elastic or plastic constitutive relationship according to the relation between the stresses $\bar{\sigma}_{max}$ and σ_s. Repeat the above process until the whole external force is applied. Eventually, the obtained displacement, stress, and strain are the final solutions of the elastic–plastic problem. The whole computing procedure is described in Figure 1.

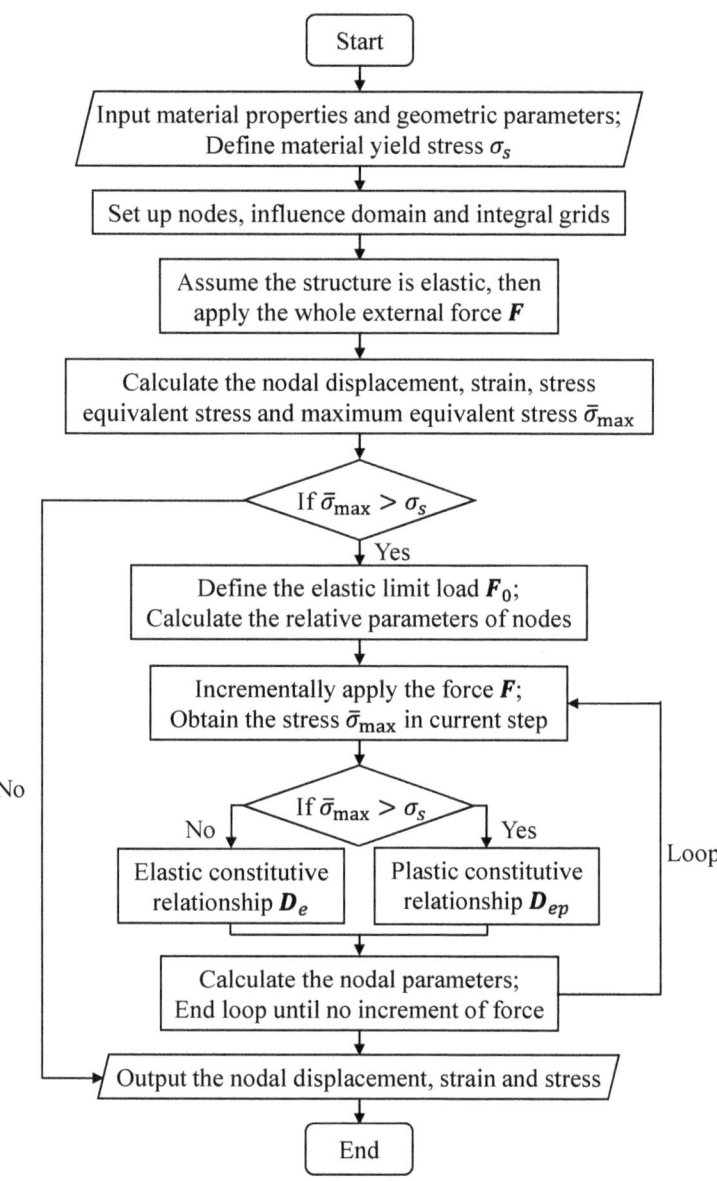

Figure 1. Flow chart of the computing procedure.

To guarantee that the computed solutions are more accurate, in each load step the Equation (41) is modified to

$$K(\sigma_{i-1})\Delta U_i = F_i - \int_\Omega B^T \sigma_{i-1} d\Omega, \qquad (43)$$

where the second term on the right side is the equivalent node load, and F_i is the total equivalent node load in the $i-th$ load step,

$$F_i = F_0 + \Delta F_1 + \Delta F_2 + \cdots + \Delta F_i. \qquad (44)$$

Based on Equation (40), the above expression can be rewritten as

$$F_i = \frac{\sigma_s}{\overline{\sigma}_{max}} F + \frac{i}{N}(1 - \frac{\sigma_s}{\overline{\sigma}_{max}})F, \; (i = 1, 2, \ldots, N). \quad (45)$$

3. Numerical Examples

Since there are no analytical solutions for nonlinear elastic–plastic problems, the ABAQUS program is used as a reference in this paper. In this section, to validate the numerical advantages of the IICVEFG method, three numerical examples under different constraints and forces are simulated and analysed. The solutions obtained from the IICVEFG method are compared with the solutions obtained from the ABAQUS program and the non-interpolating ICVEFG method [38].

For the following examples, the linear basis function and the 4×4 Gauss points are used in the IICVEFG and ICVEFG methods. The singular weight function and cubic spline weight function are used in the IICVEFG and ICVEFG methods, respectively [23,30]. In the ABAQUS program, the C3D8R element is selected. Additionally, the external load is applied with $N = 100$ steps. In this paper, two-dimensional elastic–plastic problems are regarded as plane stress problems, and the tangent modulus E' in Equation (11) is given as $E' = 0.2E$.

For error analysis, define the error between the ABAQUS program and other numerical methods, and the traditional relative error at a specific node, respectively,

$$e_i^{ABAQUS} = \frac{1}{n}\sum_{I=1}^{n}(u_I^{ABAQUS} - u_I^i)^2, \quad (46)$$

$$e = \left| \frac{u_I^i - u_I^{ABAQUS}}{u_I^{ABAQUS}} \right|, \quad (47)$$

where n is the number of the nodes, and i represents the IICVEFG and ICVEFG methods in this paper.

For convergence analysis, define the following variance between the different node distributions,

$$E_{ij} = \frac{1}{n}\sum_{I=1}^{n}[(u_I^i - u_I^{ij})^2 + (u_I^j - u_I^{ij})^2], \quad (48)$$

where u_I^{ij} represents the average displacement value of node I under two different kinds of node distributions i and j.

3.1. A cantilever Beam Constrained with a Concentrated Force

The first example is a cantilever beam; the free end is constrained with a concentrated force, as displayed in Figure 2. The geometric parameters are: $L = 8$ m, $h = 1$ m and the depth is the unit length. The material parameters are: $E = 1.0 \times 10^5$ Pa, $\nu = 0.25$, and $\sigma_s = 25$ Pa. The concentrated load is $P = -1$ N.

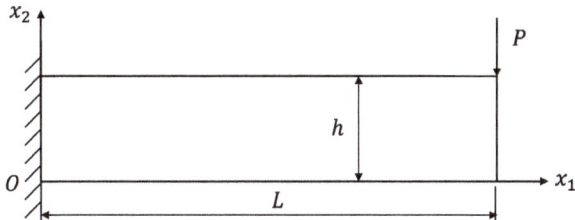

Figure 2. Cantilever beam constrained with a concentrated force.

For this example, we mainly discuss the influence of the parameter scale d_{max} and different node distributions (as described in Figure 3) on the presented IICVEFG method. In the ABAQUS program, 64×8 square four-node elements are. From Figure 3, it is clear that, with the decrease in the d_{max} value and the increase in the total number of nodes, the numerical solutions obtained from the IICVEFG method at point $(8, 0)$ are closer to the solutions of the ABAQUS program. From Figure 4 and the error analysis of Figure 5, we can also see that under $d_{max} = 2$ and a 65×9 node distribution, the numerical deflection u_2 of the nodes on the x_1 axis of the IICVEFG method is consistent with the ABAQUS solutions.

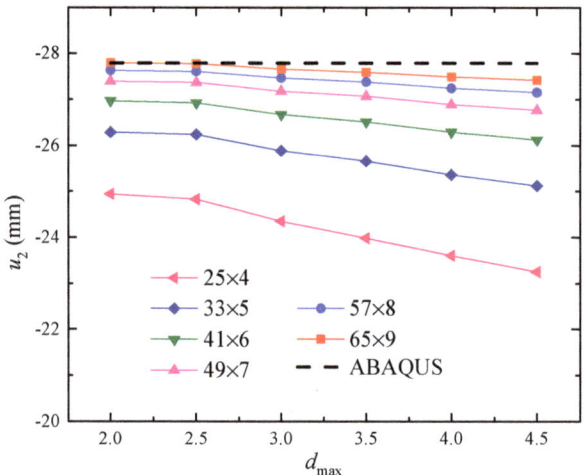

Figure 3. The influence of d_{max} and node distributions on the IICVEFG method.

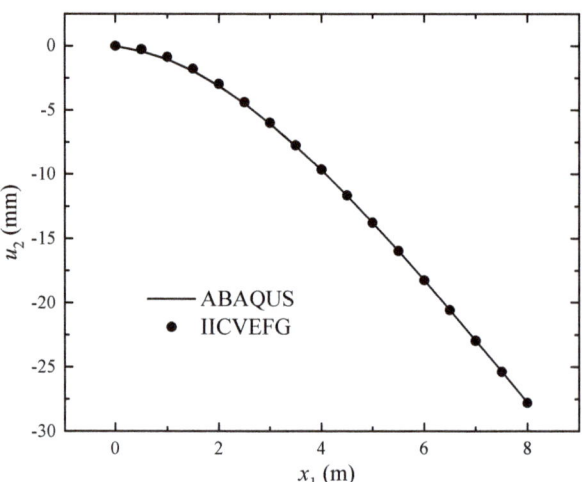

Figure 4. The deflection u_2 of the nodes on the x_1 axis.

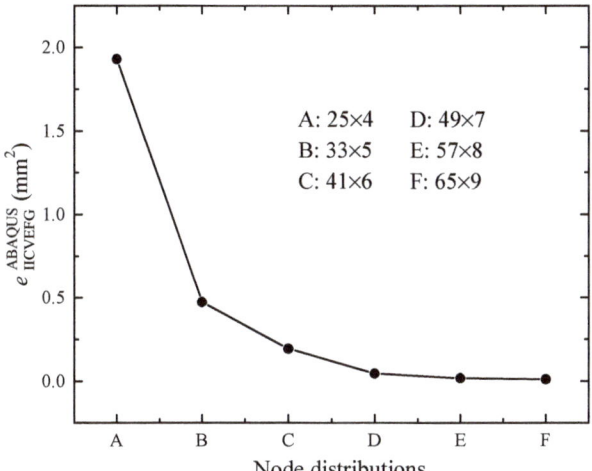

Figure 5. The error analysis under different node distributions.

Figure 6 shows the convergence of the IICVEFG method between different node distributions. We can conclude that the greater the number of total nodes is, the smaller the variance is. Therefore, the IICVEFG method has good numerical convergence. We should note that the IICVEFG method may spend more CPU computing time as the number of total nodes increases.

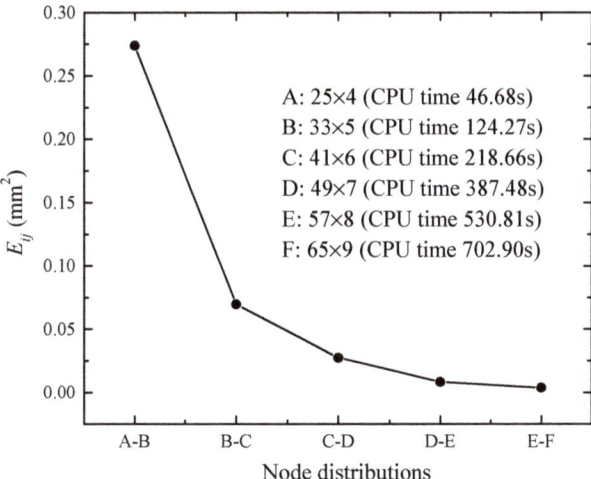

Figure 6. The convergence analysis and CPU time.

Figure 7 describes the relation between the load and the deflection u_2 at the point (8, 0.5). When loaded to about $P = -0.6$ N, the structure starts to enter plastic stage. Until about $P = -0.8$ N, the whole structure is in the plastic stage.

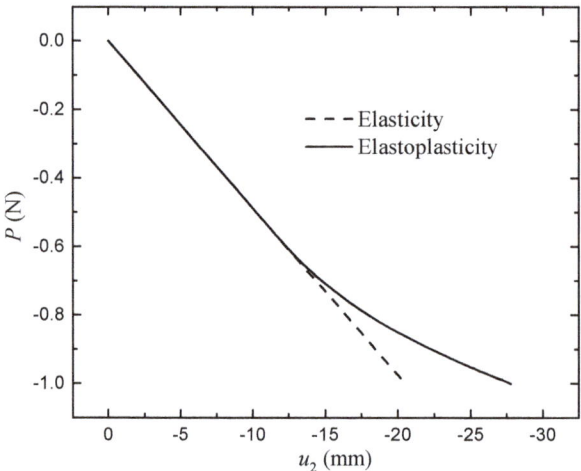

Figure 7. The relation between the load and the deflection.

3.2. A Cantilever Beam Constrained with a Distributed Load

The second example is a cantilever beam where the upper boundary is constrained with a distributed load, as described in Figure 8. The geometric and material parameters are the same as in the first example. The distributed load is $p = -1\ \text{N/m}$.

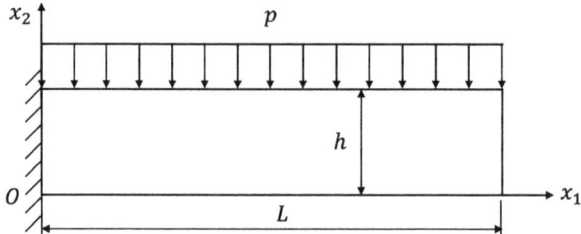

Figure 8. Cantilever beam constrained with a distributed load.

For this example, we mainly discuss the merits of the IICVEFG method in terms of computing accuracy and efficiency, as compared to the non-interpolating ICVEFG method. In the IICVEFG method, 17×4 nodes are used. The grid distribution in the ABAQUS program is same as the first example.

Under different parameter scalings $d_{\max}$, Figure 9 shows the relative errors of the deflection u_2 at point $(8, 0)$ between the IICVEFG method and ABAQUS program. It is clear that when $d_{\max} = 2$, the relative error is close to zero. Thus, we choose these data for the following discussion. It widely known that the greater the value of $d_{\max}$ is, the more CPU time the IICVEFG method requires.

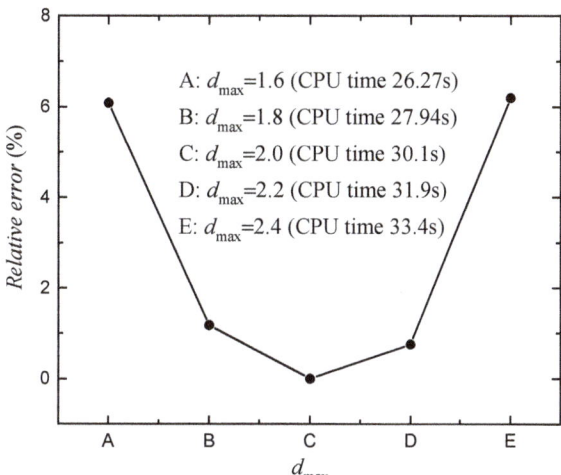

Figure 9. The relative errors and CPU time under different $d_{\max}$.

Taking the ICVEFG method as a comparison method, the suitable node distribution, $d_{\max}$, and penalty factor α should be chosen. For this example, 21×11 nodes and $d_{\max} = 3.9$ are used. The penalty factor α is chosen according to Figure 10. From the relative error analysis, there are two observations: (1) The solutions of the IICVEFG method have no relation with the penalty factor α, because in the IICVEFG method special techniques are unnecessary when applying the essential boundary conditions; (2) With the increase in the penalty factor α the relative error is gradually reduced, and when $\alpha = 1.0 \times 10^{12}$ the relative error is sufficiently small and close to the error of the IICVEFG method. It is worth mentioning that this selection process is time consuming. Therefore, the IICVEFG method has a greater computing accuracy and efficiency than the ICVEFG method.

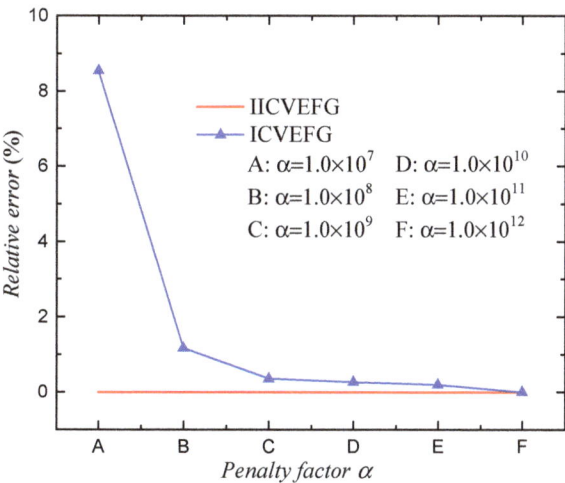

Figure 10. The influence of penalty factor α.

After deciding the values of the relative parameters, the deflection u_2 of the nodes on the x_1 axis are acquired from the ABAQUS program, as well as the IICVEFG and ICVEFG methods. The results are shown in Figure 11. The solutions are in good agreement with each other. Moreover, for a single calculation, the CPU time spent in the IICVEFG method is 30.1 s, which is much less than the 538.0 s spent in the ICVEFG method under similar accuracy.

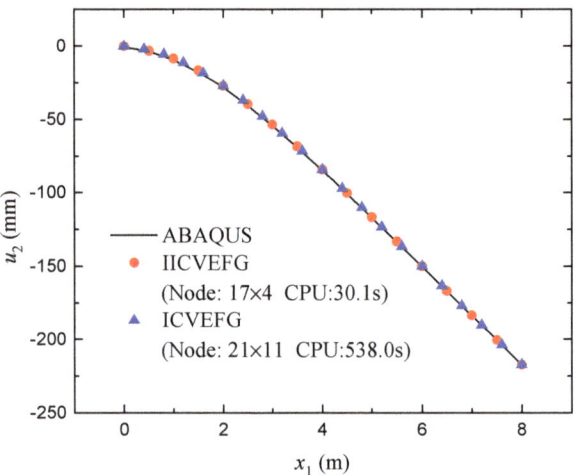

Figure 11. The deflection u_2 of the nodes on the x_1 axis.

Identically to the first example, the relation between the load and the deflection u_2 at the point $(8, 0)$ is shown in Figure 12. For this example, the structure begins to produce the plastic deformation when $p = -0.2$ N/m, and up to $p = -0.4$ N/m the structure is completely in the plastic stage.

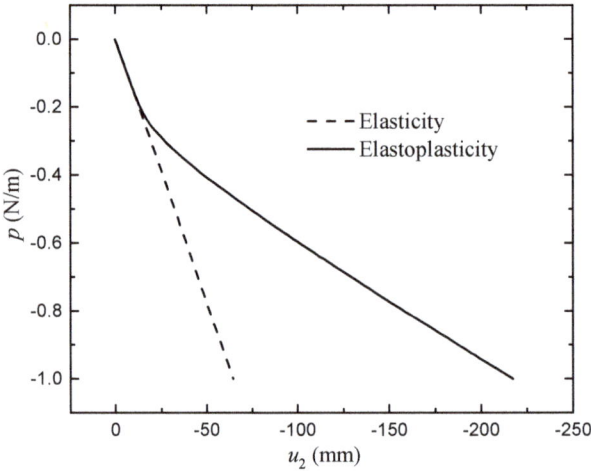

Figure 12. The relation between the load and the deflection.

3.3. A Rectangular Plate with a Central Hole under a Distributed Traction

The final example is a rectangular plate with a circular hole in the centre. This structure bears a distributed traction at the right boundary, as described in Figure 13. The geometric parameters are: $L = 10$ m, $h = 4$ m, $r = 1$ m, and the depth is the unit length. The material parameters are: $E = 1.0 \times 10^5$ Pa, $\nu = 0.25$, and $\sigma_s = 250$ Pa. The traction load is $p = 1000$ N/m.

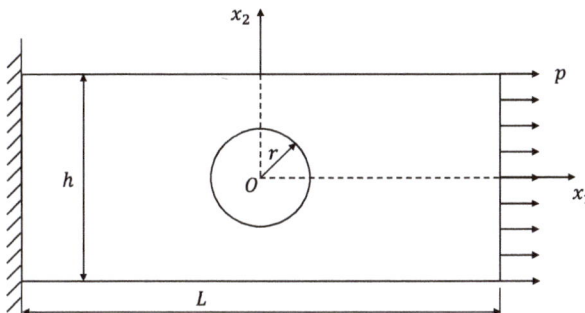

Figure 13. Rectangular plate with a central hole under a distributed traction.

For this example, we mainly discuss the applicability of the IICVEFG model for complex structures. First, for the IICVEFG and ICVEFG methods, the numerical solutions were obtained under the same node distribution 23×15. In the IICVEFG and ICVEFG methods $d_{max} = 2$. Moreover, in the ICVEFG method $\alpha = 1.0 \times 10^9$. As a reference, 40×8 grids are distributed in the ABAQUS program.

Figure 14 shows the displacement u_1 of the nodes on $x_2 = -2$ m. We can see that the solutions obtained from the IICVEFG and ICVEFG methods are in good agreement with the solutions of the ABAQUS program. The relative errors at point $(5, -2)$ acquired from the IICVEFG and ICVEFG methods are 0.144% and 0.1611%, respectively. Furthermore, under similar computing accuracy, the IICVEFG method requires 408.84 s to compute, which is less than the 474.78 s for the ICVEFG method.

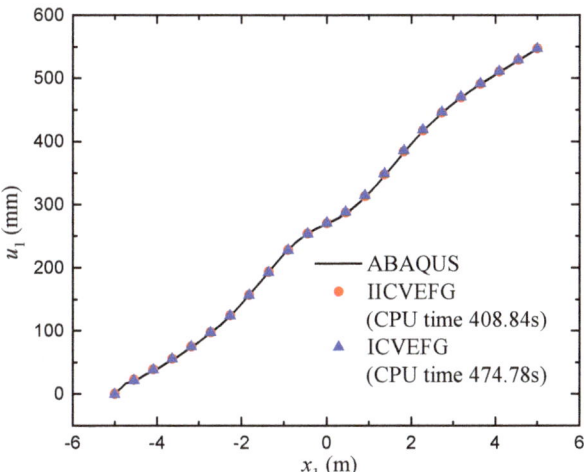

Figure 14. The displacement u_1 of the nodes on $x_2 = -2$ m.

Figure 15 describes the grid distribution in the ABAQUS program, node distribution in the IICVEFG method, and the corresponding distributions of displacement u_1. We can see that the displacement distributions obtained from the ABAQUS program and IICVEFG method are similar.

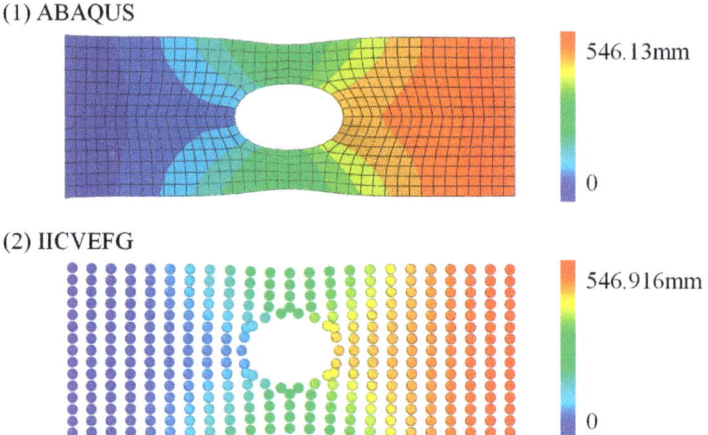

Figure 15. The displacement distributions.

For this example, the relation of the traction and the displacement u_1 at point (5, 0) is also discussed in Figure 16. Around the value $p = 100$ N/m the plastic deformation occurs; and around $p = 300$ N/m the deformation of the whole structure is plastic deformation.

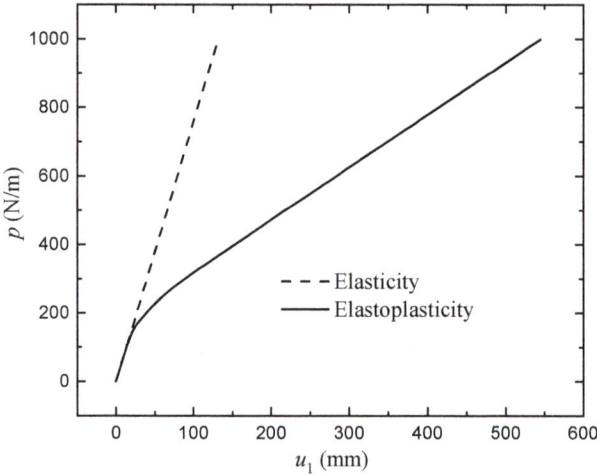

Figure 16. The relation between the displacement and traction.

4. Conclusions

In this paper, a more efficient and accurate numerical model for the two-dimensional nonlinear elastic–plastic problems is established, based on the IICVEFG method and the incremental tangent stiffness matrix method. Through numerical analyses we found that, in the IICVEFG method, the variance is smaller as the number of total nodes increases. Thus, the IICVEFG method has good convergence. The solutions of the IICVEFG method are consistent with the solutions of the ABAQUS program. In addition, the error between the IICVEFG method and ABAQUS program is less than that between the ICVEFG method and ABAQUS program. Furthermore, under similar accuracy constraints, the CPU time spent on the IICVEFG method is 30.1 s, which is much less than 538.0 s spent on the ICVEFG method. Thus, the IICVEFG method has greater numerical accuracy and efficiency than the non-interpolating ICVEFG method for different elastic–plastic problems. This validates that the IICVEFG method is sufficiently adaptable.

Author Contributions: Conceptualization, Y.D. (Ying Dai); Funding acquisition, Y.D. (Yajie Deng); Methodology, Y.D. (Yajie Deng); Software, Y.D. (Yajie Deng), X.S. and J.T.; Supervision, Y.D. (Ying Dai); Visualization, X.S. and J.T.; Writing—original draft, Y.D. (Yajie Deng); Writing—review and editing, Y.D. (Ying Dai). All authors have read and agreed to the published version of the manuscript.

Funding: This research was funded by the National Science Foundation of China, grant number 12002240.

Institutional Review Board Statement: Not applicable.

Informed Consent Statement: Not applicable.

Data Availability Statement: Not applicable.

Acknowledgments: The authors sincerely acknowledge the financial support from the National Science Foundation of China (No. 12002240).

Conflicts of Interest: The authors declare no conflict of interest.

References

1. Mcmeeking, R.M.; Rice, J.R. Finite-element formulations for problems of large elastic-plastic deformation. *Int. J. Solids Struct.* **1975**, *11*, 601–616. [CrossRef]
2. Barry, W.; Saigal, S. A three-dimensional element-free Galerkin elastic and elastoplastic formulation. *Int. J. Numer. Meth. Eng.* **1999**, *46*, 671–693. [CrossRef]
3. Schreyer, H.L.; Kulak, R.F.; Kramer, J.M. Accurate Numerical Solutions for Elastic-Plastic Models. *J. Press. Vess-T* **1979**, *101*, 226–234. [CrossRef]
4. Rong, B.; Rui, X.T.; Tao, T.; Wang, G.P. Theoretical modeling and numerical solution methods for flexible multibody system dynamics. *Nonlinear Dyn.* **2019**, *98*, 1519–1553. [CrossRef]
5. Ostiguy, G.L.; Sassi, S. Effects of initial geometric imperfections on dynamic behavior of rectangular plates. *Nonlinear Dyn.* **1992**, *3*, 165–181. [CrossRef]
6. Mahdiabadi, M.K.; Tiso, P.; Brandt, A.; Rixen, D.J. A non-intrusive model-order reduction of geometrically nonlinear structural dynamics using modal derivatives. *Mech. Syst. Signal Process.* **2021**, *147*, 107126. [CrossRef]
7. Vaiana, N.; Losanno, D.; Ravichandran, N. A novel family of multiple springs models suitable for biaxial rate-independent hysteretic behavior. *Comput. Struct.* **2021**, *244*, 106403. [CrossRef]
8. Vaiana, N.; Sessa, S.; Rosati, L. A generalized class of uniaxial rate-independent models for simulating asymmetric mechanical hysteresis phenomena. *Mech. Syst. Signal Process.* **2021**, *146*, 106984. [CrossRef]
9. Vaiana, N.; Sessa, S.; Paradiso, M.; Rosati, L. Accurate and efficient modeling of the hysteretic behavior of sliding bearings. In Proceedings of the 7th International Conference on Computational Methods in Structural Dynamics and Earthquake Engineering Methods in Structural Dynamics and Earthquake Engineering, Crete, Greece, 24–26 June 2019.
10. Belytschko, T.; Lu, Y.Y.; Gu, L. Element-free Galerkin methods. *Int. J. Numer. Meth. Eng.* **1994**, *37*, 229–256. [CrossRef]
11. Belytschko, T.; Krongauz, Y.; Organ, D.; Fleming, M.; Krysl, P. Meshless methods: An overview and recent development. *Comput. Methods Appl. Mech. Eng.* **1996**, *139*, 3–47. [CrossRef]
12. Chen, J.S.; Pan, C.; Wu, C.T.; Liu, W.K. Reproducing kernel particle methods for large deformation analysis of non-linear structures. *Comput. Methods Appl. Mech.* **1996**, *139*, 195–227. [CrossRef]
13. Cheng, Y.M.; Bai, F.N.; Liu, C.; Peng, M.J. Analyzing nonlinear large deformation with an improved element-free Galerkin method via the interpolating moving least-squares method. *Int. J. Comput. Mater. Sci. Eng.* **2016**, *5*, 1650023. [CrossRef]
14. Fleming, M.; Chu, Y.A.; Moran, B.; Belytschko, T. Enriched element-free Galerkin methods for crack tip fields. *Int. J. Numer. Meth. Eng.* **1997**, *40*, 1483–1504. [CrossRef]
15. Memari, A.; Mohebalizadeh, H. Quasi-static analysis of mixed-mode crack propagation using the meshless local Petrov-Galerkin method. *Eng. Anal. Bound. Elem.* **2019**, *106*, 397–411. [CrossRef]
16. Jiang, F.; Oliveira, M.S.A.; Sousa, A.C.M. Mesoscale SPH modeling of fluid flow in isotropic porous media. *Comput. Phys. Commun.* **2007**, *176*, 471–480. [CrossRef]
17. Moradi, D.R.; Radhi, A.; Behdinan, K. Damped dynamic behavior of an advanced piezoelectric sandwich plate. *Compos. Struct.* **2020**, *243*, 112243. [CrossRef]
18. Liu, M.B.; Liu, G.R. Smoothed particle hydrodynamics (SPH): An overview and recent developments. *Arch. Comput. Methods Eng.* **2010**, *17*, 25–76. [CrossRef]
19. Liu, W.K.; Chen, Y.; Jun, S.; Chen, J.S.; Belytschko, T.; Pan, C.; Uras, R.A.; Cheng, C.T. Overview and applications of the reproducing kernel particle methods. *Arch. Comput. Methods Eng.* **1996**, *3*, 3–80. [CrossRef]

20. Peng, M.J.; Li, D.M.; Cheng, Y.M. The complex variable element-free Galerkin (CVEFG) method for elasto-plasticity problems. *Eng. Struct.* **2011**, *33*, 127–135. [CrossRef]
21. Liew, K.M.; Feng, C.; Cheng, Y.M.; Kitipornchai, S. Complex variable moving least-squares method: A meshless approximation technique. *Int. J. Numer. Meth. Eng.* **2007**, *70*, 46–70. [CrossRef]
22. Cheng, Y.M.; Li, J.H. Complex variable meshless method for fracture problems. *Sci. China Ser. G* **2006**, *49*, 46–59. [CrossRef]
23. Bai, F.N.; Li, D.M.; Wang, J.F.; Cheng, Y.M. An improved complex variable element-free Galerkin method for two-dimensional elasticity problems. *Chin. Phys. B* **2012**, *21*, 020204. [CrossRef]
24. Li, D.M.; Liew, K.M.; Cheng, Y.M. An improved complex variable element-free Galerkin method for two-dimensional large deformation elastoplasticity problems. *Comput. Methods Appl. Mech.* **2014**, *269*, 72–86. [CrossRef]
25. Zhang, L.W.; Deng, Y.J.; Liew, K.M. An improved element-free Galerkin method for numerical modeling of the biological population problems. *Eng. Anal. Bound. Elem.* **2014**, *40*, 181–188. [CrossRef]
26. Wang, J.F.; Sun, F.X.; Cheng, Y.M. An improved interpolating element-free Galerkin method with nonsingular weight function for two-dimensional potential problems. *Chin. Phys. B* **2012**, *21*, 090204. [CrossRef]
27. Sun, F.X.; Wang, J.F.; Cheng, Y.M.; Huang, A.X. Error estimates for the interpolating moving least-squares method in n-dimensional space. *Appl. Numer. Math.* **2015**, *98*, 79–105. [CrossRef]
28. Ren, H.P.; Cheng, Y.M. The interpolating element-free Galerkin (IEFG) method for two-dimensional elasticity problems. *Int. J. Appl. Mech.* **2011**, *3*, 735–758. [CrossRef]
29. Deng, Y.J.; Liu, C.; Peng, M.J.; Cheng, Y.M. The interpolating complex variable element-free Galerkin method for temperature field problems. *Int. J. Appl. Mech.* **2015**, *7*, 1550017. [CrossRef]
30. Deng, Y.J.; He, X.Q. An improved interpolating complex variable meshless method for bending problem of Kirchhoff plates. *Int. J. Appl. Mech.* **2017**, *9*, 1750089. [CrossRef]
31. Ren, H.P.; Cheng, J.; Huang, A.X. The complex variable interpolating moving least-squares method. *Appl. Math. Comput.* **2012**, *219*, 1724–1736. [CrossRef]
32. Deng, Y.J.; He, X.Q.; Dai, Y. The improved interpolating complex variable element free Galerkin method for two-dimensional potential problems. *Int. J. Appl. Mech.* **2019**, *11*, 1950104. [CrossRef]
33. Deng, Y.J.; He, X.Q.; Sun, L.G.; Yi, S.H.; Dai, Y. An improved interpolating complex variable element free Galerkin method for the pattern transformation of hydrogel. *Eng. Anal. Bound. Elem.* **2020**, *113*, 99–109. [CrossRef]
34. Yu, S.Y.; Peng, M.J.; Cheng, H.; Cheng, Y.M. The improved element-free Galerkin method for three-dimensional elastoplasticity problems. *Eng. Anal. Bound. Elem.* **2019**, *104*, 215–224. [CrossRef]
35. Cheng, Y.M. *Meshless Methods*; Science Press: Beijing, China, 2015.
36. Cheng, Y.M.; Bai, F.N.; Peng, M.J. A novel interpolating element-free Galerkin (IEFG) method for two-dimensional elastoplasticity. *Appl. Math. Model.* **2014**, *38*, 5187–5197. [CrossRef]
37. Sun, F.X.; Wang, J.F.; Cheng, Y.M. An improved interpolating element-free Galerkin method for elastoplasticity via nonsingular weight functions. *Int. J. Appl. Mech.* **2016**, *8*, 1650096. [CrossRef]
38. Cheng, Y.M.; Wang, J.F.; Bai, F.N. A new complex variable element-free Galerkin method for two-dimensional potential problems. *Chin. Phys. B* **2012**, *21*, 090203. [CrossRef]

Article

Mathematical Models and Data Analysis of Residential Land Leasing Behavior of District Governments of Beijing in China

Jing Cheng

Architecture and Civil Engineering Research Centre, City University of Hong Kong Shenzhen Research Institute, Shenzhen 518057, China; jingcheng7-c@my.cityu.edu.hk; Tel.: +86-138-1825-8328

Abstract: To analyze the leasing behavior of residential land in Beijing, the mathematical models of the price and the total area of the leased residential land are presented. The variables of the mathematical models are proposed by analyzing the factors influencing the district government's leasing behavior for residential land based on the leasing right for residential land in Beijing, China. The regression formulae of the mathematical models are obtained with the ordinary least squares method. By introducing the data of the districts in Beijing from 2004 to 2015 into the mathematical models, the numerical results of the coefficients in the mathematical models are obtained by solving the equations of the regression formulae. After discussing the numerical results of the influencing factors, the district government behavior for leasing residential land in Beijing, China, is investigated. The numerical results show the factors concerning the government and how these factors influence the leased price and the total leased area of residential land for this large city in China. Finally, policy implications for the district government regarding residential land leasing in Beijing are proposed.

Keywords: mathematical model; leased price; total leased area; data analysis; residential land; Beijing

Citation: Cheng, J. Mathematical Models and Data Analysis of Residential Land Leasing Behavior of District Governments of Beijing in China. *Mathematics* **2021**, *9*, 2314. https://doi.org/10.3390/math9182314

Academic Editor: Yumin Cheng

Received: 6 September 2021
Accepted: 15 September 2021
Published: 18 September 2021

Publisher's Note: MDPI stays neutral with regard to jurisdictional claims in published maps and institutional affiliations.

Copyright: © 2021 by the author. Licensee MDPI, Basel, Switzerland. This article is an open access article distributed under the terms and conditions of the Creative Commons Attribution (CC BY) license (https://creativecommons.org/licenses/by/4.0/).

1. Introduction

For a country, the leasing of residential land is related to people's life and the economic development of the country. With the developments in China in the past 30 years, the land and real estate markets also have been developing rapidly, and the mode of residential land leasing has been fixed. To analyze how the mode is fixed, considering that land leasing is a kind of government behavior, it is necessary to analyze the factors influencing government behavior for leasing residential land in China to enhance the efficient use of residential land and achieve sustainable development. Therefore, studying the reasonable allocation of land resources is necessary for regional urban planning [1], land policies and planning [2], and the development of cities [3].

In China, for the metropolitans, such as Beijing, Shenzhen and Shanghai, the district governments of these cities decide the leasing behavior of the land use rights, and then land markets are mainly controlled by the district governments [4,5]. The central and local governments are responsible for managing the different parts of the urban housing and land markets [6]. Various policies are formulated by the central government to promote the marketization of land, while the local governments implement these polices to maximize long-term profits and ensure long-term sustainable development [7]. The policies for land leasing are affected by the fiscal incentives; thus, the local governments considered attracting the land investments [8]. Li et al. [9] considered multi-objective functions to discuss the optimization of land-use arrangement. Therefore, when the local governments lease land, the factors influencing land leasing should be considered [10].

Some factors affecting the land leasing of the local governments are discussed by using mathematical models. Land price [11,12], land leasing mode [13], political competition among local officials [14], the economy of the city and so on are considered. The listing, tender and auction of land leasing modes stipulated by the Chinese land law affect the local governments' decisions on leasing land [13]. The increase in gross domestic product

(GDP) of a city can make the local government increase the land leasing [12]. The behavior of land leasing of the local government and the prices of the land and houses can also be influenced by local public goods, such as public transit [15], airports [16], subway stations [17] and so on. In suburban districts of large Chinese cities, subway stations make the local governments obtain more profits from leasing land near these stations [18], because they impact the consumer amenities and economic activities positively [17]. The shorter the distances to subway stations are, the higher the land prices are [19]. Land or houses near pure air, high-quality primary and middle schools, main universities and environmental conveniences raise their prices [15]. Land prices can also be influenced by the distance between the land location and the center of a city. The shorter this distance is, the higher the prices of the land leases are [16].

For the influencing factors of leased land area, the shorter the distance of the land location to the city center is, the larger the total area of the leased land is [20]. The distance of the land to the city center or the closest subway station has a negative correlation with the total area of leased land [21]. The district location and the highway number in this district have influences on the total leased area of industrial land [5]. Furthermore, the total area of leased land is also influenced by the distance of the land to the city or district center, metro station and highway number [22].

In general, in the mathematical models of the leased land, the regression formulae are obtained with the ordinary least squares (OLS) method [23–25]. With the further development of the OLS method, the general least squares method, moving least squares method [26,27], improved moving least squares method [28,29] and complex variable moving least squares method [30] are presented. The general least squares method can also be used in the mathematical models of the leased land to obtain the regression formulae. The moving least squares method, improved moving least squares method and complex variable moving least squares method are presented to propose new meshless methods to solve science and engineering problems governed by the partial differential equations.

Beijing, as the capital, is one of the largest Chinese cities. It has a high GDP, land price as well as house price. The population of Beijing reached more than 20 million. With the rapid economic development of Beijing, the pressures on land supply increased, and the contradiction between land resources and population growth became sharp. As mentioned above, the district governments in Beijing decide the planning and leasing of residential land, which shows that in Beijing, the data of the districts in Beijing should be used to study the leasing behavior regarding residential land. Currently, the corresponding research on the influencing factors of the leasing prices for house and land are mainly based on the data of a city or province. Few papers have been published studying the factors affecting the leasing behavior of residential land of district governments in Beijing by using the data of the districts, because it is difficult to obtain the corresponding data at the district level. The corresponding research mainly considered the factors of basic land and location, while the district factors, such as political and economic influences, were not discussed; thus, more factors from different aspects should be considered. Furthermore, most of the literature discussed land leasing prices, while few researchers applied the price and the total area of leased land together to study the land leasing behavior of the local governments.

In this paper, the mathematical models of the price and the total area of the leased residential land are presented to analyze the leasing behavior of residential land in Beijing. The variables of the mathematical models are proposed based on the leasing right for residential land in Beijing, China. The regression formulae of the mathematical models are obtained with the OLS method. The data of the districts in Beijing from 2004 to 2015 are used to obtain the numerical results of the coefficients in the models. The district government's behavior towards leasing residential land in Beijing, China, is investigated by discussing the numerical results of the models.

2. Methodology

The methodology in this paper is to discuss the factors influencing the leasing behavior of the district governments for leasing residential land by using the mathematical models of the price and the total area of leased residential land. Linear regression relationships are applied in the models proposed in this paper, and the regression formulae of the coefficients in the models are obtained from the OLS method.

By using the data of all districts in Beijing from 2004 to 2015, numerical results can be obtained from the regression formulae of the mathematical models. From the results, the relationship between the price (or total area) of residential land leased and the corresponding influencing factors are analyzed.

The mathematical models of the price and the total area of leased residential land presented in this paper are for every piece of land for all districts in Beijing for a year. The dependent variables are residential land price and total area, and the corresponding independent ones are the factors affecting the local district governments' behavior on leasing residential land.

From the literature published before, all possible factors are considered in the mathematical models in this paper. From the macro level of a district and micro level of a piece of leased land, the land attributes, district-level economic status and geographic location of the leased land are discussed.

The regression formulae of the mathematical models are obtained from the OLS method in which the best approximation is used to obtain the most optimal solutions, and then the correct numerical solutions can be obtained from the models.

According to the data of the price and the total area of leased residential land and the corresponding influencing factors in the districts of Beijing from 2004 to 2015, the numerical results can be obtained from the regression formulae. The variance inflation factor (VIF) is applied to avoid multicollinearity among the independent variables of the mathematical models.

From the numerical results, the factors influencing the local district governments on leasing residential land are discussed, and how the price and the total area of leased residential land being changed with the factors is analyzed. Finally, policy implications for the local district governments are proposed, and the metropolitans of developing countries implementing public ownership of land can learn from and benefit from these implications.

3. Mathematical Models

3.1. The Dependent and Independent Variables

The dependent variables considered in this paper are the price and the total area of residential land leased. Then the mathematical models of the price and the total area are proposed, respectively.

The independent variables considered are the factors influencing the local district governments on leasing residential land. These factors are proposed based on the literature from the macro level of a district and micro level of a piece of leased land, such as land attributes, district-level economy, geographic location of the leased land and so on. Thus, land attributes, district-level attributes and location attributes, of factors affecting residential land leasing, are considered.

With regard to land attributes, the factors considered in this paper are the area and the floor area ratio (FAR) of the residential land, the mode of land leasing and the corresponding district location. The land area is the built area of a certain leased residential land. The FAR of the land is the ratio of the built area to the area of a piece of residential land. These two factors will be considered by the government because the area and FAR of the leased land are needed for different land leasing types. The land leasing mode can affect land leasing, and the price of land leased by listing mode can be higher [13]. The area and price of residential land are different in the various districts in Beijing. In Beijing, three categories, i.e., center districts, suburban ones and county, are considered for the 18 districts from 2004 to 2015. Districts such as Dongcheng, Xicheng, Chaoyang, Haidian, Chongwen, Xuanwu,

Fengtai and Shijingshan, are the center ones; the districts of Daxing, Changping, Fangshan, Shunyi, Mentougou, Tongzhou, Pinggu and Huairou are suburban ones, whereas Yanqing and Miyun are counties. The district location can influence land prices in that the land prices in the central districts are higher than those in other districts [16]. The geographic distribution of the 18 districts in Beijing is shown in Figure 1.

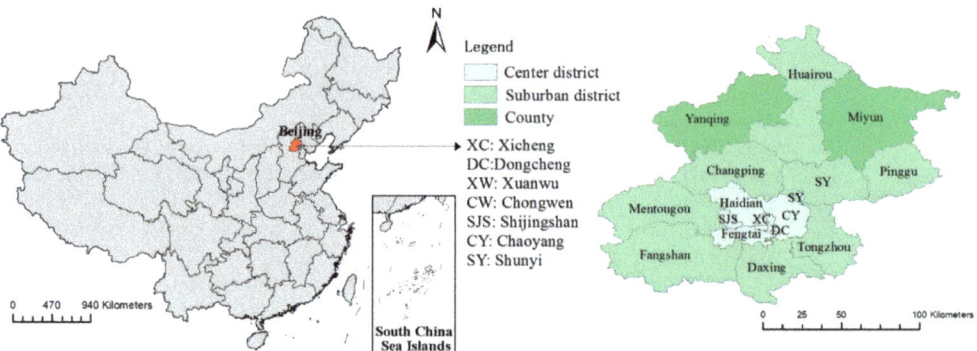

Figure 1. The distribution of the center districts, suburban districts and counties [3].

With regard to district-level attributes, factors such as GDP and term of office for the district head are involved. Land supply is impacted by the urban economy, such as GDP [12]. The district heads can lease a certain piece of land at a certain time according to the planning and development of the district.

The location attributes consider the location of the leased residential land, and the distances of the land to city center, district center, subway station, highway, university, high school, park and industrial park. The transportation status and the location of the leased land are crucial for the land leasing behavior of the government. Tiananmen Square is regarded as the center of Beijing. The location of the government of the district is regarded as the district center. The subway and highway are basic transport infrastructure, and can provide excellent conditions for residential development. University and high school show the educational level of a district, which can also have significant impacts on land price and house price [15]. For the key high schools, currently in China, school district housing becomes more and more popular among parents, thereby giving their children high-quality education in a more favorable atmosphere. Parks can supply an excellent environment and be of convenience for the nearby residents, and usually increase the house price [31,32]. The industrial parks have negative impacts on residential land price, because generally the residences are far from industrial parks due to the great noise and pollution.

These factors mentioned above consider the macro level of a district and micro level of a piece of leased land, such as land attributes, district-level economy, geographic location of the leased land and so on, and all possible factors are included based on the literature. These factors will be regarded as the variables of the mathematical models to study the factors affecting the behavior of the district government for leasing residential land.

3.2. Mathematical Model of Leased Residential Land Price

Based on above variables, the mathematical models for the price and the total area of leased residential land are presented. Similar to the hedonic model, the mathematical models are proposed based on the linear regression, and the OLS method is applied to obtain the coefficients of the models. The VIF is tested to avoid multicollinearity among the independent variables, so that the VIFs are smaller than 7.

The mathematical model of the price of leased residential land is

$$\ln LP_{it} = a + \sum_{m=1}^{M} \alpha_m A_{mit} + \sum_{j=1}^{J} \beta_j D_{jit} + \sum_{k=1}^{K} \gamma_k L_{kit} + Yr\_dum + Dis\_dum + u_{it} \quad (1)$$

where LP_{it} denotes the price of each piece of leased residential land; A_{mit}, D_{jit} and L_{kit} denote the land attributes, the district-level attributes and the location attributes, respectively; M, J and K are the numbers of the land attributes, the district-level attributes and the location attributes, respectively; Yr_dum and Dis_dum denote dummy variables of the year and the district, respectively; i is the district, t is the year, a is a constant, and u_{it} denotes the error term. The district and the year may influence the results; thus, the district dummy and year dummy variables are added to control the variables of years and districts. In Table 1, a detailed description of the variables in Equation (1) is presented.

Table 1. The definitions and summary statistics of the variables for the price model.

Category	Variable	Description	Obs.	Mean	Std. Dev.
	$\ln(LP_{it})$	Transaction price of every piece of leased land of district i in year t. (Yuan)	187	7.95×10^8	8.99×10^8
A_{1it}	$\ln(Area_{it})$	Built areas of the land leasing for district i in year t. (m^2)	187	75,839.24	69,095.43
A_{2it}	$\ln(FAR_{it})$	FAR of the land for district i in year t.	187	2	0.72
A_{3it}	$MOD1_{it}$	Land leasing mode for district i in year t =1 when the mode is listing; =0 otherwise. (Auction is for comparison.)	187 / 132 / 55	0.71	0.46
A_{4it}	$MOD2_{it}$	Land leasing mode for district i in year t =1 when the mode is tender; =0 otherwise. (Auction is for comparison.)	187 / 54 / 133	0.29	0.45
A_{5it}	$LOC1_{it}$	Location of district i =1 when i is center district; =0 otherwise. (County is for comparison.)	187 / 59 / 128	0.32	0.47
A_{6it}	$LOC2_{it}$	Location of district i =1 when i is suburban district; =0 otherwise. (County is for comparison.)	187 / 114 / 73	0.61	0.49
D_{1it}	$\ln(GDP_{it})$	GDP for district i in year t. (Yuan)	187	8.51×10^{10}	9.55×10^{10}
D_{2it}	DM_{it}	Term of office for district head of district i in year t.	187	4	1.91
L_{1it}	$\ln(TA_{it})$	Distance of the land for district i in year t to Tiananmen Square. (m)	187	28,788.91	18,217.55
L_{2it}	$\ln(GOV_{it})$	Distance of the land for district i in year t to the government of district i. (m)	187	8752.82	9588.75
L_{3it}	$\ln(SUB_{it})$	Distance of the land for district i in year t to the nearest subway. (m)	187	13,181.63	15,094.78
L_{4it}	$\ln(HIGH_{it})$	Distance of the land for district i in year t to the nearest highway. (m)	187	3398.24	5569.69
L_{5it}	$\ln(UNI_{it})$	Distance of the land for district i in year t to the nearest university. (m)	187	14,376.65	15,060.32
L_{6it}	$\ln(HS_{it})$	Distance of the land for district i in year t to the nearest key high school. (m)	187	6099.26	6151.21
L_{7it}	$\ln(PAR_{it})$	Distance of the land for district i in year t to the nearest park. (m)	187	5681.05	3802.66
L_{8it}	$\ln(IP_{it})$	Distance of the land for district i in year t to the nearest industrial park. (m)	187	3603.74	4155.92

The vector form of Equation (1) is

$$\ln LP_{it} = a + \mathbf{a}\mathbf{A} + u_{it} \tag{2}$$

where

$$\mathbf{a} = (\alpha_1, \alpha_2, \ldots, \alpha_M, \beta_1, \beta_2, \ldots, \beta_J, \gamma_1, \gamma_2, \ldots, \gamma_K, 1, 1) \tag{3}$$

is the coefficient vector, and

$$\mathbf{A} = (A_{1it}, A_{2it}, \ldots, A_{Mit}, D_{1it}, D_{2it}, \ldots, D_{Jit}, L_{1it}, L_{2it}, \ldots, L_{Kit}, Yr\_dum, Dis\_dum)^{\mathrm{T}} \tag{4}$$

is the variable (or factor) vector.

Then we know that the expectation and variance equal to zero, i.e.,

$$\mathrm{E}(\ln LP_{it} - a - \mathbf{a}\mathbf{A}) = 0 \tag{5}$$

$$\mathrm{E}(A_j(\ln LP_{it} - a - \mathbf{a}\mathbf{A})) = 0 \tag{6}$$

where A_j is the weight coefficient.

Considering the sampling data, we define the estimator $\hat{\mathbf{a}}$ of the vector $\mathbf{a}$ as

$$\hat{\mathbf{a}} = (\hat{a}_1, \hat{a}_2, \ldots, \hat{a}_M) \tag{7}$$

From Equations (5) and (6) we have

$$\frac{1}{N}\sum_{n=1}^{N}(\ln LP_{itn} - \hat{a} - \hat{\mathbf{a}}\mathbf{A}_n) = 0 \tag{8}$$

$$\frac{1}{N}\sum_{n=1}^{N} A_{jn}(\ln LP_{itn} - \hat{a} - \hat{\mathbf{a}}\mathbf{A}_n) = 0 \tag{9}$$

where N denotes the number of sample data.

From Equation (8) we obtain

$$\bar{y} = \hat{a} + \hat{\mathbf{a}}\overline{\mathbf{A}}_n \tag{10}$$

then

$$\hat{a} = \bar{y} - \hat{\mathbf{a}}\overline{\mathbf{A}}_n \tag{11}$$

where

$$\bar{y} = \frac{1}{N}\sum_{n=1}^{N}\ln LP_{itn} \tag{12}$$

$$\overline{\mathbf{A}}_n = \frac{1}{N}\sum_{n=1}^{N} \mathbf{A}_n \tag{13}$$

In Equation (9), considering the arbitrariness of sample number, we can obtain

$$\sum_{n=1}^{N} A_{jn}(\ln LP_{itn} - \hat{a} - \hat{\mathbf{a}}\mathbf{A}_n) = 0 \tag{14}$$

From Equations (11) and (14) we have

$$\sum_{n=1}^{N} A_{jn}\left(\ln LP_{itn} - (\bar{y} - \hat{\mathbf{a}}\overline{\mathbf{A}}_n) - \hat{\mathbf{a}}\mathbf{A}_n\right) = 0 \tag{15}$$

i.e.,

$$\sum_{n=1}^{N} A_{jn}(\ln LP_{itn} - \bar{y}) = \hat{\mathbf{a}}\sum_{n=1}^{N} A_{jn}(\mathbf{A}_n - \overline{\mathbf{A}}_n) \tag{16}$$

By solving Equation (16) we have

$$\hat{a}_i = \frac{\sum\limits_{n=1}^{N} A_{jn}(\ln LP_{itn} - \bar{y})}{\sum\limits_{n=1}^{N} A_{jn}(A_n - \overline{A}_n)} \quad (17)$$

Then we can obtain the estimator $\hat{a}$.

3.3. Mathematical Model of Leased Residential Land Area

The mathematical model of the total area of leased residential land is

$$\ln(LA_{it}) = a + \sum_{l=1}^{L} \alpha_l M_{lit} + Yr\_dum + Dis\_dum + u_{it} \quad (18)$$

where LA_{it} denotes the total area of leased residential land; M_{lit} denotes the location attributes; and L denotes the number of location attributes. The detailed description and statistics of the variables in Equation (18) are shown in Table 2. The corresponding estimator $\hat{a}$ in this model can be obtained in a similar way mentioned above.

Table 2. The definitions and summary statistics of the variables for the total area model.

Category	Variable	Description	Obs.	Mean	Std. Dev.
	$\ln(LA_{it})$	Built area of total leased land of district i in year t. (m²)	216	65,658.12	130,448.1
M_{1it}	$\ln(DCC_{it})$	Distance between district i in year t and Tiananmen Square. (m)	216	17,538.98	17,704.8
M_{2it}	$Subway_{it}$	Numbers of subway stations in district i in year t.	216	8.7	13.26
M_{3it}	$Highway_{it}$	Numbers of highway entrances and exits in district i in year t.	216	84.3	103.22
M_{4it}	$\ln(DIP_{it})$	Distance between district i in year t and the nearest industrial park. (m)	216	181.21	744.76
M_{5it}	$LOC1_{it}$	Location of district i =1 when i is center district; is center district; =0 otherwise. (County is for comparison.)	216 96 120	0.44	0.50
M_{6it}	$LOC2_{it}$	Location of district i =1 when i is suburban district; =0 otherwise. (County is for comparison.)	216 96 120	0.44	0.50

The mathematical models proposed in this study for the price and the total area of leased residential land are based on multivariate regression analysis. The relationship between the price of every piece of leased residential land (or the area of total leased residential land) with each influencing factor is linear. The OLS method is used to obtain the regression formulae of the mathematical models. From mathematical theory, the OLS method is one of the most accurate mathematical methods to fit the most optimal value; thus, the correct regression results can be obtained from the formulae in this paper. Then, the validation for the mathematical models is shown theoretically.

4. Data and Regression Results

To obtain the regression results, the data of all districts in Beijing from 2004 to 2015 are searched or computed by the author one by one.

The basic data, such as GDP and term of office of the district head, of all the districts in Beijing, were obtained from the yearbooks of all 18 districts.

The data of leased residential land, such as transaction price, built area, FAR and leasing modes, in Beijing, were obtained from the official website of the Beijing Planning and Land Resources Bureau. The distribution of residential land leased in Beijing from 2004 to 2015 is given in Figure 2.

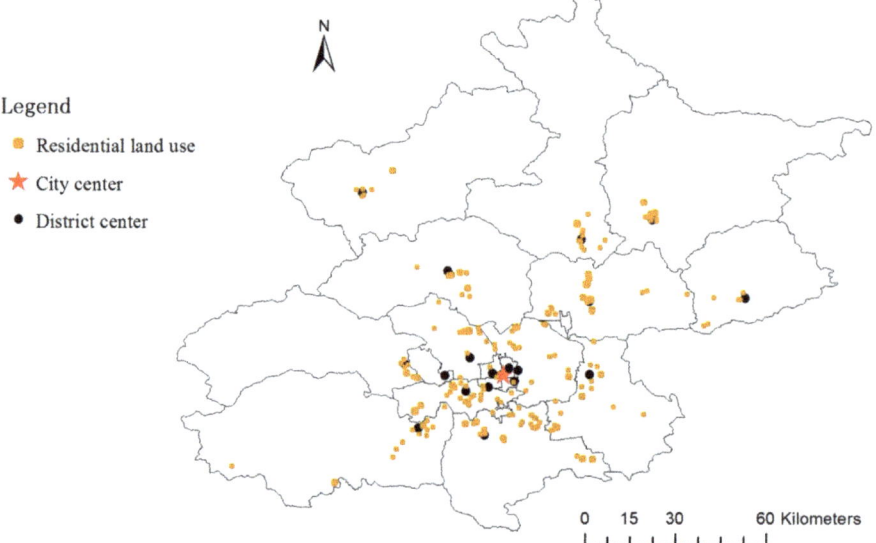

Figure 2. Residential land leasing from 2004 to 2015.

The longitude and latitude of all locations, such as the piece of land, the centers of Beijing and the 18 districts, subway stations, highway entrances and exits, university, high school, park and industrial park, were obtained from Google Maps. In total, 44 key high schools, 60 main universities, 50 parks and 72 industrial parks in Beijing were considered. The distributions of the subway stations and highways in 2004 and 2015 are shown in Figures 3 and 4, respectively, and the distribution of the municipal key high schools, main universities, parks and industrial parks considered in this paper is presented in Figure 5.

The distances between the location of a leased land and Tiananmen Square, district government, the nearest subway, the nearest highway entrance and exit, the nearest key high school, the nearest university, the nearest park and the nearest industrial park were computed with ArcGIS, which is geographic information system software.

After collecting the above data, from the mathematical models, the regression results of the leased residential land price and total leased area at the district level were obtained. The corresponding numerical results are presented in Tables 3 and 4.

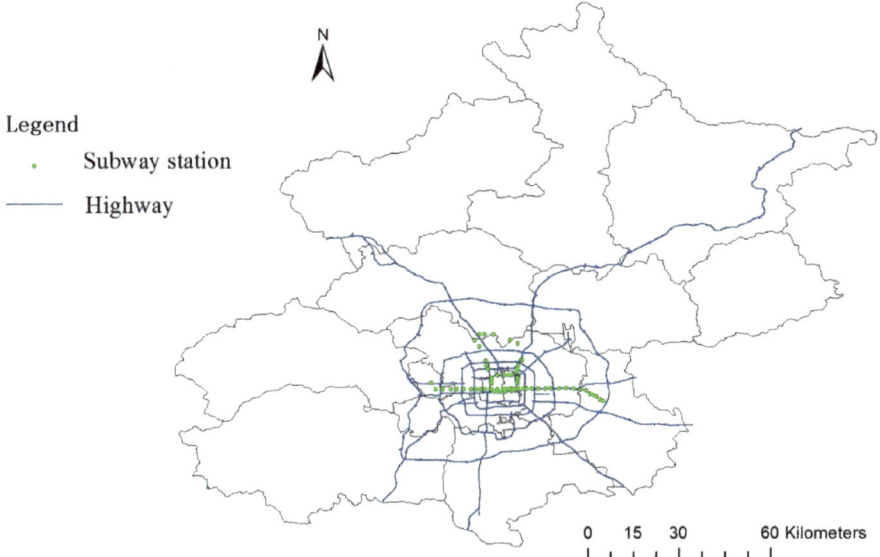

Figure 3. The subway stations and highways in 2004.

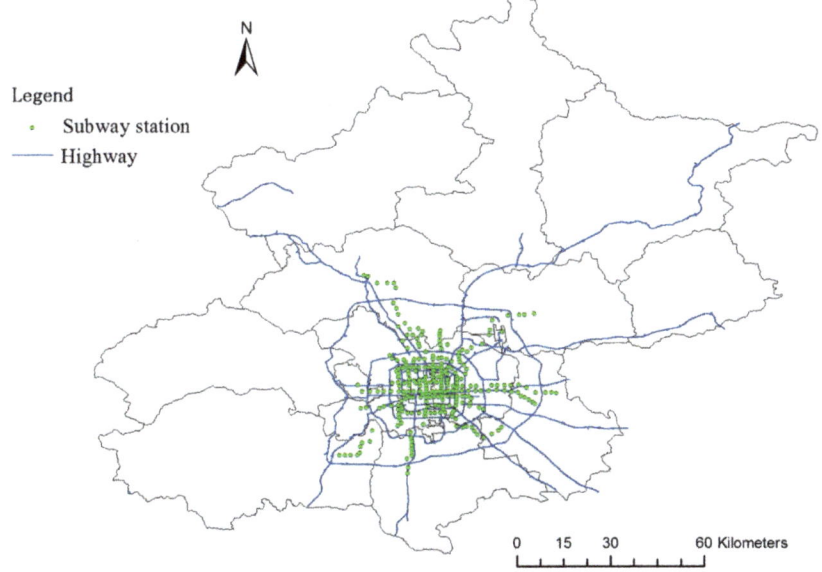

Figure 4. The subway stations and highways in 2015 [3].

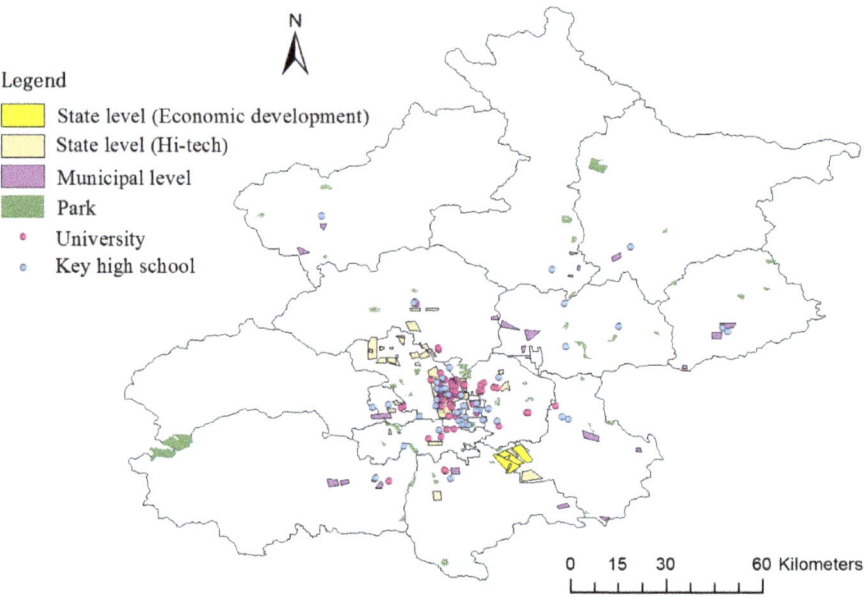

Figure 5. The distribution of the main universities, key high schools, parks and industrial parks.

Table 3. The results for the price model.

Variable	Coefficient	Robust Standard Errors
Residential land attributes		
$\ln(Area_{it})$	1.05599 ***	0.03843
$\ln(FAR_{it})$	0.46383 ***	0.14348
$MOD1_{it}$	−0.16323	0.45901
$MOD2_{it}$	−0.06821	0.35298
$LOC1_{it}$	0.05951	0.74614
$LOC2_{it}$	0.41961	0.70880
District-level attributes		
$\ln(GDP_{it})$	−0.09871	0.36908
DM_{it}	−0.03325	0.03341
Location attributes		
$\ln(TA_{it})$	−1.02350 ***	0.24363
$\ln(GOV_{it})$	−0.06071	0.05973
$\ln(SUB_{it})$	−0.05064	0.05986
$\ln(HIGH_{it})$	0.09980 *	0.05807
$\ln(UNI_{it})$	−0.05349	0.07592
$\ln(HS_{it})$	0.04179	0.06062
$\ln(PAR_{it})$	0.13204 **	0.06517
$\ln(IP_{it})$	0.00667	0.01617
Constant	21.25886 **	8.96312
District dummy	Yes	
Year dummy	Yes	
Observations	187	
R^2	0.9298	

Notes: ***: Significant at the 1 percent level; **: significant at the 5 percent level; *: significant at the 10 percent level.

Table 4. The results for the total area model.

Variable	Coefficient	Robust Standard Errors
Location attributes		
$\ln(DCC_{it})$	0.51405 **	0.20171
$Subway_{it}$	0.03815	0.06362
$Highway_{it}$	0.03179	0.05952
$\ln(DIP_{it})$	−0.20298	0.16756
$LOC1_{it}$	4.36266 *	2.58414
$LOC2_{it}$	4.17678 ***	1.59481
Constant	−4.84172 *	2.65913
District dummy	Yes	
Year dummy	Yes	
Observations	216	
R^2	0.4677	

Notes: ***: Significant at the 1 percent level; **: significant at the 5 percent level; *: significant at the 10 percent level.

5. Discussion

Firstly, we discuss the numerical results in Table 3 for the price of residential land leasing.

For the land attributes, the area and FAR of the leased residential land are very significant. When the area of it increases by 1%, the price of the leased residential land increases by 1.06%. Then, the district government hopes to lease residential land of which the area is large, because more profits can be earned. When the FAR of the leased residential land increases by 1%, the price of the land increases by 0.46%. From an economic viewpoint, a high floor ratio indicates a high intensive land use, and then the real estate developers can make large profits from the land. Thus, the district government prefers to lease the residential land of which the FAR is high.

About the location attributes, the distance of the location of the leased land to Tiananmen Square is very significant. When the distance increases by 1%, the price of the leased residential land decreases by 1.04%. The residential land that is closer to the Tiananmen Square has a higher price, because the accessibility to the public transportation system around the city center is better, as well as the convenience level of the neighborhood. Thus, the district government tends to lease residential land near the city center.

The distances from the land to the nearest park and the nearest highway entrance and exit are significant. When the distance from the leased land to the nearest park increases by 1%, the price of the land increases by 0.13%. When the distance from the land to the nearest highway entrance and exit increases by 1%, the land price increases by 0.1%. A green space provides a healthy environment and is convenient to relax in for residents. The parks can reduce the distance between residents and nature, and are helpful for the residents to relieve stress and breathe fresh air. The highways as for transportation, and can provide the convenience for residents to travel inside and outside cities. Thus, the district government is likely to lease residential land in proximity to parks and highways.

Then, we discuss the numerical results in Table 4 for the total area of residential land leasing.

The location of the district and the distance from the district to Tiananmen Square is significant. The total area of leased residential land is larger in the center and suburban districts than that in the counties. The total area of leased residential land increases by 0.51% when the distance from the district to Tiananmen Square increases by 1%. The government leases more residential land near the city center. Residential land is also more popular in center districts and suburban districts than that in counties. The reasons may be that the high-quality public transportation system is more favorable for the residential development, as well as the convenience level of the neighborhood. The government can earn more revenues from leasing residential land in the center and suburban areas, and near the city center.

In conclusion, the land area, the FAR, the distances between the land to the city center, the nearest park and the nearest highway entrance and exit have influences on the price of the residential land. The district location and the distance between the district and the city center affect the total area of residential land leasing in Beijing. The high land leasing price also results in great profits for the district government; thus, the district government hopes to lease the residential land with a high price. Under the control of the central government regarding house prices, the land leasing price should not increase rapidly.

According to the analysis above, we can see that the district government in Beijing hopes to lease residential land that has a large area or high FAR. Besides the land attributes, the location factors also have influences on the district government for leasing residential land. The district government prefers to lease residential land near the center of the city, park and highway; indeed, the government leases more residential land near the city center and in the center and suburban districts.

Compared with other similar studies, the residential land leasing price has a positive relationship with the area and FAR, which is in agreement with the results of Yang et al. [13]. The residential land leasing prices near the city center [13] and parks [20] are much higher, which is identical with the results in this study. It is shown that the numerical results in this paper are in agreement with those in other similar studies. The validation for the mathematical models presented in this paper is shown numerically.

Then the policy implications can be obtained from the above discussions.

Firstly, when the district government plans to lease residential land, the centers of the city and the districts should be considered as important factors to promote the pattern of combination of a center business district and high-standard residences near the center and sub-centers of the city for the development of the city in the long run.

Secondly, the district government is concerned more about the original attributes of the land, such as the land area and the FAR, when leasing residential land. Thus, the quality of the land plays an important role, and a large area and high FAR could increase profits for the governments.

Thirdly, the transportation infrastructure, such as highways, is vital for the district government to lease residential land, which is helpful for the government to develop the residences in suburban districts, promote the construction of development of suburban districts and achieve a relatively balanced residential development between the center and suburban districts.

Other developing countries implementing public ownership of land have a similar background of economic and residential development to that in China, and possibly face similar problems in residential land leasing given this background. Thus, the policy implications proposed from this study can be applied to other developing countries and other metropolitans in China, and provide a reference for them to figure out how to balance land leasing and have more sustainable development of the land use and economy.

6. Conclusions

Mathematical models of the price and the total area of the leased residential land are presented in this study to analyze the leasing behavior of residential land in Beijing. The factors influencing the district government's leasing behavior for residential land are considered as the variables of the models. By introducing the data of the districts in Beijing from 2004 to 2015 into the models, the numerical results of the coefficients of the influencing factors in the mathematical models are obtained by solving the equations of the regression formulae. By discussing the numerical results of the influencing factors, the district government's behavior regarding the leasing of residential land in Beijing, China, is investigated.

According to the results, area, FAR, the distance of the land to the city center, the nearest park and the nearest entrance and exit of highway affect the price of residential land; and the district location and the distance of the location of land to the city center affect total area of residential land.

According to the results in this study, the district governments in metropolitans can draw on these factors when residential land is being leased. The district governments should also consider additional factors previously overlooked, and the district governments can formulate land policy more efficiently for sustainable development of the districts, even the whole city.

Further, some recommendations on land use for an efficient and equitable land-use policy and long-term, financially sustainable urban development are proposed. The district governments can make better land leasing decisions in the coming decades based on the results in this study. Moreover, the policy implications of this study give a reference for other large cities in China and other counties under public land ownership.

Funding: This research received no external funding.

Institutional Review Board Statement: Not applicable.

Informed Consent Statement: Not applicable.

Data Availability Statement: All data, models, or code generated or used during the study are available from the corresponding author by request: GDP and tenure of the district mayor of 18 districts in Beijing from 2004 to 2015; land leasing data for residential land use in Beijing from 2004 to 2015; data of the distances in this study; data of city center, district centers, subway stations, highways, main universities, key high schools, public parks, and industrial parks; and other data supporting this study and related statistical methodology models.

Conflicts of Interest: The author declares no conflict of interest.

References

1. Liu, Y.S.; Zhang, Z.W.; Zhou, Y. Efficiency of construction land allocation in China: An econometric analysis of panel data. *Land Use Policy* **2018**, *74*, 261–272. [CrossRef]
2. Liu, Y.S.; Li, J.T.; Yang, Y.Y. Strategic adjustment of land use policy under the economic transformation. *Land Use Policy* **2018**, *74*, 5–14. [CrossRef]
3. Cheng, J. Analysis of commercial land leasing of the district governments of Beijing in China. *Land Use Policy* **2021**, *100*, 104881. [CrossRef]
4. Lin, C.S.G.; Ho, P.S.S. The state, land system, and land development processes in contemporary China. *Ann. Assoc. Am. Geogr.* **2005**, *95*, 411–436. [CrossRef]
5. Cheng, J. Data analysis of the factors influencing the industrial land leasing in Shanghai based on mathematical models. *Math. Probl. Eng.* **2020**, *2020*, 9346863. [CrossRef]
6. Fu, Q.; Lin, N. Local state marketism: An institutional analysis of China's urban housing and land market. *Chin. Sociol. Rev.* **2013**, *46*, 3–24. [CrossRef]
7. Liu, T.; Cao, G.Z.; Yan, Y.; Wang, Y.R. Urban land marketization in China: Central policy, local initiative, and market mechanism. *Land Use Policy* **2016**, *57*, 265–276. [CrossRef]
8. Li, H.; Kung, K.S.J. Fiscal incentives and policy choices of local governments: Evidence from China. *J. Dev. Econ.* **2015**, *116*, 89–104.
9. Li, F.X.; Gong, Y.A.; Cai, L.Y.; Sun, C.Y.; Chen, Y.M.; Liu, Y.X.; Jiang, P.H. Sustainable land-use allocation: A multiobjective particle swarm optimization model and application in Changzhou, China. *J. Urban Plan. Dev.* **2018**, *144*, 04018010. [CrossRef]
10. Cheng, J. Analyzing the factors influencing the choice of the government on leasing different types of land uses: Evidence from Shanghai of China. *Land Use Policy* **2020**, *90*, 104303. [CrossRef]
11. Buxon, M.; Taylor, E. Urban land supply, governance and the pricing of land. *Urban Policy Res.* **2011**, *29*, 5–22. [CrossRef]
12. Du, J.F.; Peiser, B.R. Land supply, pricing and local governments' land hoarding in China. *Reg. Sci. Urban Econ.* **2014**, *48*, 180–189. [CrossRef]
13. Yang, Z.; Ren, R.R.; Liu, H.Y.; Zhang, H. Land leasing and local government behaviour in China: Evidence from Beijing. *Urban Stud.* **2015**, *52*, 841–856. [CrossRef]
14. Solé-Ollé, A.; Viladecans-Marsal, E. Lobbying, political competition, and local land supply: Recent evidence from Spain. *J. Public Econ.* **2012**, *96*, 10–19. [CrossRef]
15. Sun, W.Z.; Zheng, S.Q.; Wang, R. The capitalization of subway access in home value: A repeat-rentals model with supply constraints in Beijing. *Transp. Res. Part A* **2015**, *80*, 104–115. [CrossRef]
16. Li, L.H. The dynamics of the Shanghai land market—An intra city analysis. *Cities* **2011**, *28*, 372–380. [CrossRef]
17. Zheng, S.Q.; Hu, X.K.; Wang, J.H.; Wang, R. Subways near the subway: Rail transit and neighborhood catering businesses in Beijing. *Transp. Policy* **2016**, *51*, 81–92. [CrossRef]
18. Yang, J.W.; Chen, J.X.; Le, X.H.; Zhang, Q. Density-oriented versus development-oriented transit investment: Decoding metro station location selection in Shenzhen. *Transp. Policy* **2016**, *51*, 93–102. [CrossRef]

19. Xu, T.; Zhan, M.; Aditjandra, P.T. The impact of urban rail transit on commercial property value: New evidence from Wuhan, China. *Transp. Res. Part A* **2016**, *91*, 223–235. [CrossRef]
20. Zheng, S.Q.; Kahn, M.E. Land and residential property markets in a booming economy: New evidence from Beijing. *J. Urban Econ.* **2008**, *63*, 743–757. [CrossRef]
21. Zheng, S.Q.; Kahn, M.E. Does government investment in local public goods spur gentrification? Evidence from Beijing. *Real Estate Econ.* **2014**, *41*, 1–48. [CrossRef]
22. Murakami, J.; Chang, Z. Polycentric development under public leasehold: A spatial analysis of commercial land use rights. *Reg. Sci. Urban Econ.* **2018**, *71*, 25–36. [CrossRef]
23. Cheng, J. Residential land leasing and price under public land ownership. *J. Urban Plan. Dev.* **2021**, *147*, 05021009. [CrossRef]
24. Wu, S.S.; Cheng, J.; Lo, S.M.; Chen, C.C.; Bai, Y.X. Coordinating urban constructions and district level population density for balanced development: An explorative structural equation modeling analysis on Shanghai. *J. Clean. Prod.* **2021**, *312*, 127646. [CrossRef]
25. Cheng, J. Mathematical model and analysis of residential land leasing in non-center districts of Shanghai. *Chin. J. Eng. Math.* **2020**, *37*, 403–414. (In Chinese)
26. Ren, H.P.; Cheng, J.; Huang, A.X. The complex variable interpolating moving least-squares method. *Appl. Math. Comput.* **2012**, *219*, 1724–1736. [CrossRef]
27. Wu, Q.; Peng, P.P.; Cheng, Y.M. The interpolating element-free Galerkin method for elastic large deformation problems. *Sci. China Technol. Sci.* **2021**, *64*, 364–374. [CrossRef]
28. Zheng, G.D.; Cheng, Y.M. The improved element-free Galerkin method for diffusional drug release problems. *Int. J. Appl. Mech.* **2020**, *12*, 2050096. [CrossRef]
29. Wu, Q.; Peng, M.J.; Cheng, Y.M. The interpolating dimension splitting element-free Galerkin method for 3D potential problems. *Eng. Comput.* **2021**, 1–15. [CrossRef]
30. Cheng, H.; Peng, M.J.; Cheng, Y.M. The hybrid complex variable element-free Galerkin method for 3D elasticity problems. *Eng. Struct.* **2020**, *219*, 110835. [CrossRef]
31. Chen, Y.W. Environmental externalities of urban river pollution and restoration: A hedonic analysis in Guangzhou (China). *Landsc. Urban Plan.* **2017**, *157*, 170–179. [CrossRef]
32. Chen, T.T.; Lang, W.; Li, X. Exploring the impact of urban green space on residents' health in Guangzhou, China. *J. Urban Plan. Dev.* **2020**, *146*, 05019022. [CrossRef]

Article

A Dimension Splitting-Interpolating Moving Least Squares (DS-IMLS) Method with Nonsingular Weight Functions

Jufeng Wang [1,*], Fengxin Sun [2] and Rongjun Cheng [3]

1 College of Finance & Information, Ningbo University of Finance & Economics, Ningbo 315175, China
2 Faculty of Science, Ningbo University of Technology, Ningbo 315016, China; fengxin@nbut.edu.cn
3 Faculty of Maritime and Transportation, Ningbo University, Ningbo 315211, China; chengrongjun@nbu.edu.cn
* Correspondence: wjf@nit.zju.edu.cn

Abstract: By introducing the dimension splitting method (DSM) into the improved interpolating moving least-squares (IMLS) method with nonsingular weight function, a dimension splitting–interpolating moving least squares (DS-IMLS) method is first proposed. Since the DSM can decompose the problem into a series of lower-dimensional problems, the DS-IMLS method can reduce the matrix dimension in calculating the shape function and reduce the computational complexity of the derivatives of the approximation function. The approximation function of the DS-IMLS method and its derivatives have high approximation accuracy. Then an improved interpolating element-free Galerkin (IEFG) method for the two-dimensional potential problems is established based on the DS-IMLS method. In the improved IEFG method, the DS-IMLS method and Galerkin weak form are used to obtain the discrete equations of the problem. Numerical examples show that the DS-IMLS and the improved IEFG methods have high accuracy.

Keywords: meshless method; dimension splitting-interpolating moving least squares (DS-IMLS) method; improved interpolating element-free Galerkin (IEFG) method; potential problem

1. Introduction

The construction of approximation functions in the meshless method is only related to nodes and independent of the mesh, so the meshless method has the advantages of no grid reconstruction and high computational accuracy [1–4]. The meshless method has become an essential numerical method in scientific and engineering calculation problems [5–8].

Many meshless methods have been proposed based on different construction methods of the shape function or discretization approach of the problem to be solved. The smoothed particle hydrodynamics (SPH) method [9], moving least squares (MLS) approximation [10], point interpolation method (PIM) [11], and radial basis function [12–15] are the widely used method to construct the meshless approximation. The major drawbacks of the SPH method include tensile instability and lack of approximation consistency. The MLS can provide an approximation with high smoothness on the whole problem domain. However, the major shortcoming of the MLS is a lack of Kronecker delta function property. The meshless method based on the MLS cannot enforce the essential boundary conditions directly. The approximation of the PIM satisfies the properties of delta function. However, when the node arrangement is not very suitable, the matrix singularity is likely to occur in the calculation of the shape function for PIM.

The meshless method is mainly constructed based on the strong form and weak form. The strong form-based method has also been applied to various problems [16,17]. This method has the advantages of easy adaptive refinement and low computation cost [18–21]. Since no background mesh is required, this method is a real meshless method. However, the strong form-based meshless collation method also has the drawbacks of poor accuracy

and stability. The element-free Galerkin (EFG) method [22], reproducing kernel particle method [23,24], local Petrov–Galerkin method [25], and boundary integral equation method [26] belong to the weak-from meshless method. Sometimes meshless methods based on weak forms may have weak computational efficiency.

The MLS approximation, which is developed from the traditional least squares (LS) method [27–30], is one of the most important methods for constructing trial functions in meshless methods. Based on the MLS approximation, Belytschko et al. proposed the EFG method [31], which has a wide range of applications and high calculation accuracy. In addition to the EFG method, many MLS-based meshless methods have been proposed, such as meshless local Petrov–Galerkin [32] and boundary knot method [33].

To reduce the ill condition of the matrix in the calculation of MLS approximation, Liew and Cheng et al. proposed an improved MLS approximation by using the weighted orthogonal function [34,35]. Based on this improved orthogonal MLS approximation, the boundary element-free method [36] and improved MLS Ritz method [37] were developed. To improve the computational efficiency, by using the theory of complex variables, Liew and Cheng et al. proposed the complex variable moving least-squares (CVMLS) method [38]. The meshless method based on the CVMLS method can improve calculation efficiency and accuracy [39,40].

Because the MLS method is not interpolable at the nodes, the MLS-based meshless method cannot directly enforce the essential boundary as the finite element method, which increases the additional computational burden. For this reason, Lancaster et al. proposed the interpolated moving least-squares (IMLS) method [10] by selecting singular special weight functions. Based on IMLS, the interpolating element-free Galerkin (IEFG) method [41] and other interpolation-type meshless methods [32,42–45] were proposed. Wang et al. studied the error convergence of the IMLS method [46,47]. The meshless method based on the IMLS method has a good calculation effect [48–51]. However, the singularity of the weight function in the IMLS method is not conducive to numerical calculation. To overcome the deficiency, Cheng et al. proposed an improved IMLS method with nonsingular weights [52,53]. The meshless method based on the improved IMLS has the advantages of nonsingular weight function and direct application of essential boundary [54–56].

The dimension-splitting method (DSM) was first applied in the finite element method. This method divides high-dimensional problems into a series of lower-dimensional problems and then iteratively solves them, which can effectively improve the computational complexity of the numerical methods [4,57,58]. By introducing DSM into the meshless method, Cheng et al. first proposed the dimension splitting meshless method, which showing high calculation accuracy and efficiency [59–61]. When a high order polynomial basis function is used, there are many matrix multiplications and inversion of high order matrices in the MLS approximation, especially in the calculations for the higher-order derivatives of the approximation function. It leads to a considerable accumulation of calculation errors and is not conducive to improving accuracy. This paper aims to propose a new hybrid method to obtain the shape function of the meshless method by incorporating the DSM into the improved IMLS method.

The main contributions of this paper are as follows. (1) By coupling the DSM and improved IMLS methods, this paper aims to propose a new hybrid method to obtain the shape function of the meshless method, which is called the "dimension splitting – interpolating moving least squares (DS-IMLS) method". (2) Similar to the weight function in the improved IMLS method, the weight function in the DS-IMLS method is also nonsingular, and the approximation satisfies the properties of the Kronecker delta function, so the meshless method based on the DS-IMLS method does not require additional numerical methods to enforce essential boundary conditions. (3) When a high order polynomial basis function is used, there are many matrix multiplications and inversion of high order matrices in MLS. This may lead to a considerable accumulation of calculation errors. We expect that the order of the inverse matrix can be reduced when finding the shape function in the hybrid method. Based on the DSM, for two-dimensional space, the shape function is calculated from a series of one-dimensional spaces, and then the order of the matrix that needs to be inverted will be greatly reduced in the DS-IMLS method when calculating the shape function. (4) We hope that the DS-IMLS method has high calculation accuracy for anisotropic node distribution. Even if the difference between the nodes spacings in the x and y directions is very large, the DS-IMLS method still has a good calculation effect. The performance of the method is verified through several numerical examples.

This paper is organized as follows. In Section 2, we describe the improved IMLS method with nonsingular weight functions. Incorporating the DSM to the improved IMLS method, the DS-IMLS method is presented in Section 3. Then based on the Galerkin weak form and the DS-IMLS method, Section 4 describes the improved IEFG method for the two-dimensional potential problems. The numerical examples to verify the performance are prescribed in Section 5. Finally, a summary and conclusions are provided in Section 6.

2. The Improved IMLS Method with Nonsingular Weight Functions

To improve the deficiency that the weight function must be singular in the IMLS method [10], Wang and Cheng et al. proposed an improved IMLS method with nonsingular weight functions [52]. The improved IMLS method can apply any nonsingular weight function used in the MLS approximation. To meet the interpolation characteristics, the improved IMLS method performs the following interpolation transformation:

$$b_i(\tilde{x})_x = p_i(\tilde{x}) - \sum_{k=1}^{n} I(x, x_k) p_i(x_k), \ i = 1, 2, \cdots, m, \tag{1}$$

$$\tilde{u}(\tilde{x})_x = u(\tilde{x}) - \sum_{k=1}^{n} I(x, x_k) u(x_k), \tilde{x} \in \Omega, \tag{2}$$

where $u(x)$ is an unknown function to be approximated, $p_i(x)$ is the basis function, and x_k represents the node whose influence domain covering x. The $I(x, x_k)$ is a Kronecker δ function on the nodes. In 1D space, it can be chosen as

$$I(x, x_k) = \prod_{j \neq k} \frac{x - x_j}{x_k - x_j}, \ x \in R^1. \tag{3}$$

Let $w(x - x_k)$ denote the nonsingular weight function. Then, taking $b_i(\tilde{x})_x$ and $\tilde{u}(\tilde{x})_x$ as the basis function and a function to be approximated, respectively, the approximation function of $u(x)$ can be obtained from the traditional MLS method as

$$u^h(x) = \Phi(x) u = \sum_{k=1}^{n} \phi_k(x) u(x_k), \tag{4}$$

where $\phi_k(x)$ is the shape function defined by

$$\Phi(x) = (\phi_1(x), \phi_2(x), \cdots, \phi_n(x)) = I(x) + p^T(x) A^{-1}(x) B(x), \tag{5}$$

with

$$u^T = (u(x_1), \ u(x_2), \cdots, u(x_n)), \tag{6}$$

$$I(x) = (I(x, x_1), I(x, x_2), \ldots, I(x, x_n)), \tag{7}$$

$$p^T(x) = (s_2(x), s_3(x), \cdots, s_m(x)), \tag{8}$$

$$s_i(x) = p_i(x) - \sum_{k=1}^{n} I(x, x_k) p_i(x_k). \tag{9}$$

$$A(x) = P^T(x) W(x) P(x), \tag{10}$$

$$B(x) = P^T(x) W(x) \varphi(x), \tag{11}$$

$$\boldsymbol{\varphi}(x) = [\delta_{ij} - I(x, x_j)]_{n \times n}, \qquad (12)$$

$$\boldsymbol{W}(x) = \begin{bmatrix} w(x - x_1) & 0 & \cdots & 0 \\ 0 & w(x - x_2) & \cdots & 0 \\ \vdots & \vdots & \ddots & \vdots \\ 0 & 0 & \cdots & w(x - x_n) \end{bmatrix}, \qquad (13)$$

$$\boldsymbol{P}(x) = \begin{bmatrix} b_2(x_1)_x & b_3(x_1)_x & \cdots & b_m(x_1)_x \\ b_2(x_2)_x & b_3(x_2)_x & \cdots & b_m(x_2)_x \\ \vdots & \vdots & \ddots & \vdots \\ b_2(x_n)_x & b_3(x_n)_x & \cdots & b_m(x_n)_x \end{bmatrix}. \qquad (14)$$

3. The DS-IMLS Method

The MLS approximation is one of the most important methods to construct shape functions in the meshless method and is widely used in scientific and engineering problems. The process of seeking the shape function of the MLS approximation involves matrix multiplication and inversion. Especially in calculating high-order derivatives such as second-order derivatives, there are many high-order matrix operations when using the quadratic basis function. It leads to the accumulation of calculation errors and the reduction of the accuracy of high-order derivatives of the approximation function. By introducing the idea of the dimension splitting method into the improved IMLS method with nonsingular weight functions, a dimension splitting – interpolating moving least squares (DS-IMLS) method with nonsingular weight functions is proposed in this section.

For two-dimensional problems, the problem domain is divided into a series of low-dimensional regions by the DSM (as shown in Figure 1). Suppose the problem domain Ω is split into L layers in the x direction, and $\Omega^{(k)}$ denotes the k−th layer satisfying $x = x_k$ with relevant boundary $\Gamma^{(k)}$, $k = 1, 2, \cdots, L$. For the problem domain, it follows that

$$\Omega = \bigcup_{k=1}^{L} \{x = x_k\} \times [x_k, x_{k+1}). \qquad (15)$$

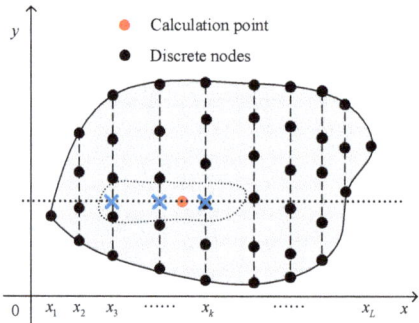

Figure 1. Problem domain and node distribution for the DS-IMLS method.

Based on the idea of the DSM, the unknown $u(x,y)$ is first regarded as a one-dimensional function of x. Then, imposing the improved IMLS method with nonsingular weight functions on the node distribution $\{x_1, x_2, \cdots, x_L\}$, the approximation function on x can be obtained as

$$u^h(x,y) = \sum_{k=1}^{n} \Phi_k(x) u(x_k, y), \tag{16}$$

where $\Phi_k(x)$ is the shape function determined by the improved IMLS method in one-dimensional space from Equation (4), and suppose x_k is one of the n nodes whose influence domain covers x.

Next, the function $u(x_k, y)$ is treated as the function on y, and is approximated by the improved IMLS method on the split plane $\Omega^{(k)}$. Suppose the plane $\Omega^{(k)}$ is discretized as $\{y_1^{(k)}, y_2^{(k)}, \cdots, y_{m_k}^{(k)}\}$, where m_k is the number of the nodes on $\Omega^{(k)}$. Then we have

$$u(x_k, y) = \sum_{i=1}^{n_k} \widetilde{\Phi}_i^{(k)}(y) u(x_k, y_i^{(k)}), \tag{17}$$

where $y_i^{(k)}$ is a node whose influence domain contains (x_k, y), and n_k is the number, and $\widetilde{\Phi}_i^{(k)}(y)$ is the shape function deduced from the splitting plane $\Omega^{(k)}$.

Coupling Equations (16) and (17), the approximation function of $u(x,y)$ can be

$$u^h(x,y) = \sum_{k=1}^{n} \sum_{i=1}^{n_k} \Phi_k(x) \widetilde{\Phi}_i^{(k)}(y) u(x_k, y_i^{(k)}). \tag{18}$$

Let $\overline{m} = \sum_{k=1}^{n} n_k$. Suppose that the global number of $(x_k, y_i^{(k)})$ in all discrete nodes of the problem domain is v_s, $s = 1, 2, \cdots, \overline{m}$. Then Equation (18) can be rewritten as

$$u^h(x,y) = \widetilde{\boldsymbol{\Phi}} \boldsymbol{u} = (\Phi_1(x)\widetilde{\boldsymbol{\varphi}}_1(y), \Phi_2(x)\widetilde{\boldsymbol{\varphi}}_2(y), \cdots, \Phi_n(x)\widetilde{\boldsymbol{\varphi}}_n(y))\boldsymbol{u}, \tag{19}$$

where $\widetilde{\boldsymbol{\Phi}}$ is the shape function of the DS-IMLS method, and

$$\begin{aligned}
\boldsymbol{u} &= (\widetilde{\boldsymbol{u}}_k)_{1 \times \overline{m}} = (u_{v_1}, u_{v_2}, \cdots, u_{v_m})^{\mathrm{T}}, \\
\widetilde{\boldsymbol{u}}_k &= \left(u(x_k, y_1^{(k)}), u(x_k, y_2^{(k)}), \cdots, u(x_k, y_{n_k}^{(k)})\right)_{1 \times n_k},
\end{aligned} \tag{20}$$

$$\widetilde{\boldsymbol{\varphi}}_k(y) = \left(\widetilde{\Phi}_1^{(k)}(y), \widetilde{\Phi}_2^{(k)}(y), \cdots, \widetilde{\Phi}_{n_k}^{(k)}(y)\right). \tag{21}$$

The derivatives of the approximation function can be easily obtained as

$$u^h_{,x}(x,y) = \widetilde{\boldsymbol{\Phi}}_{,x} \boldsymbol{u} = (\Phi_{1,x}(x)\widetilde{\boldsymbol{\varphi}}_1(y), \Phi_{2,x}(x)\widetilde{\boldsymbol{\varphi}}_2(y), \cdots, \Phi_{n,x}(x)\widetilde{\boldsymbol{\varphi}}_n(y))\boldsymbol{u}, \tag{22}$$

$$u^h_{,y}(x,y) = \widetilde{\boldsymbol{\Phi}}_{,y} \boldsymbol{u} = (\Phi_1(x)\widetilde{\boldsymbol{\varphi}}_{1,y}(y), \Phi_2(x)\widetilde{\boldsymbol{\varphi}}_{2,y}(y), \cdots, \Phi_n(x)\widetilde{\boldsymbol{\varphi}}_{n,y}(y))\boldsymbol{u}, \tag{23}$$

where the subscript is defined as

$$u^h_{,x}(x,y) = \frac{\partial}{\partial x} u^h(x,y). \tag{24}$$

The radii of the influence domain of nodes for the approximation of Equations (16) and (17) are, respectively, defined as

$$\gamma_1 = \mathrm{dmax}_1 \cdot d_1, \tag{25}$$

$$\gamma_2 = \mathrm{dmax}_2 \cdot d_2, \tag{26}$$

where d_1 and d_2 represent the distances between adjacent nodes in the x direction and on the split plane, respectively. The dmax_1 and dmax_2 are the influence domain parameter determining the radii. To ensure the existence of the shape function, the radius of the influence domain should be large enough. We can adopt the adaptive algorithm to determine the radius so there is an appropriate number in the influence domain in the program.

Thus, the DS-IMLS method is proposed. In the DS-IMLS method, the weight function is not singular, and the approximation satisfies the Kronecker delta property. Since the DSM is used to divide the problem into a series of lower-dimensional problems, the complexity of the matrix calculation for calculating the approximation function and its derivative is reduced.

4. The Improved IEFG Method Based on the DS-IMLS Method

Consider the following two-dimensional potential problems

$$-\nabla^2 u(x,y) = f(x,y), \ (x,y) \in \Omega \subset R^2, \tag{27}$$

with the essential boundary condition

$$u(x,y) = \overline{u}(x,y), \ (x,y) \in \Gamma_u, \tag{28}$$

where Γ_u is the boundary of Ω, f and $\overline{u}$ are given functions.

The Galerkin weak form of Equation (27) is

$$\int_\Omega \delta u \left[\nabla^2 u(x,y) + f(x,y) \right] d\Omega = 0, \tag{29}$$

where δu denotes the variation of function u.

From the partial integral, it follows that

$$-\int_\Omega \delta(\nabla u)^T \cdot \nabla u \, d\Omega + \int_\Omega \delta u \cdot f(x,y) d\Omega = 0, \tag{30}$$

where

$$\nabla u = \left(\frac{\partial u}{\partial x}, \frac{\partial u}{\partial y} \right)^T. \tag{31}$$

From the DS-IMLS method, the function $u(x,y)$ can be approximated as

$$u(x,y) \approx u^h(x,y) = \tilde{\mathbf{\Phi}} \mathbf{u} = (\Phi_1(x)\tilde{\varphi}_1(y), \Phi_2(x)\tilde{\varphi}_2(y), \cdots, \Phi_n(x)\tilde{\varphi}_n(y))\mathbf{u}. \tag{32}$$

Substituting Equation (32) into Equation (30) yields

$$\int_\Omega \delta \mathbf{u}^T \left(\mathbf{B}\mathbf{B}^T \right) \mathbf{u} \, d\Omega = \int_\Omega \delta \mathbf{u}^T \tilde{\mathbf{\Phi}} \cdot f(x,y) d\Omega, \tag{33}$$

where

$$\mathbf{B}^T = \begin{bmatrix} \Phi_{1,x}(x)\tilde{\varphi}_1(y) & \Phi_{2,x}(x)\tilde{\varphi}_2(y) & \cdots & \Phi_{n,x}(x)\tilde{\varphi}_n(y) \\ \Phi_1(x)\tilde{\varphi}_{1,y}(y) & \Phi_2(x)\tilde{\varphi}_{2,y}(y) & \cdots & \Phi_n(x)\tilde{\varphi}_{n,y}(y) \end{bmatrix}. \tag{34}$$

According to the arbitrariness of $\delta \mathbf{u}$, the discretized equation of Equation (27) is

$$\mathbf{K}\mathbf{u} = \mathbf{F}, \tag{35}$$

where

$$\mathbf{K} = \int_\Omega \mathbf{B}\mathbf{B}^T d\Omega, \tag{36}$$

$$F = \int_\Omega \widetilde{\mathbf{\Phi}} \cdot f(x,y) \mathrm{d}\Omega. \tag{37}$$

The shape functions of the DS-IMLS method have the interpolating property. Then the numerical solutions for two-dimensional potential problems can be obtained by directly substituting the essential boundary condition into Equation (35). Thus, the improved IEFG method based on the DS-IMLS method is presented for the potential problems.

5. Numerical Example

This section presents some examples to illustrate the effectiveness of the DS-IMLS method and the improved IEFG method. Three examples are given for studying the convergence and errors of the approximation function of the DS-IMLS method by using the known functions. In addition, two potential problems are solved by the improved IEFG method based on the DS-IMLS method. All numerical results are compared with those of the MLS or EFG methods. Both the MLS and DS-IMLS methods use second-order complete polynomial basis functions and cubic spline weight functions. In the MLS method, the node rectangular influence field of the following form is adopted:

$$\varepsilon_i = \mathrm{dmax}_0 \cdot \Delta, \tag{38}$$

where Δ is a two-dimensional column vector representing the average distance between nodes in the x and y directions. To study the error, the average and maximum errors of the following form are defined:

$$e_{\mathrm{mean}} = \frac{1}{M} \sum_{k=1}^{M} \left| u_k - u_k^h \right|, \tag{39}$$

$$e_{\mathrm{max}} = \max_{1 \le k \le M} \left\{ \left| u_k - u_k^h \right| \right\} \tag{40}$$

where $u_k = u(x_k, y_k)$ and $u_k^h = u^h(x_k, y_k)$ are, respectively, the exact and numerical solutions at the node (x_k, y_k), and M is the number of the discrete points used to calculate the errors.

The procedure for obtaining the approximation of the DS–IMS method and the solution of the improved IEFG method is as follows:

(1) Input the parameters of the governing equation and geometric parameters.
(2) Split the problem domain into L layers in the dimension splitting direction and determine the radius of influence domain for point x_i. Suppose the set of splitting points is $\{x_1, x_2, \cdots, x_L\}$.
(3) Discretize the plane $\Omega^{(k)}$ by $\left\{ y_1^{(k)}, y_2^{(k)}, \cdots, y_{m_k}^{(k)} \right\}, k = 1, 2, \cdots, L$.
(4) For any given (x, y), get all nodes $\{x_1, x_2, \cdots, x_n\}$ whose influence field covers x, and denote the subscript set as $\mathbf{v}_1$. Then calculate the corresponding shape functions $\Phi_k(x)$ by the improved IMLS method from $\{x_1, x_2, \cdots, x_n\}$ and $\mathbf{v}_1$.
(5) For every $k \in \mathbf{v}_1$, find all nodes in $\left\{ y_1^{(k)}, y_2^{(k)}, \cdots, y_{m_k}^{(k)} \right\}$ whose influence domain covers y. Suppose the global number is $\bar{\mathbf{v}}_i$. Then calculate the $\widetilde{\Phi}_i^{(k)}(y)$ by introducing the improved IMLS method into $\left\{ y_1^{(k)}, y_2^{(k)}, \cdots, y_{m_k}^{(k)} \right\}$ and $\bar{\mathbf{v}}_i$.
(6) Coupling Steps (4) and (5), the approximation function of $u(x,y)$ can be obtained as $u^h(x,y) = \sum_{k=1}^{n} \sum_{i=1}^{n_k} \Phi_k(x) \widetilde{\Phi}_i^{(k)}(y) u(x_k, y_i^{(k)})$. Thus, the approximation of the DS-IMLS method is presented.
(7) Substitute the approximation and its derivatives into Equation (30), and then obtain the discrete equation of the potential problems.
(8) Substitute the essential boundary condition into Equation (35) and solve Equation (35), and then obtain the node value u. Thus, the solution of the improved IEFG method for two-dimensional potential problems is obtained.

5.1. The Examples of the DS-IMLS Method

Example 1. Let $u(x,y) = \sin(xy)$, $0 \leq x, y \leq \pi$.

The approximation function is constructed from the known function $u(x,y)$ by the DS-IMLS method or MLS approximation. When $\text{dmax}_1 = \text{dmax}_2 = 3$, and 21×21 regular nodes distribution is used, the numerical approximations of the functions u, u_x, u_{xx} on the line $y = x$ are shown in Figure 2, and the approximations of u_y, u_{yy} are given in Figure 3. The corresponding approximated values of the second derivatives obtained by the MLS method are shown in Figure 4. It can be seen from these figures that the approximation function and its first and second derivatives of the DS-IMLS method are very consistent with the exact solutions and have higher accuracy than the MLS method.

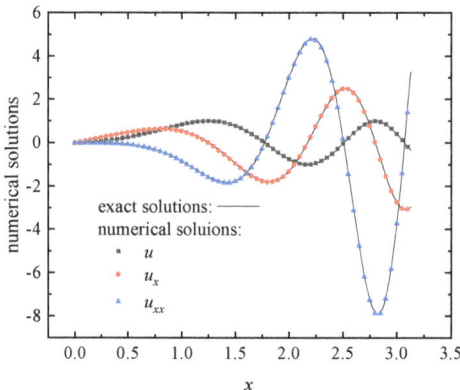

Figure 2. The numerical approximations of the functions u, u_x, u_{xx} obtained by the DS-IMLS method.

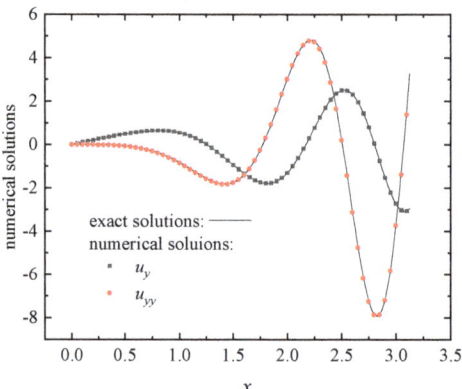

Figure 3. The numerical approximations of the functions u_y, u_{yy} obtained by the DS-IMLS method.

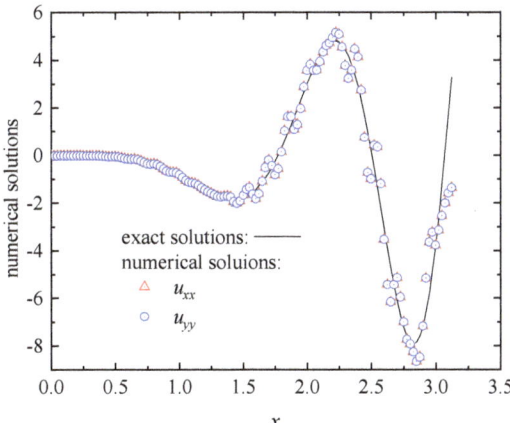

Figure 4. The numerical approximations of u_{xx}, u_{yy} obtained by the MLS method.

In order to analyze the influence of influence domain parameters on the error, 30×30 regular points are used to calculate the average and maximum errors. The approximation functions of the DS-IMLS and MLS methods are constructed based on the 21×21 regular nodes distribution. When $dmax_2 = 3$, the average and maximum errors of the nodes for different influence domain parameters $dmax_1$ are shown in Figure 5a. When fixing $dmax_1 = 3$, the corresponding errors are shown in Figure 5b. The errors of the MLS method for different influence domain parameter values are depicted in Figure 6. For the quadratic basis function, the DS-IMLS method has higher stability on the influence domain parameters and has high calculation accuracy when the value is greater than 3.

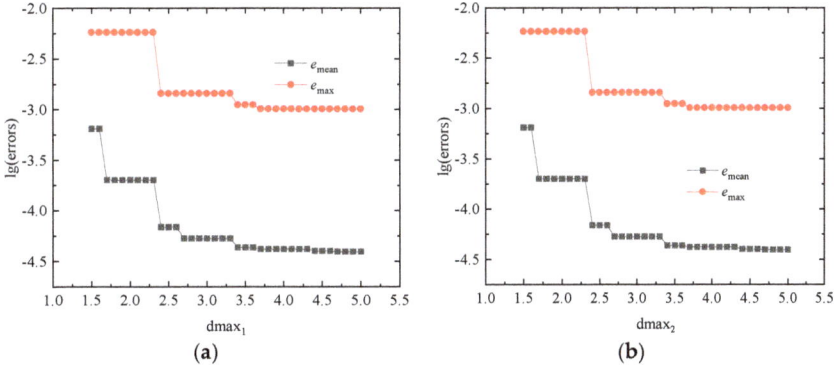

Figure 5. The average and maximum errors obtained by the DS-IMLS method for (**a**) different values of $dmax_1$ with fixed $dmax_2 = 3$; (**b**) different values of $dmax_2$ with fixed $dmax_1 = 3$.

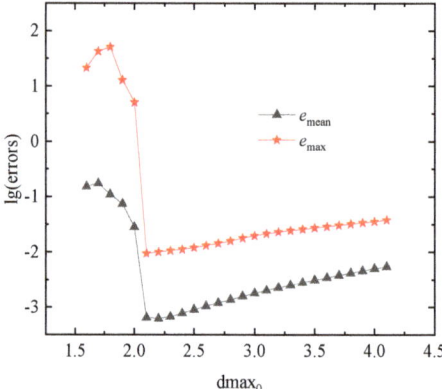

Figure 6. The average and maximum errors obtained by the MLS method for different influence domain parameters dmax_0.

To analyze the convergence of the approximation function with respect to node spacing, when $5 \times 5, 9 \times 9, 13 \times 13, 17 \times 17,$ and 21×21 regular node distributions are respectively adopted, the average discrete point errors e_{mean} of the DS-IMLS and MLS methods at 30×30 points are shown in Figure 7. The corresponding maximum point errors e_{max} are given in Figure 8. Here, $\text{dmax}_0 = 2.1$, and $\text{dmax}_1 = \text{dmax}_2 = 3$. It can be seen that the approximation function of the DS-IMLS method gradually converges to the exact solution with the increase of the number of nodes and has a higher convergence order than the MLS method. Let $\text{rand}()$ represent the uniformly distributed random numbers on $(0,1)$ generated by Matlab and d be the node spacing. When the perturbation of $\frac{2 \times \text{rand}() - 1}{5} \times d$ is added on the nodes $\{x_1, x_2, \cdots, x_L\}$ and $\{y_1^{(k)}, y_2^{(k)}, \cdots, y_{m_k}^{(k)}\}$, the errors of e_{mean} and e_{max} under the irregular node distribution are plotted in Figure 9. This figure shows that the approximation of the DS-IMLS method also has high accuracy under irregular nodes distribution.

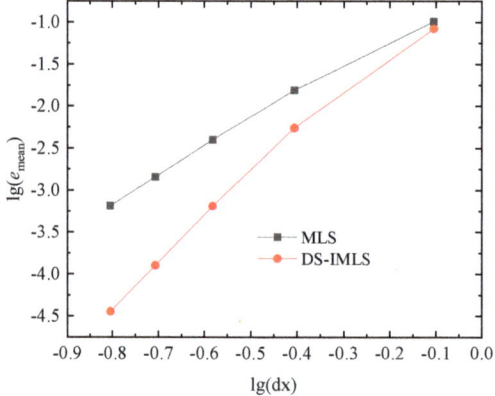

Figure 7. The average discrete point errors e_{mean} of the DS-IMLS and MLS methods for the different node distances dx of $5 \times 5, 9 \times 9, 13 \times 13, 17 \times 17, 21 \times 21$ regular node distributions.

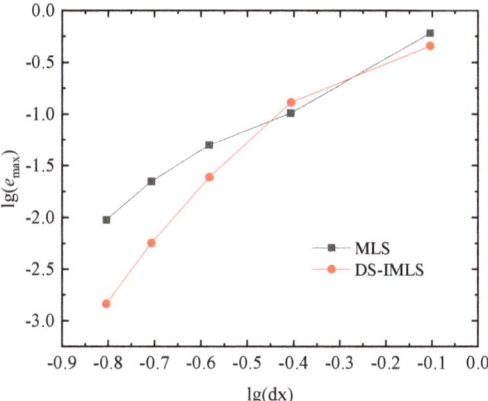

Figure 8. The maximum errors e_{max} of the DS-IMLS and MLS methods for the different node distances dx of 5×5, 9×9, 13×13, 17×17, 21×21 regular node distributions.

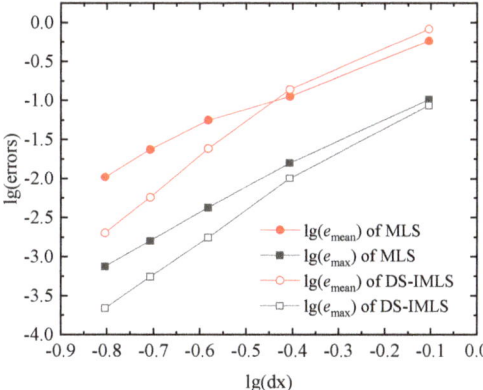

Figure 9. The errors e_{mean} and e_{max} of the MLS and DS-IMLS methods under the irregular node distribution obtained by small random disturbance.

Example 2. Let $u(x,y) = \frac{e^{2x}}{\ln(1+y)}$, $0 \leq x, y \leq 1$.

In this example, 21×21 regular nodes distribution is used to construct the approximation function. The numerical approximations of the u, u_x, u_{xx} on the line $y = x$ are plotted in Figure 10 by using the DS-IMLS method with $dmax_1 = dmax_2 = 3$. The corresponding numerical results of the second derivatives obtained by the DS-IMLS and MLS methods are shown in Figure 11. We can see that the approximation function and its derivatives of the DS-IMLS method fit the exact solution very well.

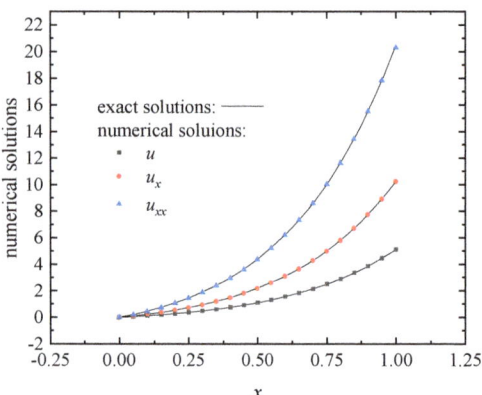

Figure 10. The numerical approximations of the functions u, u_x, u_{xx} on line $y = x$ obtained by the DS-IMLS method for Example 2.

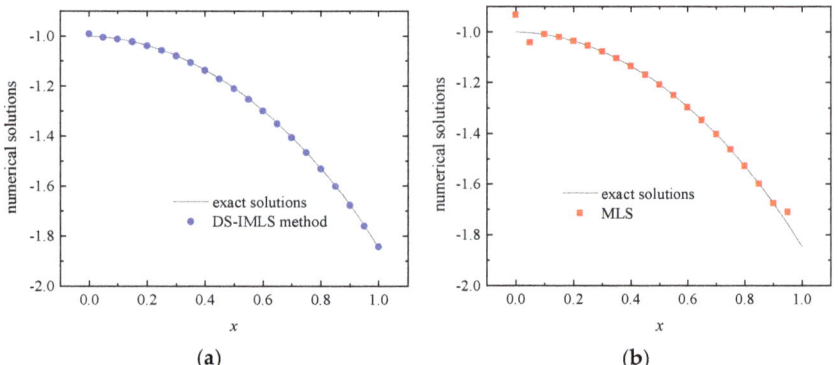

Figure 11. The numerical approximations of u_{yy} on line $y = x$ obtained by the DS-IMLS (**a**) and MLS (**b**) methods for Example 2.

When fixing dmax$_2$ = 3, the average and maximum point errors of the 30 × 30 regular calculation point are shown in Figure 12a for different values of dmax$_1$. Fixing dmax$_1$ = 3, the corresponding errors for different values of dmax$_2$ are listed in Figure 12b. The effect of the influence domain parameter on the MLS method is shown in Figure 13. It can still be seen that when the value of the influence domain parameter reaches 3, the DS-IMLS method has better calculation accuracy.

When dmax$_0$ = 2.1, and dmax$_1$ = dmax$_2$ = 3, the errors e_{mean} and e_{max} for the different node distance dx of 5×5, 9×9, 13×13, 17×17, 21×21 regular node distributions are respectively shown in Figures 14 and 15 by the DS-IMLS and MLS methods. The DS-IMLS method has a higher order of convergence than the MLS method.

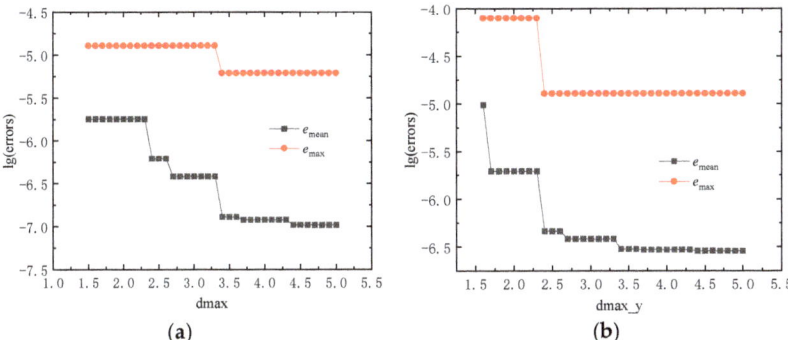

Figure 12. The errors on the 30 × 30 regular calculation point obtained by the DS-IMLS method for (**a**) different dmax$_1$ with dmax$_2$ = 3; (**b**) different dmax$_2$ with dmax$_1$ = 3.

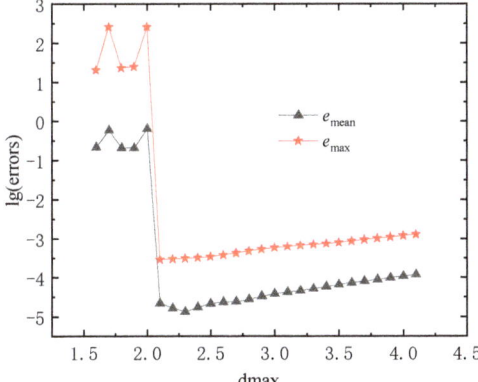

Figure 13. The errors obtained by the MLS method for different influence domain parameters dmax$_0$.

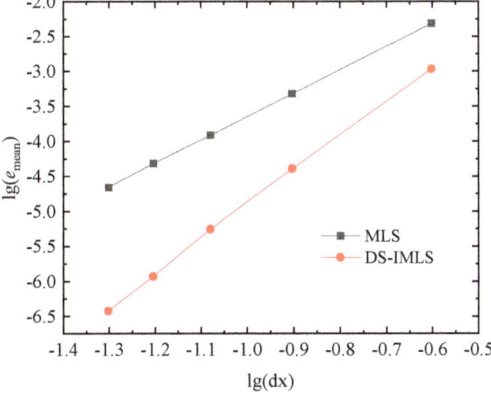

Figure 14. The errors e_{mean} of the DS-IMLS and MLS methods for different node distances dx of 5×5, 9×9, 13×13, 17×17, 21×21 regular node distributions.

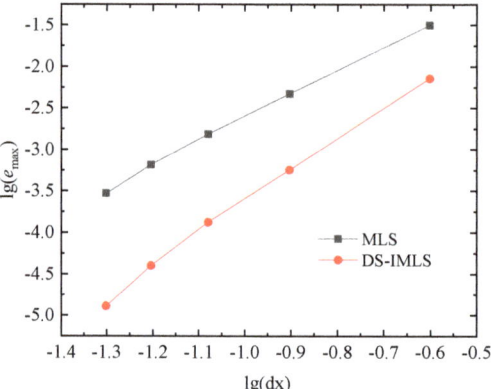

Figure 15. The maximum errors $e_{\max}$ of the DS-IMLS and MLS methods for the different node distance dx for Example 2.

Example 3. Let $u(x,y) = (x^3 - x^2)\sin(\pi y)$, $0 \leq x, y \leq 1$.

When 21×21 regular nodes distribution is used and $dmax_1 = dmax_2 = 3$, the approximation and its first and second derivatives u_x, u_{xx} on the line $y = x$ are plotted in Figure 16. The partial derivatives of the approximation function concerning y are shown in Figure 17. The approximation of the DS-IMLS method is also consistent with the exact function. Let $dmax_0 = 2.1$. When using the 5×5, 9×9, 13×13, 17×17, and 21×21 regular node distributions, the errors e_{mean} and e_{max} obtained by the DS-IMLS and MLS methods are shown in Figures 18 and 19, respectively. These two figures show that the approximation functions of the DS-IMLS and MLS methods are convergent to the exact solutions, and the DS-IMLS method has a higher convergence rate.

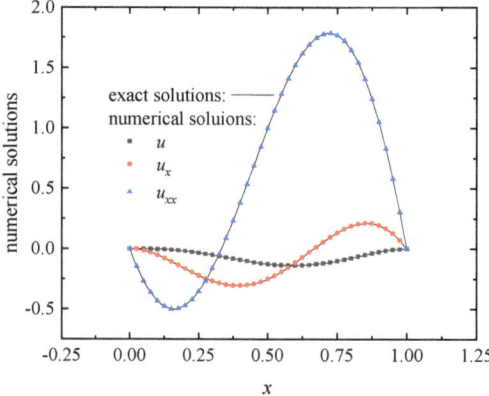

Figure 16. The approximations of the functions u, u_x, u_{xx} on the line $y = x$ obtained by the DS-IMLS method for Example 3.

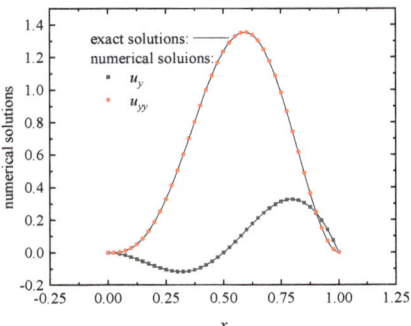

Figure 17. The approximations of the functions u_y, u_{yy} on the line $y = x$ obtained by the DS-IMLS method for Example 3.

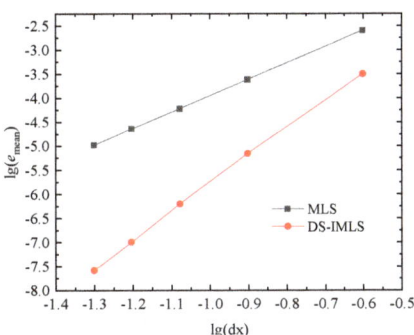

Figure 18. The errors e_{mean} obtained by the DS-IMLS and MLS methods for the different node distances dx of 5×5, 9×9, 13×13, 17×17, 21×21 regular node distributions of Example 3.

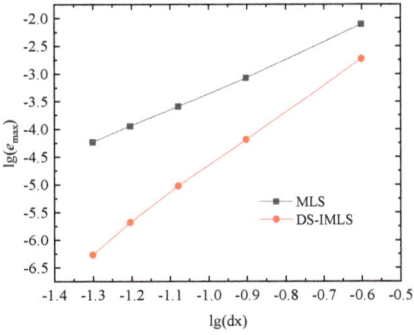

Figure 19. The maximum errors $e_{\max}$ obtained by the DS-IMLS and MLS methods for the different node distances dx of Example 3.

5.2. The Examples for the Improved IEFG Method Based on the DS-IMLS Method

Example 4. Considering a temperature field governed by Laplace's equation

$$\nabla^2 T = \frac{\partial^2 T}{\partial x^2} + \frac{\partial^2 T}{\partial y^2} = 0, \; 0 < x < 5, \quad 0 < y < 10. \tag{41}$$

The essential boundary conditions are used and deduced from the analytical temperature solution of

$$T(x,y) = \frac{100\sin(\pi x/10)\sinh(\pi y/10)}{\sinh(\pi)}. \tag{42}$$

When 21×21 regular nodes distribution is used and $\mathrm{dmax}_1 = \mathrm{dmax}_2 = 3, \mathrm{dmax}_1 = 2.1$, the improved IEFG method of this paper and EFG methods are used to solve this potential problem. In the EFG method, the Lagrange multiplier method is applied to enforce the essential boundary condition. The exact and numerical solutions obtained with the improved IEFG and EFG methods on the line $y = x$ are listed in Figure 20. The corresponding absolute errors of numerical solutions of the improved IEFG and EFG methods are plotted in Figure 21. It is clear that the solutions of the improved IEFG and EFG methods are very consistent with the analytical solutions, but the improved IEFG method based on the DS-IMLS method has a smaller calculation error than the EFG method.

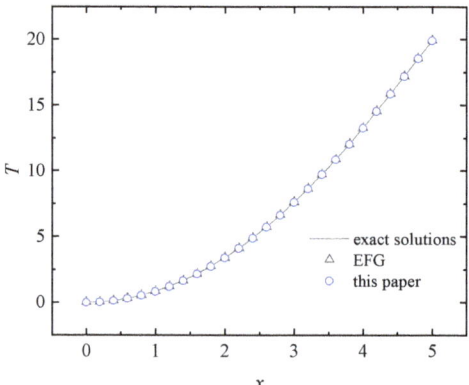

Figure 20. The exact and numerical solutions on the line $y = x$ obtained by the improved IEFG and EFG methods.

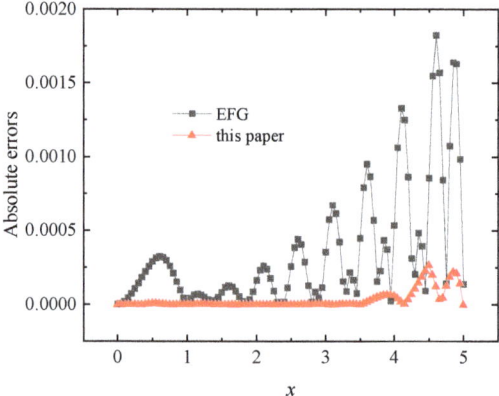

Figure 21. The absolute errors of numerical solutions on the line $y = x$ obtained by the improved IEFG and EFG methods.

Example 5. Considering a potential problem governed by

$$\nabla^2 u = \frac{\partial^2 u}{\partial x^2} + \frac{\partial^2 u}{\partial y^2} = f(x,y),\ 0 < x, y < 1, \tag{43}$$

with

$$\begin{aligned}f(x,y) &= (x-1)x^2 \cos(\pi y)\left[2 - \pi^2(y-1)y\right] \\ &+ 2(3x-1)(y-1)y\cos(\pi y) - 2\pi(x-1)x^2(2y-1)\sin(\pi y).\end{aligned} \tag{44}$$

The essential boundary conditions are used, and the analytical solution is

$$u(x,y) = \left(x^3 - x^2\right)\left(y^2 - y\right)\cos(\pi y). \tag{45}$$

Let $dmax_1 = dmax_2 = 3$, $dmax_1 = 2.1$. Using the 21×21 regular nodes distribution, the numerical solutions on the line $y = x$ solved by the improved IEFG and EFG methods are shown in Figure 22. The corresponding absolute errors are shown in Figure 23. For the two-dimensional potential problem, this example again illustrates that the improved IEFG method based on the DS-IMLS method has a smaller calculation error than the EFG method.

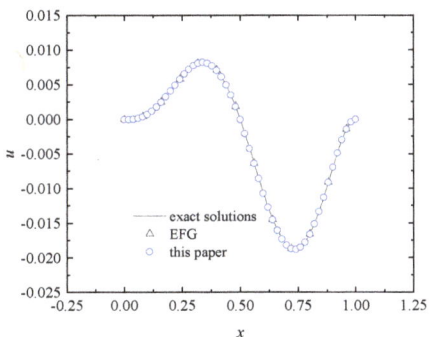

Figure 22. The exact and numerical solutions on the line $y = x$ obtained by the EFG and improved IEFG methods of this paper for Example 5.

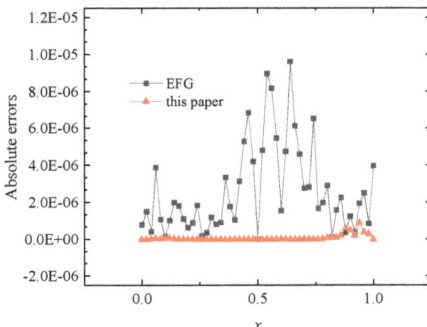

Figure 23. The absolute errors of solutions on the line $y = x$ obtained by the EFG and improved IEFG methods of this paper for Example 5.

Example 6. The example considered is a potential problem with a trapezoidal field as shown in Figure 24. The source term is

$$f(x,y) = 2(x-1)x^2 + (6x-2)(y-1)y. \tag{46}$$

The analytical solution is

$$u(x,y) = \left(x^3 - x^2\right)\left(y^2 - y\right). \tag{47}$$

Let $\text{dmax}_1 = \text{dmax}_2 = 2$, $\text{dmax}_1 = 2.1$. When the 11×11 regular nodes (shown in Figure 24) and the essential boundary condition are used, the numerical and exact solutions on the line $y = \frac{x}{3}$ are shown in Figure 25. We can see that the numerical solution of this paper is in good agreement with the exact solution. When using different node distributions shown in Table 1, the corresponding average errors e_{mean} of the 31×31 node distribution are given in Table 1. When 11×81 regular nodes are used, the EFG method cannot obtain the numerical solutions. It can be seen from the table that both the EFG and improved IEFG methods have high calculation accuracy. When the difference of the node spacings in the x and y directions is very large, the improved IEFG method can still obtain high accuracy, but the EFG method may not obtain a numerical solution. Moreover, reducing the spacing dx of dimension splitting is more conducive for the improved IEFG method of this paper to improve the accuracy than reducing the node spacing on the split plane. When $11 \times 11, 21 \times 11, \cdots, 81 \times 11$ nodes are adopted, the relationships between the average error e_{mean} and CPU time for the EFG and the method of this paper are shown in Figure 26. It can be seen from the figure that when the node spacing in X and Y directions is quite different, the IEFG method based on the DS-IMLS method has high calculation efficiency.

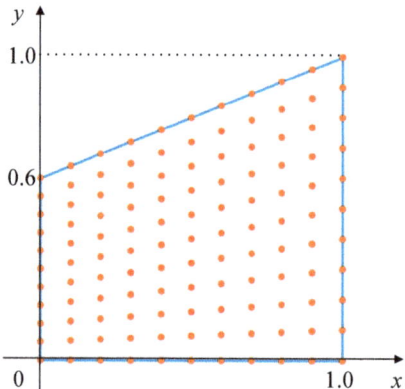

Figure 24. A trapezoidal field for Example 6.

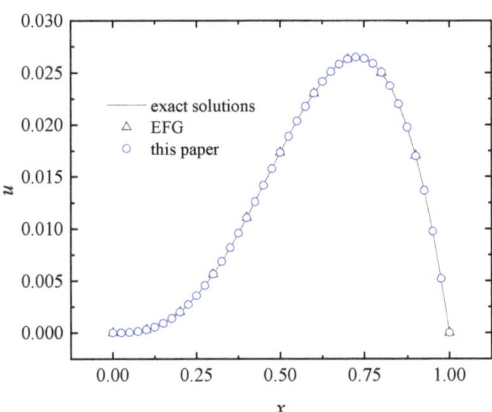

Figure 25. The exact and numerical solutions on the line $y = \frac{1}{3}x$ obtained by the EFG and improved IEFG methods of this paper for Example 6.

Table 1. The average errors e_{mean} of the EFG and improved IEFG methods for different nodes.

Nodes	EFG	Improved IEFG	Nodes	EFG	Improved IEFG	Nodes	EFG	Improved IEFG
11 × 11	2.03 × 10^{-5}	9.56 × 10^{-6}	11 × 11	1.44 × 10^{-5}	9.56 × 10^{-6}	11 × 11	2.03 × 10^{-5}	9.56 × 10^{-6}
21 × 11	3.12 × 10^{-6}	1.49 × 10^{-6}	11 × 21	1.28 × 10^{-5}	9.77 × 10^{-6}	21 × 21	2.21 × 10^{-6}	1.39 × 10^{-6}
41 × 11	1.24 × 10^{-6}	3.13 × 10^{-7}	11 × 41	5.79 × 10^{-5}	5.11 × 10^{-5}	41 × 41	3.32 × 10^{-7}	2.88 × 10^{-7}
81 × 11	1.12 × 10^{-6}	8.66 × 10^{-8}	11 × 81	NaN	1.69 × 10^{-4}	81 × 81	5.06 × 10^{-8}	8.43 × 10^{-8}

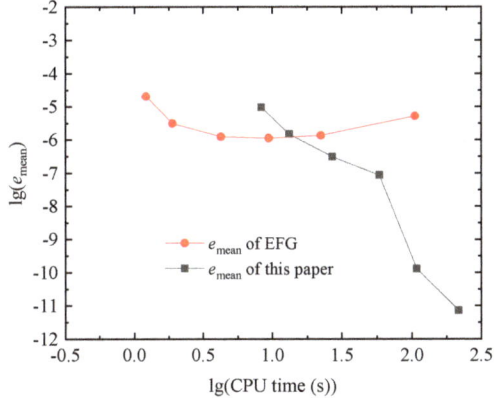

Figure 26. The relationships between the average error e_{mean} and CPU time for the EFG and the method of this paper under the 11 × 11, 21 × 11, · · · , 81 × 11 nodes.

6. Conclusions

By introducing the DSM into the improved IMLS method with a nonsingular weight function, this paper presents a new hybrid method to obtain the shape function of the meshless method, which is called the dimension splitting–interpolating moving least squares (DS-IMLS) method. Then based on the Galerkin weak form and the DS-IMLS method, the improved IEFG method for the two-dimensional potential problems is also presented. The weight function used in the DS-IMLS method is nonsingular, and the approximation function has the characteristics of the Kronecker delta function. Then the improved IEFG method based on the DS-IMLS method can directly impose essential boundary conditions.

Since the DSM can decompose the problem into a series of lower-dimensional problems, the DS-IMLS method can reduce the matrix dimension and complexity in calculating the shape function. The derivatives of the approximation function in the DS-IMLS method can be easily calculated. For a two-dimensional space, the shape function is calculated from a series of one-dimensional spaces, and then the order of the matrix that needs to be inverted will be greatly reduced. The DS-IMLS method has high calculation accuracy for anisotropic node distribution. When the difference between the node spacings in the x and y directions is very large, the DS-IMLS method still has a good calculation effect. Several examples demonstrated that the approximation function and its derivatives of the DS-IMLS and the improved IEFG methods have high accuracy in the regular problem domain.

Author Contributions: Conceptualization, J.W. and F.S.; methodology, J.W. and F.S.; software, J.W. and F.S.; writing—original draft preparation, J.W. and F.S.; writing—review and editing, J.W. and R.C. All authors have read and agreed to the published version of the manuscript.

Funding: This research was funded by the Natural Science Foundation of Zhejiang Province, China (Grant Nos. LY20A010021, LY20G030025, LY19A010002, LY18F020026), and the Ningbo Natural Science Foundation of China (Grant No. 202003N4142).

Institutional Review Board Statement: Not applicable.

Informed Consent Statement: Not applicable.

Data Availability Statement: Not applicable.

Conflicts of Interest: The authors declare no conflict of interest.

References

1. Gu, Y.; Fan, C.; Xu, R. Localized method of fundamental solutions for large-scale modeling of two-dimensional elasticity problems. *Appl. Math. Lett.* **2019**, *93*, 8–14. [CrossRef]
2. Zhang, T.; Li, X. Variational multiscale interpolating element-free Galerkin method for the nonlinear darcy–forchheimer model. *Comput. Math. Appl.* **2020**, *79*, 363–377. [CrossRef]
3. Gu, Y.; Fan, C.; Qu, W.; Wang, F. Localized method of fundamental solutions for large-scale modelling of three-dimensional anisotropic heat conduction problems–theory and Matlab code. *Comput. Struct.* **2019**, *220*, 144–155. [CrossRef]
4. Wang, J.; Sun, F. A hybrid variational multiscale element-free Galerkin method for convection-diffusion problems. *Int. J. Appl. Mech.* **2019**, *11*, 1950063. [CrossRef]
5. Lin, J.; Xu, Y.; Zhang, Y. Simulation of linear and nonlinear advection–diffusion–reaction problems by a novel localized scheme. *Appl. Math. Lett.* **2020**, *99*, 106005. [CrossRef]
6. Gu, Y.; Sun, H. A meshless method for solving three-dimensional time fractional diffusion equation with variable-order derivatives. *Appl. Math. Model.* **2020**, *78*, 539–549. [CrossRef]
7. Abbaszadeh, M.; Khodadadian, A.; Parvizi, M.; Dehghan, M.; Heitzinger, C. A direct meshless local collocation method for solving stochastic Cahn–Hilliard–cook and stochastic swift–Hohenberger equations. *Eng. Anal. Bound. Elem.* **2019**, *98*, 253–264. [CrossRef]
8. Selim, B.A.; Liu, Z. Impact analysis of functionally-graded graphene nanoplatelets-reinforced composite plates laying on Winkler-Pasternak elastic foundations applying a meshless approach. *Eng. Struct.* **2021**, *241*, 112453. [CrossRef]
9. Almasi, F.; Shadloo, M.S.; Hadjadj, A.; Ozbulut, M.; Tofighi, N.; Yildiz, M. Numerical simulations of multi-phase electro-hydrodynamics flows using a simple incompressible smoothed particle hydrodynamics method. *Comput. Math. Appl.* **2021**, *81*, 772–785. [CrossRef]
10. Lancaster, P.; Salkauskas, K. Surfaces generated by moving least squares methods. *Math. Comput.* **1981**, *37*, 141–158. [CrossRef]
11. Li, Y.; Liu, G.R. An element-free smoothed radial point interpolation method (EFS-RPIM) for 2d and 3d solid mechanics problems. *Comput. Math. Appl.* **2019**, *77*, 441–465. [CrossRef]
12. Li, J.; Feng, X.; He, Y. Rbf-based meshless local Petrov Galerkin method for the multi-dimensional convection–diffusion-reaction equation. *Eng. Anal. Bound. Elem.* **2019**, *98*, 46–53. [CrossRef]
13. Lin, J.; Yu, H.; Reutskiy, S.; Wang, Y. A meshless radial basis function based method for modeling dual-phase-lag heat transfer in irregular domains. *Comput. Math. Appl.* **2021**, *85*, 1–17. [CrossRef]
14. Cavoretto, R.; De Rossi, A. Adaptive meshless refinement schemes for RBF-PUM collocation. *Appl. Math. Lett.* **2019**, *90*, 131–138. [CrossRef]
15. Khan, M.N.; Hussain, I.; Ahmad, I.; Ahmad, H. A local meshless method for the numerical solution of space-dependent inverse heat problems. *Math. Methods Appl. Sci.* **2021**, *44*, 3066–3079. [CrossRef]

16. Fu, Z.; Chu, W.; Yang, M.; Li, P.; Fan, C. Estimation of tumor characteristics in a skin tissue by a meshless collocation solver. *Int. J. Comput. Methods* **2021**, *18*, 2041009. [CrossRef]
17. Wang, L.; Qian, Z. A meshfree stabilized collocation method (SCM) based on reproducing kernel approximation. *Comput. Methods Appl. Mech. Eng.* **2020**, *371*, 113303. [CrossRef]
18. Beel, A.; Kim, T.; Jiang, W.; Song, J. Strong form-based meshfree collocation method for wind-driven ocean circulation. *Comput. Methods Appl. Mech. Eng.* **2019**, *351*, 404–421. [CrossRef]
19. Almasi, A.; Beel, A.; Kim, T.; Michopoulos, J.G.; Song, J. Strong-form collocation method for solidification and mechanical analysis of polycrystalline materials. *J. Eng. Mech.* **2019**, *145*, 04019082. [CrossRef]
20. Almasi, A.; Kim, T.; Laursen, T.A.; Song, J. A strong form meshfree collocation method for frictional contact on a rigid obstacle. *Comput. Methods Appl. Mech. Eng.* **2019**, *357*, 112597. [CrossRef]
21. Park, S.I.; Lee, S.; Almasi, A.; Song, J. Extended IFC-based strong form meshfree collocation analysis of a bridge structure. *Autom. Constr.* **2020**, *119*, 103364. [CrossRef]
22. Li, X.; Dong, H. An element-free Galerkin method for the obstacle problem. *Appl. Math. Lett.* **2021**, *112*, 106724. [CrossRef]
23. Abbaszadeh, M.; Dehghan, M. The reproducing kernel particle Petrov–Galerkin method for solving two-dimensional nonstationary incompressible boussinesq equations. *Eng. Anal. Bound. Elem.* **2019**, *106*, 300–308. [CrossRef]
24. Liu, Z.; Wei, G.; Wang, Z. Numerical analysis of functionally graded materials using reproducing kernel particle method. *Int. J. Appl. Mech.* **2019**, *11*, 1950060. [CrossRef]
25. Abbaszadeh, M.; Dehghan, M. Direct meshless local Petrov–Galerkin (DMLPG) method for time-fractional fourth-order reaction–diffusion problem on complex domains. *Comput. Math. Appl.* **2020**, *79*, 876–888. [CrossRef]
26. Zhu, T.; Zhang, J.; Atluri, S.N. A local boundary integral equation (LBIE) method in Comput. Mech., and a meshless discretization approach. *Comput. Mech.* **1998**, *21*, 223–235. [CrossRef]
27. Cheng, J. Residential land leasing and price under public land ownership. *J. Urban Plan. Dev.* **2021**, *147*, 05021009. [CrossRef]
28. Cheng, J. Analysis of commercial land leasing of the district governments of Beijing in China. *Land Use Policy* **2021**, *100*, 104881. [CrossRef]
29. Cheng, J. Analyzing the factors influencing the choice of the government on leasing different types of land uses: Evidence from Shanghai of China. *Land Use Policy* **2020**, *90*, 104303. [CrossRef]
30. Cheng, J. Data analysis of the factors influencing the industrial land leasing in shanghai based on mathematical models. *Math. Probl. Eng.* **2020**, *2020*. [CrossRef]
31. Belytschko, T.; Lu, Y.Y.; Gu, L. Element-free Galerkin methods. *Int. J. Numer. Methods Eng.* **1994**, *37*, 229–256. [CrossRef]
32. Singh, R.; Singh, K.M. Interpolating meshless local Petrov-Galerkin method for steady state heat conduction problem. *Eng. Anal. Bound. Elem.* **2019**, *101*, 56–66. [CrossRef]
33. Wang, F.; Gu, Y.; Qu, W.; Zhang, C. Localized boundary knot method and its application to large-scale acoustic problems. *Comput. Methods Appl. Mech. Eng.* **2020**, *361*, 112729. [CrossRef]
34. Liew, K.M.; Cheng, Y.; Kitipornchai, S. Boundary element-free method (BEFM) and its application to two-dimensional elasticity problems. *Int. J. Numer. Methods Eng.* **2006**, *65*, 1310–1332. [CrossRef]
35. Zheng, G.; Cheng, Y. The improved element-free Galerkin method for diffusional drug release problems. *Int. J. Appl. Mech.* **2020**, *12*, 2050096. [CrossRef]
36. Peng, M.; Cheng, Y. A boundary element-free method (BEFM) for two-dimensional potential problems. *Eng. Anal. Bound. Elem.* **2009**, *33*, 77–82. [CrossRef]
37. Zhang, L.W.; Liew, K. An improved moving least-squares ritz method for two-dimensional elasticity problems. *Appl. Math. Comput.* **2014**, *246*, 268–282. [CrossRef]
38. Liew, K.M.; Feng, C.; Cheng, Y.; Kitipornchai, S. Complex variable moving least-squares method: A meshless approximation technique. *Int. J. Numer. Methods Eng.* **2007**, *70*, 46–70. [CrossRef]
39. Chen, L.; Li, X. A complex variable boundary element-free method for the Helmholtz equation using regularized combined field integral equations. *Appl. Math. Lett.* **2020**, *101*, 106067. [CrossRef]
40. Cheng, H.; Peng, M.; Cheng, Y.; Meng, Z. The hybrid complex variable element-free Galerkin method for 3d elasticity problems. *Eng. Struct.* **2020**, *219*, 110835. [CrossRef]
41. Liu, D.; Cheng, Y.M. The interpolating element-free Galerkin (IEFG) method for three-dimensional potential problems. *Eng. Anal. Bound. Elem.* **2019**, *108*, 115–123. [CrossRef]
42. Chen, S.S.; Xu, C.J.; Tong, G.S. A meshless local natural neighbour interpolation method to modeling of functionally graded viscoelastic materials. *Eng. Anal. Bound. Elem.* **2015**, *52*, 92–98. [CrossRef]
43. Chen, S.; Wang, W.; Zhao, X. An interpolating element-free Galerkin scaled boundary method applied to structural dynamic analysis. *Appl. Math. Model.* **2019**, *75*, 494–505. [CrossRef]
44. Wang, Q.; Zhou, W.; Feng, Y.T.; Ma, G.; Cheng, Y.; Chang, X. An adaptive orthogonal improved interpolating moving least-square method and a new boundary element-free method. *Appl. Math. Comput.* **2019**, *353*, 347–370. [CrossRef]
45. Wang, J.; Sun, F.; Xu, Y. Research on error estimations of the interpolating boundary element free-method for two-dimensional potential problems. *Math. Probl. Eng.* **2020**, *2020*, 6378745. [CrossRef]
46. Sun, F.X.; Wang, J.F.; Cheng, Y.M.; Huang, A.X. Error estimates for the interpolating moving least-squares method in n-dimensional space. *Appl. Numer. Math.* **2015**, *98*, 79–105. [CrossRef]

47. Wang, J.F.; Sun, F.; Cheng, Y.; Huang, A.X. Error estimates for the interpolating moving least-squares method. *Appl. Math. Comput.* **2014**, *245*, 321–342. [CrossRef]
48. Abbaszadeh, M.; Dehghan, M. Numerical and analytical investigations for neutral delay fractional damped diffusion-wave equation based on the stabilized interpolating element free Galerkin (IEFG) method. *Appl. Numer. Math.* **2019**, *145*, 488–506. [CrossRef]
49. Wu, Q.; Liu, F.B.; Cheng, Y.M. The interpolating element-free Galerkin method for three-dimensional elastoplasticity problems. *Eng. Anal. Bound. Elem.* **2020**, *115*, 156–167. [CrossRef]
50. Abbaszadeh, M.; Dehghan, M. Investigation of heat transport equation at the microscale via interpolating element-free Galerkin method. *Eng. Comput.* **2021**, 1–17.
51. Wang, J.; Sun, F. An interpolating meshless method for the numerical simulation of the time-fractional diffusion equations with error estimates. *Eng. Comput.* **2019**, *37*, 730–752. [CrossRef]
52. Wang, J.; Wang, J.; Sun, F.; Cheng, Y. An interpolating boundary element-free method with nonsingular weight function for two-dimensional potential problems. *Int. J. Comput. Methods* **2013**, *10*, 1350043. [CrossRef]
53. Sun, F.; Wang, J.; Cheng, Y. An improved interpolating element-free Galerkin method for elastoplasticity via nonsingular weight functions. *Int. J. Appl. Mech.* **2016**, *8*, 1650096. [CrossRef]
54. Wu, S.; Xiang, Y. A coupled interpolating meshfree method for computing sound radiation in infinite domain. *Int. J. Numer. Methods Eng.* **2018**, *113*, 1466–1487. [CrossRef]
55. Li, X. An interpolating boundary element-free method for three-dimensional potential problems. *Appl. Math. Model.* **2015**, *39*, 3116–3134. [CrossRef]
56. Liu, F.; Wu, Q.; Cheng, Y. A meshless method based on the nonsingular weight functions for elastoplastic large deformation problems. *Int. J. Appl. Mech.* **2019**, *11*, 1950006. [CrossRef]
57. Chen, H.; Li, K.; Wang, S. A dimension split method for the incompressible Navier–Stokes equations in three dimensions. *Int. J. Numer. Methods Fluids* **2013**, *73*, 409–435. [CrossRef]
58. Wang, J.; Sun, F. A hybrid generalized interpolated element-free Galerkin method for stokes problems. *Eng. Anal. Bound. Elem.* **2020**, *111*, 88–100. [CrossRef]
59. Meng, Z.; Cheng, H.; Ma, L.; Cheng, Y. The dimension splitting element-free Galerkin method for 3d transient heat conduction problems. *Sci. China Phys. Mech. Astron.* **2019**, *62*, 1–12. [CrossRef]
60. Wu, Q.; Peng, M.J.; Fu, Y.D.; Cheng, Y.M. The dimension splitting interpolating element-free Galerkin method for solving three-dimensional transient heat conduction problems. *Eng. Anal. Bound. Elem.* **2021**, *128*, 326–341. [CrossRef]
61. Wu, Q.; Peng, M.; Cheng, Y. The interpolating dimension splitting element-free Galerkin method for 3d potential problems. *Eng. Comput.* **2021**, 1–15. [CrossRef]

Article

Analysis of a Novel Two-Dimensional Lattice Hydrodynamic Model Considering Predictive Effect

Huimin Liu [1], Rongjun Cheng [1,*] and Tingliu Xu [1,2]

[1] Faculty of Maritime and Transportation, Ningbo University, Ningbo 315211, China; liuhuimin725@126.com (H.L.); xutingliu@nbu.edu.cn (T.X.)
[2] Merchant Marine College, Shanghai Maritime University, Shanghai 201306, China
* Correspondence: chengrongjun@nbu.edu.cn

Abstract: In actual driving, the driver can estimate the traffic condition ahead at the next moment in terms of the current traffic information, which describes the driver's predictive effect. Due to this factor, a novel two-dimensional lattice hydrodynamic model considering a driver's predictive effect is proposed in this paper. The stability condition of the novel model is obtained by performing the linear stability analysis method, and the phase diagram between the driver's sensitivity coefficient and traffic density is drawn. The nonlinear analysis of the model is conducted and the kink-antikink of modified Korteweg-de Vries (mKdV) equation is derived, which describes the propagation characteristics of the traffic density flow waves near the critical point. The numerical simulation is executed to explore how the driver's predictive effect affects the traffic flow stability. Numerical results coincide well with theoretical analysis results, which indicates that the predictive effect of drivers can effectively avoid traffic congestion and the fraction of eastbound cars can also improve the stability of traffic flow to a certain extent.

Keywords: traffic flow; two-dimensional lattice hydrodynamic model; driver's predictive effect

1. Introduction

For the past few years, infrastructure construction of urban traffic networks has developed rapidly. However, with the rapid development of economy, the desire for convenient transportation of people is increasing, and the measures of road construction alone are insufficient for the growing needs of travel. Since traffic congestion is a common problem that needs to be solved urgently, several academics have committed considerable efforts to easing urban traffic congestion. Thereby, a large number of traffic flow models are proposed to explore the evolution law of traffic flow, such as car-following models [1–9], macro models [10–15], and lattice hydrodynamic models [16–23]. With the improvement of people's living standard, as well as the rapid development of high-tech, some intelligent transportation models [24–28] have been proposed. The establishment and analysis of traffic flow model, whether for the development of traffic flow theory, or for the reality of traffic management, planning, and control, are greatly meaningful.

At present, most of scholars specializing in traffic flow theory have investigated the one-dimensional lattice hydrodynamic model, such as the self-stabilization effect [29,30], the flow difference effect [31], the density difference effect [32], and so on. There are both single-lane and two-lane models, so the investigation of one-dimensional lattice hydrodynamic model has been relatively mature. However, the actual urban road traffic is a network structure. Thereby, the exploration of a two-dimensional lattice hydrodynamic model is more significant and valuable. So far, there are still extremely few scholars who are involved in these fields. In 1999, Nagatani et al. [33] first extended the one-dimensional lattice hydrodynamic model to two dimensions without any reference, and performed analysis and numerical simulation. Redhu et al. [34] conducted a two-dimensional lattice hydrodynamic model to research the influence of the overtaking effect on the stability

of traffic flow in two-dimensional traffic flow in a two-dimensional scene. Liu et al. [35] investigated the role of shared lane signs in two-dimensional actual traffic. Li et al. [36] executed a new feedback control signal to discuss, not only in detail but clearly, the effect of driver's memory effect on two-dimensional actual traffic.

In actual driving, drivers tend to make predictions about the upcoming congestion based on the current traffic conditions. Therefore, it is crucial to thoroughly investigate the influence of prediction effect on the conditions of road traffic. At present, relevant studies have been carried out by scholars. Wang et al. [37] proposed a lattice hydrodynamic model of driver's prediction effect in a single lane to explore traffic flow characteristics considering such driver's behavior. Zhang et al. [38] also extended the driver's prediction effect to the two-lane lattice model, and investigated the influence of this driver's behavior on the two-lane road traffic. Kaur et al. [39] introduced the driver's prediction effect into the single-lane lattice hydrodynamic model with overtaking effect. However, in the two-dimensional lattice hydrodynamic model, up to now, there has been no academics investigated on the influence of the prediction effect on the two-dimensional traffic flow. Therefore, in this paper, a novel two-dimensional lattice hydrodynamic considering prediction effect is put forward to fill this gap.

The remaining content of this paper is the following parts. The second part provides detailed information on the origin and development of the model. In the third part, the linear analysis is conducted and the deduced stability conditions were plotted as stability curves. In the fourth section, we perform the nonlinear analysis to derive the mKdV equation that is a nonlinear differential equations describing the evolution of density waves. Then, the novel model is simulated numerically and the results are compared with those of theoretical analysis. In the last section, the appropriate conclusions are given according to the previous theoretical analysis and numerical simulation results.

2. Methods: The Novel Two-Dimensional Lattice Model Considering Driver's Predictive Effect

In 1998, a lattice hydrodynamic model for describing road traffic was first established by Nagatani et al. [16]. The optimal velocity function in the micro model is cleverly referenced by lattice model despite doing so as a macro model. Therefore, the model has the characteristics of both the macro model and the micro model. Furthermore, the model is comparatively easier to simulate due to discrete space variables and continuous time variables in this model. In order to make the model closer to the real road traffic, the two-dimensional lattice hydrodynamic model is extended from the one-dimensional model by Nagatani et al. [33].

The continuity equations of vehicles heading east and north are respectively given by Equations (1) and (2).

$$\partial_t \rho_x(x,y,t) + \partial_x \rho_x(x,y,t) u(x,y,t) = 0, \tag{1}$$

$$\partial_t \rho_y(x,y,t) + \partial_x \rho_y(x,y,t) v(x,y,t) = 0. \tag{2}$$

where $\partial_t = \partial/\partial t$, $\partial_x = \partial/\partial x$ and $\partial_y = \partial/\partial y$. $\rho_x(x,y,t) [\rho_y(x,y,t)]$ and $u(x,y,t) [v(x,y,t)]$ indicate the density and speed of eastbound cars (northbound cars) on the two-dimensional lattice.

The continuity equations express the conservation of vehicles and reflect the relationship between the local density and the local average speed. In addition to the continuity equation, the model also contains the motion equation describing the traffic currents. Equations (3) and (4) are established on the condition that traffic flow is regulated by the optimal speed with a delay time. The motion equation of eastbound and northbound cars respectively are

$$\rho_x(x,y,t+\tau) u(x,y,t+\tau) = c\rho_0 V(\rho(x+x_0,y,t)), \tag{3}$$

$$\rho_y(x,y,t+\tau) v(x,y,t+\tau) = (1-c)\rho_0 V(\rho(x,y+y_0,t)). \tag{4}$$

where c and $1 - c$ are the proportion of vehicles driving east and north, respectively. ρ_0 is on the behalf of the total average density as in the two-dimensional. $\rho(x, y, t)$ represents the local density and $\rho(x, y, t) = \rho_x(x, y, t) + \rho_y(x, y, t)$. x_0 and y_0 are respectively the average headway of eastbound cars and northbound cars. τ refers to the delay time mentioned above, which represents the time lag required for the traffic current to reach the optimal current after the change of traffic flow. When $c = 0$ or 1, all vehicles will go straight or turn left. At this moment, thus, the two-dimensional model is transformed into a one-dimensional hydrodynamic traffic model.

As shown in Figure 1, we treat each crossroads as a grid. As we all know, some cars will continue to drive straight and others will take the left at the crossroads. q represents traffic flow rate. If a certain intersection is the j, m lattice, vehicles going straight through this intersection will enter the $j + 1, m$ lattice, and turning left, will enter the $j, m + 1$ lattice. The above equations are discretized differentially and the delay time τ is rewritten as the driver's sensitivity a where $a = 1/\tau$, the model equations of driving north and driving east are as follows:

$$\partial_t \rho^x_{j,m}(t) + c\rho_0 \left(q^x_{j,m}(t) - q^x_{j-1,m}(t) \right) = 0, \tag{5}$$

$$\partial_t \rho^y_{j,m}(t) + (1-c)\rho_0 \left(q^y_{j,m}(t) - q^y_{j,m-1}(t) \right) = 0, \tag{6}$$

$$\partial_t q^x_{j,m}(t) = ac\rho_0 V \left(\rho^x_{j+1,m}(t) \right) - aq^x_{j,m}(t), \tag{7}$$

$$\partial_t q^y_{j,m}(t) = a(1-c)\rho_0 V \left(\rho^y_{j,m}(t) \right) - aq^y_{j,m}(t). \tag{8}$$

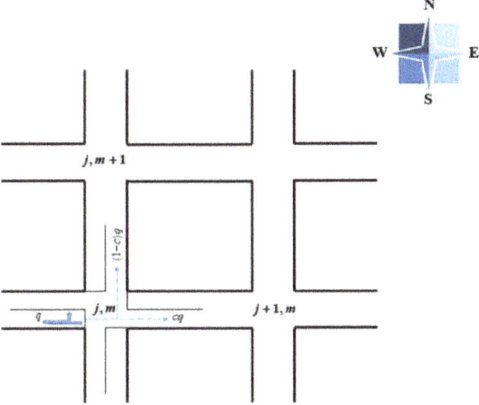

Figure 1. Schematic model of traffic flow on a two-dimensional highway.

With the development of traffic intelligence, drivers can acquire more information about vehicles around them, which is conducive for drivers to fully understand the current road traffic conditions and make accurate predictions. In order to investigate the consequence of driver predictive effect on the stability of two-dimensional traffic flow, we improved the above model. When the continuity equations (i.e., Equations (5) and (6)) remain unchanged, the equations of traffic currents (i.e., Equations (7) and (8)) to the north and east with the introduction of the prediction terms are respectively as follows:

$$\partial_t q^x_{j,m}(t) = ac\rho_0 V \left[\rho^x_{j+1,m}(t) + \beta \left(\rho^x_{j+1,m}(t+\tau) - \rho^x_{j+1,m}(t) \right) \right] - aq^x_{j,m}(t), \tag{9}$$

$$\partial_t q^y_{j,m}(t) = a(1-c)\rho_0 V \left[\rho^y_{j,m+1}(t) + \beta \left(\rho^y_{j,m+1}(t+\tau) - \rho^y_{j,m+1}(t) \right) \right] - aq^y_{j,m}(t). \tag{10}$$

To simplify the expression, we perform the Taylor expansion for $\rho(t+\tau)$ with ignoring the nonlinear terms and then do the same for $V[\rho(t) + \beta(\rho(t+\tau) - \rho(t))]$, which obtains the formula

$$V[\rho(t) + \beta(\rho(t+\tau) - \rho(t))] = V(\rho(t)) + V'(\rho(t))\beta\tau\partial_t\rho(t). \tag{11}$$

Under the condition of $\rho = \rho^x + \rho^y$, according to eliminating the flow rate (i.e., q) Equations (5), (6), (9), (10) and (12) are simultaneously conducted.

$$\begin{aligned}
&\partial_t^2 \rho_{j,m}(t) + a\partial_t \rho_{j,m}(t) \\
&+ ac^2 \rho_0^2 [V(\rho_{j+1,m}(t)) - V(\rho_{j,m}(t))] \\
&+ ac^2 \rho_0^2 \beta\tau [V'(\rho_{j+1,m}(t))\partial_t \rho_{j+1,m}(t) - V'(\rho_{j,m}(t))\partial_t \rho_{j,m}(t)] \\
&+ a(1-c)^2 \rho_0^2 [V(\rho_{j,m+1}(t)) - V(\rho_{j,m}(t))] \\
&+ a(1-c)^2 \rho_0^2 \beta\tau [V'(\rho_{j,m+1}(t))\partial_t \rho_{j,m+1}(t) - V'(\rho_{j,m}(t))\partial_t \rho_{j,m}(t)] = 0
\end{aligned} \tag{12}$$

Moreover, as with most lattice models, the following OV function is selected.

$$V(\rho) = \frac{v_{\max}}{2}\left[\tanh\left(\frac{2}{\rho_0} - \frac{\rho}{\rho_0^2} - \frac{1}{\rho_c}\right) + \tanh\left(\frac{1}{\rho_c}\right)\right]. \tag{13}$$

This monotone minus function has an upper bound, and an inflection point of $\rho = \rho_c$ when $\rho_0 = \rho_c$.

3. Discussion

3.1. Linear Stability Analysis

The driver may suddenly accelerate or decelerate during driving, generating in a slight change in vehicle density, which is equivalent to adding a small disturbance to the overall stable traffic flow. The stability analysis mainly investigates the impact of small- and medium-sized disturbances on the overall traffic flow, so as to grasp the evolution mechanism of them with clarity, improve the stability of traffic flow and alleviate traffic congestion.

When the traffic flow attains a steady state, we believe that the density of vehicles in the traffic flow is uniform. That is to say, Equation (13) has the equilibrium solution demonstrated Equation (14).

$$\rho_{j,m}(t) = \rho_0. \tag{14}$$

In the state of stable traffic flow, we assume that a certain traffic jam occurs at site j, m, which leads to the density of traffic flow at this location deviating from the steady density. Set the deviation quantity namely the small disturbance at this position as $y_{j,m}$, then the density at site j, m is met in Equation (15).

$$\rho_{j,m}(t) = \rho_0 + y_{j,m}(t). \tag{15}$$

After that, we substitute Equation (15) into Equation (13) and rearrange it to get the Equation (16).

$$\begin{aligned}
&\partial_t^2 y_{j,m}(t) + a\partial_t y_{j,m}(t) \\
&+ ac^2 \rho_0^2 [(y_{j+1,m}(t) - y_{j,m}(t))V'(\rho_0)] \\
&+ ac^2 \rho_0^2 \beta\tau [\partial_t (y_{j+1,m}(t) - y_{j,m}(t))V'(\rho_0)] \\
&+ a(1-c)^2 \rho_0^2 [(y_{j,m+1}(t) - y_{j,m}(t))V'(\rho_0)] \\
&+ a(1-c)^2 \rho_0^2 \beta\tau [\partial_t (y_{j,m+1}(t) - y_{j,m}(t))V'(\rho_0)] = 0
\end{aligned} \tag{16}$$

where $V'(\rho_0) = \frac{\partial V(\rho)}{\partial \rho}\big|_{\rho = \rho_0}$.

Next, since density waves travel at the same speed in both the west and south directions, we expand $y_{j,m}(t)$ into Fourier series. Then substituting the expansion equation $y_{j,m}(t) = \exp(ik(j+m) + zt)$ into Equation (16) to get the Equation (17) written as

$$z^2 + az + a\left(c^2 + (1-c)^2\right)\rho_0^2\left[\left(e^{ik} - 1\right)V'(\rho_0) + \beta\tau z\left(e^{ik} - 1\right)V'(\rho_0)\right] = 0, \quad (17)$$

For simplicity, letting $z = z_1(ik) + z_2(ik)^2 + \cdots$ and substituting it into Equation (17). For solving for z_1 and z_2, we rearrange the equation according to the coefficients of ik and $(ik)^2$. Setting the coefficient of them equal to zero, we acquire z_1 demonstrated as Equation (18) and z_2 containing z_1. Finally substitute Equation (18) into z_2 obtain the following result.

$$z_1 = -\left(c^2 + (1-c)^2\right)\rho_0^2 V'(\rho_0), \quad (18)$$

$$z_2 = -\left[\frac{1}{2} + \left(\frac{1}{a} + \beta\tau\right)\left(c^2 + (1-c)^2\right)\rho_0^2 V'(\rho_0)\right]\left(c^2 + (1-c)^2\right)\rho_0^2 V'(\rho_0). \quad (19)$$

If z_2 is a negative value, the uniform steady-state flow becomes unstable for long-wavelength modes. The steady state traffic flow remains steady when it is disturbed by a small amount, and there will be no traffic jam. When z_2 is a positive value, the uniform flow is stable. The system will be unstable after a period of evolution, resulting in the generation of time-travel stop wave. According to the above results and combined with the existing traffic flow stability theory, it is generally accepted that the steady-state flow becomes unstable when $z_2 < 0$. On the contrary, the traffic flow system would remain stable when $z_2 > 0$. In other words, the stability conditions have been satisfied. Thus, we achieve the curve of neutral stability as

$$a = -\frac{2\left(c^2 + (1-c)^2\right)\rho_0^2 V'(\rho_0)}{1 - 2\left(c^2 + (1-c)^2\right)\rho_0^2 V'(\rho_0)\beta\tau}, \quad (20)$$

The stability condition, consequently, for uniform traffic flow, is illuminated as inequality Equation (21).

$$a > -\frac{2\left(c^2 + (1-c)^2\right)\rho_0^2 V'(\rho_0)}{1 - 2\left(c^2 + (1-c)^2\right)\rho_0^2 V'(\rho_0)\beta\tau}, \quad (21)$$

When $c = 0$ or 1, the model is one-dimensional lattice model with the consideration of driver predictive effect, and the stability condition is converted to inequality Equation (22).

$$a > -\frac{2\rho_0^2 V'(\rho_0)}{1 - 2\rho_0^2 V'(\rho_0)\beta\tau}. \quad (22)$$

The stability conditions of inequality Equation (22) are consistent with those obtained in the one-dimensional predictive effect model by Wang et al. [37], which proves the correctness of our theoretical analysis to some extent.

Figures 2 and 3 show the neutral stability curves (dashed line) and coexisting curves (solid line) under the relevant parameters of the two factors investigated in this paper. As illustrated in the figure, above the coexisting curve and below the neutral stability curve are stable areas with smooth traffic and unstable areas with heavy traffic of traffic flow, respectively. Between these two curves is the metastable region of the vehicular system determined by the critical disturbance amplitude.

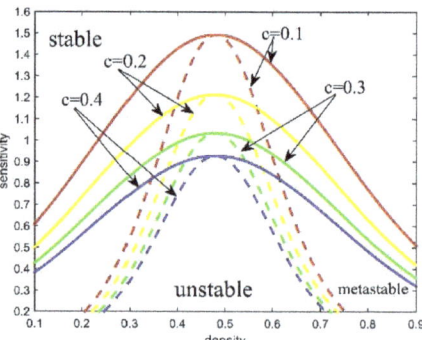

Figure 2. Phase diagrams in the density-sensitivity space for different c.

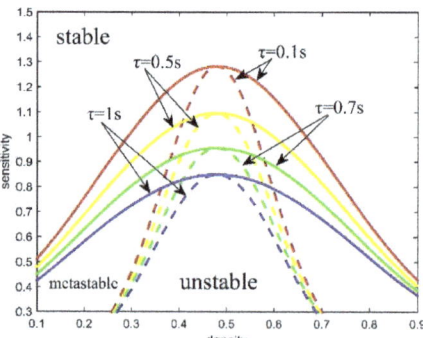

Figure 3. Phase diagrams in the density-sensitivity space for different τ.

When parameters ρ_0, β and τ are determined, we can obtain from Equation (20), the driver sensitivity coefficient a increases as the fraction of eastbound cars c increases if $0 < c < 0.5$ while a decreases as c increases if $0.5 < c < 1$. In addition, if c is regarded as a function of c, $c = 0.5$ is the axis of symmetry of this function. In other words, the neutral stability curves determined by $c = C$ and $c = 1 - C$ ($0 < c < 1$) coincide when other parameters are determined. Figure 2 display the curves for $c = 0.1, 0.2, 0.3, 0.4$ with $\beta = 0.3$, $\tau = 0.4$ s and $v_{\max} = 2$ m/s. From this picture, we can see that the stability region increases with the increase of c ($0 < c < 0.5$). This indicates that the uniform distribution of traffic flow will play an inhibitory role on traffic congestion.

Figure 3 demonstrates that the curves for $\tau = 0.1$ s, 0.4 s, 0.7 s, 1 s with $\beta = 0.3$, $c = 0.2$ and $v_{\max} = 2$ m/s. We can discover that with the increase of the predictive time τ stability region increases from this diagram. At this time, the probability of traffic congestion is greatly reduced. By observing the stability conditions of Equation (21), we can find that β and τ have the same influence on a; in other words, the prediction weight β also plays a vigorous role in the stability of traffic flow. To sum up, the predictive effect of drivers does curb traffic congestion.

3.2. Nonlinear Analysis

The nonlinear phenomenon of traffic flow is analyzed by considering the changing behavior of the time slowing variable and space slowing variable near the critical point (ρ_c, a_c) of the unstable traffic flow region. The slow variables of time and space X and T are imported respectively for a small positive scaling parameter $\varepsilon (0 < \varepsilon << 1)$ as

$$X = \varepsilon(j + m + bt), \quad T = \varepsilon^3 t, \tag{23}$$

where b means the undetermined parameters. Then we set the density of each lattice $\rho_{j,m}(t)$ to satisfy Equation (23).

$$\rho_{j,m}(t) = \rho_c + \varepsilon R(X, T). \tag{24}$$

According to the above Equations (23) and (24), each item in Equation (12) is expanded to the fifth term of ε by performing the Taylor expansion method. To make the expression simple and obvious, we set $\lambda = \left(c^2 + (1-c)^2\right)$. Then, we can acquire the following expression:

$$\begin{aligned} & \varepsilon^2 \left[(ab + a\lambda \rho_c^2 V'(\rho_c)) \partial_X R \right] \\ & + \varepsilon^3 \left[\left(b^2 + \frac{a\lambda \rho_c^2 V'(\rho_c)}{2} + a\lambda b \beta \tau \rho_c^2 V'(\rho_c) \right) \partial_X^2 R \right] \\ & + \varepsilon^4 \left[a \partial_T R + \left(\frac{a\lambda \rho_c^2 V'(\rho_c)}{6} + \frac{a\lambda b \beta \tau \rho_c^2 V'(\rho_c)}{2} \right) \partial_X^3 R + \frac{a\lambda \rho_c^2 V'''(\rho_c)}{6} \partial_X R^3 \right] \\ & + \varepsilon^5 \left[\begin{array}{c} (2b + a\lambda \beta \tau \rho_c^2 V'(\rho_c)) \partial_T \partial_X R + \left(\frac{a\lambda \rho_c^2 V'(\rho_c)}{24} + \frac{a\lambda b \beta \tau \rho_c^2 V'(\rho_c)}{6} \right) \partial_X^4 R \\ + \left(\frac{a\lambda \rho_c^2 V'''(\rho_c)}{12} + \frac{a\lambda b \beta \tau \rho_c^2 V'''(\rho_c)}{6} \right) \partial_X^2 R^3 \end{array} \right] = 0 \end{aligned} \tag{25}$$

where $V'(\rho_c) = \frac{\partial V(\rho)}{\partial \rho}\big|_{\rho = \rho_c}$ and $V'''(\rho_c) = \frac{\partial^3 V(\rho)}{\partial \rho^3}\big|_{\rho = \rho_c}$.

Moreover, there is $a = (1 - \varepsilon^2) a_c$ at the unstable region near the critical point (ρ_c, a_c). Then, in order to simplify Equation (25), we set the coefficient of the quadratic term of ε equal to zero to obtain $b = -\lambda \rho_c^2 V'(\rho_c)$. Furthermore, substituting $a = (1 - \varepsilon^2) a_c$ and $b = -\lambda \rho_c^2 V'(\rho_c)$ into Equation (25), an evolutionary equation with only fourth and fifth terms of ε can be deduced as

$$\varepsilon^4 (-g_1 \partial_X^3 R + g_2 \partial_X R^3 + \partial_T R) + \varepsilon^5 (g_4 \partial_X^4 R + g_5 \partial_X^2 R^3 - g_3 \partial_X^2 R) = 0, \tag{26}$$

where the coefficients $g_i(1, 2, \ldots, 5)$ are shown as

$$g_1 = \frac{a\lambda \rho_c^2 V'(\rho_c)}{6} + \frac{a\lambda b \beta \tau \rho_c^2 V'(\rho_c)}{2}, \tag{27}$$

$$g_2 = \frac{a\rho_c^2 V'''(\rho_c)}{6}, \tag{28}$$

$$g_3 = \frac{a\lambda \rho_c^2 V'(\rho_c)}{2} + a\lambda b \beta \tau \rho_c^2 V'(\rho_c), \tag{29}$$

$$g_4 = \frac{a\lambda \rho_c^2 V'(\rho_c)}{24} + \frac{a\lambda b \beta \tau \rho_c^2 V'(\rho_c)}{6}, \tag{30}$$

$$g_5 = \frac{a\lambda \rho_c^2 V'''(\rho_c)}{12} + \frac{a\lambda b \beta \tau \rho_c^2 V'''(\rho_c)}{6}, \tag{31}$$

For the sake of deriving the standard mKdV equation, we make the following equivalent substitution.

$$T = \frac{1}{g_1} T', R = \sqrt{\frac{g_1}{g_2}} R'. \tag{32}$$

Subsequently, substituting Equation (32) into Equation (26) and adding the correction term of $O(\varepsilon)$ into the model, the Equation (26) is turned into Equation (33).

$$\partial_{T'} R' = \partial_X^3 R' - \partial_X R'^3 + \varepsilon M[R']. \tag{33}$$

where $M[R'] = \frac{g_3}{g_1} \partial_X^2 R' + \frac{g_4}{g_1} \partial_X^4 R' + \frac{g_5}{g_2} \partial_X^2 R'^3$ and this item means the higher order infinitesimal term.

Additionally, after ignoring the correction term $O(\varepsilon)$, the kink-antikink density wave solution of the mKdV equation is Equation (34).

$$R'_0(X, T') = \sqrt{s}\tanh\left(\sqrt{\frac{s}{2}}(X - sT')\right), \quad (34)$$

where s denotes the propagation speed of the above kink-antikink solitary wave.

Then, the following condition must be satisfied to help us obtain the value of the propagation velocity s for the kink solution

$$(R'_0, M[R'_0]) = \int_{-\infty}^{+\infty} dX' R'_0 M[R'_0] = 0. \quad (35)$$

where $M[R'_0] = M[R']$, we get the general solution form of velocity s through solving the Equation (33) as

$$s = \frac{5g_2 g_3}{2g_2 g_4 - 3g_1 g_5}, \quad (36)$$

By replacing the velocity s in Equation (32) with Equation (34), the following equation can be obtained.

$$R(X, T) = \sqrt{\frac{g_1 s}{g_2}}\tanh\left(\sqrt{\frac{s}{2}}(X - sg_1 T)\right), \quad (37)$$

Since then, the general kink-antikink solution of the mKdV equation can be expressed as Equation (38).

$$\rho_j(t) = \rho_c + \varepsilon\sqrt{\frac{g_1 s}{g_2}}\tanh\left(\sqrt{\frac{s}{2}}(X - sg_1 T)\right). \quad (38)$$

Evidently, the amplitude A of the density soliton is

$$A = \varepsilon\sqrt{\frac{g_1 s}{g_2}}. \quad (39)$$

Generally speaking, we commonly exert $\rho_j = \rho_c - A$ and $\rho_j = \rho_c + A$ to describe the densities of the freely moving phase and congested phase, respectively. This kink-antikink soliton represents the coexistence phases containing the freely moving phase with low density and the congested phase with high density.

4. Results

For convenience of numerical simulation, the Equation (12) is rewritten into the following difference form:

$$\begin{aligned}
&\rho_{j,m}(t + 2\Delta t) - 2\rho_{j,m}(t + \Delta t) + \rho_{j,m}(t) + a\Delta t\left(\rho_{j,m}(t + \Delta t) - \rho_{j,m}(t)\right) \\
&+ a\Delta t^2 c^2 \rho_0^2 \left[\begin{array}{l} V(\rho_{j+1,m}(t)) + \beta\tau\left(\frac{\rho_{j+1,m}(t + \Delta t) - \rho_{j+1,m}(t)}{\Delta t}\right)V'(\rho_{j+1,m}(t)) \\ -\left(V(\rho_{j,m}(t)) + \beta\tau\left(\frac{\rho_{j,m}(t + \Delta t) - \rho_{j,m}(t)}{\Delta t}\right)V'(\rho_{j,m}(t))\right) \end{array}\right] \\
&+ a\Delta t^2 (1-c)^2 \rho_0^2 \left[\begin{array}{l} V(\rho_{j,m+1}(t)) + \beta\tau\left(\frac{\rho_{j,m+1}(t + \Delta t) - \rho_{j,m+1}(t)}{\Delta t}\right)V'(\rho_{j,m+1}(t)) \\ -\left(V(\rho_{j,m}(t)) + \beta\tau\left(\frac{\rho_{j,m}(t + \Delta t) - \rho_{j,m}(t)}{\Delta t}\right)V'(\rho_{j,m}(t))\right) \end{array}\right] = 0
\end{aligned} \quad (40)$$

We select a 140×140 grid to take different values of the corresponding parameters, and conduct numerical simulation to get the spatial-temporal evolution diagram and spatial distribution diagram of density wave after $t = 10{,}300$ s.

Figure 4 shows the space-time evolution of density waves with different values of with $a = 0.86$, $\rho_c = 0.2$, and $\tau = 0.7$ s. When we set $c = 0.1, 0.2, 0.3, 0.4$, there are torque–reverse torque density waves in all four figures of Figure 4, because there is a certain degree of congestion on the roads and the stability condition is not satisfied. Nevertheless, since the frequency and amplitude of the four images are gradually decreasing, we can conclude that the density wave tends to be stable gradually with the increase of c. In other words, the increase of the proportion of eastbound vehicles will play a constructive role in the stability of traffic flow and restrain the occurrence of traffic congestion.

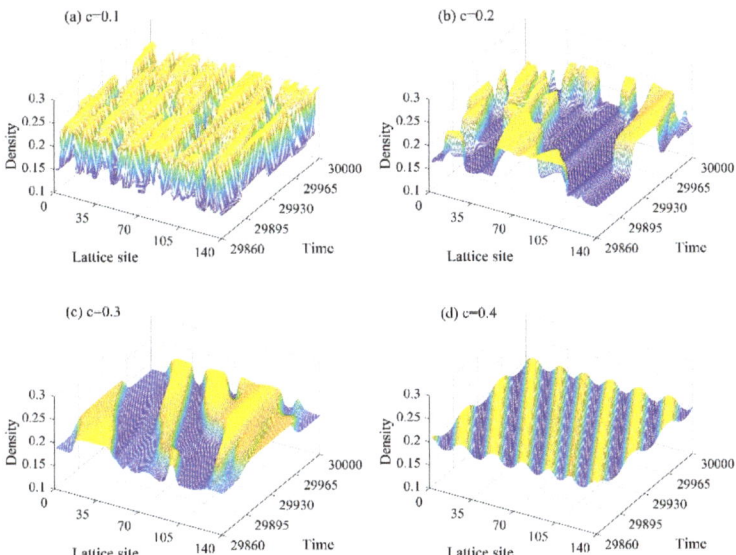

Figure 4. Space–time evolution of density under different value of parameter c.

Figure 5 depicts the density wave spatial distribution diagram corresponding to Figure 4, namely the instantaneous traffic flow distribution on each lattice at $t = 10{,}300$ s. Figure 5 can more briefly and clearly reflect the variation rule of the amplitude and frequency of density wave with the parameter c. From these changes, we can see that the increase of parameter c makes the density wave gradually tend to be stable, that is to say, the decrease of eastbound vehicles will deteriorate the traffic congestion.

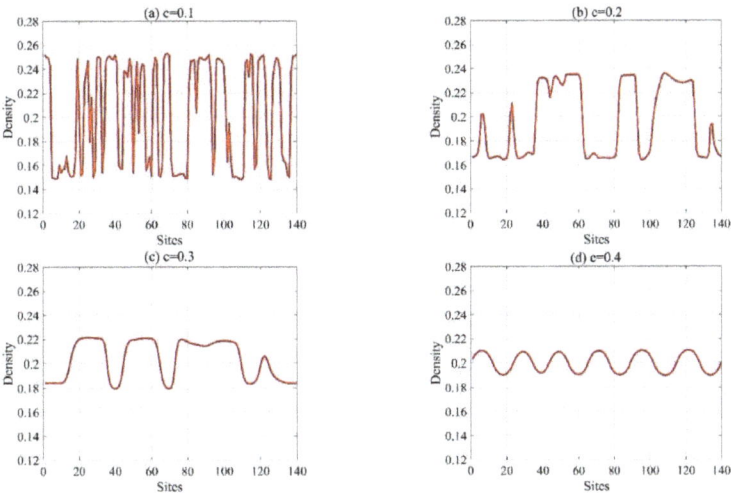

Figure 5. Density profile at $t = 10{,}300$ s corresponding to Figure 4.

Figure 6 is the plots of density versus density difference at the (100,100) lattice corresponding to Figure 4. With the increase of c, the loop area gradually decreases, which further verifies the above conclusion.

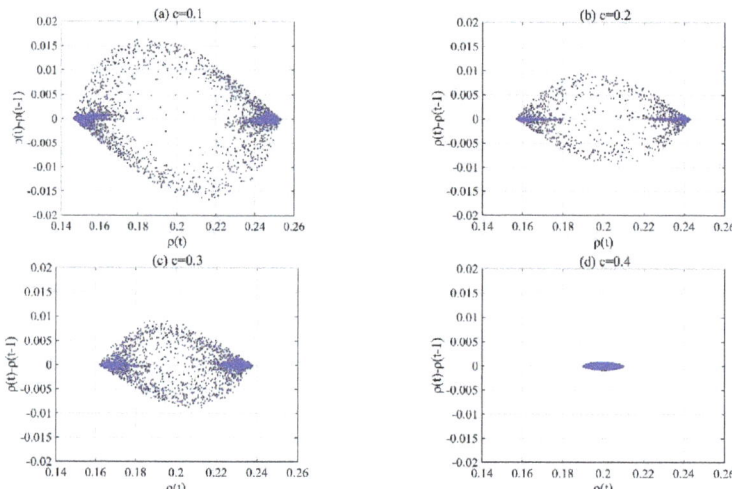

Figure 6. Plots of density versus density difference corresponding to Figure 4.

Figure 7 clearly illustrates the influence of the driver's prediction effect on the time evolution of density wave with different values of τ which are the driver's prediction time. Other parameters are selected as $a = 0.86$, $\rho_c = 0.2$, and $c = 0.4$. First of all, we can find intuitively that the first two pictures in Figure 7 have relatively large amplitudes, which means the traffic is relatively unstable. Then we can see that the amplitude of the latter one changes significantly and that the last one is a plane with almost no fluctuations. Thereby, the density wave becomes more and more stable as τ increases and the increase of prediction time will reduce the occurrence of traffic flow instability phenomena.

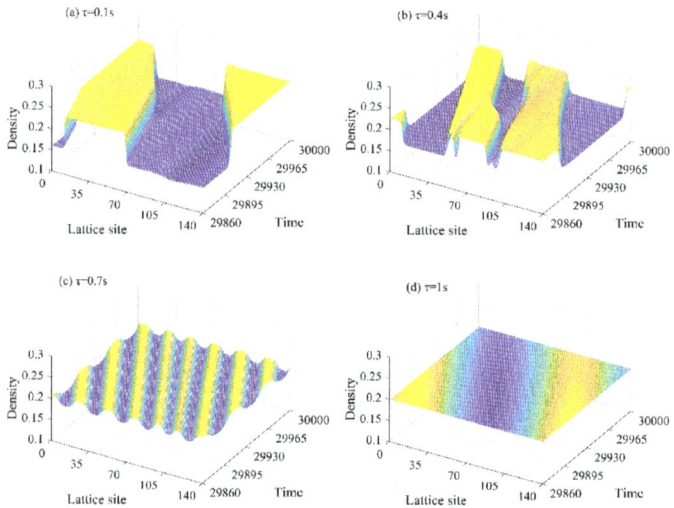

Figure 7. Space–time evolution of density under different value of parameter τ.

What is described in Figure 8 is the two-dimensional density spatial distribution diagram corresponding to Figure 8. It can be clearly seen from the figure that the amplitude of density wave becomes smaller and smaller with the increase of the predicted time τ until it finally becomes a straight line with almost no oscillation, which means that the traffic flow reaches a stable state. In conclusion, the predictive effect will promote the stability of traffic flow and will inhibit the occurrence of traffic jams.

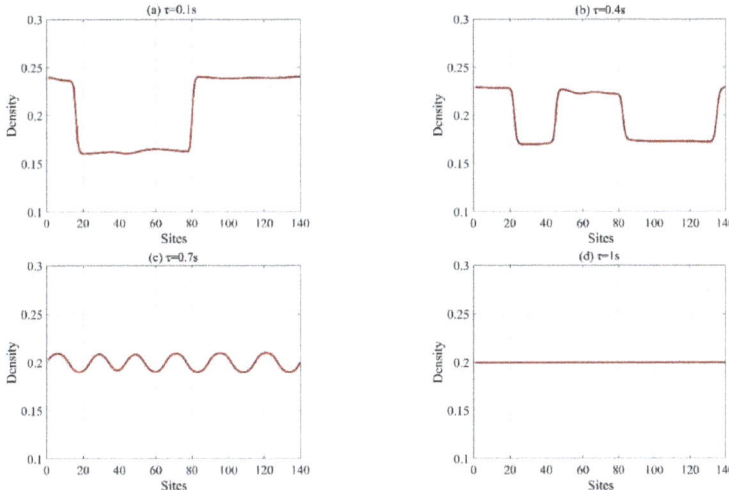

Figure 8. Density profile at $t = 10{,}300$ s corresponding to Figure 7.

Similar to Figure 6, Figure 9 is the plots of density versus density difference at the (100,100) lattice corresponding to Figure 7. With the increase of τ, the area of loop obviously decreases and eventually becomes an solitary point, which is consistent with the conclusion obtained above.

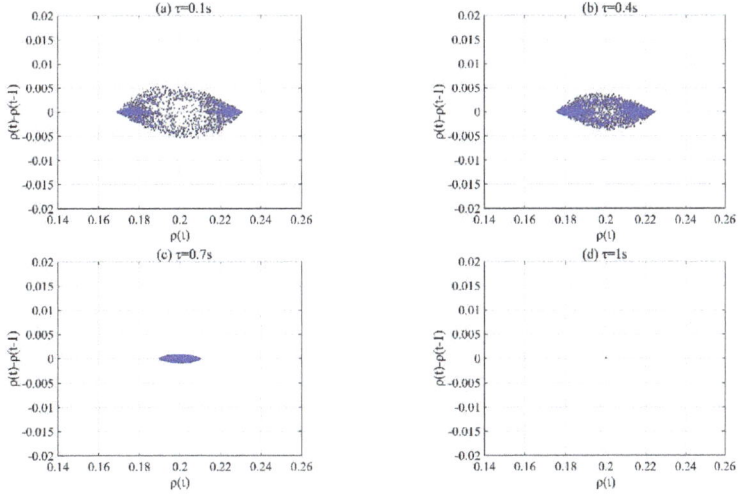

Figure 9. Plots of density versus density difference corresponding to Figure 7.

5. Conclusions

On the foundation of the discrete macro model proposed by Nagatani [16], this paper imports the driver's prediction effect, and obtains a new two-dimensional lattice hydrodynamic model. Through theoretical analysis and numerical simulation of the model, the influence of the prediction effect on the stability of two-dimensional traffic flow is investigated. The results of linear analysis illustrate that the traffic becomes smoother with the gradual increase of the proportion of eastbound vehicles or the driver's prediction effect time. Furthermore, the mKdV equation and its kink-antikink solution are derived when approaching the critical point in the unstable region. In addition, we plot phase diagrams to demonstrate the effect of corresponding parameters on traffic flow stability. By comparison, we find that the numerical simulation results are in agreement with the theoretical analysis. They unanimously manifest that a reasonable proportion of eastbound vehicles and effective prediction of drivers will reduce the occurrence of traffic congestion. In general, the two-dimensional model established in this paper can well reflect the evolution of the prediction effect on the vehicle moving forward and blocking in the actual traffic. The novel model we proposed provides a theoretical basis for solving the problem of traffic congestion and traffic flow prediction and control in reality.

Author Contributions: Methodology, H.L. and R.C.; validation, T.X.; formal analysis, H.L.; writing—original draft preparation, H.L.; writing—review and editing, R.C.; supervision, T.X.; funding acquisition, R.C. All authors have read and agreed to the published version of the manuscript.

Funding: This research was funded by the National Natural Science Foundation of China (grant no. 71571107) and the K.C. Wong Magna Fund in Ningbo University, China.

Data Availability Statement: Not applicable.

Conflicts of Interest: The authors declare no conflict of interest.

References

1. Yu, S.; Shi, Z. Analysis of car-following behaviors considering the green signal countdown device. *Nonlinear Dyn.* **2015**, *82*, 731–740. [CrossRef]
2. Zhu, W.; Li, D. A new car-following model for autonomous vehicles flow with mean expected velocity field. *Phys. A Stat. Mech. Appl.* **2018**, *492*, 2154–2165.
3. Zhu, W.; Zhang, H. Analysis of mixed traffic flow with human-driving and autonomous cars based on car-following model. *Phys. A Stat. Mech. Appl.* **2018**, *496*, 274–285. [CrossRef]
4. Ou, H.; Tang, T. An extended two-lane car-following model accounting for inter-vehicle communication. *Phys. A Stat. Mech. Appl.* **2018**, *495*, 260–298. [CrossRef]
5. Ngoduy, D. Effect of the car-following combinations on the instability of heterogeneous traffic flow. *Transp. B Transp. Dyn.* **2015**, *3*, 44–58. [CrossRef]
6. Zhu, M.; Wang, X. Human-like autonomous car-following model with deep reinforcement learning. *Transp. Res. Part C Emerg. Technol.* **2018**, *97*, 348–368. [CrossRef]
7. Ma, L.; Qu, S. A sequence to sequence learning based car-following model for multi-step predictions considering reaction delay. *Transp. Res. Part C Emerg. Technol.* **2020**, *120*, 102785. [CrossRef]
8. An, S.; Xu, L.; Qian, L. Car-following model for autonomous vehicles and mixed traffic flow analysis based on discrete following interval. *Phys. A Stat. Mech. Appl.* **2020**, *560*, 125246. [CrossRef]
9. Xue, Y.; Zhang, Y.; Fan, D. An extended macroscopic model for traffic flow on curved road and its numerical simulation. *Nonlinear Dyn.* **2019**, *95*, 3295–3307. [CrossRef]
10. Peng, G.; Song, W.; Peng, Y. A novel macro model of traffic flow with the consideration of anticipation optimal velocity. *Phys. A Stat. Mech. Appl.* **2014**, *398*, 76–82. [CrossRef]
11. Cheng, R.; Ge, H.; Wang, J. An extended continuum model accounting for the driver's timid and aggressive attributions. *Phys. Lett. A* **2017**, *381*, 1302–1312. [CrossRef]
12. Cheng, R.; Wang, Y. An extended lattice hydrodynamic model considering the delayed feedback control on a curved road. *Phys. A Stat. Mech. Appl.* **2019**, *513*, 510–517. [CrossRef]
13. Zhai, Q.; Ge, H.; Cheng, R. An extended continuum model considering optimal velocity change with memory and numerical tests. *Phys. A Stat. Mech. Appl.* **2018**, *490*, 774–785.
14. Cheng, R.; Ge, H.; Wang, J. The nonlinear analysis for a new continuum model considering anticipation and traffic jerk effect. *Appl. Math. Comput.* **2018**, *332*, 493–505.

15. Davoodi, N.; Soheili, A.; Hashemi, S. A macro-model for traffic flow with consideration of driver's reaction time and distance. *Nonlinear Dyn.* **2016**, *83*, 1621–1628. [CrossRef]
16. Nagatani, T. Modified KdV equation for jamming transition in the continuum models of traffic. *Phys. A Stat. Mech. Appl.* **1998**, *261*, 599–607. [CrossRef]
17. Nagatani, T. Jamming transition and the modified Kortweg-de Vries equation in a two-lane traffic flow. *Phys. A Stat. Mech. Appl.* **1999**, *265*, 297–310. [CrossRef]
18. Nagatani, T. TDGL and MKdV equations for jamming transition in the lattice models of traffic. *Phys. A Stat. Mech. Appl.* **1999**, *264*, 581–592. [CrossRef]
19. Cao, J.; Shi, Z. Analysis of a novel two-lane lattice model on a gradient road with the consideration of relative current. *Commun. Nonlinear Sci. Numer. Simul.* **2016**, *33*, 1–18. [CrossRef]
20. Peng, G.; Kuang, H.; Qing, L. A new lattice model of traffic flow considering driver's anticipation effect of the traffic interruption probability. *Phys. A Stat. Mech. Appl.* **2018**, *507*, 374–380. [CrossRef]
21. Zhao, H.; Xia, D.; Yang, S. The delayed-time effect of traffic flux on traffic stability for two-lane freeway. *Phys. A Stat. Mech. Appl.* **2020**, *105*, 106308. [CrossRef]
22. Wang, T.; Cheng, R.; Ge, H. Analysis of a novel two-lane lattice hydrodynamic model considering the empirical lane changing rate and the self-stabilization effect. *IEEE Access* **2019**, *540*, 123066. [CrossRef]
23. Wang, J.; Sun, F.; Ge, H. An improved lattice hydrodynamic model considering the driver's desire of driving smoothly. *Phys. A Stat. Mech. Appl.* **2019**, *515*, 119–129. [CrossRef]
24. Wu, X.; Zhao, X.; Song, H.; Xin, S.; Yu, S. Effects of the prevision relative velocity on traffic dynamics in the ACC strategy. *Phys. A Stat. Mech. Appl.* **2019**, *515*, 192–198. [CrossRef]
25. Bando, M.; Hasebe, K.; Nakayama, A.; Shibata, A.; Sugiyama, Y. Dynamical model of traffic congestion and numerical simulation. *Phys. Rev. E* **1995**, *51*, 1035–1042. [CrossRef]
26. Zhu, W.; Yu, R. Nonlinear analysis of traffic flow on a gradient highway. *Phys. A Stat. Mech. Appl.* **2012**, *391*, 964–965. [CrossRef]
27. Gupta, A.; Sharma, S.; Redhu, P. Analyses of lattice traffic model on a Gradient highway. *Commun. Theor. Phys.* **2014**, *62*, 393–404. [CrossRef]
28. Zhou, J.; Shi, Z.; Cao, J. An extended traffic flow model on a gradient highway with the consideration of the relative velocity. *Nonlinear Dyn.* **2014**, *78*, 1765–1779. [CrossRef]
29. Zhang, G. The self-stabilization effect of lattice's historical flow in a new lattice hydrodynamic model. *Nonlinear Dyn.* **2018**, *91*, 809–817. [CrossRef]
30. Peng, G.; Zhao, H.; Li, X. The impact of self-stabilization on traffic stability considering the current lattice's historic flux for two-lane freeway. *Phys. A Stat. Mech. Appl.* **2019**, *515*, 31–37. [CrossRef]
31. Wang, T.; Gao, Z.; Zhao, X. Flow difference effect in the two-lane lattice hydrodynamic model. *Chin. Phys. B* **2012**, *7*, 211–219. [CrossRef]
32. Gupta, A.; Redhu, P. Analysis of a modified two-lane lattice model by considering the density difference effect. *Commun. Nonlinear Sci. Numer. Simul.* **2014**, *19*, 1600–1610. [CrossRef]
33. Nagatani, T. Jamming transition in a two-dimensional traffic flow model. *Phys. Rev. E* **1999**, *59*, 4857–4864. [CrossRef] [PubMed]
34. Redhu, P.; Gupta, A. The role of passing in a two-dimensional network. *Nonlinear Dyn.* **2016**, *86*, 389–399. [CrossRef]
35. Liu, Y.; Wong, C. A two-dimensional lattice hydrodynamic model considering shared lane marking. *Phys. Lett. A* **2020**, *384*, 126668. [CrossRef]
36. Li, L.; Cheng, R.; Ge, H. New feedback control for a novel two-dimensional lattice hydrodynamic model considering driver's memory effect. *Phys. A Stat. Mech. Appl.* **2021**, *561*, 125295. [CrossRef]
37. Wang, T.; Zang, R.; Xu, K.; Zhang, J. Analysis of predictive effect on lattice hydrodynamic traffic flow model. *Phys. A Stat. Mech. Appl.* **2019**, *526*, 120711. [CrossRef]
38. Zhang, J.; Xu, K.; Li, S.; Wang, T. A new two-lane lattice hydrodynamic model with the introduction of driver's predictive effect. *Phys. A Stat. Mech. Appl.* **2020**, *551*, 124249. [CrossRef]
39. Kaur, D.; Sharma, S. The impact of the predictive effect on traffic dynamics in a lattice model with passing. *Eur. Phys. J. B Condens. Matter Complex Syst.* **2020**, *93*, 35. [CrossRef]

Article

Structural Optimization and Application Research of Alkali-Activated Slag Ceramsite Compound Insulation Block Based on Finite Element Method

Xiaona Fan, Yu Guo, Qin Zhao and Yiyun Zhu *

Department of Civil Engineering, Xi'an University of Technology, Xi'an 710048, China; 1190711008@stu.xaut.edu.cn (X.F.); 2180721123@stu.xaut.edu.cn (Y.G.); zhaoqin6688@xaut.edu.cn (Q.Z.)
* Correspondence: zyyun@xaut.edu.cn; Tel.: +86-138-9180-8287

Abstract: The research and application of new wall materials have been attracting increasing attention owing to the continuous promotion of sustainable development in the building industry. An alkali-activated slag ceramsite compound insulation block (AASCCIB) is used as the research object. Based on the finite element method, the effects of different numbers of hole rows and hole ratios on the thermal and mechanical performances of AASCCIBs are analyzed using ANSYS CFX. On this basis, the AASCCIB with the optimal comprehensive performance is determined by a multi-objective optimization analysis. Finally, the improvement effect of the AASCCIB wall on the indoor thermal environment relative to an ordinary block (OB) wall is quantitatively analyzed using ANSYS CFX. The results show that the von Mises equivalent stress and heat transfer coefficient of the AASCCIB decrease with the increase in the hole ratio when the hole shape and number of hole rows are constant. AASCCIB B_1 has the optimal comprehensive performance among six AASCCIBs, with the heat transfer coefficient and average von Mises equivalent stress of 0.446 W/(m^2·K) and 9.52 MPa, respectively. Compared with the indoor lowest and average temperatures of the building with the OB wall, those of the building with the AASCCIB wall increased by at least 1.39 and 0.82 °C on the winter solstice, respectively. The indoor temperature difference decreased by at least 0.83 °C. In addition, the indoor highest temperature, average temperature, and temperature difference decreased by at least 1.75, 0.79, and 1.89 °C on the summer solstice, respectively.

Keywords: finite element method; alkali-activated slag ceramsite compound insulation block; ANSYS CFX; thermal and mechanical performances; indoor thermal environment

Citation: Fan, X.; Guo, Y.; Zhao, Q.; Zhu, Y. Structural Optimization and Application Research of Alkali-Activated Slag Ceramsite Compound Insulation Block Based on Finite Element Method. *Mathematics* **2021**, *9*, 2488. https://doi.org/10.3390/math9192488

Academic Editor: Yumin Cheng

Received: 5 September 2021
Accepted: 29 September 2021
Published: 4 October 2021

Publisher's Note: MDPI stays neutral with regard to jurisdictional claims in published maps and institutional affiliations.

Copyright: © 2021 by the authors. Licensee MDPI, Basel, Switzerland. This article is an open access article distributed under the terms and conditions of the Creative Commons Attribution (CC BY) license (https://creativecommons.org/licenses/by/4.0/).

1. Introduction

With the progress of science and technology and improvement in living standards, higher requirements for living conditions have been imposed. Instead of limiting the demand for buildings to shelter from wind, rain, and warmth, people emphasize the need for a comfortable, energy-saving, and environmentally friendly living environment [1,2]. However, improvements in indoor thermal comfort are often accompanied by increases in building energy consumption and environmental pollution [3,4]. It is reported that buildings account for 40% of the total global energy consumption, and this proportion is still increasing [5,6]. In addition, approximately 40% of the total human greenhouse gas emission is attributed to the building industry [7,8]. Therefore, how to achieve improvements in indoor comfort without significantly increasing energy consumption and greenhouse gas emissions is a thorny issue that countries must face and solve.

In China, wall materials account for approximately 70% of housing construction materials. Clay bricks are the predominant wall material. However, it is statistically demonstrated that more than 1 billion cubic meters of arable land and 70 million tons of coal are consumed each year by the production of clay bricks [9]. If the growth of clay brick production is uncontrolled, the contradiction between supply and demand of resources, as well as energy, will become more acute. Obviously, it is required to promote the innovation of wall materials to realize the sustainable development of buildings. The self-insulation block is a new type of wall material [10]. It occupies a large share of the construction market because of its good heat insulation and thermal insulation, lightweight, high strength, long service life, simple construction, etc. [11]. Commonly, cement is chosen as the cementitious material for self-insulation blocks [12]. The production and processing of cement, however, consumes large amounts of energy and emits a lot of greenhouse gases. The production of 1 t of cement requires 5000 MJ of energy and emits 1 t of CO_2 [13]. Thus, the cementitious material alternative to cement is sought.

In recent years, alkali-activated slag cementitious material (AASCM) obtained using slag (industrial waste) attracted increasing attention [11]. Compared to the traditional cement production process, the AASCM production process transfers from "two grindings and one burning" to "one grinding". This reduces the energy consumption and greenhouse gas emissions of cementitious materials in the production process [14,15]. Additionally, AASCM has the advantages of high strength, high-temperature resistance, frost resistance, corrosion resistance, etc. [15]. Evidently, it is important to achieve sustainable development of building materials by choosing AASCM to replace traditional cement.

Ceramsite is a typical representative of artificial light aggregates and new energy-saving building materials [16]. It is obtained by an industrial solid waste via high-temperature calcination. It has the advantages of recycling waste, environmental protection, convenient production, and low price [17]. It also has a low thermal conductivity, high strength, lightweight, high-temperature resistance, acid and alkali resistance, etc. [18]. Considering these excellent characteristics of ceramsite, it can be used as an aggregate in studies on new wall materials.

To sum up, it is an inevitable choice for wall material development in studies on alkali-activated slag ceramsite self-insulation blocks (AASCSIBs). To improve the thermal performance of the alkali-activated slag ceramsite single self-insulation block, the alkali-activated slag ceramsite self-insulation hollow block (AASCSIHB) is generally filled with an insulation material. That is, an alkali-activated slag ceramsite compound insulation block (AASCCIB) is prepared. Therefore, conducting research on AASCCIBs will promote the integrated development of energy efficiency and functionality of buildings.

Nevertheless, there are a few reports on AASCCIBs [11,19] which focus on the preparation and performance of the block. In other words, there are very few studies devoted to the structural optimization and application feasibility of AASCCIBs [19], especially those dedicated to the comprehensive optimization of mechanical and thermal performances and the exploration of the thermal insulation effect. Undoubtedly, the above limitations restrict the application and promotion of AASCCIBs.

The most commonly used research approach in the structural optimization and application effect analysis of blocks is numerical simulation [20–22]. Various numerical analysis methods are used, including the finite difference method (FDM) [23,24], boundary element method (BEM) [25,26], finite volume method (FVM) [27,28], and finite element method (FEM) [29,30]. The FDM is a dominant numerical method for solving the motion of objects in computational fluids. However, it is challenging to solve the boundary conditions using this method. The BEM transforms the solution of the entire domain into a solution on a regional boundary. This numerical method reduces the computational effort, but is inefficient for the computation of the complex-shape flow field. In addition, the method is generally suitable for only solving homogeneous linear problems. The largest advantage of the FVM is that it provides an accurate integral conservation even with coarse meshes. However, the accuracy of the FVM is only second-order. The FEM is a numerical technique used to obtain approximate solutions to boundary value problems of partial differential equations. The basic idea of the method is to discretize the continuous solution domain, i.e., to divide the continuum into a finite number of tiny blocks with regular shapes. The method is not only applicable to complex geometries and boundary conditions, but also has a high computational accuracy and wide applicability. Furthermore, it has a standardized calculation format and can be easily applied programmatically. Thus, the FEM is a powerful, effective, and accurate numerical method.

ANSYS integrates the analyses of structure, fluid, electric, magnetic, and acoustic fields [31]. As far as professional computer-aided engineering software is concerned, ANSYS is the only analysis and design software worldwide that has passed the IS09001 quality certification. Additionally, the advantages of ANSYS are reflected in the broad scope of analysis, powerful coupling analysis functions, and convenient co-simulation platform. ANSYS CFX, a branch of ANSYS, is dedicated to fluid dynamics simulation [31]. Notably, it is the first commercial software in the world to develop and use a fully implicit multi-grid coupled solver technique. Moreover, it has advanced algorithms, rich physical models, and accurate calculation results. Considering the above analysis, ANSYS CFX is recommended for the structural optimization and application effect analysis of AASCCIBs.

In summary, this study aims to optimize the structure and analyze the thermal insulation effect of the AASCCIB using the FEM. The specific work is as follows:

- Six types of AASCCIBs with different internal structures are designed based on different numbers of hole rows and hole ratios.
- Based on the FEM, the thermal and mechanical performances of six AASCCIBs are simulated using ANSYS CFX. Moreover, the AASCCIB with the optimal comprehensive performance is determined though a multi-objective optimization analysis.
- The improvement effect of the AASCCIB wall on the indoor thermal environment relative to an ordinary block (OB) wall is quantitatively analyzed using ANSYS CFX.

2. Methods

2.1. Structural Design of AASCCIBs

Based on the literature [32], the dimensions of the selected blocks were length × width × height = 390 mm × 240 mm × 190 mm. Furthermore, because the thermal resistance of a hollow block with a rectangular hole was larger than those of diamond, square, and circle at the same hole ratio [33], the hole shape was rectangular in this study. On this basis, six types of hollow blocks with different internal structures were designed based on different numbers of hole rows and hole ratios. The diagram of the AASCSIHBs is shown in Figure 1.

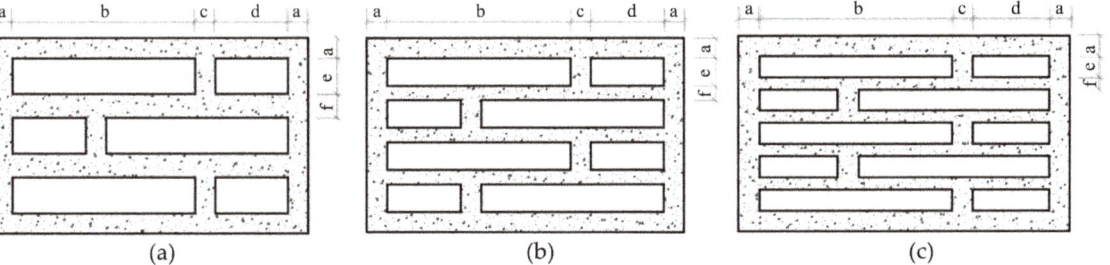

Figure 1. Diagram of AASCSIHBs. (**a**) Three rows of holes; (**b**) Four rows of holes; (**c**) Five rows of holes.

The distance between rows of the rectangular holes was the same. The distance between the rectangular holes parallel to the length direction of the block was referred to as horizontal rib, and the value was c. The distance between the rectangular holes perpendicular to the width direction of the block was referred to as vertical rib, with a value of f. The length and width of the larger rectangle in each row of the hole were b and e, respectively. The length and width of the smaller rectangle were denoted by d and e, respectively. In addition, a was taken as 25 mm according to the reference [32]. The detailed dimensions of the AASCSIHBs are shown in Table 1.

Table 1. Detailed dimensions of AASCSIHBs.

Number	Number of Hole Rows	a	b	c	d	e	f	Hole Ratio/%
A_1	Three rows	25	225	25	90	44	29	44.4
A_2		25	225	25	90	42	32	42.4
B_1	Four rows	25	225	25	90	34	18	45.8
B_2		25	225	25	90	31	22	41.7
C_1	Five rows	25	225	25	90	26	15	43.8
C_2		25	225	25	90	25.2	16	42.9

Note: The hole ratio was the ratio of the hole area to the cross-sectional area of the block.

2.2. Numerical Simulation of Thermal and Mechanical Performances of AASCCIBs

To improve the thermal performance of the block, the holes of the AASCSIHB were filled with an extruded polystyrene (XPS) foam board, which yielded the AASCCIB. Based on the FEM, the thermal and mechanical performances of the six AASCCIBs were numerically analyzed.

2.2.1. Mathematical Model

The heat transfer calculations for this study were performed on a single block wall. In addition, a single block in the wall was selected for the heat transfer analysis of the wall.

According to Fourier's law and energy conservation equation, the differential equation of heat conduction in the three-dimensional (3D) Cartesian coordinates system was established. In the heat transfer analysis, the heat input and output to the differential cube over time $d\tau$ were as follows [34]:

The heat input was:

$$dQ_x = q_x dydz \cdot d\tau, \ dQ_y = q_y dxdz \cdot d\tau, \ dQ_z = q_z dxdy \cdot d\tau \quad (1)$$

The heat output was:

$$dQ_{x+dx} = (q_x + \frac{\partial q_x}{\partial x}dx)dydz \cdot d\tau \quad (2)$$

$$dQ_{y+dy} = (q_y + \frac{\partial q_y}{\partial y}dy)dxdz \cdot d\tau \quad (3)$$

$$dQ_{z+dz} = (q_z + \frac{\partial q_z}{\partial z}dz)dydx \cdot d\tau \quad (4)$$

The net heat between input and output was as follows:

$$(dQ_x - dQ_{x+dx}) + (dQ_y - dQ_{y+dy}) + (dQ_z - dQ_{z+dz}) \\ = -(\frac{\partial q_x}{\partial x} + \frac{\partial q_y}{\partial y} + \frac{\partial q_z}{\partial z})dxdydz \cdot d\tau \quad (5)$$

According to Fourier's law [35],

$$q_x = -\lambda \frac{\partial T}{\partial x}, \ q_y = -\lambda \frac{\partial T}{\partial y}, \ q_z = -\lambda \frac{\partial T}{\partial z} \quad (6)$$

By substituting Equation (6) into Equation (5), we obtained Equation (7).

$$-(\frac{\partial q_x}{\partial x} + \frac{\partial q_y}{\partial y} + \frac{\partial q_z}{\partial z})dxdydz \cdot d\tau \\ = \left[\frac{\partial}{\partial x}(\lambda \frac{\partial T}{\partial x}) + \frac{\partial}{\partial y}(\lambda \frac{\partial T}{\partial y}) + \frac{\partial}{\partial z}(\lambda \frac{\partial T}{\partial z})\right]dxdydz \cdot d\tau \quad (7)$$

The heat generation of the infinitesimal cube over time $d\tau$ was $q_v dx dy dz \cdot d\tau$ [34].

The increment in the thermodynamic internal energy of the microelement over time $d\tau$ was $\rho c \frac{\partial T}{\partial \tau} \cdot dx dy \cdot d\tau$ [34].

According to the law of conservation of energy,

$$\left[\frac{\partial}{\partial x}(\lambda \frac{\partial T}{\partial x}) + \frac{\partial}{\partial y}(\lambda \frac{\partial T}{\partial y}) + \frac{\partial}{\partial z}(\lambda \frac{\partial T}{\partial z})\right] dxdydz \cdot d\tau + q_v dx dy dz \cdot d\tau \qquad (8)$$
$$= \rho c \frac{\partial T}{\partial \tau} \cdot dx dy dz \cdot d\tau$$

i.e., $\left[\frac{\partial}{\partial x}(\lambda \frac{\partial T}{\partial x}) + \frac{\partial}{\partial y}(\lambda \frac{\partial T}{\partial y}) + \frac{\partial}{\partial z}(\lambda \frac{\partial T}{\partial z})\right] + q_v = \rho c \frac{\partial T}{\partial \tau}$ \qquad (9)

Considering that, p, c, and λ are constants, as well as there being no internal heat source inside the wall, Equation (9) was simplified to Equation (10). That is, the mathematical model was established.

$$\frac{\partial^2 T}{\partial x^2} + \frac{\partial^2 T}{\partial y^2} + \frac{\partial^2 T}{\partial z^2} = 0 \qquad (10)$$

where T is the temperature, °C. x, y, and z are the 3D Cartesian system coordinates.

The mechanical performance in this study was analyzed using the constitutive model with the von Mises yield criterion. The core concept of this criterion was that when the second invariant ($J_{2'}$) of the stress deviation tensor of a point in a stressed object reached a constant value, the point entered the plastic state.

This criterion can be expressed by the principal stresses [36]:

$$J_{2'} = \left[(\sigma_1 - \sigma_2)^2 + (\sigma_2 - \sigma_3)^2 + (\sigma_3 - \sigma_1)^2\right] = c \qquad (11)$$

A unidirectional tensile experiment showed that $c = \frac{\sigma_s^2}{3}$ [36].
According to a pure shear experiment, it was found that $c = K^2$ [36].
Thus, the von Mises yielding criterion in the principal coordinate system was:

$$(\sigma_1 - \sigma_2)^2 + (\sigma_2 - \sigma_3)^2 + (\sigma_3 - \sigma_1)^2 = 2\sigma_s^2 = 6K^2 \qquad (12)$$

In addition, according to the von Mises yield criterion, the material began to yield when the equivalent force reached a constant value, which can be expressed as [37]:

$$\overline{\sigma} = \frac{1}{\sqrt{2}}\sqrt{(\sigma_x - \sigma_y)^2 + (\sigma_y - \sigma_x)^2 + (\sigma_z - \sigma_x)^2 + 6(\tau_{xy}^2 + \tau_{yz}^2 + \tau_{zx}^2)} = \sigma_s \qquad (13)$$

where $\overline{\sigma}$ is the equivalent stress (Pa), σ_i (σ_{ii}) is the normal stress (Pa), σ_s is the yield point, τ_{ij} is the shear stress (Pa), K is the shear yield strength (Pa), The first and second subscripts of the stress components indicated the normal direction of the action plane and direction of the stress action, respectively.

2.2.2. Development of the Finite Element Model

1. Basic assumptions and geometric model The following assumptions were used before the thermal model was developed:
   (1) The block performs a one-dimensional heat transfer.
   (2) The temperatures on both sides of the block are constant.
   (3) The main material of block and the filling material are closely connected. The material performances do not vary with the thermal environment.

Using AASCCIB B_1 as an example, a geometric model for the thermal analysis was developed (Figure 2).

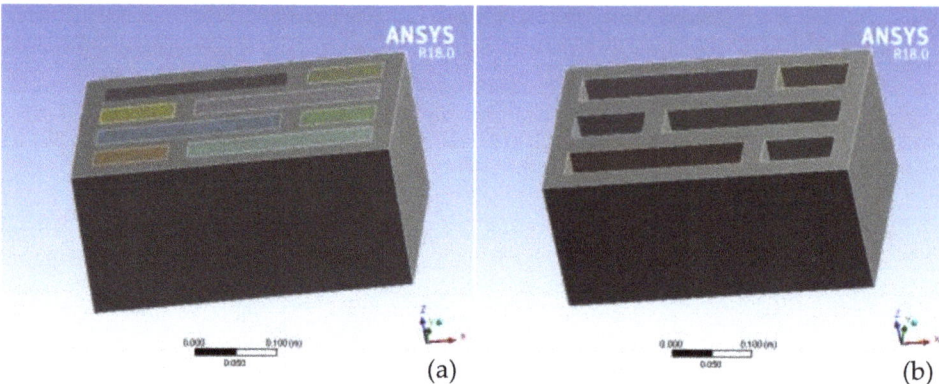

Figure 2. (**a**) Geometric model for the thermal analysis; (**b**) geometric model for the mechanical analysis.

The thermal insulation material (XPS) inside the holes of self-insulation hollow blocks had a small influence on the overall mechanical performances of the compound insulated block. Therefore, the self-insulation hollow block was selected instead of the compound insulation block for the mechanical performance analysis. The geometric model for the mechanical analysis was developed using AASCSIHB A_1 as an example (Figure 2).

2. Mesh division

The mesh division of the developed geometric models was conducted. The results are shown in Figure 3.

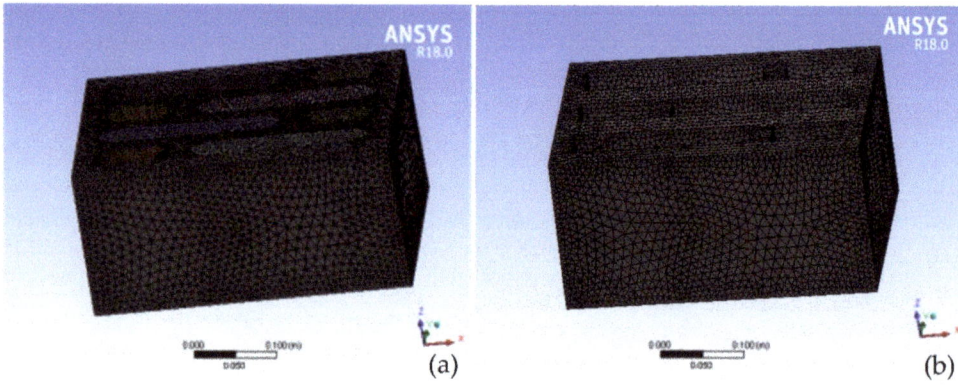

Figure 3. (**a**) Mesh model for the thermal analysis; (**b**) mesh model for the mechanical analysis.

3. Material parameter and boundary condition setting

The physical parameters of the AASCCIB are listed in Table 2. The block surfaces in contact with air were subjected to convective heat transfer boundary conditions (the third boundary condition). The other surfaces of the block were set with adiabatic boundary conditions. The expressions for the third boundary condition were as follows [38]:

$$-\lambda_1 \frac{\partial t}{\partial y}\Big|_{y=0} = h_i(t_{i1} - t_{e1}) \tag{14}$$

$$-\lambda_1 \frac{\partial t}{\partial y}\Big|_{y=h_i} = h_i(t_{e2} - t_{i2}) \tag{15}$$

$$-\lambda_2 \frac{\partial t}{\partial y}\bigg|_{y=0} = h_e(t_{i1} - t_{e1}) \tag{16}$$

$$-\lambda_2 \frac{\partial t}{\partial y}\bigg|_{y=h_e} = h_e(t_{i1} - t_{i2}) \tag{17}$$

where λ_1 and λ_2 are the thermal conductivities of the hollow block and air layer, respectively (W/(m·K)). h_i is the internal surface coefficient of heat transfer with a value of 8.7 W/(m²·K) [39], h_e is the external surface coefficient of heat transfer with a value of 23.0 W/(m²·K) [39], t_{i1} is the indoor air temperature of 281.15 K [40]. t_{i2} is the outdoor air temperature of 276.25 K [41], and t_{e1} and t_{e2} are the temperatures of the internal and external surfaces of the wall, respectively(K).

Table 2. Physical parameters of the AASCCIB.

Note	Thermal Conductivity W/(m·K)	Density kg/m³	Specific Heat Capacity J/(kg·K)	Elastic Modulus MPa	Poisson's Ratio
Shell of AASCSIHB	0.35	1600	1.05	27920	0.2
XPS	0.03	35	1.38	/	/

In the mechanical analysis, a static analysis was used to inform the effect of geometric nonlinearity. All degrees of freedom at the bottom of the finite element model were constrained, and a uniform load (P) of 10 MPa was applied to the upper surface of the model (Figure 4).

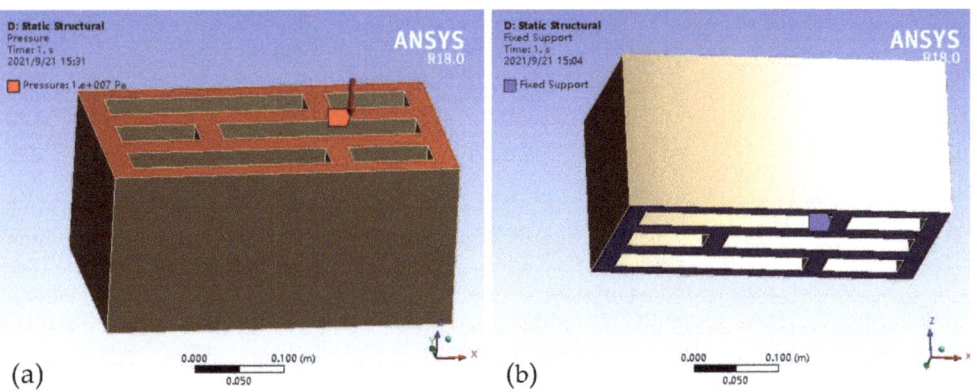

Figure 4. (a) Load on the upper surface of the model; (b) constraint on the bottom of the model.

2.3. Multi-Objective Optimization of AASCCIBs

2.3.1. Multi-Objective Optimization Method

In this study, the heat transfer coefficient, equivalent stress, and hole ratio represented the thermal, mechanical, and economic performances, respectively. Thermal, mechanical, and economic performances were included in the comprehensive performance. To obtain the AASCCIB with the optimal comprehensive performance, multi-objective optimization was conducted on the compound insulation blocks with different internal structures. The function expression of the weighted summation method was as follows [42]:

$$Max[f(x)] = \sum_{i=1}^{m} \omega_i f_i(x) \tag{18}$$

where $f(x)$ is the objective function, ω_i is the weight coefficient, and $f_i(x)$ is the subobjective function.

2.3.2. Calculation of the Weight Coefficient

The weight coefficients of the block were calculated using a hierarchical analysis. According to the relative importance, weights were assigned to each influencing factor (heat transfer coefficient, equivalent stress, and porosity). In addition, a scale of 1 to 9 was used for importance comparisons of pairwise factors (Table 3). The elements were compared to each other to obtain the judgment matrix A, as shown in Formula (19) [43]:

$$A = (a_{ij})_{n \times n} \tag{19}$$

where A is the judgment matrix and a_{ij} is the scale.

Table 3. Scale values.

Comparison of the Importance of Factor i and Factor j	Scale (a_{ij})
i and j are equally important	1
	3
i is more important than j — Gradual increase	5
	7
	9
The median value of two adjacent scales	2, 4, 6, 8

The maximum eigenvalue of the judgment matrix was calculated, and then a consistency test was performed. The Formulas were as follows [43]:

$$Ax = \lambda_{\max} x \tag{20}$$

$$CI = \frac{\lambda_{\max} - n}{n - 1} \tag{21}$$

$$CR = \frac{CI}{RI} \tag{22}$$

where CI is the consistency index, RI is the average consistency index, $\lambda_{\max}$ is the maximum eigenvalue, n is the order of the judgment matrix, and CR is the consistency ratio.

The elements of the matrix A were normalized to obtain the matrix γ. The rows of the matrix γ were summed to obtain the column matrix W. Finally, the matrix W was normalized to obtain the ranking weight vector ω. That is, the percentages of thermal, mechanical, and economic performances that affected the comprehensive performance of the blocks were obtained.

2.3.3. Factor Normalization

The units, sizes, and orders of magnitude of the influencing factors were not consistent, which did not help evaluate the comprehensive performance of the blocks. Therefore, it was necessary to standardize the influencing factors using a normalization method. The calculation Formula for the normalization method was as follows [44]:

$$y_i = x_i / \sum_{i=1}^{n} x_i \tag{23}$$

where y_i is the dimensionless constant, and $\sum_{i=1}^{n} y_i$ is equal to 1 [44].

2.4. Influence of AASCCIB Wall on the Indoor Thermal Environment

Through the ANSYS CFX simulation, the improvement effect of the AASCCIB wall on the indoor thermal environment relative to the OB wall was informed.

This study considered rural buildings in Southern Shanxi, China, as the simulation object. The main reason was that Southern Shanxi, China, is located in the zone of hot-summer and cold-winter, where it is hot in summer and wet with cold in winter. Moreover, the region is close to severe-cold and cold zones, where the average daily temperature reaches about −10 °C in winter [45]. Obviously, the indoor thermal environment of rural buildings in this region needs to be improved urgently. Based on the above analysis, this study took rural buildings in Southern Shanxi, China, as the simulation object.

2.4.1. Mathematical Model

According to Section 2.2.1, the 3D unsteady differential equation for heat conduction in the Cartesian coordinate system was as follows:

$$\left[\frac{\partial}{\partial x}(\lambda_x \frac{\partial T}{\partial x}) + \frac{\partial}{\partial y}(\lambda_y \frac{\partial T}{\partial y}) + \frac{\partial}{\partial z}(\lambda_z \frac{\partial T}{\partial z})\right] + q_v = \rho c \frac{\partial T}{\partial \tau} \quad (24)$$

This equation had to be solved in domain Ω. The boundary conditions for this domain were as follows [46]:

$$T = \overline{T} \text{(On the } \Gamma_1 \text{ boundary)} \quad (25)$$

$$\lambda_x \frac{\partial T}{\partial x} n_x + \lambda_y \frac{\partial T}{\partial y} n_y + \lambda_z \frac{\partial T}{\partial z} n_z = q \text{ (On the } \Gamma_2 \text{ boundary)} \quad (26)$$

$$\lambda_x \frac{\partial T}{\partial x} n_x + \lambda_y \frac{\partial T}{\partial y} n_y + \lambda_z \frac{\partial T}{\partial z} n_z = h(T_a - T) \text{ (On the } \Gamma_2 \text{ boundary)} \quad (27)$$

$$\Gamma_1 + \Gamma_2 + \Gamma_3 = \Gamma \quad (28)$$

where ρ is the density (kg/m^3), c is the specific heat capacity (W/(kg·K), τ is the time (s), q_v is the heat flux (W/m^2), T is the temperature (°C), λ_i is the thermal conductivity along the i-axis direction (W/(m·K), n_i is the cosine of the outer normal of the boundary along the i-axis direction. q is the heat flux density on the Γ_2 boundary, (W/m^2), $\overline{T}$ is the temperature on the Γ_1 boundary (°C), T_a is the external ambient temperature under natural convection conditions (°C), T_a is the absolute temperature of the boundary layer under forced convection conditions (°C), and Γ is the whole boundary of domain Ω.

2.4.2. Development of the Finite Element Model

1. Basic assumptions and geometric models To simplify the model calculation, the following assumptions were used before modeling:

    (1) The air in each indoor room is considered as a whole. Its heat transfer mode is natural convection heat transfer.
    (2) The indoor door is open. The door is half-open.
    (3) The influence of indoor human activities and electrical appliances on the indoor temperature is ignored.

We conducted a field study on rural buildings in Ankang (climatic conditions and building characteristics were representative of rural regions in Southern Shanxi [45]) during the period from 2017 to 2019. Based on the field research and reference [40], a representative floor plan for rural buildings in Southern Shanxi, China, was constructed (Figure 5). Further, the geometric model of the representative building was developed using ANSYS CFX, as shown in Figure 6.

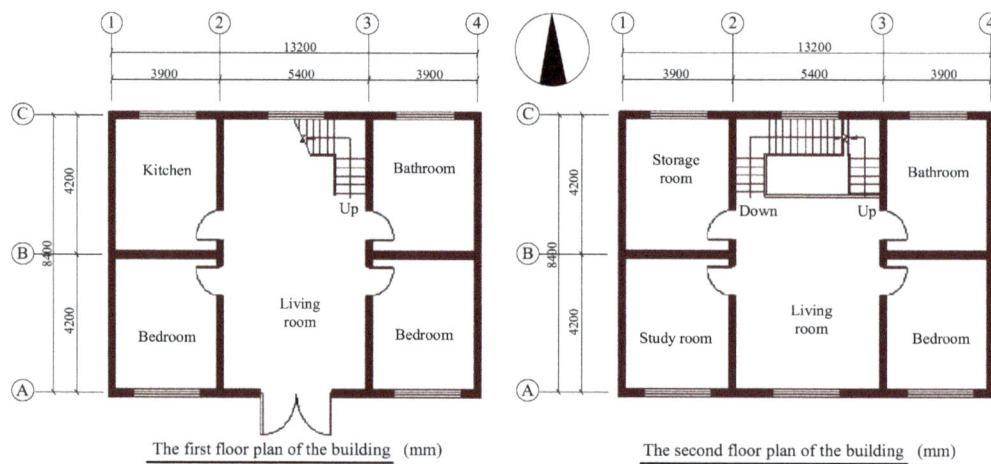

Figure 5. Floor plan of the representative building.

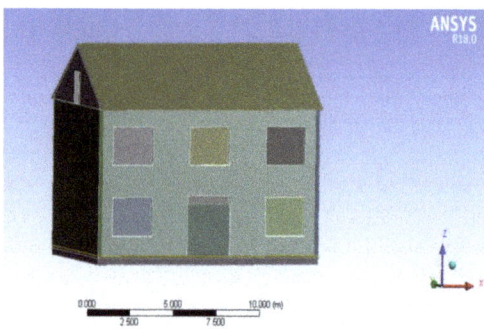

Figure 6. Geometric model of the representative building.

2. Mesh division

In the mesh division, the external surface of the air and internal surface of the external wall, window, door, and roof were mesh-refined. The minimum element size was 0.009 m, and the maximum was 0.967 m. The refined mesh model is illustrated in Figure 7.

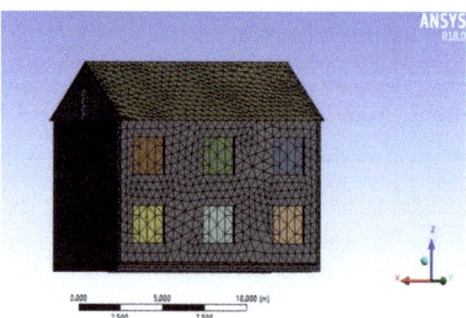

Figure 7. Refined mesh model.

3. Material parameter setting

Based on the field investigation, experimental research, and reference [39], the thermal parameters of the envelope of the building with OB walls and building with AASCCIB walls were obtained (Table 4).

Table 4. Thermal parameters of the envelope.

Item	Material Layer	Thickness mm	Thermal Conductivity W/(m·K)	Density Kg/m^3	Specific Heat Capacity J/(kg·K)
External wall (OB wall)	Cement mortar	20	0.93	1800	1050
	Solid clay brick	240	0.81	1800	1050
	Cement mortar	20	0.93	1800	1050
External wall (AASCCIB wall)	Cement mortar	20	0.93	1800	1050
	AASCCIB	240	0.11	867	1050
	Cement mortar	20	0.93	1800	1050
Partition wall	Cement mortar	20	0.93	1800	1050
	Solid clay brick	240	0.81	1800	1050
	Cement mortar	20	0.93	1800	1050
Floor	Cement mortar	20	0.93	1800	1050
	Reinforced concrete	100	1.74	2500	920
	Cement mortar	20	0.93	1800	1050
Roof	Clay tile	20	1.00	2000	800
	Wooden rafter	100	0.17	650	2120
Ground	Pebble concrete	100	1.51	2300	920
	Compacted clay	300	1.16	2000	1010
Window	Single-layer clear glass	3	0.76	2500	840
Door	Wood	150	0.35	500	2510

4. Boundary condition setting

The combined outdoor temperature considered the combined effect of solar radiation and outdoor air temperature on the external envelope of the building. Thus, the comprehensive outdoor temperature was chosen as the boundary condition for the external surface of the wall. Considering that outdoor meteorological parameters generally vary periodically, the comprehensive outdoor temperature was expressed as a sine or cosine function. Further, the comprehensive outdoor temperature was fitted as a periodic sine or cosine function by Fourier series expansion [45]. In addition, the initial temperature of the indoor air body was set to 278.6 K, and the initial temperature of the external surface of the wall was set to 277.1 K in the simulation.

$$t_z(\tau) = A_o + \sum_{n=1}^{\infty} A_n \sin(n\omega\tau + \phi_n) \tag{29}$$

where A_o is the zero-order outdoor disturbance (°C), A_n is the amplitude of the external disturbance of the n-th sine wave (°C), nw is the frequency of the external disturbance of the n-th sine wave, $nw = 2\pi n/T$ (rad), ϕ_n is the initial phase of the external disturbance of the n-th sine wave (rad). T is the period of the function (h), and n is the order of the harmonic.

Formula (29) was expanded by the sine, which yielded Formula (30).

$$t_z(\tau) = A_o + \sum_{n=1}^{\infty} [A_n \sin(n\omega\tau + \phi_n) + A_n \cos(n\omega\tau + \phi_n)] \tag{30}$$

Assuming that $\frac{a_0}{2} = A_0$, $a_n = A_n \sin \phi_n$, and $b_n = A_n \cos \phi_n$,

$$t_z(\tau) = \frac{a_0}{2} + \sum_{n=1}^{\infty} [a_n \cos(n\omega\tau) + b_n \sin(n\omega\tau)] \tag{31}$$

In addition, φ_n was determined by a_n and b_n,

$$b_n > 0 \text{ and } a_n > 0, \ \varphi_n = \arctan\left(\frac{a_n}{b_n}\right) \tag{32}$$

$$b_n > 0 \text{ and } a_n < 0, \ \varphi_n = \arctan\left(\frac{a_n}{b_n}\right) + \frac{\pi}{2} \tag{33}$$

$$b_n < 0, \ \varphi_n = \arctan\left(\frac{a_n}{b_n}\right) + \pi \tag{34}$$

$$b_n < 0 \text{ and } a_n = a_n, \ \varphi_n = \frac{\pi}{2} \tag{35}$$

$$b_n < 0 \text{ and } a_n = -a_n, \ \varphi_n = \frac{3\pi}{2} \tag{36}$$

Because the external disturbance function of the building envelope was extremely complex, the variation in the external disturbance function was expressed by a series of discrete data with equal intervals.

If the basic period interval $(0, T)$ was divided into N equal parts, the interval only had N discrete point values.

$$t_{zj} = t_z(j\Delta\tau), \ j = 0, 1, 2 \cdots N-1, \ \Delta\tau = \frac{T}{N} \tag{37}$$

The rectangular superposition summation method was used to obtain the function expressions of $\frac{a_0}{2}$, a_n, and b_n.

$$\frac{a_0}{2} = A_0 = \frac{1}{T}\sum_{j=0}^{N-1} t_{zj}\Delta\tau \tag{38}$$

$$a_n = \frac{2}{T}\sum_{j=0}^{N-1} t_{zj}\cos(n\omega j\Delta\tau)\Delta\tau \tag{39}$$

$$b_n = \frac{2}{T}\sum_{j=0}^{N-1} t_{zj}\sin(n\omega j\Delta\tau)\Delta\tau \tag{40}$$

where N is the number of measurement points in a period with a value of 24, T is the period, with a value of 24 (h), n is the order of the harmonics with a value of 4. j is the serial number of the sampled values, and $\Delta\tau$ is the sampling time interval with a value of 1 (h).

Therefore, Formula (31) was transformed into Formula (41).

$$t_z(j\Delta\tau) = A_0 + \sum_{n=1}^{\infty} A_n \sin(n\omega j\Delta\tau + \phi_n) \tag{41}$$

Based on the above analysis, according to the reference [47] and Formula (41), the fourth-order Fourier series expressions for the outdoor comprehensive temperature of different orientations in Ankang region were obtained.

The expressions for the integrated outdoor temperature on the summer solstice were as follows:

$$\begin{aligned} t_{sa.E(\tau)} = &\ 31.2 + 11.4727\sin(\pi/12 + 4.1200) + 2.5263\sin(\pi/6 + 2.1621) \\ &+ 1.8760\sin(\pi/4 + 0.5465) + 1.1061\sin(\pi/3 + 4.33.0) \end{aligned} \tag{42}$$

$$\begin{aligned} t_{sa.S(\tau)} = &\ 30.8 + 11.7485\sin(\pi/12 + 3.9708) + 1.8033\sin(\pi/6 + 1.5524) \\ &+ 1.0295\sin(\pi/4 + 0.2122) + 0.1788\sin(\pi/3 + 3.0834) \end{aligned} \tag{43}$$

$$t_{sa.W(\tau)} = 32.0 + 14.4902\sin(\pi/12 + 3.8151) + 2.5095\sin(\pi/6 + 6.1048)$$
$$+ 2.4431\sin(\pi/4 + 0.9260) + 1.3697\sin(\pi/3 + 2.9265) \quad (44)$$

$$t_{sa.N(\tau)} = 30.0 + 11.0814\sin(\pi/12 + 3.9156) + 1.8842\sin(\pi/6 + 1.2830)$$
$$+ 0.4152\sin(\pi/4 + 0.4529) + 0.2020\sin(\pi/3 + 3.7802) \quad (45)$$

The expressions for the integrated outdoor temperature on the winter solstice were as follows:

$$t_{sa.E(\tau)} = 3.5 + 4.8927\sin(\pi/12 + 3.5682) + 1.1911\sin(\pi/6 + 0.5243)$$
$$+ 1.2650\sin(\pi/4 + 2.9131) + 0.4420\sin(\pi/3 + 2.5141) \quad (46)$$

$$t_{sa.S(\tau)} = 4.7 + 7.0167\sin(\pi/12 + 3.7357) + 3.0627\sin(\pi/6 + 0.3954)$$
$$+ 2.5353\sin(\pi/4 + 2.8359) + 0.4178\sin(\pi/3 + 4.3601) \quad (47)$$

$$t_{sa.W(\tau)} = 4.1 + 6.2322\sin(\pi/12 + 3.0653) + 2.3717\sin(\pi/6 + 0.1049)$$
$$+ 2.2533\sin(\pi/4 + 2.5014) + 0.9370\sin(\pi/3 + 3.8372) \quad (48)$$

$$t_{sa.N(\tau)} = 3.4 + 4.8795\sin(\pi/12 + 3.5414) + 1.2075\sin(\pi/6 + 0.4287)$$
$$+ 1.3490\sin(\pi/4 + 2.8836) + 0.3785\sin(\pi/3 + 2.4847) \quad (49)$$

5. Validation of the model

The correctness of the model was verified to ensure that the simulation results were accurate. The measured data were compared to simulated data. The measured data were the indoor temperatures of a representative rural building in Ankang, Southern Shanxi, China. The results are presented in Figure 8. Each temperature value in the Figure is the average temperature of the room.

Figure 8 shows that the measured temperature was highly consistent with the simulation temperature. The R-squared between the measured and simulated temperatures was 0.91. At the same time, it was found that there was a small deviation between the simulated temperature and measured temperature. This deviation mainly originated from the simplifications and assumptions in modeling and accuracy error of the test instrument. Therefore, it was effective to use ANSYS CFX software to develop a finite element model of the building.

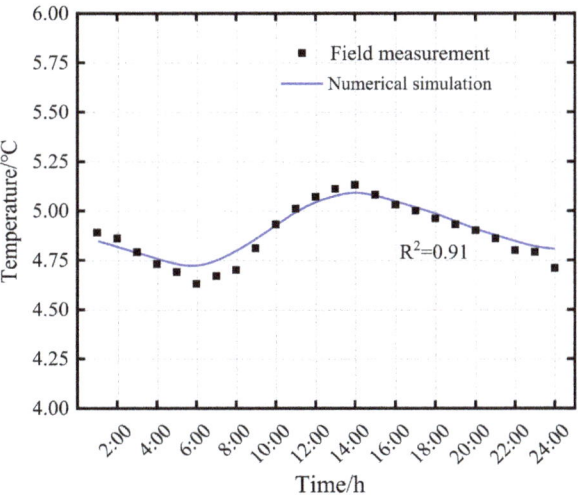

Figure 8. Comparison of measured and simulation results.

3. Results and Analysis

3.1. Analysis of Thermal and Mechanical Performances of AASCCIBs

Through the simulation by ANSYS CFX, the effects of the different numbers of holes and hole ratios on the thermal and mechanical performances of AASCCIBs were evaluated.

3.1.1. Thermal Performances

Contour plots of temperature and heat flux for the AASCCIB are presented in Figure 9 (for AASCCIB B_1 as an example).

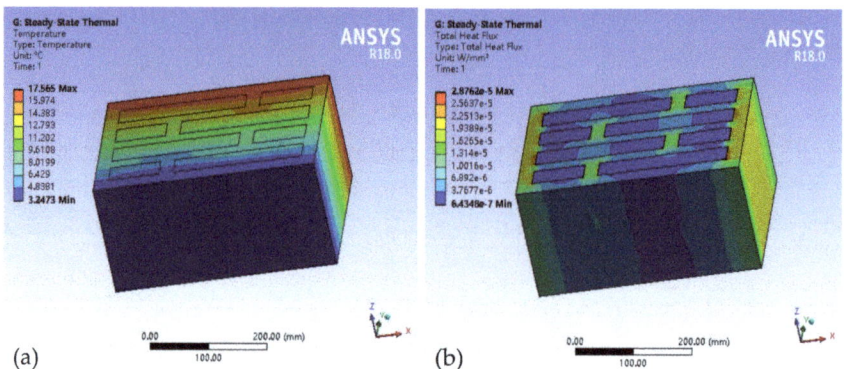

(a)   (b)

Figure 9. (**a**) Temperature contour plot; (**b**) heat flux contour plot.

Figure 9a shows that the temperature contour plot of the AASCCIB obeyed the fundamental law of heat transfer. The temperature decreased step-by-step from indoor to outdoor along the Y direction. As shown in Figure 9b, there was a concentration of heat flux at the vertical ribs, which could easily produce the thermal bridge effect. The main reason was that the heat transfer coefficient of the vertical ribs was larger than that of the other parts, which led to a quick heat transfer from the vertical rib of the block.

In addition, the temperature difference and heat flux intensity on both sides of the flat wall of the AASCCIB were obtained by numerical simulations. Furthermore, the heat transfer coefficient of the AASCCIBs was obtained by Formula (50) [48]. The results are listed in Table 5.

$$K = \frac{q}{\Delta t} \quad (50)$$

where K is the heat transfer coefficient (W/(m^2·K)), q is the heat flux intensity, (W/m^2), and Δt is the temperature difference between the internal and external surfaces of the wall (K).

Table 5. Simulated thermal performances.

Number	Number of Hole Rows	Hole Ratio %	Temperature Difference °C	Heat Flux Intensity W/m^2	Heat Transfer Coefficient W/(m^2·K)
A_1	Three rows	44.4	13.871	6.360	0.459
A_2		42.4	13.848	6.452	0.466
B_1	Four rows	45.8	13.881	6.185	0.446
B_2		41.7	13.841	6.531	0.472
C_1	Five rows	43.8	13.885	6.163	0.444
C_2		42.9	13.871	6.225	0.449

Table 5 shows that the heat transfer coefficient of the AASCCIB decreased with the increase in the hole ratio when the hole type and number of hole rows were constant.

This was because the increased hole ratio led to the increase in filler thickness when the hole shape and number of hole rows were constant. This directly increased the block heat transfer hindrance, thereby decreasing the heat transfer coefficient.

In addition, the simulated heat transfer coefficient was compared to the theoretical values to validate the finite element model.

The theoretical value of the average heat transfer coefficient of the AASCCIB was calculated by Formulas (51) to (55) [39]:

$$R = \frac{d}{\lambda} \tag{51}$$

$$R = R_1 + R_2 + \cdots R_n \tag{52}$$

$$R_0 = R_i + R + R_e \tag{53}$$

$$\overline{R} = \left[\frac{F_0}{F_1/R_{0,1} + F_2/R_{0,2} + \cdots F_n/R_{0,n}} - (R_i + R_e) \right] \cdot \phi \tag{54}$$

$$\overline{K} = \frac{1}{\overline{R}} \tag{55}$$

where R is the thermal resistance of materials ((m^2·K)/W), d is the thickness of each layer material (m), λ is the thermal conductivity of each layer material (W/(m·K)), R_0 is the total thermal resistance of the flat wall ((m^2·K)/W), R_i is the internal surface resistance of heat transfer with the value of 0.11 (m^2·K)/W [39], R_e is the external surface resistance of heat transfer with the value of 0.04 (m^2·K)/W [39], $\overline{R}$ is the average heat transfer resistance of the combined flat wall ((m^2·K)/W), F_0 is the total heat transfer area perpendicular to the direction of heat flux (m^2), $F_1, F_2, \ldots F_n$ is the area of each heat transfer region parallel to the direction of heat flux (m^2), $R_{0,1}, R_{0,2}, \ldots R_{0,n}$ is each heat transfer area parallel to the direction of the heat flux ((m^2·K)/W), ϕ is the correction factor with the value of 0.86 [39], and $\overline{K}$ is the average heat transfer coefficient of the combined wall (W/(m^2·K)).

A calculation diagram of the average thermal resistance is shown in Figure 10. A division diagram of the heat transfer channels is shown in Figure 11.

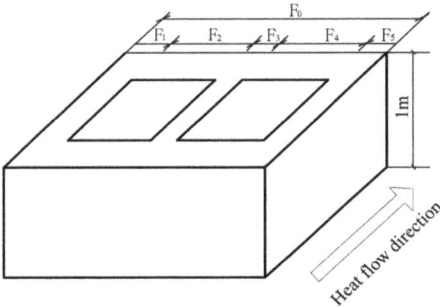

Figure 10. Calculation diagram of the average thermal resistance.

The average heat transfer coefficient of the AASCCIB was obtained using Formulas (51) to (55).

$$R_{0,1} = \frac{0.24}{0.35} = 0.686 = R_{0,7} \tag{56}$$

$$R_{0,2} = \frac{0.025}{0.35} \times 2 + \frac{0.029}{0.35} \times 2 + \frac{0.044}{0.03} \times 3 = 4.709 = R_{0,4} = R_{0,6} \tag{57}$$

$$R_{0,3} = \frac{0.025}{0.35} \times 2 + \frac{0.029}{0.35} \times 2 + \frac{0.044}{0.03} \times 2 + \frac{0.044}{0.35} = 3.368 \tag{58}$$

$$R_{0,5} = \frac{0.025}{0.35} \times 2 + \frac{0.044}{0.35} \times 2 + \frac{0.044}{0.03} + \frac{0.029}{0.35} \times 2 = 2.027 \tag{59}$$

$$R_1 = R_7 = 0.686 + 0.15 = 0.836 \tag{60}$$

$$R_2 = R_4 = R_6 = 4.709 + 0.15 = 4.859 \tag{61}$$

$$R_3 = 3.518 + 0.15 = 3.518 \tag{62}$$

$$R_5 = 2.027 + 0.15 = 2.177 \tag{63}$$

$$\overline{R} = \left[\frac{F_0}{\frac{F_1}{R_1} + \frac{F_2}{R_2} + \frac{F_3}{R_3} + \frac{F_4}{R_4} + \frac{F_5}{R_5} + \frac{F_6}{R_6} + \frac{F_7}{R_7}} - 0.15 \right] \times 0.86 = 2.30 \tag{64}$$

$$\overline{K} = \frac{1}{\overline{R}} = \frac{1}{2.30} = 0.435 \tag{65}$$

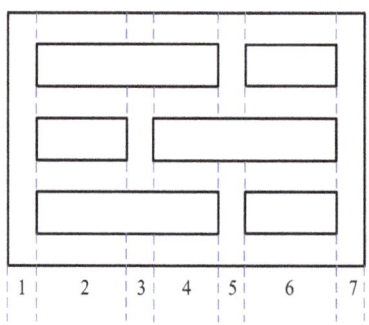

Figure 11. Division diagram of the heat transfer channels.

Based on the above calculation, the average heat transfer coefficient of AASCCIB A_1 was 0.435 W/(m²·K). In addition, using the above calculation method, the average heat transfer coefficients of AASCCIBs A_2, B_1, B_2, C_1, and C_2 were 0.444, 0.424, 0.448, 0.434, and 0.442 W/(m²·K).

The simulated and calculated values of the heat transfer coefficient were compared, as shown in Figure 12.

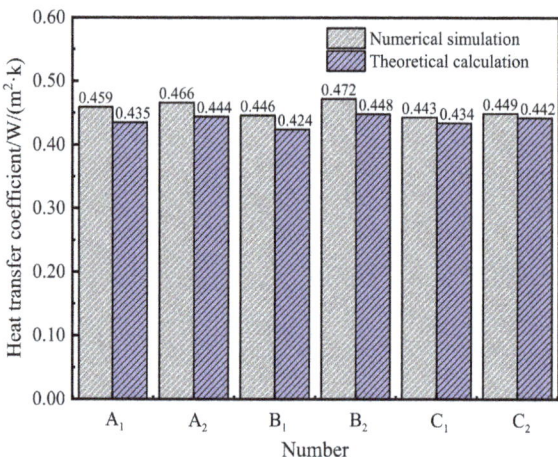

Figure 12. Comparison of simulated and calculated values of heat transfer coefficient.

Figure 12 shows that the calculated and simulated values of the average heat transfer coefficient were almost equal. The relative error of AASCCIB A_1 was the largest (5.5%). The main reason for this error was the series of assumptions in the modeling. Therefore, the finite element building model obtained using ANSYS CFX was considered effective.

3.1.2. Mechanical Performances

Contour plots of deformation and von Mises equivalent stress for AASCSIHB are presented in Figure 13 (for AASCSIHB A_1 as an example). The simulation results of the von Mises equivalent stress of the AASCSIHBs are listed in Table 6.

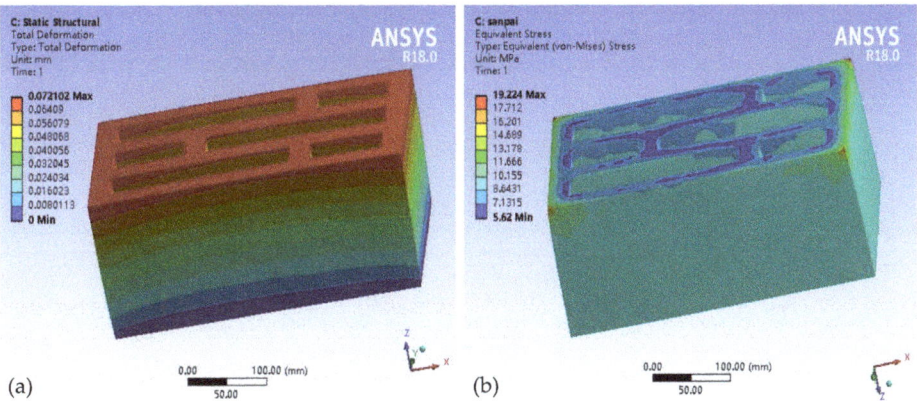

Figure 13. (**a**) Deformation contour plot; (**b**) von Mises equivalent stress contour plot.

Table 6. Simulation results of the von Mises equivalent stress.

Number	Number of Hole Rows	Hole Ratio %	Maximum von Mises Equivalent Stress/MPa	Minimum von Mises Equivalent Stress/MPa	Average von Mises Equivalent Stress/MPa
A_1	Three rows	44.4	19.22	5.62	9.553
A_2		42.4	18.70	5.59	9.559
B_1	Four rows	45.8	18.81	5.73	9.517
B_2		41.7	19.27	5.64	9.524
C_1	Five rows	43.8	18.80	5.67	9.496
C_2		42.9	18.78	5.67	9.502

Figure 13a presents that a large deformation at the edge of the block due to the principal stresses acted on it. Figure 13b shows that the minimum von Mises equivalent stress appeared in the cross ribs and inner wall of the block. The maximum von Mises equivalent stress appeared at the corners of the block (stress concentration area), and the area where stress concentration occurred was small. In summary, in this study, the maximum von Mises equivalent stress had no decisive influence on the overall bearing capacity and stability of the member.

Table 6 indicates that the average von Mises equivalent stress tended to decrease with the increase in the hole ratio when the hole shape and number of hole rows were fixed. The main reason was that the thickness of the middle rib of the block decreased with the increase in the hole ratio when the hole shape and the number of hole rows were constant. This reduced the compressive performance and connectivity between the concrete rib and wall of the block, thereby leading to a decrease in the average von Mises equivalent stress of the block.

3.2. Determination of Optimal AASCCIBs

According to Formula (19) and Table 3, judgment matrix A was obtained:

$$A = \begin{pmatrix} 1 & 2 & 3 \\ \frac{1}{2} & 1 & 2 \\ \frac{1}{3} & \frac{1}{2} & 1 \end{pmatrix} \quad (66)$$

Based on Formulas (20) and (21), λ_{max} and CI were 3.092 and 0.0046, respectively. According to reference [49], RI was 0.58. Based on Formula (22), CR was 0.0089. As CR was below 0.1, judgment matrix A satisfied the consistency test.

Matrix A was transformed to obtain the ranking weight vector ω (ω= (0.539 0.297 0.164)^T). Thus, the percentages of thermal, mechanical, and economic performances that affected the comprehensive performance of the AASCCIB were 53.9%, 29.7%, and 16.4%, respectively.

The heat transfer coefficient, Mises equivalent stress, and porosity were transformed to dimensionless using the normalization method. The results are listed in Table 7. The weighted comprehensive value of AASCCIBs was obtained by Formula (18). The results are presented in Figure 14.

Table 7. Dimensionless calculation results of each influence factor.

Number	Number of Hole Rows	Heat Transfer Coefficient	Equivalent Stress	Hole Ratio
A_1	Three rows	0.168	0.1671	0.170
A_2		0.170	0.1673	0.162
B_1	Four rows	0.163	0.1665	0.175
B_2		0.173	0.1666	0.160
C_1	Five rows	0.162	0.1662	0.168
C_2		0.164	0.1663	0.164

Note: A smaller heat transfer coefficient indicates better thermal performance. Therefore, the dimensionless value of the heat transfer coefficient was multiplied by −1 [44], to make the monotonicity of the three sub-factor functions of heat transfer coefficient, equivalent stress, and hole ratio consistent.

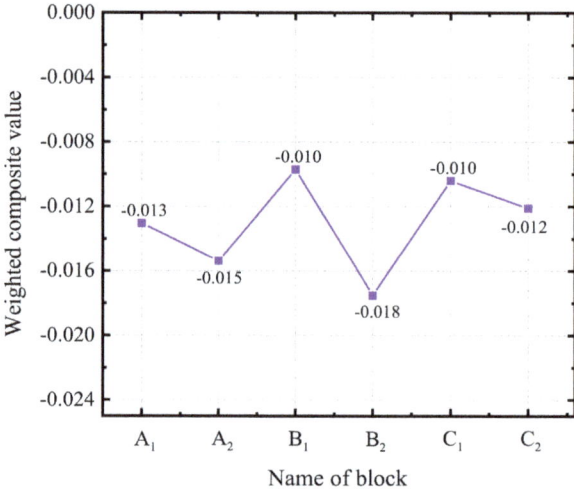

Figure 14. Weighted comprehensive value of each AASCCIB.

Figure 14 shows that the weighted comprehensive value of AASCCIB B_1 was largest. Thus, compared with several other AASCCIBs, AASCCIB B_1 had the optimal comprehensive performance. Therefore, AASCCIB B_1 was chosen to build the wall in the following modeling. The heat transfer coefficient and average von Mises equivalent stress of AASCCIB B_1 were 0.446 W/(m^2·K) and 9.52 MPa, respectively.

3.3. Improvement Effect of AASCCIB Wall on the Indoor Thermal Environment

Through the ANSYS CFX simulation, the indoor temperature changes of the building with the OB wall and building with the AASCCIB wall were informed. China is located in the northern hemisphere of the Earth. The day with the shortest sunshine time and the lowest solar altitude angle is the winter solstice. From the perspective of passive heat collection, the amount of solar radiation on this day is the lowest of the year. On the contrary, the summer solstice is the day with the longest sunshine time and the highest solar altitude angle, i.e., the solar radiation on this day is the highest in the year. Therefore, in the simulation analysis of the thermal insulation performance of the wall, the winter solstice (summer solstice) was selected as the date of the outdoor boundary condition. In addition, the indoor temperature of the room with the worst thermal comfort on the first floor (second floor) was used as the temperature of the first floor (second floor) in this study. The simulation results are presented in Figure 15.

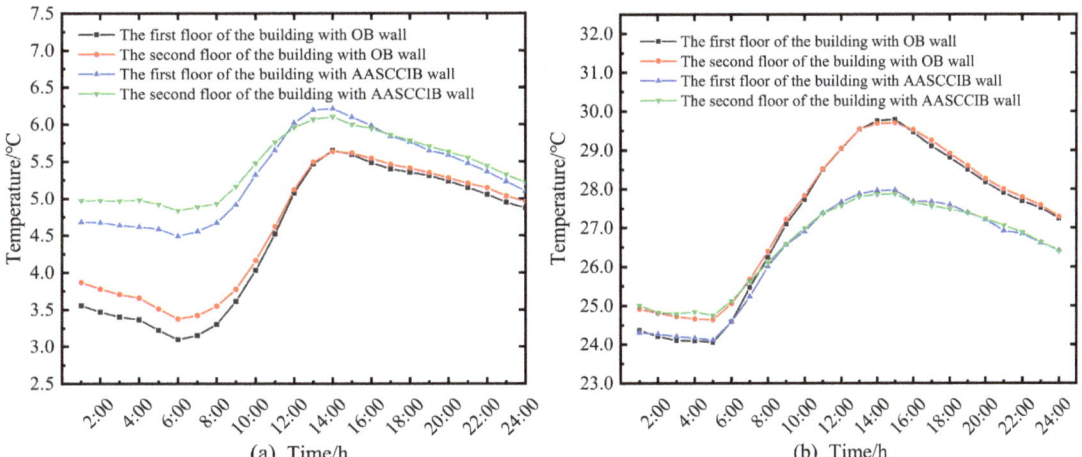

Figure 15. Indoor temperature of the building. (**a**) On the winter solstice; (**b**) on the summer solstice.

As shown in Figure 15a, the indoor temperatures of the rooms on the first and second floors of the building with the OB wall were lowest at 6:00 and highest at 14:00. The indoor lowest, highest, and average temperatures of the room on the first floor were 3.10, 5.65, and 4.47 °C, respectively. The indoor lowest, highest, and average temperatures of the room on the second floor were 3.37, 5.63, and 4.61 °C, respectively. For the building with the AASCCIB wall, the indoor temperatures of the rooms on the first and second floors were lowest at 6:00 and highest at 14:00. The indoor lowest, highest, and average temperatures of the room on the first floor were 4.49, 6.21, and 5.31 °C, respectively. The indoor lowest, highest, and average temperatures of the room on the second floor were 4.83, 6.10, and 5.43 °C, respectively. Compared with the indoor lowest and average temperatures of the building with the OB wall, those of the building with AASCCIB walls increased by at least 1.39 and 0.82 °C. In addition, the indoor temperature difference decreased by at least 0.83 °C.

Figure 15b shows that the indoor temperatures of the rooms on the first and second floors of the building with the OB wall were lowest at 5:00, 24.06, and 24.64 °C, respectively. The indoor temperatures of the rooms on the first and second floors were highest at 17:00, 29.89, and 29.81 °C, respectively. The average indoor temperatures of the rooms on the first and second floors were 27.37 and 27.54 °C, respectively. For the building with the AASCCIB wall, the indoor temperatures of the rooms on the first and second floors were lowest at 5:00, 24.11, and 24.75 °C, respectively. The indoor temperatures of the rooms on the first and second floors were highest at 15:00, 28.14, and 28.03 °C, respectively. The average indoor temperatures of the rooms on the first and second floors were 26.58 and 26.70 °C, respectively. Compared with the indoor highest temperature of the building with the OB wall, that of the building with the AASCCIB wall decreased by at least 1.75 °C. The indoor average temperature and temperature difference decreased by at least 0.79 and 1.89 °C, respectively.

In summary, the indoor thermal environment of the building with AASCCIB walls was significantly improved compared to that of the building with the OB wall. This was manifested by the increase in the indoor lowest and average temperatures on the winter solstice. The indoor temperature difference decreased. On the summer solstice, the indoor highest temperature, average temperature. and temperature difference decreased.

4. Conclusions and Outlook

In this study, six types of AASCCIBs with different internal structures were designed. Based on the FEM, the thermal and mechanical performances of the six AASCCIBs were simulated using ANSYS CFX. The AASCCIB with the optimal comprehensive performance was determined through multi-objective optimization. The improvement effect of the AASCCIB wall on the indoor thermal environment relative to the OB wall was quantitatively analyzed using ANSYS CFX. The conclusions of this study can be summarized as follows:

1. The von Mises equivalent stress and heat transfer coefficient of the AASCCIB decreased with the increase in hole ratio when the hole shape and number of hole rows were constant.
2. AASCCIB B_1 had the optimal comprehensive performance among the six AASCCIBs. The heat transfer coefficient and average von Mises equivalent stress of AASCCIB B_1 were 0.446 W/(m^2·K) and 9.52 MPa, respectively.
3. Compared with the indoor lowest and average temperatures of the building with the OB wall, those of the building with the AASCCIB wall increased by at least 1.39 and 0.82 °C on the winter solstice, respectively. The indoor temperature difference decreased by at least 0.83 °C. In addition, the indoor highest temperature, average temperature, and temperature difference decreased by at least 1.75, 0.79, and 1.89 °C on the summer solstice, respectively.

This study quantitatively elucidated the improvement effect of the AASCCIB walls on the indoor thermal environment relative to the OB walls. However, the positive effect of the AASCCIB walls on the building energy consumption was unclear. To promote the development of wall materials and building energy efficiency, the reduction effect of the AASCCIB wall on the building energy consumption will be quantitatively analyzed in a follow-up study.

Author Contributions: Funding acquisition, Y.Z.; Methodology, X.F., Y.G. and Q.Z.; Software, X.F., Y.G. and Q.Z.; Writing—original draft, X.F. and Y.G.; Data curation, X.F. All authors have read and agreed to the published version of the manuscript.

Funding: This research was supported by the National Natural Science Foundation of China (grant no. 52078419 and 51678483).

Institutional Review Board Statement: Not applicable.

Informed Consent Statement: Not applicable.

Data Availability Statement: Not applicable.

Conflicts of Interest: The authors declare no conflict of interest.

References

1. Li, Y.; He, J. Evaluating the improvement effect of low-energy strategies on the summer indoor thermal environment and cooling energy consumption in a library building: A case study in a hot-humid and less-windy city of China. In *Building Simulation*; Tsinghua University Press: Beijing, China, 2021; Volume 14, pp. 1423–1437.
2. Ujanová, P.; Rychtáriková, M.; Mayor, T.S.; Hyder, A. A Healthy, Energy-Efficient and Comfortable Indoor Environment, a Review. *Energies* **2019**, *12*, 1414. [CrossRef]
3. Ahn, J. Improvement of the Performance Balance between Thermal Comfort and Energy Use for a Building Space in the Mid-Spring Season. *Sustainability* **2020**, *12*, 9667. [CrossRef]
4. Zhu, Y.Y.; Fan, X.N.; Wang, C.J.; Sang, G.C. Analysis of Heat Transfer and Thermal Environment in a Rural Residential Building for Addressing Energy Poverty. *Appl. Sci.* **2018**, *8*, 2077. [CrossRef]
5. Kalua, A. Urban Residential Building Energy Consumption by End-Use in Malawi. *Buildings* **2020**, *10*, 31. [CrossRef]
6. Xu, X.; Mumford, T.; Zou, P. Life-cycle building information modelling (BIM) engaged framework for improving building energy performance. *Energy Build.* **2020**, *231*, 110496. [CrossRef]
7. Alsheyab, M. Recycling of construction and demolition waste and its impact on climate change and sustainable development. *Int. J. Environ. Sci. Technol.* **2021**, *1*, 1–10.
8. Liu, H.W.; Li, J.; Su, Y.F.; Wang, Y.S. Estimation Method of Carbon Emissions in the Embodied Phase of Low Carbon Building. *Adv. Civ. Eng.* **2020**, *2020*, 8853536.
9. Li, R.Y.; Li, Y.Y. Discussion on the innovation of new wall materials. *Charming China* **2014**, *22*, 263.
10. Li, P.; Sun, D.S.; Ding, Y.; Wang, A.G. Thermal Testing and Simulation of Self-thermal Insulation Block. *China Concr. Cem. Pro.* **2015**, *8*, 63–66.
11. Jiao, Z.; Wang, Y.; Zheng, W.; Huang, W.; Zhou, X. Use of Industrial Waste Slag in Alkali-Activated Slag Ceramsite Concrete Hollow Blocks. *Appl. Sci.* **2018**, *8*, 2358. [CrossRef]
12. Rashad, A.M. Recycled waste glass as fine aggregate replacement in cementitious materials based on Portland cement. *Constr. Build. Mater.* **2014**, *72*, 340–357. [CrossRef]
13. Imbabi, M.; Carrigan, C.; Mckenna, S. Trends and developments in green cement and concrete technology. *Int. J. Sustain. Built Environ.* **2012**, *1*, 194–216. [CrossRef]
14. Awoyera, P.; Adesina, A. A critical review on application of alkali activated slag as a sustainable composite binder. *Case Studies Constr. Mater.* **2019**, *11*, e00268. [CrossRef]
15. Rodríguez, E.D.; Mejia, R.; Puertas, F. Alternative concrete based on alkali-activated slag. *Mater. Constr.* **2008**, *58*, 53–67.
16. Liu, S.X.; Shen, L.L.; Niu, F.S. Researching Status and Prospect of Lightweight Aggregates Obtained from Solid Wastes in China. *Adv. Mater. Res.* **2011**, *163–167*, 624–628. [CrossRef]
17. Xie, J.; Liu, J.; Liu, F.; Wang, J.; Huang, P. Investigation of a new lightweight green concrete containing sludge ceramsite and recycled fine aggregates. *J. Clean. Prod.* **2019**, *235*, 1240–1254. [CrossRef]
18. Li, M.; Zhou, D.Y.; Jiang, Y.Q. Preparation and Thermal Storage Performance of Phase Change Ceramsite Sand and Thermal Storage Light-weight Concrete. *Renew. Energy* **2021**, *175*, 143–152. [CrossRef]
19. Sang, G.C.; Du, X.Y.; Zhang, Y.K.; Zhao, C.Y.; Cui, X.L.; Cui, H.Z.; Zhang, L.; Zhu, Y.Y.; Guo, T. A novel composite for thermal energy storage from alumina hollow sphere/paraffin and alkali-activated slag. *Ceram. Int.* **2021**, *47*, 15947. [CrossRef]
20. Akgul, B.A.; Karapınar, E. Investigation and Evaluation of Thermal Analysis for Different Wall Structures with Finite Element Method, Simulation of Temperature Distribution and Reaction in the Wall Types. *Euro. J. Math. Eng. Nat. Med. Sci.* **2021**, *8*, 132–144.
21. Ait-Taleb, T.; Abdelbaki, A.; Zrikem, Z. Simulation of coupled heat transfers in a hollow tile with two vertical and three horizontal uniform rectangular cavities heated from below or above. *Energy Build.* **2014**, *84*, 628–632. [CrossRef]
22. Boukendil, M.; Abdelbaki, A.; Zrikem, Z. Simulation of the temperature field for massive concrete structures using an interval finite element method. *Eng. Comput.* **2020**, *37*, 2467–2486.
23. Hawkes, P.W.; Kasper, E. 11-The Finite-Difference Method (FDM). *Principl. Electr. Opt.* **1996**, *116*, 159–174.
24. Mazumder, S. The Finite Difference Method—ScienceDirect. *Numer. Methods Partial Differ. Equ.* **2016**, *12*, 51–101.
25. Cheng, Y.M.; Bai, F.N.; Peng, M.J. A novel interpolating element-free Galerkin (IEFG) method for two-dimensional elastoplasticity. *Appl. Math. Model.* **2014**, *38*, 5187–5197. [CrossRef]
26. Mukherjee, S.; Liu, Y. The Boundary Element Method. *Int. J. Comp. Meth-Sing.* **2013**, *10*, 1350037. [CrossRef]
27. Mazumder, S. The Finite Volume Method (FVM). *Numer. Meth. Part. Differ. Equ.* **2016**, *1*, 277–338.
28. Teng, C.; Yang, Q.; Peng, H. Numerical Thermal Optimization of the Hole Structures of Pottery Grain Concrete Hollow Blocks. *Mater. Rev.* **2011**, *25*, 280–284.
29. Gao, H.; Wei, G. Complex Variable Meshless Manifold Method for Transient Heat Conduction Problems. *Int. J. Appl. Mech.* **2017**, *9*, 1750067. [CrossRef]
30. Gao, H.; Wei, G. Numerical solution of Potential Problems using Radial Basis Reproducing Kernel Particle Method. *Results Phys.* **2019**, *13*, 102122. [CrossRef]
31. Muttalli, R.S.; Agrawal, S.; Warudkar, H. CFD Simulation of Centrifugal Pump Impeller Using ANSYS-CFX. *Int. J. Innov. Res. Sci. Eng. Technol.* **2014**, *3*, 15553–15561. [CrossRef]
32. MOHURD. *Self-Insulation Concrete Compound Blocks: JG/T 407-2013*; China Architecture Building Press: Beijing, China, 2013.

33. Zheng, J.S.; Zhang, G.Z. Design and heat transfer performance of warming compound blocks with slag concrete. *New Build. Mater.* **2012**, *39*, 63–65.
34. Bathe, K.J. *Finite Element Procedures*; Prentice-Hall: Hoboken, NJ, USA, 2006.
35. Sardari, P.T.; Mohammed, H.I.; Mahdi, J.M.; Ghalambaz, M.; Gillott, M.; Walker, G.S.; Grant, D.; Giddings, D. Localized heating element distribution in composite metal foam-phase change material: Fourier's law and creeping flow effects. *Int. J. Energy Res.* **2021**, *45*, 13380–13396. [CrossRef]
36. Arif, M.; Kaushik, S.K. Convexity studies of two anisotropic yield criteria in principal stress space. *Eng. Comput.* **1999**, *16*, 215–229.
37. Li, Q.; Steven, G.P.; Xie, Y.M. On equivalence between stress criterion and stiffness criterion in evolutionary structural optimization. *Struct. Optim.* **1999**, *18*, 67–73. [CrossRef]
38. Pazera, E. Heat Transfer in Periodically Laminated Structures-Third Type Boundary Conditions. *Int. J. Comput. Meth.* **2021**, *18*, 2041011. [CrossRef]
39. MOHURD. *Code for Thermal Design of Civil Building: CB50176-2016*; China Architecture Building Press: Beijing, China, 2016.
40. MOHURD. *Design Standard for Energy Efficiency of Rural Residential Buildings: GB50176-2016*; China Architecture Building Press: Beijing, China, 2016.
41. MOHURD. *Design Standards for Energy Efficiency of Residential Buildings in Hot Summer and Cold Winter Zones: JGJ134-2010*; China Architecture Building Press: Beijing, China, 2010.
42. Sánchez-Zarco, X.G.; González-Bravo, R.; Ponce-Ortega, J.M. Multi-objective Optimization Approach to Meet Water, Energy, and Food Needs in an Arid Region Involving Security Assessment. *ACS Sustain. Chem. Eng.* **2021**, *9*, 4771–4790. [CrossRef]
43. Hamka, M.; Harjono, H. Application of fuzzy preference relations method in AHP to improve judgment matrix consistency. In *IOP Conference Series: Materials Science and Engineering*; IOP Publishing: Bristol, UK, 2020; Volume 821, p. 12035.
44. Yang, Z.T.; Liu, Y.; Yin, G.S.; Shi, M.H.; Wei, P.F. Optimization design and analysis of multi-row ceramsite concrete composite block structure. *Bull. Chin. Ceram. Soc.* **2020**, *39*, 113–123.
45. Zhao, Q.; Fan, X.N.; Wang, Q.; Sang, G.C.; Zhu, Y.Y. Research on Energy-Saving Design of Rural Building Wall in Qinba Mountains Based on Uniform Radiation Field. *Math. Probl. Eng.* **2020**, *2020*, 9786895. [CrossRef]
46. Chandrupatla, T.R.; Belegundu, A.D. *Introduction to Finite Element in Engineering*; Prentice-Hall: Hoboken, NJ, USA, 1991.
47. Zhang, Q.Y.; Huang, J. *Standard Meteorological Database Used for Buildings in China*; Mechanical Industry Press: Beijing, China, 2004.
48. Samoshkin, S.L.; Meyster, A.O.; Yukhnevskiy, M.A. Methodical issues of determination of the average heat transfer coefficient of the passenger car body. *Vest. Rail. Res. Ins.* **2020**, *78*, 344–350. [CrossRef]
49. Guo, T.M.; Hu, S.T.; Liu, G.D. Evaluation Model of Specific Indoor Environment Overall Comfort Based on Effective-Function Method. *Energies* **2017**, *10*, 1634. [CrossRef]

Article

A Dimension Splitting Generalized Interpolating Element-Free Galerkin Method for the Singularly Perturbed Steady Convection–Diffusion–Reaction Problems

Fengxin Sun [1,*], Jufeng Wang [2], Xiang Kong [1] and Rongjun Cheng [3]

1. Faculty of Science, Ningbo University of Technology, Ningbo 315016, China; kongx@nbut.edu.cn
2. College of Finance & Information, Ningbo University of Finance & Economics, Ningbo 315175, China; wjf@nit.zju.edu.cn
3. Faculty of Maritime and Transportation, Ningbo University, Ningbo 315211, China; chengrongjun@nbu.edu.cn
* Correspondence: fengxin@nbut.edu.cn

Abstract: By introducing the dimension splitting method (DSM) into the generalized element-free Galerkin (GEFG) method, a dimension splitting generalized interpolating element-free Galerkin (DS-GIEFG) method is presented for analyzing the numerical solutions of the singularly perturbed steady convection–diffusion–reaction (CDR) problems. In the DS-GIEFG method, the DSM is used to divide the two-dimensional CDR problem into a series of lower-dimensional problems. The GEFG and the improved interpolated moving least squares (IIMLS) methods are used to obtain the discrete equations on the subdivision plane. Finally, the IIMLS method is applied to assemble the discrete equations of the entire problem. Some examples are solved to verify the effectiveness of the DS-GIEFG method. The numerical results show that the numerical solution converges to the analytical solution with the decrease in node spacing, and the DS-GIEFG method has high computational efficiency and accuracy.

Keywords: meshless method; dimension splitting method; dimension splitting generalized interpolating element-free Galerkin method; convection–diffusion–reaction problem

1. Introduction

Since the construction of the approximation function is independent of the mesh, the meshless method, which has developed rapidly in recent years, can completely abandon the mesh reconstruction to ensure high calculation accuracy [1–3]. The meshless method has become an essential numerical method in scientific and engineering computation [4–7].

When studying surface fitting, Lancaster and Salkauskas proposed the moving least squares (MLS) approximation [8], which is based on the traditional least squares (LS) method [9–12]. The MLS is one of the most important methods for constructing trial functions in meshless methods [13]. Based on the MLS approximation, Belytschko et al. proposed the element-free Galerkin (EFG) method [14], which has a wide range of applications and high calculation accuracy. Since the shape function of the MLS approximation does not satisfy the Kronecker delta property [15], additional numerical techniques are required to impose essential boundary conditions, such as Lagrange multipliers, a penalty method, which may increase the computational burden. For this reason, Lancaster et al. proposed the interpolated moving least-squares (IMLS) method [8] by selecting singular special weight functions. Since the singularity of the weight function is not conducive to numerical calculation, Cheng et al. proposed an improved interpolated moving least squares (IIMLS) method with nonsingular weights for potential problems [16]. The improved meshless method based on the IIMLS has the advantages of nonsingular weight function and direct application of an essential boundary [17,18].

Many meshless methods have been presented [19], such as the smooth particle hydrodynamics method, element-free Galerkin (EFG) method, reproducing kernel particle method, hp-cloud method, and meshless local Petrov–Galerkin (MLPG) method. Peridynamics (PD) is also an important meshless method for solving solid and fluid mechanics problems [20,21]. When the EFG method is used to solve some fluid problems, the numerical solution is prone to non-physical oscillation [22–24]. By coupling the variational multiscale method and EFG method, Ouyang et al. established the variational multiscale EFG method (VMEFG) [25]. The VMEFG method has been successfully applied in many physical problems [26–28]. However, the disadvantage of VMEFG is that the bubble function in the stabilization factor must be based on the mesh and is difficult to construct in high-dimensional cases. Li et al. proposed the general element-free Garlerkin (GEFG) method [22] for Stokes problems. The GEFG method overcomes the non-physical oscillation of the solution caused by the EFG method, and also overcomes the deficiency that the stabilization factor of the VMEFG method must be related to the mesh.

Due to the complexity of the shape function, the traditional EFG method requires a large amount of calculation, especially for three-dimensional problems. Then, Cheng et al. proposed the dimension-splitting element-free Galerkin method by coupling the dimension-splitting method (DSM) and EFG method [29–31]. Since the DSM divides high-dimensional problems into a series of low-dimensional problems and then iteratively solves them, it can effectively improve the computational efficiency of numerical methods [32,33]. Therefore, the dimension-splitting element-free Galerkin method can significantly improve the computational efficiency of the EFG method [34].

The convection–diffusion–reaction (CDR) equation has a wide range of applications in the fields of physics and chemistry [35–37]. The steady CDR equation can model the transport of the quantity and represent the balance of three processes: transport by convection, diffusion and reactions [37]. As it is difficult to obtain the analytical solutions of the CDR equation in complex situations, many numerical methods have been proposed to obtain the numerical solutions [38–40]. A finite difference method [36] and two spurious oscillations at layers diminishing (SOLD) methods [37] have been presented for solving steady CDR problems. For the singularly perturbed problems, the numerical solutions are prone to instability issues [41,42]. Then, when the diffusion coefficient is very small in CDR problems, it is usually necessary to add additional stability measures to ensure that the numerical method obtains a stable solution [43]. Wu et al. presented an adaptive upwind finite difference method for the CDR problem with two small parameters [44]. The finite difference method [45], a cubic B-spline-based semi-analytical algorithm [46], and weak Galerkin method [47] are proposed for studying the numerical solutions of the CDR problems.

Due to the advantages of the meshless method, some meshless methods have been developed for the CDR problems [48,49]. Zhang and Xiang discussed the numerical solutions of the CDR equation with small diffusion by the VMEFG method [50,51]. Li et al. also applied the local Petrov Galerkin method to the multi-dimensional CDR equations based on the radial basis function [52]. Additionally, the local knot method [53] and the meshless boundary collocation method [54] have been presented to solve the numerical solution of the CDR equation.

In this paper, by constructing the trial functions from the IIMLS method and coupling the DSM and GEFG method, a dimension splitting general interpolating element-free Galerkin (DS-GIEFG) method is presented for the singularly perturbed steady CDR problems. In the DS-GIEFG method, DSM divides the two-dimensional problem into a series of one-dimensional problems. The GEFG method is used to establish the discrete equations on the low-dimensional problems. Finally, the IIMLS method is used to assemble the discrete equations on the entire problem domain. The DS-GIEFG method will have high computational efficiency and solution stability for the singularly perturbed steady CDR problem.

2. The DS-GIEFG Method for CDR Problems

By using the interpolating shape function of the IIMLS method and coupling the DSM and GEFG method, we will present the DS-GIEFG method for the singularly perturbed steady CDR problems.

2.1. The Trial Functions for the DS-GIEFG Method

The trial function of the DS-GIEFG method is presented by using the property of the PU function. From the Refs. [14,16], the following properties are satisfied:

$$\sum_{i=1}^{n} \Phi_i(y) b(y_i) = b(y) \tag{1}$$

where y_i is the discrete node, Φ_i and b are, respectively, the shape functions and the basis functions used in the IIMLS method [16].

Then, if the basis functions are chosen to be the complete polynomials of order m, the PU function can be established as follows [16]

$$\sum_{i=1}^{n} \Phi_i = 1 \tag{2}$$

Similar to the GEFG method [22], the trial function of the DS-GIEFG method is defined as

$$u^h(y) = \sum_{i=1}^{n} \Phi_i(y) \tau_i(y) \tag{3}$$

where the function $\tau_k(y)$ is

$$\tau_i(y) = \sum_{j=1}^{m_i} \theta_{ij}(y) c_{ij} \tag{4}$$

Here, the function $\theta_{ij}(y)$ and c_{ij} are, respectively, the nodal enrichment basis function and the corresponding coefficient to be determined of y_i, and m_i is the number of the local enrichment basis function. The purpose of introducing local enrichment polynomial basis functions is to increase the stability of the meshless method to fluid problems. When $m_i = 1$, the trial function (3) is consistent with that of the EFG method.

According to reference [22,55], we take the local polynomial basis function as the enrichment basis function. In one-dimensional space, $\theta_{kj}(y)$ can be taken as the following forms [22,55]:

(a) If $m_i = 1$, then $\theta_{i1}(y) = 1$.
(b) if $m_i = 2$, then $\{\theta_{i1}, \theta_{i2}\} = \{1, (y - y_i)^2\}$.
(c) if $m_i = 3$, then $\{\theta_{i1}, \theta_{i2}, \theta_{i3}\} = \{1, (y - y_i)^2, (y - y_i)^3\}$.

For example, when $m_i = 2$, the trial function of the DS-GIEFG method in one-dimensional space is:

$$u^h = \sum_{i=1}^{n} \Phi_i(y) \cdot c_{i1} + \sum_{i=1}^{n} \Phi_i(y) \cdot (y - y_i)^2 c_{i2} \tag{5}$$

In Equation (5), the first term represents the effect of the IIMLS method, and the second term is the stabilization parameter of the DS-GIEFG method for the singularly perturbed steady CDR problems.

2.2. Discretization Process on the Splitting Plane

The following two-dimensional singular perturbed steady CDR equations are considered:

$$\begin{cases} \mathbf{a} \cdot \nabla u - \varepsilon \Delta u + cu = f, & \text{in } \Omega \subset R^2, \\ u = u_D, & \text{on boundary } \Gamma. \end{cases} \quad (6)$$

Equation (6) can model the transport of the quantity $u = u(x,y)$. The prescribed function f is the source term describing chemical reactions, and u_D is a given functions for the Dirichlet condition. $\mathbf{a} = (a_1, a_2)^T$ denotes velocity field, $0 < \varepsilon \ll 1$ denotes the small diffusion coefficient, and c is the reaction coefficient.

Let L denote the number of the splitting plane. According to the idea of the DSM, the problem (6) is divided into a series of one-dimensional problems on the split surface y:

$$\begin{cases} (\mathbf{a} \cdot \nabla u - \varepsilon \Delta u + cu)|_{x=x_k} = f|_{x=x_k}, & \text{in } \Omega_k = \Omega \cap \{x = x_k\}, \\ u = u_D, & \text{on boundary } \Gamma, \end{cases} \quad (7)$$

where Ω_k ($k = 1, 2, \cdots, L$) is a splitting plane such that

$$\Omega = \bigcup_{k=1}^{L} \Omega_k \times (x_{k-1}, x_k] \quad (8)$$

Define $V^{(k)} \triangleq H^1(\Omega_k) \cap C^0(\Omega_k)$. The weak form of Equation (7) is

$$\left(\mathbf{a} \cdot \nabla u^{(k)}, v\right) + \varepsilon\left(v_y, u_y^{(k)}\right) - \varepsilon\left(v, u_{xx}^{(k)}\right) + c\left(v, u^{(k)}\right) = (v, f^{(k)}), \quad \forall v \in V^{(k)} \quad (9)$$

where $u^{(k)} = u\big|_{x=x_k}$, $u_y^{(k)} = \frac{\partial u}{\partial y}\big|_{x=x_k}$, $u_{xy}^{(k)} = \frac{\partial^2 u}{\partial x \partial y}\big|_{x=x_k}$, and other symbols are similarly defined, and the inner product is:

$$(v, u) \triangleq \int_{\Omega_k} uv\, dy \quad (10)$$

For $\Omega^{(k)}$, define the numerical solution space as

$$\mathbf{V}^h = \text{span}\left\{\Phi_i(y)\theta_{ij}(y), 1 \leq i \leq n, 1 \leq j \leq m_i, y \in \Omega^{(k)}\right\} \quad (11)$$

where $\Phi_i(y)$ is obtained by the IIMLS method on the splitting plane.

From Equation (11), the undetermined function $u^{(k)}$ is approximated by

$$u^{(k)} \approx \sum_{i=1}^{n} \sum_{j=1}^{m_i} \Phi_i(y)\theta_{ij}(y) c_{ij}^{(k)} \quad (12)$$

where $c_{ij}^{(k)}$ are parameters to be determined.

The matrix form of Equation (12) is

$$u^{(k)} = \boldsymbol{\varpi}^{(k)} \mathbf{c}^{(k)}(x) \quad (13)$$

where

$$\boldsymbol{\varpi}^{(k)} = \left(\Phi_1(y)\boldsymbol{\theta}_1^{(k)}(y), \Phi_2(y)\boldsymbol{\theta}_2^{(k)}(y), \cdots, \Phi_n(y)\boldsymbol{\theta}_n^{(k)}(y)\right)^T \quad (14)$$

$$\boldsymbol{\theta}_i^{(k)} = (\theta_{i1}(y), \theta_{i2}(y), \cdots, \theta_{im_i}(y)) \quad (15)$$

$$\mathbf{c}(x) = (c_{11}(x), c_{12}(x), \cdots, c_{1m_1}(x), \cdots, c_{n1}(x), c_{n2}(x), \cdots, c_{nm_n}(x))^T \quad (16)$$

From Equation (12), the partial derivatives can be obtained as

$$u_y^{(k)} \approx \sum_{i=1}^{n} \sum_{j=1}^{m_i} \frac{\partial}{\partial y}[\Phi_i(y)\theta_{ij}(y)]c_{ij}^{(k)} \tag{17}$$

$$u_x^{(k)} \approx \sum_{i=1}^{n} \sum_{j=1}^{m_i} \Phi_i(y)\theta_{ij}(y)c_{ij,x}^{(k)} \tag{18}$$

where $c_{ij,x}^{(k)}$ is the partial derivatives concerning x of $c_{ij}^{(k)}$ at $x = x_k$.

Then, the discrete Galerkin weak form of Equation (9) is: for $\forall \overline{u}^{(k)} \in \mathbf{V}^h$, find $\hat{u}^{(k)} \in \mathbf{V}^h$ such that

$$\left(\overline{u}^{(k)}, \mathbf{a} \cdot \nabla \hat{u}^{(k)}\right) + \varepsilon\left(\overline{u}_y^{(k)}, \hat{u}_y^{(k)}\right) - \varepsilon\left(\overline{u}^{(k)}, \hat{u}_{xx}^{(k)}\right) + c\left(\overline{u}^{(k)}, \hat{u}^{(k)}\right) = \left(\overline{u}^{(k)}, f^{(k)}\right) \tag{19}$$

Substituting Equations (12)–(18) into Equation (19), we can obtain the discrete equations:

$$-\varepsilon \mathbf{M}_0^{(k)} \mathbf{c}_{xx}^{(k)} + a_1 \mathbf{M}_0^{(k)} \mathbf{c}_x^{(k)} + \left[\varepsilon \mathbf{M}_2^{(k)} + c\mathbf{M}_0^{(k)} + a_2 \mathbf{M}_1^{(k)}\right]\mathbf{c}^{(k)} = \mathbf{F}^{(k)} \tag{20}$$

where $\mathbf{c}_{xx}^{(k)} = \left.\frac{\partial^2 \mathbf{c}(x)}{\partial x^2}\right|_{x=x_k}$, $\mathbf{c}_x^{(k)} = \left.\frac{\partial \mathbf{c}(x)}{\partial x}\right|_{x=x_k}$, $\mathbf{c}^{(k)} = \mathbf{c}(x_k)$, and

$$\mathbf{M}_2^{(k)} = \int_{\Omega^{(k)}} \frac{\partial}{\partial y}\boldsymbol{\omega}^{(k)} \cdot \left(\frac{\partial}{\partial y}\boldsymbol{\omega}^{(k)}\right)^T dy \tag{21}$$

$$\mathbf{M}_1^{(k)} = \int_{\Gamma^{(k)}} \boldsymbol{\omega}^{(k)} \cdot \left(\frac{\partial}{\partial y}\boldsymbol{\omega}^{(k)}\right)^T dy \tag{22}$$

$$\mathbf{M}_0^{(k)} = \int_{\Omega^{(k)}} \boldsymbol{\omega}^{(k)} \cdot \left(\boldsymbol{\omega}^{(k)}\right)^T dy \tag{23}$$

$$\mathbf{F}^{(k)} = \int_{\Omega^{(k)}} \boldsymbol{\omega}^{(k)} \cdot f^{(k)} dy \tag{24}$$

2.3. Assembling the Discrete Equations of the Whole Problem Domain

The discrete equations of all nodes on Ω will be assembled by using the IIMLS method in the x direction. Let

$$\mathbf{c}(x) = \sum_{s \in \wedge(x)} \phi_s(x)\mathbf{c}(x_s) = \sum_{s \in \wedge(x)} \phi_s(x)\mathbf{c}^{(s)} \tag{25}$$

where $\phi_i(x)$ denotes the shape function obtained by the IIMLS method in the x direction with the nodes x_k, $k = 1, 2, \cdots, L$, and $\wedge(x)$ is an index set of nodes satisfying x in its influence domain.

Then, it follows from Equation (25) that

$$\mathbf{c}_x^{(k)} = \sum_{s \in \wedge(x_k)} \frac{\partial}{\partial x}\phi_s(x_k)\mathbf{c}^{(s)} \tag{26}$$

$$\mathbf{c}_{xx}^{(k)} = \sum_{s \in \wedge(x_k)} \frac{\partial^2}{\partial x^2}\phi_s(x_k)\mathbf{c}^{(s)} \tag{27}$$

Substituting Equations (25)–(27) into Equation (20), it follows

$$\begin{cases} \left[\varepsilon\mathbf{M}_2^{(k)} + c\mathbf{M}_0^{(k)} + a_2\mathbf{M}_1^{(k)}\right]\mathbf{c}^{(k)} + \sum_{s\in\wedge(x_k)}\left(a_1\frac{\partial}{\partial x}\phi_s(x_k)\mathbf{M}_0^{(k)} - \varepsilon\frac{\partial^2}{\partial x^2}\phi_s(x_k)\mathbf{M}_0^{(k)}\right)\mathbf{c}^{(s)} = \mathbf{F}^{(k)} \\ k = 1, 2, \cdots, L. \end{cases} \quad (28)$$

On the boundary, the coefficient $c_{ij}^{(k)}$ of enrichment basis function will be supposed to be zero. Then, using the interpolation characteristics of the IIMLS method, and substituting the essential boundary conditions into Equation (28), we can solve the coefficients of all nodes in whole Ω. Additionally, then for $\forall (x,y) \in \Omega$, the numerical solution of u is

$$u^h(x,y) = \sum_{s\in\wedge(x)}\sum_{i=1}^{n}\sum_{j=1}^{m_i}\phi_s(x)\Phi_i(y)\theta_{ij}(y)c_{ij}^{(s)} \quad (29)$$

3. Numerical Examples

To show the effectiveness of the DS-GIEFG method of this paper, we will present some examples of singularly perturbed steady CDR problems. The examples wer solved on a notebook computer with I5-6200U CPU @2.30GHz, and the SUITESPARSE MATRIX SOFTWARE was also utilized to solve the discrete equations. For comparison, the EFG and VMEFG methods were applied to solve these examples. The weight functions used in this paper were the cubic spline functions, and the influence domains of the nodes in the meshless were rectangular regions with radii of $d_{\max} \times \Delta \mathbf{x}$, where $d_{\max}$ is a scalar constant and $\Delta \mathbf{x}$ denotes the spacing of the nodes. A flow chart for obtaining the numerical solutions of the DS-GIEFG method is listed in Figure 1. The numerical errors are defined as:

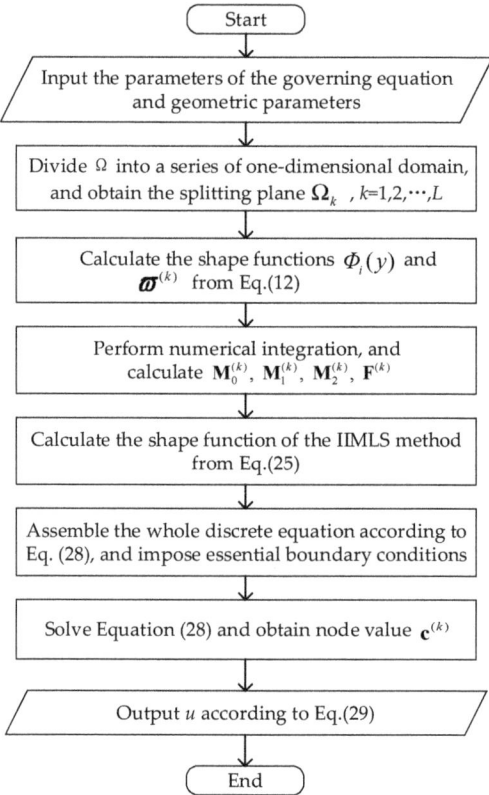

Figure 1. A flow chart for obtaining the numerical solutions of the DS-GIEFG method.

$$\left\|\text{RE}\right\| = \frac{\|u - u^h\|_{L^2(\Omega)}}{\|u\|_{L^2(\Omega)}} \tag{30}$$

$$\|e\| = \|u - u^h\|_{L^2(\Omega)} \tag{31}$$

where u are u^h denote the exact and approximated solutions, respectively.

Example 1. The first example is a convection–diffusion problem with the following exact solution [56]:

$$u(x,y) = \frac{65,536}{729} x^3 (1-x) y^3 (1-y), \ (x,y) \in \Omega = [0,1] \times [0,1] \tag{32}$$

The boundary conditions were extracted from the exact solution.

When 21×21 regular nodes distribution is used, and the parameters are $\varepsilon = 10^{-9}$, $a_1 = \frac{1}{2}$, $a_2 = \frac{-1}{3}$, $c = 0$ and $d_{\max} = 2.2$, the numerical solutions solved by the DS-GIEFG method on the lines $x = 0.1, 0.2, \cdots, 0.9$, are listed in Figure 2. We can see that the results of the DS-GIEFG method fit very well with the analytical solutions.

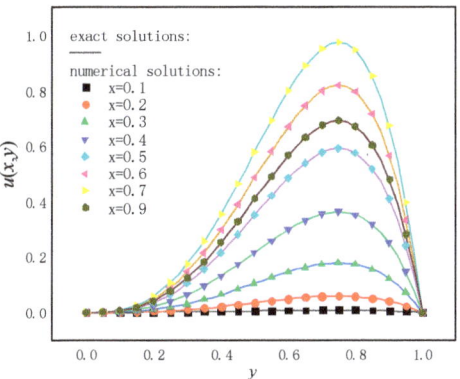

Figure 2. The numerical solutions of the DS-GIEFG method with the 21×21 regular nodes and $\varepsilon = 10^{-9}$, $a_1 = -1/3$, $a_2 = 1/2$.

For comparison, the EFG and VMEFG methods were also used to solve this example, and the boundary conditions were enforced by the penalty function method with a penalty factor of $\alpha = 10^5$. The influence scalar constants in the EFG and VMEFG methods are $d_{\max} = 2.8$. Then, under the 21×21 regular nodes distribution, the absolute errors on the whole field are shown in Figure 3. Clearly, the solution of the DS-GIEFG method has better calculation accuracy than those of the other two methods.

To show the convergence on node spacing, when 11×11, 21×21, $\cdots$, 51×51 regular node distributions were used; the relative errors of the DS-GIEFG, VMEFG and EFG methods with respect to node spacing are shown in Figure 4, and the corresponding CPU times are listed in Figure 5. Figure 4 shows that the proposed method has higher calculation accuracy and convergence order, and the numerical solution will gradually converge to the analytical solution with the reduction in node spacing. It can also be seen from Figure 5 that the proposed method has less computation time and higher computational efficiency than the EFG and VMEFG methods.

(**a**) DS-GIEFG

(**b**) VMEFG

(**c**) EFG

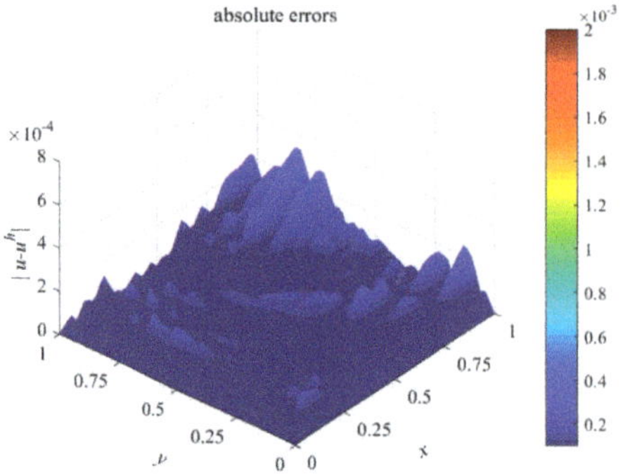

Figure 3. Absolute errors of the solutions solved by the (**a**) DS-GIEFG method, (**b**) VMEFG method and (**c**) EFG method with the same conditions of Figure 2.

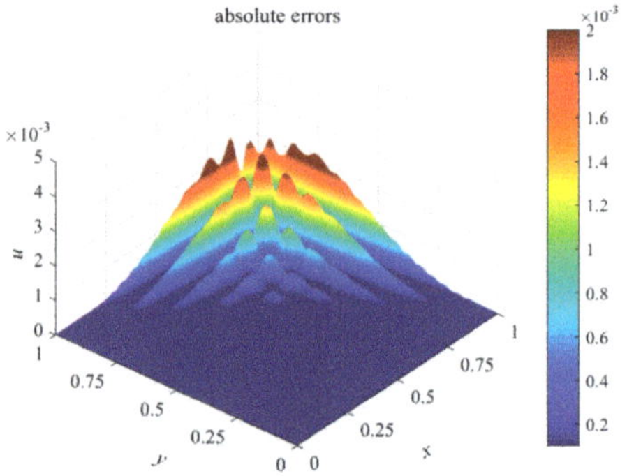

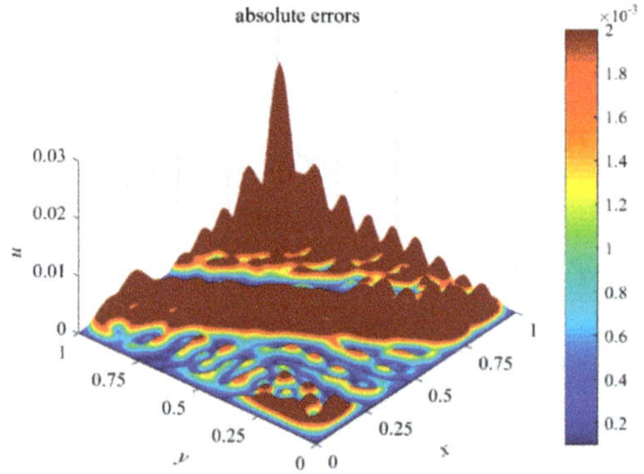

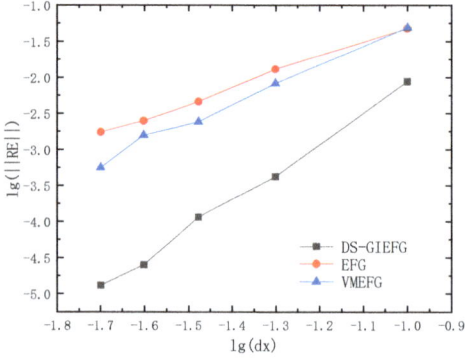

Figure 4. The variation of relative errors of the DS-GIEFG, VMEFG and EFG methods with respect to node spacing (in lg–lg scale).

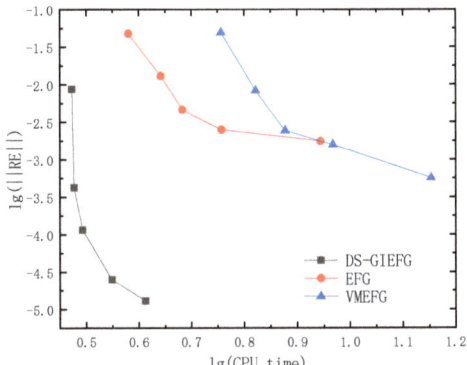

Figure 5. The variation of relative errors of the DS-GIEFG, VMEFG and EFG methods with respect to the CPU time (in lg–lg scale).

Example 2. This example [57] is defined in the field of $\Omega = [0,1] \times [0,1]$ with the exact solution of:

$$u(x,y) = 100x^2y(1-x)^2(1-y)(1-2y) \tag{33}$$

The essential boundary was used and determined by the exact solution.

The parameters were chosen to be $\varepsilon = 10^{-8}$, $a_1 = a_2 = 1$, $c = 0$ and $d_{\max} = 2.2$. When using 21×21 node distributions, the 3D surfaces of the solution obtained by the EFG, VMEFG and DS-GIEFG methods are, respectively, shown in Figure 6a–c, and the corresponding exact solution is plotted in Figure 6d. The penalty factor and scalar constant of influence domain in the EFG and VMEFG methods are $\alpha = 10^5$ and $d_{\max} = 2.6$, respectively. The corresponding snapshots of the solutions of the DS-GIEFG method on the fields of lines $x = 0.1, 0.2, \cdots, 0.9$ are listed in Figure 7. Additionally, the absolute errors of the DS-GIEFG and VMEFG methods on the whole field are shown in Figure 8. It can be seen from Figure 6a that the solution of the EFG method is unstable, and there is a non-physical oscillation for the diffusion convection problem with a very small diffusion coefficient. Figure 6 shows that both VMEFG and DS-GIEFG methods can obtain stable numerical solutions for small diffusion coefficients. Figure 8 also shows that the DS-GIEFG method can have higher calculation accuracy than the VMEFG method.

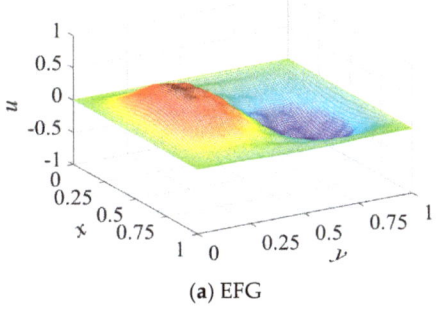

(**a**) EFG

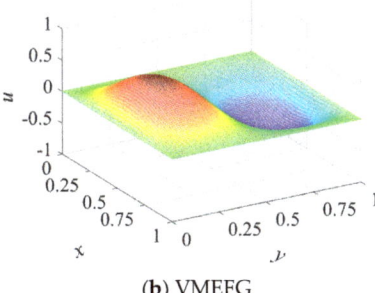

(**b**) VMEFG

Figure 6. *Cont.*

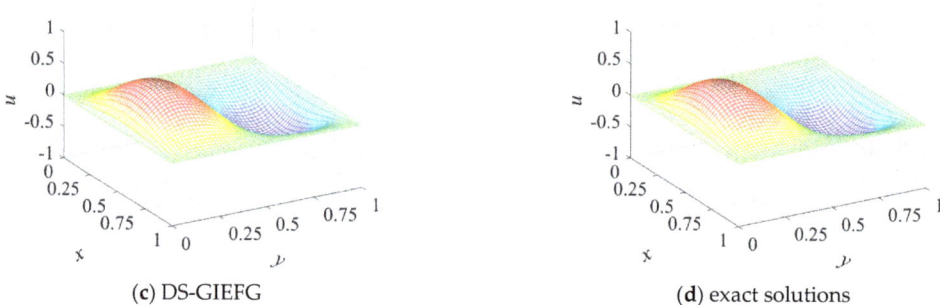

(c) DS-GIEFG   (d) exact solutions

Figure 6. The exact solutions and the numerical solutions obtained by the EFG, VMEFG and DS-GIEFG methods.

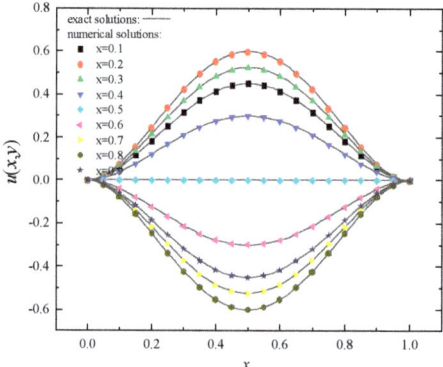

Figure 7. The snapshots of numerical solutions of the DS-GIEFG method on the lines of $x = 0.1, 0.2, \cdots, 0.9$ with 21×21 nodes.

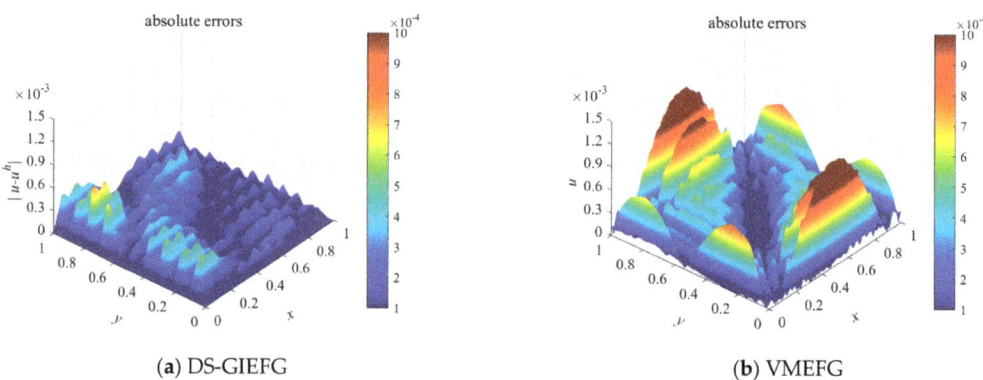

(a) DS-GIEFG   (b) VMEFG

Figure 8. The absolute errors of the VMEFG and DS-GIEFG methods on the whole field under 21×21 nodes.

When the 17×17, 33×33, 65×65, 129×129 node distributions are used, the relative errors of the EFG, VMEFG and DS-GIEFG methods in the lg–lg scale are presented in Figure 9. The results of Ref. [57] are also listed in this figure. Additionally, the corresponding CPU time of these methods is plotted in Figure 10. For this example, there is no doubt that the DS-GIEFG method in this paper has higher calculation accuracy and efficiency.

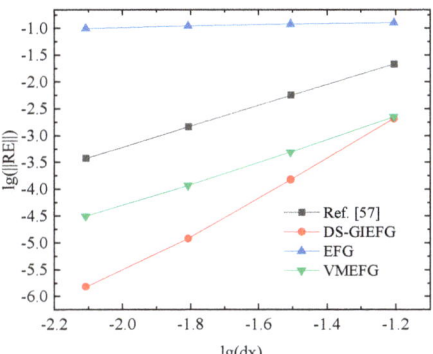

Figure 9. The variation of relative errors of different methods with respect to the node spacing (in lg–lg scale).

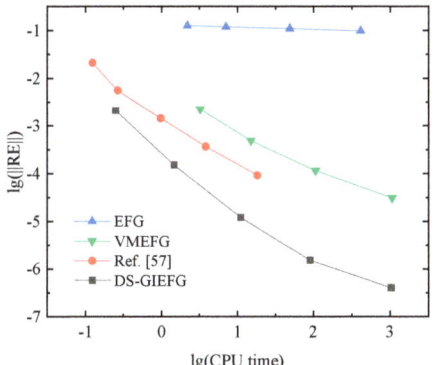

Figure 10. The variation of relative errors of different methods with respect to the CPU time (in lg–lg scale).

Example 3. This example is chosen to be an interior layer problem with the exact solution [58]:

$$u(x,y) = \frac{1}{2}x(1-x)y(1-y)\left(1 - \tan\frac{y-a}{b}\right), \ (x,y) \in \Omega = [0,1] \times [0,1] \quad (34)$$

Let $\varepsilon = 10^{-9}, a_1 = 0, a_2 = 1, c = 1, a = b = 0.05$. The other parameters are exactly the same as in Example 2. When using 51×51 nodes, the 3D surface of the exact and numerical solutions of the DS-GIEFG method are plotted in Figure 11. Additionally, the snapshots of solutions on the lines $y = 0.1, 0.2, \cdots, 0.5$ are shown in Figure 12. These two figures show that the solutions of the DS-GIEFG method are very consistent with those of the exact solutions.

When the 9×9, 17×17, 33×33, 65×65, 129×129 nodes distributions are used, the errors $||u - u^h||$ of the Ref. [58], EFG, VMEFG and DS-GIEFG methods are listed in Table 1. Additionally, the corresponding variation of the errors with respect to the CPU time is shown in Figure 13. These results once again show that the method proposed in this paper has high computational accuracy and computational efficiency.

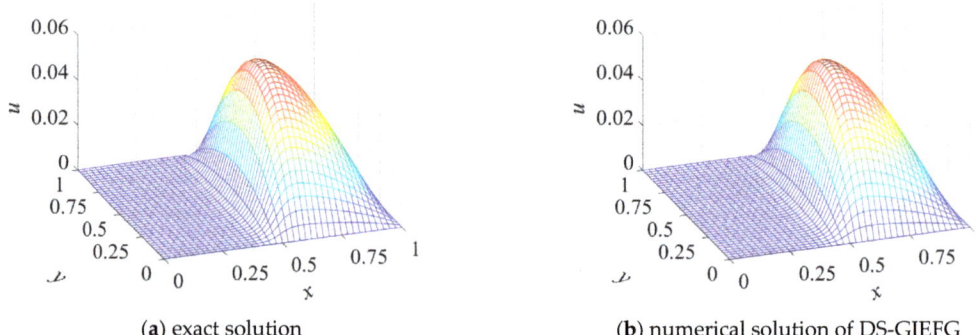

(a) exact solution (b) numerical solution of DS-GIEFG

Figure 11. The exact and numerical solutions of the DS-GIEFG method with 51 × 51 regular nodes.

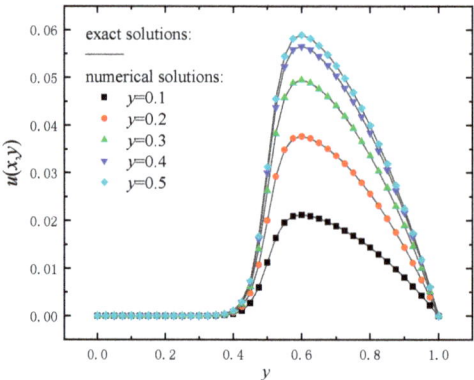

Figure 12. The snapshots of numerical solutions of the DS-GIEFG method on the lines of $y = 0.1, 0.2, \cdots, 0.5$ with 51 × 51 nodes.

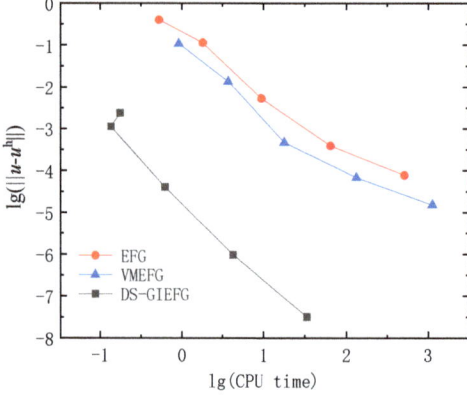

Figure 13. The variation of errors of different methods with respect to the CPU time (in lg–lg scale).

Table 1. The errors $\left\|u - u^h\right\|$ of the Ref. [58], EFG, VMEFG and DS-GIEFG methods for different nodes spacing.

Nodes	DS-GIEFG	VMEFG	EFG	Ref. [58]
9×9	7.90×10^{-4}	1.10×10^{-1}	4.02×10^{-1}	3.80×10^{-3}
17×17	1.81×10^{-4}	1.36×10^{-2}	1.14×10^{-1}	1.31×10^{-3}
33×33	1.37×10^{-5}	4.74×10^{-4}	5.29×10^{-3}	4.37×10^{-4}
65×65	9.46×10^{-8}	6.91×10^{-5}	3.89×10^{-4}	1.16×10^{-4}
129×129	1.29×10^{-8}	1.52×10^{-5}	7.75×10^{-5}	2.96×10^{-5}

4. Conclusions

To improve the computational efficiency and overcome the non-physical oscillation of the EFG method in solving singularly perturbed fluid problems, a DS-GIEFG method for singularly perturbed steady CDR problems is proposed in this paper by constructing the trial functions based on the IIMLS method and coupling the DSM and GEFG method. The stabilization parameter of the DS-GIEFG method is only related to the nodes and not to the mesh. Since the two-dimensional problem is divided into a series of one-dimensional problems, the DS-GIEFG method has high efficiency. Three numerical examples are solved by the DS-IEFG method of this paper. The numerical solutions are compared with those of the EFG and VMEFG methods. The numerical results show that the solutions of the DS-GIEFG method converge to the analytical solution with the increase in the number of nodes, and the DS-GIEFG method has higher computational efficiency and accuracy than the EFG and VMEFG methods.

Author Contributions: Conceptualization, F.S. and J.W.; methodology, F.S. and J.W.; software, J.W. and X.K.; writing—original draft preparation, J.W. and F.S.; writing—review and editing, F.S. and R.C. All authors have read and agreed to the published version of the manuscript.

Funding: This research was funded by the Natural Science Foundation of Zhejiang Province, China (Grant Nos. LY20A010021, LY18F020026, LY19A010002), and the Ningbo Natural Science Foundation of China (Nos. 20211JCGY010257 and 202003N4142).

Data Availability Statement: Not applicable.

Conflicts of Interest: The authors declare no conflict of interest.

References

1. Liu, Z.; Wei, G.; Wang, Z. Numerical analysis of functionally graded materials using reproducing kernel particle method. *Int. J. Appl. Mech.* **2019**, *11*, 1950060. [CrossRef]
2. Liu, Z.; Wei, G.; Wang, Z.; Qiao, J. The meshfree analysis of geometrically nonlinear problem based on radial basis reproducing kernel particle method. *Int. J. Appl. Mech.* **2020**, *12*, 2050044. [CrossRef]
3. Hosseini, S.; Rahimi, G. Nonlinear bending analysis of hyperelastic plates using FSDT and meshless collocation method based on radial basis function. *Int. J. Appl. Mech.* **2021**, *13*, 2150007. [CrossRef]
4. Selim, B.A.; Liu, Z. Impact analysis of functionally-graded graphene nanoplatelets-reinforced composite plates laying on Winkler-Pasternak elastic foundations applying a meshless approach. *Eng. Struct.* **2021**, *241*, 112453. [CrossRef]
5. Fu, Z.; Zhang, J.; Li, P.; Zheng, J. A semi-lagrangian meshless framework for numerical solutions of two-dimensional sloshing phenomenon. *Eng. Anal. Bound. Elem.* **2020**, *112*, 58–67. [CrossRef]
6. Wang, J.; Sun, F. A hybrid variational multiscale element-free Galerkin method for convection-diffusion problems. *Int. J. Appl. Mech.* **2019**, *11*, 1950063. [CrossRef]
7. Oruç, Ö. A meshless multiple-scale polynomial method for numerical solution of 3d convection-diffusion problems with variable coefficients. *Eng. Comput.* **2020**, *36*, 1215–1228. [CrossRef]
8. Lancaster, P.; Salkauskas, K. Surfaces generated by moving least squares methods. *Math. Comput.* **1981**, *37*, 141–158. [CrossRef]
9. Cheng, J. Residential land leasing and price under public land ownership. *J. Urban Plan. Dev.* **2021**, *147*, 05021009. [CrossRef]
10. Cheng, J. Analysis of commercial land leasing of the district governments of Beijing in China. *Land Use Policy* **2021**, *100*, 104881. [CrossRef]
11. Cheng, J. Analyzing the factors influencing the choice of the government on leasing different types of land uses: Evidence from Shanghai of China. *Land Use Policy* **2020**, *90*, 104303. [CrossRef]

12. Cheng, J. Data analysis of the factors influencing the industrial land leasing in shanghai based on mathematical models. *Math. Probl. Eng.* **2020**, *2020*, 9346863. [CrossRef]
13. Zheng, G.; Cheng, Y. The improved element-free Galerkin method for diffusional drug release problems. *Int. J. Appl. Mech.* **2020**, *12*, 2050096. [CrossRef]
14. Belytschko, T.; Lu, Y.Y.; Gu, L. Element-free Galerkin methods. *Int. J. Numer. Methods Eng.* **1994**, *37*, 229–256. [CrossRef]
15. Wang, J.; Sun, F.; Xu, Y. Research on error estimations of the interpolating boundary element free-method for two-dimensional potential problems. *Math. Probl. Eng.* **2020**, *2020*, 6378745. [CrossRef]
16. Wang, J.; Wang, J.; Sun, F.; Cheng, Y. An interpolating boundary element-free method with nonsingular weight function for two-dimensional potential problems. *Int. J. Comput. Methods* **2013**, *10*, 1350043. [CrossRef]
17. Wang, J.; Sun, F. An interpolating meshless method for the numerical simulation of the time-fractional diffusion equations with error estimates. *Eng. Comput.* **2019**, *37*, 730–752. [CrossRef]
18. Liu, F.; Wu, Q.; Cheng, Y. A meshless method based on the nonsingular weight functions for elastoplastic large deformation problems. *Int. J. Appl. Mech.* **2019**, *11*, 1950006. [CrossRef]
19. Nguyen, V.P.; Rabczuk, T.; Bordas, S.; Duflot, M. Meshless methods: A review and computer implementation aspects. *Math. Comput. Simul.* **2008**, *79*, 763–813. [CrossRef]
20. Silling, S.A.; Lehoucq, R.B. Peridynamic theory of solid mechanics. *Adv. Appl. Mech.* **2010**, *44*, 73–168.
21. Silling, S.A.; Askari, E. A meshfree method based on the peridynamic model of solid mechanics. *Comput. Struct.* **2005**, *83*, 1526–1535. [CrossRef]
22. Zhang, T.; Li, X. A generalized element-free Galerkin method for stokes problem. *Comput. Math. Appl.* **2018**, *75*, 3127–3138. [CrossRef]
23. Wang, J.; Sun, F. A hybrid generalized interpolated element-free Galerkin method for Stokes problems. *Eng. Anal. Bound. Elem.* **2020**, *111*, 88–100. [CrossRef]
24. Zhang, T.; Li, X. A novel variational multiscale interpolating element-free Galerkin method for generalized Oseen problems. *Comput. Struct.* **2018**, *209*, 14–29. [CrossRef]
25. Zhang, L.; Ouyang, J.; Zhang, X.; Zhang, W. On a multiscale element-free Galerkin method for the Stokes problem. *Appl. Math. Comput.* **2008**, *203*, 745–753.
26. Abbaszadeh, M.; Dehghan, M.; Navon, I.M. A proper orthogonal decomposition variational multiscale meshless interpolating element-free Galerkin method for incompressible magnetohydrodynamics flow. *Int. J. Numer. Methods Fluids* **2020**, *92*, 1415–1436. [CrossRef]
27. Zhang, X.; Zhang, P.; Qin, W.; Shi, X. An adaptive variational multiscale element free Galerkin method for convection–diffusion equations. *Eng. Comput.* **2021**, 1–18. [CrossRef]
28. Dehghan, M.; Abbaszadeh, M. Variational multiscale element free Galerkin (VMEFG) and local discontinuous Galerkin (LDG) methods for solving two-dimensional brusselator reaction–diffusion system with and without cross-diffusion. *Comput. Methods Appl. Mech. Eng.* **2016**, *300*, 770–797. [CrossRef]
29. Meng, Z.; Cheng, H.; Ma, L.; Cheng, Y. The dimension splitting element-free Galerkin method for 3d transient heat conduction problems. *Sci. China Phys. Mech.* **2019**, *62*, 1–12. [CrossRef]
30. Wu, Q.; Peng, M.J.; Fu, Y.D.; Cheng, Y.M. The dimension splitting interpolating element-free Galerkin method for solving three-dimensional transient heat conduction problems. *Eng. Anal. Bound. Elem.* **2021**, *128*, 326–341. [CrossRef]
31. Cheng, H.; Peng, M.; Cheng, Y.; Meng, Z. The hybrid complex variable element-free Galerkin method for 3d elasticity problems. *Eng. Struct.* **2020**, *219*, 110835. [CrossRef]
32. Li, K.; Huang, A.; Zhang, W.L. A dimension split method for the 3-d compressible Navier–Stokes equations in turbomachine. *Commun. Numer. Methods Eng.* **2002**, *18*, 1–14. [CrossRef]
33. Wu, Q.; Peng, M.; Cheng, Y. The interpolating dimension splitting element-free Galerkin method for 3d potential problems. *Eng. Comput.* **2021**, 1–15. [CrossRef]
34. Meng, Z.J.; Cheng, H.; Ma, L.D.; Cheng, Y.M. The dimension split element-free Galerkin method for three-dimensional potential problems. *Acta Mech. Sin.* **2018**, *34*, 462–474. [CrossRef]
35. Bansal, K.; Sharma, K.K. Parameter uniform numerical scheme for time dependent singularly perturbed convection-diffusion-reaction problems with general shift arguments. *Numer. Algorithms* **2017**, *75*, 113–145. [CrossRef]
36. Kaya, A. Finite difference approximations of multidimensional unsteady convection-diffusion-reaction equations. *J. Comput. Phys.* **2015**, *285*, 331–349. [CrossRef]
37. Zhao, S.; Xiao, X.; Tan, Z.; Feng, X. Two types of spurious oscillations at layers diminishing methods for convection-diffusion–reaction equations on surface. *Numer. Heat. Transf. A Appl.* **2018**, *74*, 1387–1404. [CrossRef]
38. Han, H.; Huang, Z. Tailored finite point method based on exponential bases for convection-diffusion-reaction equation. *Math. Comput.* **2013**, *82*, 213–226. [CrossRef]
39. Lin, R.; Ye, X.; Zhang, S.; Zhu, P. A weak Galerkin finite element method for singularly perturbed convection-diffusion-reaction problems. *SIAM J. Numer. Anal.* **2018**, *56*, 1482–1497. [CrossRef]
40. Fendoğlu, H.; Bozkaya, C.; Tezer-Sezgin, M. Dbem and DRBEM solutions to 2d transient convection-diffusion-reaction type equations. *Eng. Anal. Bound. Elem.* **2018**, *93*, 124–134. [CrossRef]

41. Lukyanenko, D.V.; Shishlenin, M.A.; Volkov, V.T. Asymptotic analysis of solving an inverse boundary value problem for a nonlinear singularly perturbed time-periodic reaction-diffusion-advection equation. *J. Inverse Ill Posed Probl.* **2019**, *27*, 745–758. [CrossRef]
42. Lukyanenko, D.V.; Grigorev, V.B.; Volkov, V.T.; Shishlenin, M.A. Solving of the coefficient inverse problem for a nonlinear singularly perturbed two-dimensional reaction—Diffusion equation with the location of moving front data. *Comput. Math. Appl.* **2019**, *77*, 1245–1254. [CrossRef]
43. Chandru, M.; Das, P.; Ramos, H. Numerical treatment of two-parameter singularly perturbed parabolic convection diffusion problems with non-smooth data. *Math. Methods Appl. Sci.* **2018**, *41*, 5359–5387. [CrossRef]
44. Wu, Y.; Zhang, N.; Yuan, J. A robust adaptive method for singularly perturbed convection-diffusion problem with two small parameters. *Comput. Math. Appl.* **2013**, *66*, 996–1009. [CrossRef]
45. Kaya, A.; Sendur, A. Finite difference approximations of multidimensional convection–diffusion–reaction problems with small diffusion on a special grid. *J. Comput. Phys.* **2015**, *300*, 574–591. [CrossRef]
46. Lin, J.; Reutskiy, S. A cubic b-spline semi-analytical algorithm for simulation of 3d steady-state convection-diffusion-reaction problems. *Appl. Math. Comput.* **2020**, *371*, 124944. [CrossRef]
47. Gharibi, Z.; Dehghan, M. Convergence analysis of weak Galerkin flux-based mixed finite element method for solving singularly perturbed convection-diffusion-reaction problem. *Appl. Numer. Math.* **2021**, *163*, 303–316. [CrossRef]
48. Lin, J.; Reutskiy, S.Y.; Lu, J. A novel meshless method for fully nonlinear advection–diffusion-reaction problems to model transfer in anisotropic media. *Appl. Math. Comput.* **2018**, *339*, 459–476. [CrossRef]
49. Hidayat, M.I.P. Meshless finite difference method with b-splines for numerical solution of coupled advection-diffusion-reaction problems. *Int. J. Therm. Sci.* **2021**, *165*, 106933. [CrossRef]
50. Zhang, X.; Xiang, H. Variational multiscale element free Galerkin method for convection-diffusion-reaction equation with small diffusion. *Eng. Anal. Bound. Elem.* **2014**, *46*, 85–92. [CrossRef]
51. Zhang, P.; Zhang, X.; Xiang, H.; Song, L. A fast and stabilized meshless method for the convection-dominated convection-diffusion problems. *Numer. Heat. Transf. A Appl.* **2016**, *70*, 420–431. [CrossRef]
52. Li, J.; Feng, X.; He, Y. Rbf-based meshless local Petrov Galerkin method for the multi-dimensional convection-diffusion-reaction equation. *Eng. Anal. Bound. Elem.* **2019**, *98*, 46–53. [CrossRef]
53. Wang, F.; Wang, C.; Chen, Z. Local knot method for 2d and 3d convection–diffusion–reaction equations in arbitrary domains. *Appl. Math. Lett.* **2020**, *105*, 106308. [CrossRef]
54. Liu, S.; Li, P.; Fan, C.; Gu, Y. Localized method of fundamental solutions for two-and three-dimensional transient convection-diffusion-reaction equations. *Eng. Anal. Bound. Elem.* **2021**, *124*, 237–244. [CrossRef]
55. Dehghan, M.; Abbaszadeh, M. Proper orthogonal decomposition variational multiscale element free Galerkin (POD-VMEFG) meshless method for solving incompressible Navier–Stokes equation. *Comput. Methods Appl. Mech. Eng.* **2016**, *311*, 856–888. [CrossRef]
56. Zhang, T.; Li, X. A variational multiscale interpolating element-free Galerkin method for convection-diffusion and stokes problems. *Eng. Anal. Bound. Elem.* **2017**, *82*, 185–193. [CrossRef]
57. Chen, G.; Feng, M.; Xie, C. A new projection-based stabilized method for steady convection-dominated convection-diffusion equations. *Appl. Math. Comput.* **2014**, *239*, 89–106. [CrossRef]
58. Gao, F.; Zhang, S.; Zhu, P. Modified weak Galerkin method with weakly imposed boundary condition for convection-dominated diffusion equations. *Appl. Numer. Math.* **2020**, *157*, 490–504. [CrossRef]

Deep Learning Approach to Mechanical Property Prediction of Single-Network Hydrogel

Jing-Ang Zhu, Yetong Jia, Jincheng Lei and Zishun Liu *

International Center for Applied Mechanics, State Key Laboratory for Strength and Vibration of Mechanical Structures, School of Aerospace Engineering, Xi'an Jiaotong University, Xi'an 710049, China; stephenzhu@stu.xjtu.edu.cn (J.-A.Z.); jiayetong@stu.xjtu.edu.cn (Y.J.); jinchenglei@xjtu.edu.cn (J.L.)
* Correspondence: zishunliu@mail.xjtu.edu.cn

Abstract: Hydrogel has a complex network structure with inhomogeneous and random distribution of polymer chains. Much effort has been paid to fully understand the relationship between mesoscopic network structure and macroscopic mechanical properties of hydrogels. In this paper, we develop a deep learning approach to predict the mechanical properties of hydrogels from polymer network structures. First, network structural models of hydrogels are constructed from mesoscopic scale using self-avoiding walk method. The constructed model is similar to the real hydrogel network. Then, two deep learning models are proposed to capture the nonlinear mapping from mesoscopic hydrogel network structural model to its macroscale mechanical property. A deep neural network and a 3D convolutional neural network containing the physical information of the network structural model are implemented to predict the nominal stress–stretch curves of hydrogels under uniaxial tension. Our results show that the end-to-end deep learning framework can effectively predict the nominal stress–stretch curves of hydrogel within a wide range of mesoscopic network structures, which demonstrates that the deep learning models are able to capture the internal relationship between complex network structures and mechanical properties. We hope this approach can provide guidance to structural design and material property design of different soft materials.

Keywords: deep learning; hydrogel network; mechanical property; convolutional neural network; self-avoiding walk

1. Introduction

With remarkable mechanical properties, hydrogels demonstrate high potential to be one of the advanced smart materials in the future [1,2]. Various superior properties of hydrogels have been discovered, such as high stretchability [3], biocompatibility [4], self-healing [5], and toughness [6]. On the basis of these properties, hydrogels are expected to pave the way for future applications such as drug delivery [7], flexible electronics [8,9], tissue engineering [10–12], and optical components [13–15]. Because the effect of polymer network structure on the mechanical properties of hydrogel is significant, a deeper understanding of polymer network can help us to better utilize the existed material and create new material. Therefore, it is imperative to investigate the relationship between the network structures and mechanical properties of hydrogels.

The mechanical properties of hydrogels are studied from different scales, from microscopic scale to continuum scale. The constitutive model constructed at the continuum scale is widely used and practical [16], however, some of them are lack of physical meanings and the parameters of the constitutive model are not universal to hydrogels with different ingredients proportion. It is because that the continuum scale model cannot reflect the real structure of hydrogel network. At the microscopic level, the mechanical properties of hydrogels are usually studied using molecular dynamics methods. However, it is difficult to overcome the issues of small size and time-consuming natures of the molecular dynamics simulations. The mesoscopic hydrogel model is expected to link the microscopic and the continuum scales and act as an important complement between them, providing a new theoretical framework for hydrogel research. Recent research on hydrogels at the mesoscopic scale is still in its infancy [17–21]. Obtaining valuable information from the mesoscale model can help to better understand the relationship between network structure and mechanical property. Proper hydrogel network models are in urgent need to essentially describe multiple mechanical behaviors of hydrogels. Therefore, we develop a generating method of mesoscopic hydrogel network based on self-avoiding walk (SAW) network model. There are several main advantages of mesoscopic hydrogel model, such as discrete systems, the characterization of complexity and stochasticity, and the reflection of mesoscopic structure of hydrogels. In fact, the complex physical relationship between the hydrogel network structure and its corresponding properties is often difficult to accurately express with current constitutive theories. In current studies on hydrogel mechanical property, results of phenomenological theory are not accurate enough, and numerical simulations are often time-consuming. In order to rapidly describe the mechanical properties of hydrogels, machine learning (ML) offers the benefit of extremely fast inference and requires only a basic dataset to learn the relationship between hydrogel network structure and mechanical properties.

With the development of ML, various ML algorithms have been widely applied to the field of engineering. Traditional ML algorithms have been used for data-driven solutions to mechanical problems [22–25]. There are also studies on the parameter determination of hydrogel constitutive model [26] and self-assembly hydrogel design [27]. In addition to using ML to establish implicit input-output relationships to solve regression problems, recently there is a new paradigm of physical informed neural network [28] that extends the learning capability of neural network (NN) to include physical equations and boundary conditions. Deep learning (DL) is a class of ML algorithms that uses multiple layers to progressively extract higher-level features from the raw input. DL has been successful in a wide range of applications, such as semantic segmentation, image classification, and face recognition [29–32]. The reason why DL significantly outperforms traditional ML is that the models are no longer limited to the multilayer perceptron (MLP) architecture, and are able to learn embedded and aggregated datasets. More specifically, DL methods provide a more advanced framework in which explicit feature engineering is not required and the trained model typically demonstrates higher generalization and robustness. Thereby, DL shows great potential in solving cross-scale prediction problems of structure–property relationship in the field of mechanics. Among the applications of DL algorithms in mechanics, it is proved that convolutional neural networks (CNNs) are significantly superior in damage identification and mechanical property prediction on composite materials [33–37]. In addition, Yang et al. [38] demonstrated how a deep residual network can be used to deduce the dislocation characteristics of a sample using only its surface strain profiles at small deformations for crystal plasticity prediction. Pandey and Pokharel [39] presented a DL modeling method to predict spatially resolved 3D crystal orientation evolution of polycrystalline materials under uniaxial tensile loading. Herriott and Spear [40] investigated the ability of deep learning models to predict microstructure-sensitive mechanical properties in metal additive manufacturing and Choi et al. [41] used artificial intelligence-based methods to investigate the fatigue life of the hyperelastic anisotropic elastomer W-CR material.

The advantages of CNNs for image-like data are mainly in the following aspects: firstly, by employing the concepts of receptive fields in the convolutional layer, CNNs could be a powerful tool for pattern recognition in computational mechanics and material problems that are characterized by local structural interactions [42]. Secondly, CNNs are able to effectively learn a certain representation of underlying symmetry and tend to be invariant to general affine input transformations such as translations, rotations, and small distortions [42]. These properties enable CNNs to characterize structures with heterogeneous and randomness, for instance, hydrogel network at the mesoscopic scale. Meanwhile, mesoscopic scale modeling studies often yield a large amount of high-dimensional data with corresponding physical information, which can be used to establish a modular and efficient mechanical modeling framework. However, there is still lack of using DL methods to study the mechanical properties of soft materials.

In this paper, we utilize deep neural network (DNN) and 3D CNN to reveal the implicit relationship between network structure and mechanical property of hydrogel, so as to predict mechanical property from different network structures. First, we propose a modeling method for single-network hydrogel network, that is, a self-avoiding walk network model, which approximates the real polyacrylamide (PAAm) hydrogel structure at a mesoscopic scale. Then, we develop a DNN based on MLP and a 3D CNN containing the physical information of the network, and use them to predict the nominal stress–stretch curves of hydrogels under uniaxial tension, because the stress–stretch relationship is one of the most important mechanical description that can be used to derive typical properties, such as modulus, toughness, and strength. Using a dataset of 2200 randomly generated network structures of PAAm hydrogel and their corresponding stress–stretch curves, we train and evaluate the performance of the two models. Based on the results of the error analysis and the performance of the two models on the training data, we compare and summarize their generalization capability.

The paper is organized as follows: in Section 2 we present the derivation of the constitutive model for PAAm hydrogel, the modeling method of hydrogel networks, and the basic knowledge of DNN and CNN algorithms. The modeling framework and architecture of the two DL models we developed are detailed in Section 3. Analysis and evaluation of the results for mechanical property prediction of hydrogel are demonstrated in Section 4. Finally, concluding remarks are provided in Section 5.

2. Methodology

2.1. Derivation of the Constitutive Model of Hydrogel

For effectively using hydrogel in engineering applications, it is very imperative to understand the mechanical properties of hydrogels. Although polymer physics and continuum mechanics provide a way to study the mechanical properties of hydrogels, uniaxial loading test is still a common method to test the mechanical property of hydrogel materials. In order to accurately predict the nominal stress–stretch relationship of hydrogel using DL method, a dataset of stress–stretch curves is needed for the model training. However, obtaining stress–stretch curves from experiment tests requires a lot of labor work, especially considering different polymer fractions of hydrogel. In this study, the relationship of stress and stretch is derived from the constitutive model we have proposed, which is used as the ground truth (prediction target) for DL model training.

In this study, to determine the relationship of stress and stretch whether from testing or theoretical prediction, the deformation process of hydrogel is divided into two steps: swelling process and loading process. During swelling process, because of the hydrophilia of polymer chains, the dry polymer can imbibe a large quantity of solvent and swell into hydrogel. The volume of hydrogel is the sum of absorbed solvent and dry polymer due to the law of conservation of mass. The hydrogel is assumed to be traction-free and reaches an equilibrium state at the end of the process, which represents the chemical potential is the same throughout the whole hydrogel and the external solvent. In the loading process, both ends of the dumbbell-shaped specimen are clamped. One end is held fixed on the foundation of the tensile testing machine and the other end is stretched with the elongation of the moveable clamp. The middle part of dumbbell-shaped specimen is under uniaxial tension state since two directions that are perpendicular to the loading direction are traction-free. At this state, hydrogel is no longer contacted with solvent and mechanical boundary condition is applied.

To derive the stress–stretch relationship of hydrogel during uniaxial loading, we adopt well-known free energy function due to Flory and Rehner [43,44]:

$$W = \frac{1}{2}NkT[F_{iK}F_{iK} - 3 - 2\log(\det \mathbf{F})] - \frac{kT}{v}\left[vC\log\left(1 + \frac{1}{vC}\right) + \frac{\chi}{1+vC}\right] \quad (1)$$

where W is the free energy pure reference volume, N is the number of polymeric chains per reference volume, k is the Boltzmann constant, T is the absolute temperature, $\mathbf{F}$ is the deformation gradient of the current state related to the dry state, C is the concentration of solvent in the gel, v is the volume per solvent molecule, and χ is a dimensionless parameter measuring the enthalpy of mixing. The reference state is chosen as the dry state before the polymer absorbs any solvent.

During the swelling process, all molecules in the gel are assumed to be incompressible. Therefore, the volume of the gel is the sum of the volume of the dry network and the volume of solvent:

$$1 + vC = \det \mathbf{F} \tag{2}$$

Using Legendre transformation, the free energy density function $W(\mathbf{F}, C)$ can be transformed into $\hat{W} = W(\mathbf{F}, C) - \mu C$, which is the function of chemical potential μ and deformation gradient $\mathbf{F}$. Considering the incompressible condition, the new free energy density function can be written as:

$$\hat{W}(\mathbf{F}, \mu) = \frac{1}{2} NkT[I - 3 - 2\log J] - \frac{kT}{v}\left[(J-1)\log\left(\frac{J}{J-1}\right) + \frac{\chi}{J}\right] - \frac{\mu}{v}(J-1) \tag{3}$$

where $I = F_{iK}F_{iK}$ and $J = \det \mathbf{F}$.

Based on the assumption of two steps during the deformation process, the deformation gradient tensor $\mathbf{F}$ can be decomposed as $\mathbf{F} = \mathbf{F}_0 \mathbf{F}'$. $\mathbf{F}_0$ is the deformation gradient of the free-swelling state related to the dry state. $\mathbf{F}'$ is the deformation gradient of the mechanical loading state related to the free-swelling state. For a free-swelling process, when hydrogel reaches the equilibrium, $\mathbf{F}_0 = \lambda_0 \mathbf{I}$.

Since we prefer to use the free-swelling state as the reference state during mechanical test, the free energy density function with free-swelling state as the reference state is $\hat{W}'(\mathbf{F}', \mu) = \lambda_0^{-3} \hat{W}(\mathbf{F}, \mu)$, which can be expanded as:

$$\hat{W}'(\mathbf{F}', \mu) = \frac{\lambda_0^{-3}}{2} NkT(\lambda_0^2 I' - 3 - 2\log(\lambda_0^3 J')) \\ - \frac{kT}{v}\left[(J' - \lambda_0^{-3})\log\frac{J'}{\lambda_0^3 J' - 1} + \frac{\chi}{\lambda_0^6 J'}\right] - \frac{\mu}{v}(J' - \lambda_0^{-3}) \tag{4}$$

where $I' = F'_{iK} F'_{iK}$ and $J' = \det \mathbf{F}'$. Because the volume is incompressible during the loading process, J' equals to one and stretch λ_0 is a constant. With free-swelling state as the reference state, the free energy density function can be written as:

$$\hat{W}'(\mathbf{F}', \mu) = \frac{\lambda_0^{-1}}{2} NkT I' + A \tag{5}$$

where A is a constant given as:

$$A = -\frac{\lambda_0^{-3}}{2} NkT\left(3 + 2\log(\lambda_0^3)\right) - \frac{kT}{v}\left[\left(1 - \lambda_0^{-3}\right)\log\frac{1}{\lambda_0^3 - 1} + \frac{\chi}{\lambda_0^6}\right] - \frac{\mu}{v}\left(1 - \lambda_0^{-3}\right) \tag{6}$$

During loading process, considering the volume incompressibility condition, we add a term $p(1 - \det \mathbf{F}')$ to the free energy function $\hat{W}'(\mathbf{F}', \mu)$, where p is a Lagrange multiplier, which can be determined by boundary conditions. Then the nominal stress can be calculated by:

$$s'_{ik} = \frac{\partial\left(\hat{W}'(\mathbf{F}', \mu) + p\left(1 - \det(\mathbf{F}')\right)\right)}{\partial F'_{ik}} \tag{7}$$

and we obtain the expression of nominal stress with free-swelling state as the reference state:

$$s'_{ik} = \lambda_0^{-1} NkT F'_{ik} - p\left(F'_{ik}\right)^{-T} \tag{8}$$

For a uniaxial loading process, the deformation gradient tensor $\mathbf{F}'$ is:

$$\mathbf{F}' = \begin{bmatrix} \lambda_s & & \\ & \frac{1}{\sqrt{\lambda_s}} & \\ & & \frac{1}{\sqrt{\lambda_s}} \end{bmatrix} \tag{9}$$

where λ_s is the stretch along the uniaxial direction. The nominal stress along with and perpendicular to the uniaxial direction is s_1', s_2' and s_3', respectively. As the surface perpendicular to the uniaxial direction is traction-free, therefore, the expressions of nominal stress s_1', s_2' and s_3' are as follows

$$s_1' = \lambda_0^{-1} NkT\lambda_s - p\lambda_s^{-\frac{1}{2}} \tag{10}$$

$$s_2' = s_3' = \lambda_0^{-1} NkT\lambda_s^{-1} - p\lambda_s^{\frac{1}{2}} = 0 \tag{11}$$

The Lagrange multiplier is solved from Equation (11), and $p = \lambda_0^{-1} NkT\lambda_s^{-\frac{3}{2}}$. The nominal stress along with the uniaxial direction is derived as:

$$s_1' = \lambda_0^{-1} NkT\left(\lambda_s - \lambda_s^{-2}\right) \tag{12}$$

We define the volume fraction of the polymer in the hydrogel as ϕ_V, $\phi_V = \frac{1}{J} = \frac{1}{\lambda_0^3}$. Under uniaxial loading, the nominal stress with free-swelling state as reference state is given as:

$$s_1' = \phi_V^{\frac{1}{3}} NkT\left(\lambda_s - \lambda_s^{-2}\right) \tag{13}$$

After obtaining Equation (13), the nominal stress–stretch curves with different polymer fractions could be calculated. This equation reveals the relationship between mechanical response and material property of single-network hydrogel and can be used as the dataset for DL-based model training.

2.2. Network Generation Model of Single-Network Hydrogel

At mesoscopic scale, the hydrogels can be abstracted as polymer chains comprised by a large number of points and bond vectors [45,46]. Models at the mesoscopic scale can help us extract the commonalities of polymer chains, and make the research focus on the responses of structural changes of the chain and network, rather than the specific molecular properties at the microscopic scale or the complex boundary problems at the continuum scale. In order to describe the network configuration of single-network hydrogels at a mesoscopic scale, we develop a mathematical model using SAW to characterize the randomness, uniqueness, and heterogeneity of polymer chains. In addition, the model potentially reproduces a configuration that is statistically similar to the true structure of polymer chains.

The configuration of molecular chains of single-network hydrogels can be abstracted as bond vectors connected end to end, which is geometrically similar to a walking trajectory in space. Random walk (RW) is a mathematical model describing a random process in the lattice space. RW describes a series of random steps starting from a point in a discrete lattice space. An example of RW in two-dimensional space is shown in Figure 1a. Assuming that the end of the chain is the ongoing random walk, then the next step is to choose from up, down, left, and right directions (including the direction to the point of the previous step). The probability of each direction is 1/4. After selecting the next direction, the chain takes one step to the neighboring node, then randomly selects a direction again for the next step, and so on. The RW model allows the walking trajectory to repeatedly visit the same node. Besides, the SAW model is also a commonly used mathematical model to describe the configuration of polymers. The SAW model is derived from the RW model. The main difference between the two models is that the SAW model does not allow the walking trajectory to visit the same point repeatedly. Because the SAW model does not allow to go back, each node has at most three alternative directions in two-dimensional space, as shown in Figure 1b. If some of the three directions have been previously visited by this chain or other chains in the same space, the SAW model will not select this direction at the next step, as shown in Figure 1c.

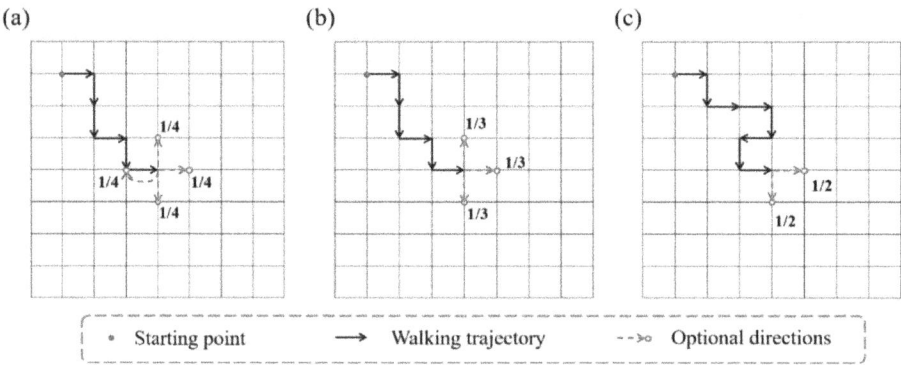

Figure 1. Schematics of RW model and SAW model. (The red dot is the starting point, the black arrow represents the walking path, and the blue arrow represents the optional direction for the next step.) (**a**) The RW model. There are four optional directions at every moment. (**b**) The SAW model cannot go back. (**c**) The SAW model cannot select points that are already occupied.

Figure 2 shows the SAW trajectory with different number of steps N. It can be seen that with N increase, the configuration of the SAW trajectory is geometrically similar to the configuration of the real polymer chain.

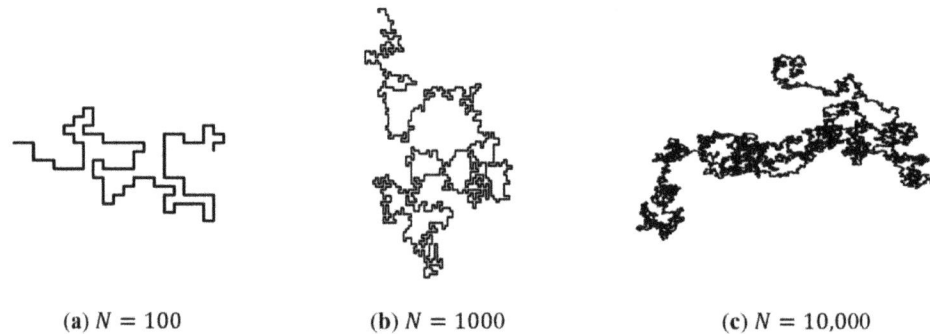

(**a**) $N = 100$ (**b**) $N = 1000$ (**c**) $N = 10{,}000$

Figure 2. The SAW path generated by the computer program. As the number of steps N increases, the configuration of the path is similar to the real polymer chain.

The SAW model is able to generate one long chain, but not multiple paths. In order to generate a complex network model reflecting the configuration of the hydrogel network, we propose a SAW-based network generation algorithm (NGA). Because polyacrylamide (PAAm) hydrogel basically does not conduct viscoelasticity or damage accumulation effect during the loading process, and it can be described as nearly elastic using hyperelastic constitutive model to its mechanical properties, we take the PAAm hydrogel as an example. The design ideas of the NGA are quite similar to the actual generation process of hydrogel network. Figure 3 shows the design logic of the NGA. Take two-dimensional space as an example, consider that each point in the discrete space can only be occupied by one particle, that is, one from monomer particles (gray dots), crosslinker particles (red dots), or water molecules (void space). Before the NGA starts, it is necessary to set the space size w, the number of monomer particles n_{mon} and the number of crosslinker particles n_{cro}, so that the polymer volume fraction of the network can be determined as:

$$\phi_V = \frac{n_{mon} + n_{cro}}{w^3} \approx \frac{n_{mon}}{w^3} \tag{14}$$

where considering $n_{mon} \gg n_{cro}$, Equation (14) gives the polymer volume fraction in the NGA. While the NGA is running, a SAW starts to wander from the original point in the space. Each step of the SAW represents a certain type of particle assembled into the chain and becomes part of the chain. In each step of the SAW, the probability of what kind of particles to be inserted depends on the number of remaining monomers and crosslinkers, as shown in Figure 3a. Each particle that has not been inserted has the same probability to be the next spatial point. Because one crosslinker of the PAAm hydrogels can link four monomers, if the nineth position is connected to the crosslinker, the tenth position will be branched out to form three new chain ends, as shown in Figure 3b. The SAW will continue on the basis of these three new chains. There is only one SAW chain at the beginning, then it will gradually bifurcate, and finally form a network structure, as shown in Figure 3c. In this study, this network model is called SAW network model, which is able to characterize the complex polymer network configuration of single-network hydrogels.

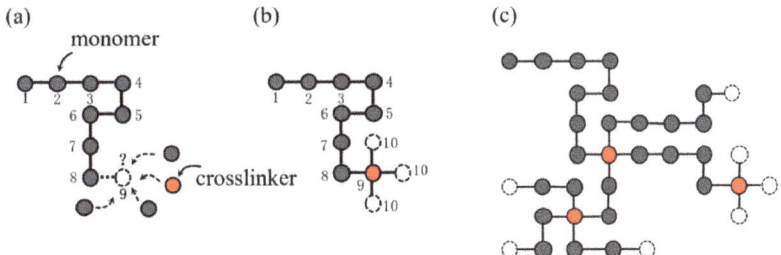

Figure 3. Schematics of SAW network generation model in 2D space. (**a**) The probability of what kind of particles to be inserted depends on the number of remaining monomers and crosslinkers. (**b**) Generation of new chain ends when inserting a crosslinker. (**c**) More chains walk in space to form a network.

Since the space size w is limited, the SAW network generated by the NGA will eventually reach the boundary of the space. Therefore, we adopt periodic boundary conditions in this model. When the SAW touches the periodic boundary of the space, it will stop right there and no longer connect to any other particles. Instead, the periodic boundary condition makes it place a new chain starting point at the corresponding position on the other side of the space (a symmetrical position) and the SAW continues. This process is similar to a SAW path that goes out from one side of the space and enters from the other side of the space at the same time.

The examples above in 2D space are to make the design logic of the NGA easy to be understood. For the real configuration of hydrogel network, the NGA should be implemented in 3D space. In 3D space, each spatial point has 26 neighbors (including six surface neighbors, twelve side neighbors, and eight corner neighbors). Although the distances from the 26 neighbors to the center point are not all equal, when the size of these 27 local points compares with the size of the entire model space, the distance difference between neighbors is negligible.

In practical experiment, polymer mass fraction ϕ_m is used as usual to measure the water content of hydrogels due to the ease of measuring the sample mass. For practical application of the NGA, polymer mass fraction ϕ_m is adopted in the algorithm. The conversion relationship between polymer volume fraction ϕ_V and polymer mass fraction ϕ_m is given by:

$$\phi_m = \frac{1}{\left(\phi_V^{-1} - 1\right)\left(\frac{M_w}{M_{mon}}\right) + 1} \tag{15}$$

where M_w is the molar mass of water. M_{mon} is the molar mass of AAm monomers. They are equal to $M_w = 18$ g/mol and $M_{mon} = 71.08$ g/mol, respectively.

For the complex network of PAAm hydrogel, the SAW network model generated by the NGA in 3D space is shown in Figure 4. The different values of the model determined by n_{mon}, n_{cro} and w result in different polymer mass fractions ϕ_m. In Figure 4, the blue lines represent polymer chains, and the red dots represent crosslinkers. When ϕ_m is low, the distribution of polymer chains in the space is sparse and inhomogeneous. This proves the structural randomness, heterogeneity, and uniqueness of the polymer network of PAAm hydrogel. With the increase of ϕ_m, the PAAm hydrogel network becomes gradually dense and is closer to the homogeneous assumption in continuum mechanics. Thus, this model has the potential in characterizing the mesoscopic configuration of single-network hydrogels and provides a powerful tool for follow-up research.

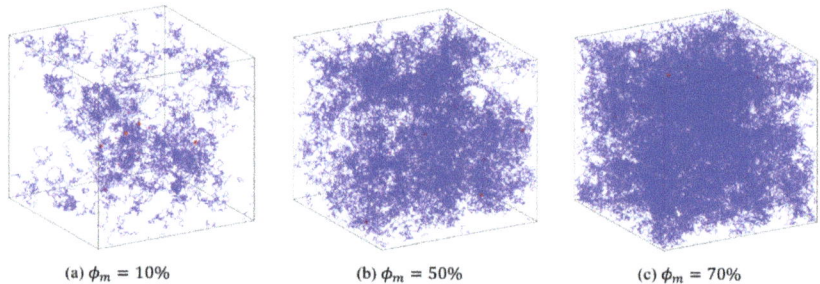

(a) $\phi_m = 10\%$ (b) $\phi_m = 50\%$ (c) $\phi_m = 70\%$

Figure 4. Configurations of PAAm hydrogels generated by SAW network model.

2.3. Deep Learning Algorithms and Approaches

Machine learning systems can be classified according to the amount and type of supervision they receive during training. There are four major categories: supervised, unsupervised, semi-supervised, and reinforcement learning. In the case of supervised learning, the input data set (containing samples and corresponding features) and labels (the correct results) are both necessary for training. On the contrary, unsupervised learning, as the name suggests, only provides unlabeled training data. For engineering problems, most of the applied ML algorithms are supervised learning with the datasets collected from experiments or simulations [47–49]. Artificial neural network (ANN) [50] is comprised of multiple interconnected computational elements called neurons. In this study, the algorithms we adopt belong to a subset of ANN. By adjusting parameters, for instance, weights and biases in a NN architecture, the algorithms we used can predict the mechanical property of hydrogel through an optimization of errors. Both the fully connected MLP and CNN belong to the class of ANN, and they differ primarily in their architecture and interconnectivity. This section gives a brief introduction to the main ML algorithms used in this work.

2.3.1. Multilayer Perceptron

The MLP architecture, generally called feedforward NN, is one of the most popular and widely used ML architectures that was proposed initially as a function approximator [51]. The aim of a MLP is to approximate a function f between input x and output $\hat{y}$

$$\hat{y} = f(x) \tag{16}$$

In order to approximate strongly non-linear functional relations, MLP adds an additional level of hierarchy to linear learning algorithms involving features and learned weights by combining activation functions:

$$a_j = \sigma(z_j) = \sigma\left(\sum_{i=1}^{m} w_{ji}x_i + b_j\right) \quad (17)$$

where i denotes the ith neuron in the previous layer, and j the jth neuron in the current layer. a_j is the output value of the current neuron. $\sigma(\cdot)$ is the activation function that usually takes a non-linear function. x_i represents one feature input of x. w_{ji} and b_j are parameters updated during the training, named weight and bias, respectively. m is the number of neurons in the previous layer. z_j is the sum of the input values and the bias, also the prediction of the linear learning model. This process is demonstrated in Figure 5, which is the typical mathematical process of a single neuron. Furthermore, matrix form can be written as:

$$a_{\mathbf{W},\mathbf{b}}(\mathbf{X}) = \sigma(\mathbf{XW} + \mathbf{b}) \quad (18)$$

where $\mathbf{X}$ represents the matrix of input features. It has one row per sample and one column per feature. The weight matrix $\mathbf{W}$ contains all the connection weights, which has one row per input neuron in the previous layer and one column per artificial neuron in the current layer. $\mathbf{b}$ is the bias vector that has one bias term per artificial neuron. The weights of the MLP are usually initialized stochastically, and then subsequently tuned during the training. One way to train the MLP is to establish a linkage of its known input–output data and to minimize its loss function from the output by appropriately changing the weights.

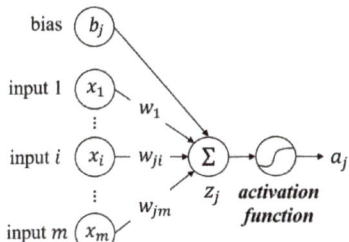

Figure 5. Process of a single neuron in MLP.

There are several alternatives to the activation functions. Frequently used activation functions in regression tasks include the sigmoid function (Equation (19)) for the outputs required between the domain (0,1) and the rectified linear unit (ReLU) as shown in Equation (20) for nonzero outputs. The two functions are illustrated in Figure 6.

$$sigmoid(z) = \frac{1}{1+e^{-z}} \quad (19)$$

$$ReLU(z) = \max(0,z) \quad (20)$$

It is the nonlinear transformation of the activation function that gives the MLP a strong nonlinear fitting capability. It should be noted that a feedforward NN can approximate any continuous functions with arbitrary complexity in the reach of arbitrary precision, using only one hidden layer containing enough neurons [52]. MLP is served as the beginning of research on more complex DL algorithms. Deep architecture has better learning capability by stacking more layers to extend the depth of the NN.

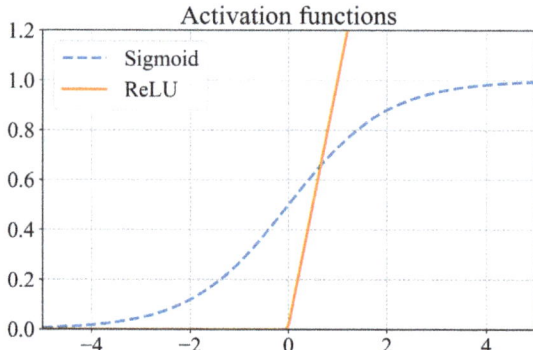

Figure 6. Plot illustrating the sigmoid and ReLU activation functions.

2.3.2. Convolutional Neural Network

Convolutional neural network is one of the most widely-used deep neural networks that is inspired by the study of the brain's visual cortex, and CNN is extremely successful in the image recognition field. It has been extended to various applications of many other disciplines including mechanics.

There are two main differences between a fully connected MLP and a CNN, i.e., the input data structure and data transfer. Input data in a CNN is assumed to be an image or can be physically interpreted as an image. The input image contains many pixels and is a 2D data structure with length and width. Of course, the image can also be a 3D structure with three dimensions of length, width, and thickness. The 3D CNN model used in this study utilizes three3Dimensional data. Instead, in the case of the MLP, the inputs to the neurons in the hidden layer are obtained by a standard matrix multiplication **XW** of the weight **W** and the input **X**. Besides, in the case of the data transfer, MLP only feedforwards the input data obeying Equation (18). However, for CNNs, the input data will be transformed through a convolutional kernel (or called a filter) into a feature map using a convolution operation. This process is symbolically written as **X** ∗ **W** (∗ symbol represents convolution operation).

A typical CNN architecture is mainly comprised of four building blocks, and they are referred to as convolutional layers, pooling layers, fully connected layers, and activation functions. Take a 2D input image as an example:

It can be seen from Figure 7 that different layers have their corresponding functions. The convolutional layer is the core of a CNN model, each convolutional layer has one or several convolutional kernels (or filters). The kernels extract the features of the input image by scanning pixels (like a camera) in a small rectangle (called receptive field) using convolution operations, and repeat until the entire image is scanned. The shift from one receptive field to the next is called the stride. By default, stride equals one for convolutional layers and two for pooling layers. Indeed, a convolutional layer can contain multiple kernels (filters) and output one feature map per kernel. New feature maps (the number of newly generated feature maps depends on the number of filters in the convolutional layer) are generated with smaller height and width compared to the previous image. One pixel is one neuron in each feature map, and all neurons in the same feature map share the same parameters (the same weights and bias). In order to ensure each input image for a layer have the same height and width as the previous layer, it is common to add zeros around the inputs (zero padding), as shown in Figure 7a. Neurons in the first convolutional layer are not connected to every single pixel but only to pixels in the corresponding receptive fields. The role of the kernel allows features to be mapped through local interactions. This architecture allows the network only to focus on small low-level features in the first layer, then with more convolution layers repeating this feature extraction process, larger high-level features are assembled, and so on. That is why CNN is more effective than MLP on the input–output relationship learning of structures depending on spatial locations.

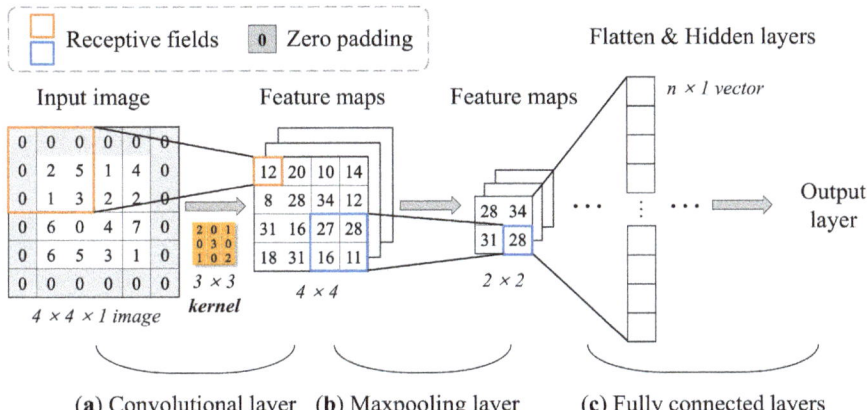

Figure 7. Computation process of an example architecture of 2D CNN with 3 × 3 kernel (it should be noted that the process of bias and activation functions is ignored here for simple illustration). (**a**) Convolutional operation of the input image. The value in the receptive field is multiplied by the value of the corresponding center symmetric position in the kernel and then obtain the summed value in the feature maps. (**b**) 2 × 2 max-pooling process. Each 2 × 2 block is replaced by the maximum value in the receptive field. (**c**) Flatten last feature maps to one-dimension vector for learning.

After the pre-activated convolutional operation, results are offset by a bias (one bias per convolutional layer). Then the feature maps are passed through nonlinear activation functions commonly referred to as ReLU. ReLU has been proven [52] to provide high computational efficiency and often achieves sufficient accuracy and performance in practice.

The max-pooling layer is usually implemented after one or multiple convolutional layers, making a key role in reducing the number of parameters thus resulting in a faster training process. Its goal is to subsample the input image for reducing the computational load by reducing the number of parameters and preventing the risk of overfitting. On the contrary to the convolution layer, a pooling neuron has no weights or bias, all it does is aggregate the inputs using an aggregate method, such as max or mean. Figure 7b simply shows how the max-pooling layer works. Subsequently, there is usually a fully connected layer at the end, which is no different from a typical MLP architecture at most times.

CNNs explain the topological structure of the input data, that is, allow stacking neural layers to extract high-level features. Actually, this hierarchical architecture is common in real images, which is one of the structural reasons why CNNs work so well on image recognition. Through the optimization process, the CNN model "learns" how the spatial arrangement of specific features are related to the outputs. Once trained, the CNN model can be used to make predictions with high computational efficiency. Compared with general projects in the DL field, the requirement of the number of datasets and features used in mechanical property prediction of hydrogels is much less. Therefore, the framework of the DL-based models employed in this study could be adjusted easily, and the increasing number of weights and biases has an acceptable impact on the computational cost. For this reason, DNN and CNN are finally used in this study to predict the macroscopic mechanical properties of hydrogel.

3. Deep Learning Modeling Framework for Single-Network Hydrogel

In this section, in order to explore the application potential of the SAW network model and the performance of the 3D CNN model in predicting the mechanical properties of hydrogels with complex network structures, we firstly design two types of data structures extracting structure–property linkages of hydrogels. Furthermore, we implement two deep learning models that are used to make predictions. For both models, the data samples are generated based on the SAW network model. The two datasets include training, validation, and testing sets, which reflect the ground truth. In this study, it should be noted that the labels are the nominal stress–stretch response of the single-network hydrogels under uniaxial tension, as mentioned above.

3.1. Dataset Generation and Preprocessing

The two deep learning models we developed are the DNN model and the 3D CNN model, respectively. It should be noted that the DNN in this study specifically refers to neural networks made up of fully connected layers (as the same architecture as MLP), to distinguish from CNN used in this study. For model comparison, we use theoretical resolution instead of experimental results as labels. Therefore, the outputs of the two models are not affected by experimental errors, which ensures the fair evaluations of the feasibility and performance of the DL models. Because each input data usually needs to maintain the same dimension for the DL models, the space size w is fixed at 33, and 2200 simulations are conducted using the SAW network model by changing the preset numbers of monomers and crosslinkers. As a result, the polymer mass fraction ϕ_m is distributed from 5% to 80%, and the corresponding water content is from 95% to 20%. The number of samples and the space size have to be large enough to reflect the randomness and heterogeneity of the SAW network with different polymer mass fractions, but small enough to prevent excessive computational costs (considering that the input data of the 3D CNN model is four-dimensional, the amount of data will grow rapidly with the increase of the space size w).

In the terms of the DNN model, the input data set is two-dimensional with one row per sample and one column per feature. We designed eight features in the DNN model to capture key physical information of the network generated by SAW. They are referred to as the number of chains, the number of monomers, the number of crosslinkers, the number of water molecules, the standard deviation of the number of monomers per chain, the number of isolated, branch, and network chains. As a result, the size of the input data of the DNN is 2176 × 8. There is a principle of feature design for the traditional MLP architecture, that is, each feature is possibly independent of other features, and potentially related to the outputs. Therefore, this is why we choose the standard deviation of the number of monomers per chain instead of the mean value (for the fifth feature), the latter can be calculated from the number of monomers (the second feature) and chains (the first feature). Similarly, the degree of cross-linking is also an important feature of the complex network structure of hydrogels, which can be calculated from the total number of monomers (the second feature) and the number of crosslinkers (the third feature). Therefore, they are no longer independent features. On the other hand, the original sample size of the 3D CNN model is 33 × 33 × 33. Through further transformation, the SAW network image is represented as a data structure that can train the 3D CNN model, as shown in Figure 8.

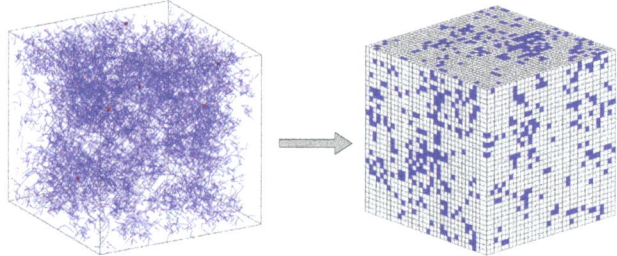

(a) 3-D SAW network of PAAm hydrogel   (b) Input image for 3D-CNN model

Figure 8. Data representation for model training.

In order to include the geometric and physical information of the SAW network model in input data, we design three sublayers and combine them with the inputs by replacing the color channels in the traditional CNN architecture. The 3D CNN model we developed incorporates both the geometric and physical features of hydrogel networks for mechanical property prediction. More specifically, the geometric features captured by the sublayers are referred to as the types of molecules, the degree (the number of edges incident to the vertex) of each molecule, and the angles of chain connections, as shown in Figure 9.

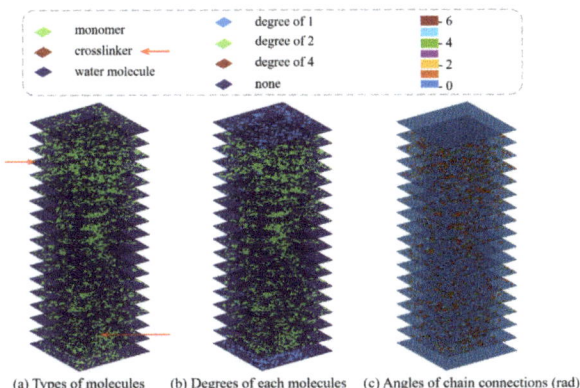

Figure 9. Schematics of slices plot illustration of three sublayers incorporating the geometric and physical features. (**a**) Representation of the type of molecules. (**b**) The degree of each molecule, that is, the number of connections per molecule. (**c**) The angle of chain connections.

As for the color channels of the input images in a typical CNN, they are generally composed of one (grayscale image) or three (colorful image with red, green, and blue, i.e., RGB) sublayers. However, the colors of input images in this study are only for representation and explanation. They have no specific physical meaning. As for the traditional CNN, the original values of a pixel range from 0 to 255, which would be exceedingly large for a CNN-based model. Therefore, the RGB values are rescaled into the range (0, 1) to speed up the convergence of a training process. This problem also occurs in the dataset with sublayers used in this study, thus the datasets to be used are normalized into the range of (0, 1) before training.

The proposed sublayers make full use of various data formats of SAW simulation outputs. Compared with the DNN model, the local spatial information of SAW network model is included in 3D CNN model. Two datasets are eventually constructed, one is two-dimensional including 2176 samples and 8 features for the DNN model, the other includes 2176 four-dimensional samples with a size of $33 \times 33 \times 33 \times 3$ including the three feature channels. The corresponding nominal stress–stretch data are generated through Equation (13). The general idea of sublayers design described here can be extended to any other desired component to obtain effective mechanical properties.

3.2. Framework of Deep Learning Models

On the basic paradigm of DL algorithms presented in previous section, we propose two architectures of the DL models, one is the DNN model based on MLP, the other is the 3D CNN model. Figure 10 gives the schematic illustration for the DNN architecture we have constructed. While Figure 11 provides a schematic of the 3D CNN architecture, where inputs are 3D images and outputs are the stress–stretch relations of single-network hydrogels under uniaxial tension.

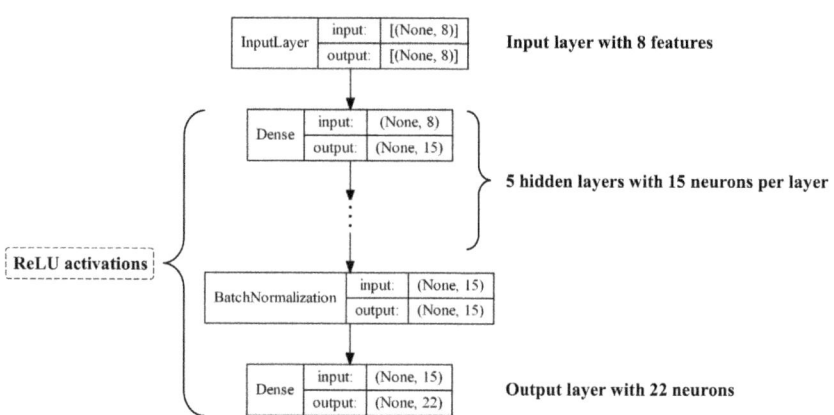

Figure 10. Architecture schematic of the DNN model.

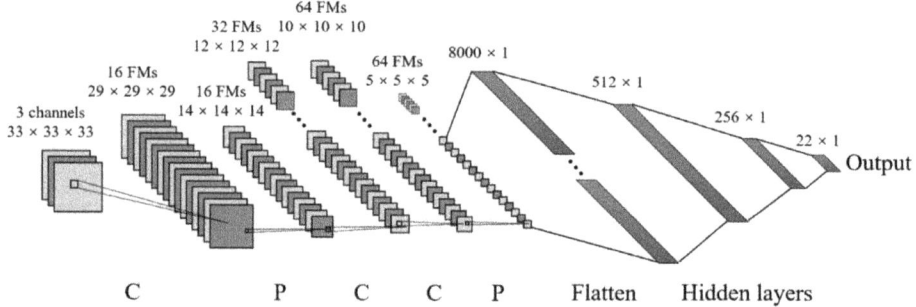

Figure 11. Three-dimensional convolutional neural network architecture (for simpler schematics, one gray rectangular represents one 3D input image). C is referred to as convolutional layer, P is max-pooling layer, and FMs denote the feature maps.

The modeling starts from dividing both datasets into three parts, 70% for training, 10% for validation and 20% for testing. The hyperparameters used for the 3D CNN model are shown in Figure 11 and Table 1. Both models output a subsample of the stress–stretch curve, taking the stress values corresponding to 22 fixed stretching values. The dimensions of the output data are both equal to 22. It should be noted that when the stretch is small, the stretching points we selected are denser, and vice versa. Because on the one hand, nonlinear effect is more obvious at small stretch, and on the other hand, the neo-Hookean-based constitutive model has a larger error at large stretch.

Table 1. Hyperparameters values used in the proposed models.

Hyperparameters	Model	
	DNN	3D CNN
Number of epochs	315	30
Batch size	32	32
Learning rate	5.6×10^{-3}	1×10^{-3}
Optimizer	SGD	Nadam
Loss function	MSE	MSE
Trainable weights	1477	430,872,6
Activation functions	ReLU	ReLU

The development of the two DL-based models is carried out on Python 3.8 and Keras with the Tensorflow backend. The training of 3D CNN is first to determine the number of convolutional, max-pooling, fully connected layers, and the hidden neurons in each layer (see Figure 11). The prediction of mechanical property is a regression task, so mean square error (MSE) is set as the loss function, which is referred as:

$$MSE = \frac{1}{m}\sum_{i=1}^{m}(\hat{y}_i - y_i)^2 \qquad (21)$$

where m denotes the number of samples. $\hat{y}_i$ and y_i are predicted and actual value of output, respectively. The optimizer of 3D CNN model takes 'Nadam' algorithm with a 0.001 learning rate. Following the input layer is a combination of the first convolution layer and max-pooling layer. There are sixteen convolution filters with a size of five in the first convolutional layer. Then two deeper convolutional with filters size of three and one max-pooling layer are followed sequentially. Considering the output is always positive (nominal stress), ReLU activation function is the best choice to reflect the nonlinear response of uniaxial tension test of hydrogel. Subsequently, a fully connected layer leads to the output of the network, which is the stress–stretch relationship. Once trained, the model is able to predict the relationship with an obviously shorter time (within one second) when fed by unseen input image. As for the DNN model, after a process of combining grid search [53] and cross validation in the hyperparameters space, the preferred hyperparameters of the model for mechanical property prediction problems are determined and detailed in Table 1. The stochastic gradient descent method is taken as the optimizer of the DNN model with a learning rate of 0.0056.

4. Results and Discussions

4.1. Analysis and Comparison of Model Performance

The configuration of the DNN model is determined using the grid search and cross validation, and the details are not mentioned here for simplicity. The configuration is shown in Figure 10 and the hyperparameters are listed in Table 1. It is worth mentioning that batch normalization is a technique for training deep neural networks that standardizes the inputs to a layer for each mini-batch [54]. Owning the effect of stabilizing the learning process and significantly reducing the number of training epochs required, batch normalization can normalize the prior inputs and ensure the gradients are more predictive, thus allow for larger range of learning rates and faster convergence. Figure 12 depicts the convergence history of training and testing set for each model. It can be seen from Figure 12a that the MSE losses of training set and testing set converge rapidly within 160 epochs, then maintain stable in the remaining epochs. One epoch can be explained as a batch of samples that goes forward from the input layer at the beginning then feeds back from the output layer to complete an iteration. When all training samples have completed one iteration, the epoch ends. The 3D CNN model is trained using 30 epochs with batch-size of 32 as shown in Figure 12b. The fluctuation of the loss may be caused by the following reasons. The first reason is that the learning rate is unchangeable in this model during the training process, whose value can be large enough to converge at the beginning, but too large to reach a stable and local minimum. As a result, the loss fluctuates around the 'valley' of the loss function. Secondly, there may be a reason that the loss function is exceedingly complex due to the high dimension and large amount of input data, and the optimizer is hard to find a good convergence point. The history of training accuracy is shown in Figure 13. Both the models we developed reach an accuracy over 90%.

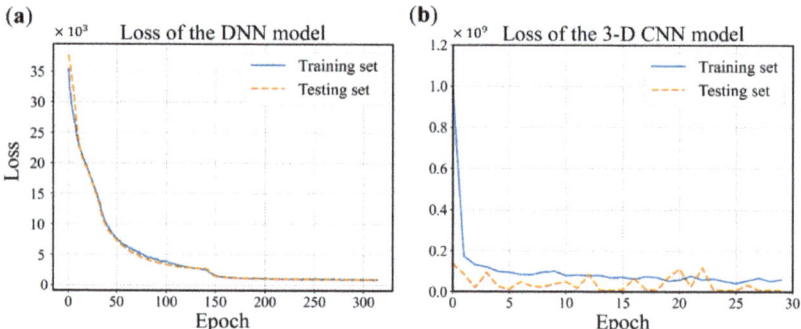

Figure 12. History of loss values. (**a**) The DNN model with 315 epochs. (**b**) The 3D CNN model with 30 epochs (0 to 29).

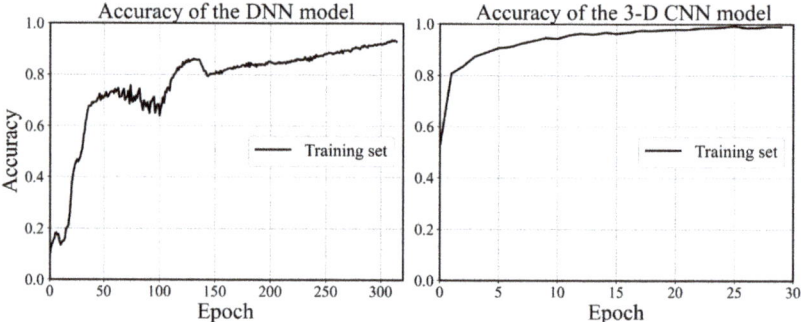

Figure 13. History of accuracy values.

By comparing the two figures in Figure 13, it is found that the accuracy of the 3D CNN model is more stable than the DNN model and is able to reach a higher value within fewer epochs. Because the number of trainable weights in the 3D CNN model is much more than the latter. The convolutional layers of our 3D CNN model focus on extracting the features of each image, while the hierarchical architecture could efficiently capture the potential feature maps relating to the outputs. Therefore, the 3D CNN model is able to reach a better convergence point on a more complex loss function.

It is noted that we employ a dropout layer after each hidden layer in the fully connected layer of the 3D CNN model. The effect of dropout on model's performance is actually negative as usual, because lots of specific data are directly dropped. However, it can effectively reduce the possibility of model overfitting. By sacrificing some accuracy on the training set to obtain better accuracy on the testing set, the model is able to conduct better robustness and generalization on new data that was unseen before.

In order to quantitatively analyze the performance of the DNN and 3D CNN model, mean square error (MSE) and mean square percentage error (MSPE) are computed. MSPE for a selected set of data represents the percentage error between the predicted values and the ground truth calculated from the constitutive model. The MSPE used in this study is defined as:

$$MSPE = \frac{1}{m} \sum_{i=1}^{m} \left(\frac{\hat{y}_i - y_i}{\bar{y}} \right)^2 \times 100\% \qquad (22)$$

where $\bar{y}$ denotes the average nominal stress of all the samples in the dataset. The MSE, MSPE and prediction accuracy R^2 of the two models we proposed are summarized in Table 2. It can be seen that the MSPE values of both models are no more than 4% and the R^2 values reach highly over 91%, which confirms that the 3D CNN model has more potential for the structure–property linkage problem. Besides, with only 1600 training samples, the proposed models can achieve quite gratifying performance. The 3D CNN model shows a remarkable ability to extract structural features of the network. The 3D CNN provides a direct and reliable method to identify the three-dimensional network information of single-network hydrogels at the mesoscopic scale, and has the capability to establish a highly accurate structure–property linkage. Our model can be used to predict the mechanical property based on the basic material structure, which is a universal method bridging the mesoscopic network to macroscopic mechanical properties.

Table 2. Evaluation indicators of the deep learning models.

Model	Values of Indicators					
	Training Set			Testing Set		
	MSE	MSPE	R^2	MSE	MSPE	R^2
DNN	9.3×10^3 kPa	3.61%	92.87%	9.1×10^4 kPa	3.55%	91.00%
3D CNN	7.1×10^3 kPa	0.30%	99.23%	5.7×10^3 kPa	0.24%	99.65%

4.2. Evaluation of Model Generalization

Considering that the nominal stress–stretch curve is usually a comprehensive demonstration of mechanical properties, more specific descriptors such as modulus and strength can be derived from the relationship. Therefore, we decide to evaluate the model based on the mechanical response under uniaxial tension, and explore the potential of the proposed model in the issue of predicting mechanical properties.

Our model architecture is inspired by the recent full convolutional architecture in traditional computer vision applications. According to empirical observations, convolutional architecture is an efficient and stable method because it is a local operation, allowing itself to implicitly quantify and learn the local spatial effects of the mesoscopic network. Obtaining the performance of the DL-based model on unseen data is essential to ensure its compatibility of application. In order to test the generalization ability of the models, we utilize the SAW network model to newly generate multiple network models, and transform these new samples to input images for 3D CNN model according to the process described previously. Then we pass them to the models we proposed to predict the stress–stretch relationship.

To evaluate the generalization ability and robustness of the proposed DL-based modeling framework, Figures 14 and 15 provide the comparisons between the predicted results and the actual results, respectively. It can be seen that both the two models keep good consistency. Despite the nonlinear behavior of the stress–stretch curve for hydrogel, they can fit a favorable nonlinear trend. There are 22 principle stretch values we firstly determined, and the predicted output could contain 22 corresponding nominal stress values. The model can accurately capture the initial nonlinear growth of the nominal stress. In the case of the DNN model, one can easily see that the predictions tend to be more accurate when the water content is low, which indicates that the DNN model has a better performance on the homogenous hydrogel network. With the increase of water content, the predictions become unstable and begin to distort. In addition, the distortion happens only in the first few data points. Because the weights of hidden layers more possibly tend to be close to zeros when labels are close to zeros. The traditional DNN extracts the features of the overall structure instead of the local structure, so its performance is not good enough in the prediction of heterogeneous polymer network. In the case of the 3D CNN model, the fitting accuracy of samples under different water content is significantly higher than that of DNN model. It is indicated that the admirable learning ability ensures 3D CNN to learn complex behavior patterns from the mesoscopic structure. It also has a high fidelity for sparsely heterogeneous and random networks. The prediction results of the two models show that the DL-based model can still accurately predict the mechanical property of the unseen samples of hydrogel network. The proposed modeling framework has good application prospects for multi-scale modeling.

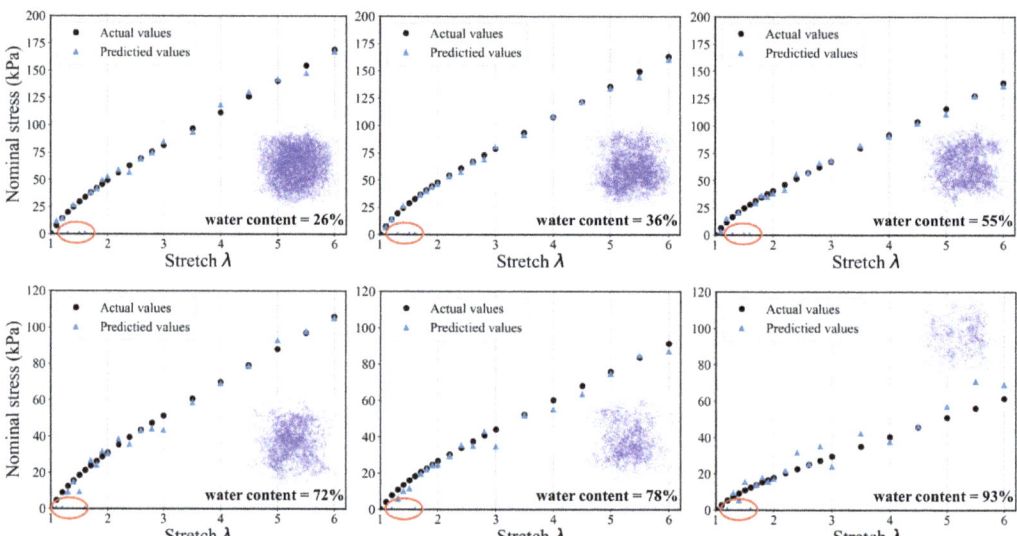

Figure 14. A randomly generated set of six SAW models and corresponding stress–stretch curves for the DNN model prediction compared to the actual results. (The data points in the red circle represent prediction distortion).

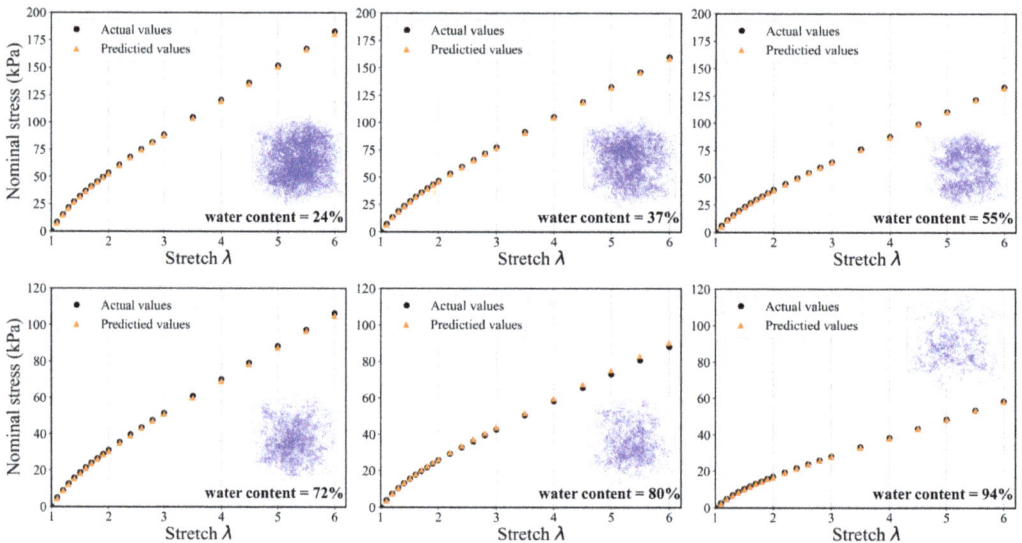

Figure 15. A randomly generated set of six SAW models and corresponding stress–stretch curves for the 3D CNN model prediction compared to the actual results.

To the best of our knowledge, this is the first time that a three-dimensional CNN is implemented to establish structure–property linkage of a single-network hydrogel based on the SAW model. Therefore, the proposed modeling framework in this study provides important insight and guidance, and the proposed model can serve as a pre-trained model to accelerate extensive prediction of mechanical properties, especially for the 3D complex structure. Besides, the DL-based modeling method described previously in this paper expands data-driven strategy to the soft material design and research of material property. It allows a more efficient determination of parameters in the mechanical model, such as the constitutive models, under the lack of experimental data sets. In addition, the ideas of sublayers design we present previously also guide how CNNs could be employed for problems in mechanics and other engineering disciplines. More mechanical properties (components of stiffness) in higher dimensions are required in the field of describing the mechanical behavior of materials. Given the success of 3D CNN model in our current 3D problem, it would be a promising strategy to identify various mechanical properties as different channels in a CNN input sublayer.

5. Conclusions

In order to predict the mechanical property of hydrogel, this paper firstly introduces the RW model, then develops a modeling method for the mesoscopic network of single-network hydrogels based on the SAW model with PAAm hydrogel as an example. Secondly, a DL-based modeling strategy is proposed on the basis of this approach. We developed two deep learning models, a DNN and a 3D CNN, respectively, for the construction of structure–property linkage of hydrogel. A grid search and cross validation of the hyperparameter space of the neural network architecture was employed to find the desirable DNN model, and eight features were designed to overall characterize the mesoscopic network model. In the 3D CNN model, feature extraction of 3D structure was achieved by designing the size of kernels and feature maps of the convolutional layers. It should be noted that we redesigned the color channels of the input images of the 3D CNN model to incorporate the physical and geometric information. The proposed 3D CNN model is able to learn input images that contain sublayers of physical information. These two models can quantitatively predict the relationship between mesoscopic network and the macroscopic mechanical properties. We trained the models using stress–stretch curves generated based on hydrogel theory and Neo-Hookean constitutive model, and then tested the generalization ability and robustness on the testing set. For the new SAW network samples, both DNN and 3D CNN models give accurate predictions, especially the 3D CNN shows a promising capability.

Furthermore, from the results of model evaluation, it can be found that the proposed DNN model can provide a good prediction for lower water content hydrogel, but it shows a large fluctuation error when water content is high, which indicates the weakness of the DNN model for inhomogeneous and sparse network polymer. In contrast, the 3D CNN performs more superior than the conventional DNN approach, which reflects the potential of the model in 3D polymer structural analysis problems. The 3D CNN can capture potential structural features of hydrogel, especially for multiscale material problems. The proposed method can be easily extended to study similar problems, such as the structural design and the material property design to improve the mechanical performance of different soft materials.

Author Contributions: Conceptualization, J.-A.Z.; methodology, J.-A.Z. and Y.J.; model building, J.-A.Z.; analysis, J.-A.Z. and Y.J.; writing—original draft preparation, J.-A.Z.; writing—review and editing, J.-A.Z., Y.J., J.L. and Z.L.; visualization, J.-A.Z.; supervision, Z.L.; project administration, Z.L.; funding acquisition, Z.L. All authors have read and agreed to the published version of the manuscript.

Funding: This work was supported by the National Natural Science Foundation of China [Grant Numbers 11820101001, 12172273].

Institutional Review Board Statement: Not applicable.

Informed Consent Statement: Not applicable.

Conflicts of Interest: The authors declare no conflict of interest.

References

1. Liu, Z.; Toh, W.; Ng, T.Y. Advances in Mechanics of Soft Materials: A Review of Large Deformation Behavior of Hydrogels. *Int. J. Appl. Mech.* **2015**, *7*, 1530001. [CrossRef]
2. Huang, R.; Zheng, S.; Liu, Z.; Ng, T.Y. Recent Advances of the Constitutive Models of Smart Materials—Hydrogels and Shape Memory Polymers. *Int. J. Appl. Mech.* **2020**, *12*, 2050014. [CrossRef]
3. Sun, J.Y.; Zhao, X.H.; Illeperuma, W.R.K.; Chaudhuri, O.; Oh, K.H.; Mooney, D.J.; Vlassak, J.J.; Suo, Z.G. Highly stretchable and tough hydrogels. *Nature* **2012**, *489*, 133–136. [CrossRef] [PubMed]
4. Wei, Z.; Yang, J.H.; Liu, Z.Q.; Xu, F.; Zhou, J.X.; Zrinyi, M.; Osada, Y.; Chen, Y.M. Novel Biocompatible Polysaccharide-Based Self-Healing Hydrogel. *Adv. Funct. Mater.* **2015**, *25*, 1352–1359. [CrossRef]
5. Taylor, D.L.; Panhuis, M.I.H. Self-Healing Hydrogels. *Adv. Mater.* **2016**, *28*, 9060–9093. [CrossRef] [PubMed]
6. Gong, J.P. Why are double network hydrogels so tough? *Soft Matter* **2010**, *6*, 2583–2590. [CrossRef]
7. Li, J.; Mooney, D.J. Designing hydrogels for controlled drug delivery. *Nat. Rev. Mater.* **2016**, *1*, 16071. [CrossRef]
8. Liu, L.; Li, X.; Ren, X.; Wu, G.F. Flexible strain sensors with rapid self-healing by multiple hydrogen bonds. *Polymer* **2020**, *202*, 122657. [CrossRef]
9. Tian, K.; Bae, J.; Bakarich, S.E.; Yang, C.; Gately, R.D.; Spinks, G.M.; Panhuis, M.I.H.; Suo, Z.; Vlassak, J.J. 3D Printing of Transparent and Conductive Heterogeneous Hydrogel-Elastomer Systems. *Adv. Mater.* **2017**, *29*, 1604827. [CrossRef]
10. Yuk, H.; Varela, C.E.; Nabzdyk, C.S.; Mao, X.; Padera, R.F.; Roche, E.T.; Zhao, X. Dry double-sided tape for adhesion of wet tissues and devices. *Nature* **2019**, *575*, 169–174. [CrossRef]
11. Lyu, Y.; Azevedo, H.S. Supramolecular Hydrogels for Protein Delivery in Tissue Engineering. *Molecules* **2021**, *26*, 873. [CrossRef] [PubMed]
12. Censi, R.; Di Martino, P.; Vermonden, T.; Hennink, W.E. Hydrogels for protein delivery in tissue engineering. *J. Control. Release* **2012**, *161*, 680–692. [CrossRef] [PubMed]
13. Xing, J.; Yang, B.; Dang, W.; Li, J.; Bai, B. Preparation of Photo/Electro-Sensitive Hydrogel and Its Adsorption/Desorption Behavior to Acid Fuchsine. *Water Air Soil Pollut.* **2020**, *231*, 231. [CrossRef]
14. Shuai, S.; Zhou, S.; Liu, Y.; Huo, W.; Zhu, H.; Li, Y.; Rao, Z.; Zhao, C.; Hao, J. The preparation and property of photo- and thermo-responsive hydrogels with a blending system. *J. Mater. Sci.* **2020**, *55*, 786–795. [CrossRef]
15. Chen, X.; Li, H.; Lam, K.Y. A multiphysics model of photo-sensitive hydrogels in response to light-thermo-pH-salt coupled stimuli for biomedical applications. *Bioelectrochemistry* **2020**, *135*, 107584. [CrossRef] [PubMed]
16. Xiao, R.; Qian, J.; Qu, S. Modeling Gel Swelling in Binary Solvents: A Thermodynamic Approach to Explaining Cosolvency and Cononsolvency Effects. *Int. J. Appl. Mech.* **2019**, *11*, 1950050. [CrossRef]
17. Ghareeb, A.; Elbanna, A. An adaptive quasicontinuum approach for modeling fracture in networked materials: Application to modeling of polymer networks. *J. Mech. Phys. Solids* **2020**, *137*, 103819. [CrossRef]
18. Tauber, J.; Kok, A.R.; van der Gucht, J.; Dussi, S. The role of temperature in the rigidity-controlled fracture of elastic networks. *Soft Matter* **2020**, *16*, 9975–9985. [CrossRef]
19. Yin, Y.; Bertin, N.; Wang, Y.; Bao, Z.; Cai, W. Topological origin of strain induced damage of multi-network elastomers by bond breaking. *Extrem. Mech. Lett.* **2020**, *40*, 100883. [CrossRef]
20. Lei, J.; Li, Z.; Xu, S.; Liu, Z. Recent advances of hydrogel network models for studies on mechanical behaviors. *Acta Mech. Sin.* **2021**, *37*, 367–386. [CrossRef]
21. Lei, J.; Li, Z.; Xu, S.; Liu, Z. A mesoscopic network mechanics method to reproduce the large deformation and fracture process of cross-linked elastomers. *J. Mech. Phys. Solids* **2021**, *156*, 104599. [CrossRef]
22. Dong, J.; Qin, Q.-H.; Xiao, Y. Nelder-Mead Optimization of Elastic Metamaterials via Machine-Learning-Aided Surrogate Modeling. *Int. J. Appl. Mech.* **2020**, *12*, 2050011. [CrossRef]
23. Jie, Y.; Rui, X.; Qun, H.; Qian, S.; Wei, H.; Heng, H. Data-driven Computational Mechanics:a Review. *Chin. J. Solid Mech.* **2020**, *41*, 1–14.
24. Bessa, M.A.; Bostanabad, R.; Liu, Z.; Hu, A.; Apley, D.W.; Brinson, C.; Chen, W.; Liu, W.K. A framework for data-driven analysis of materials under uncertainty: Countering the curse of dimensionality. *Comput. Methods Appl. Mech. Eng.* **2017**, *320*, 633–667. [CrossRef]
25. Ibanez, R.; Abisset-Chavanne, E.; Aguado, J.V.; Gonzalez, D.; Cueto, E.; Chinesta, F. A Manifold Learning Approach to Data-Driven Computational Elasticity and Inelasticity. *Arch. Comput. Methods Eng.* **2018**, *25*, 47–57. [CrossRef]
26. Zheng, S.; Liu, Z. The Machine Learning Embedded Method of Parameters Determination in the Constitutive Models and Potential Applications for Hydrogels. *Int. J. Appl. Mech.* **2021**, *13*, 2150001. [CrossRef]
27. Li, F.; Han, J.; Cao, T.; Lam, W.; Fan, B.; Tang, W.; Chen, S.; Fok, K.L.; Li, L. Design of self-assembly dipeptide hydrogels and machine learning via their chemical features. *Proc. Natl. Acad. Sci. USA* **2019**, *116*, 11259–11264. [CrossRef]
28. Haghighat, E.; Raissi, M.; Moure, A.; Gomez, H.; Juanes, R. A physics-informed deep learning framework for inversion and surrogate modeling in solid mechanics. *Comput. Methods Appl. Mech. Eng.* **2021**, *379*, 113741. [CrossRef]
29. Pavel, M.S.; Schulz, H.; Behnke, S. Object class segmentation of RGB-D video using recurrent convolutional neural networks. *Neural Netw.* **2017**, *88*, 105–113. [CrossRef]
30. Yu, S.; Jia, S.; Xu, C. Convolutional neural networks for hyperspectral image classification. *Neurocomputing* **2017**, *219*, 88–98. [CrossRef]

31. Shin, H.-C.; Roth, H.R.; Gao, M.; Lu, L.; Xu, Z.; Nogues, I.; Yao, J.; Mollura, D.; Summers, R.M. Deep Convolutional Neural Networks for Computer-Aided Detection: CNN Architectures, Dataset Characteristics and Transfer Learning. *IEEE Trans. Med Imaging* **2016**, *35*, 1285–1298. [CrossRef]
32. Khan, A.; Sohail, A.; Zahoora, U.; Qureshi, A.S. A survey of the recent architectures of deep convolutional neural networks. *Artif. Intell. Rev.* **2020**, *53*, 5455–5516. [CrossRef]
33. Zobeiry, N.; Reiner, J.; Vaziri, R. Theory-guided machine learning for damage characterization of composites. *Compos. Struct.* **2020**, *246*, 112407. [CrossRef]
34. Abueidda, D.W.; Almasri, M.; Ammourah, R.; Ravaioli, U.; Jasiuk, I.M.; Sobh, N.A. Prediction and optimization of mechanical properties of composites using convolutional neural networks. *Compos. Struct.* **2019**, *227*, 111264. [CrossRef]
35. Yang, C.; Kim, Y.; Ryu, S.; Gu, G.X. Prediction of composite microstructure stress-strain curves using convolutional neural networks. *Mater. Des.* **2020**, *189*, 108509. [CrossRef]
36. Yang, Z.; Yabansu, Y.C.; Al-Bahrani, R.; Liao, W.-K.; Choudhary, A.N.; Kalidindi, S.R.; Agrawal, A. Deep learning approaches for mining structure-property linkages in high contrast composites from simulation datasets. *Comput. Mater. Sci.* **2018**, *151*, 278–287. [CrossRef]
37. Cecen, A.; Dai, H.; Yabansu, Y.C.; Kalidindi, S.R.; Song, L. Material structure-property linkages using three-dimensional convolutional neural networks. *Acta Mater.* **2018**, *146*, 76–84. [CrossRef]
38. Yang, Z.; Papanikolaou, S.; Reid, A.C.E.; Liao, W.K.; Choudhary, A.N.; Campbell, C.; Agrawal, A. Learning to Predict Crystal Plasticity at the Nanoscale: Deep Residual Networks and Size Effects in Uniaxial Compression Discrete Dislocation Simulations. *Sci. Rep.* **2020**, *10*, 8262. [CrossRef] [PubMed]
39. Pandey, A.; Pokharel, R. Machine learning based surrogate modeling approach for mapping crystal deformation in three dimensions. *Scr. Mater.* **2021**, *193*, 1–5. [CrossRef]
40. Herriott, C.; Spear, A.D. Predicting microstructure-dependent mechanical properties in additively manufactured metals with machine- and deep-learning methods. *Comput. Mater. Sci.* **2020**, *175*, 109599. [CrossRef]
41. Choi, J.; Quagliato, L.; Lee, S.; Shin, J.; Kim, N. Multiaxial fatigue life prediction of polychloroprene rubber (CR) reinforced with tungsten nano-particles based on semi-empirical and machine learning models. *Int. J. Fatigue* **2021**, *145*, 106136. [CrossRef]
42. Douglass, M.J.J. Hands-on Machine Learning with Scikit-Learn, Keras, and Tensorflow, 2nd edition. *Phys. Eng. Sci. Med.* **2020**, *43*, 1135–1136. [CrossRef]
43. Flory, P.J.; Rehner, J. Statistical mechanics of cross-linked polymer networks I Rubberlike elasticity. *J. Chem. Phys.* **1943**, *11*, 512–520. [CrossRef]
44. Flory, P.J.; Rehner, J. Statistical mechanics of cross-linked polymer networks II Swelling. *J. Chem. Phys.* **1943**, *11*, 521–526. [CrossRef]
45. Li, Z.; Liu, Z.; Ng, T.Y.; Sharma, P. The effect of water content on the elastic modulus and fracture energy of hydrogel. *Extrem. Mech. Lett.* **2020**, *35*, 100617. [CrossRef]
46. Li, Z.; Liu, Z. Energy transfer speed of polymer network and its scaling-law of elastic modulus—New insights. *J. Appl. Phys.* **2019**, *126*, 215101. [CrossRef]
47. Liu, R.; Kumar, A.; Chen, Z.; Agrawal, A.; Sundararaghavan, V.; Choudhary, A. A predictive machine learning approach for microstructure optimization and materials design. *Sci. Rep.* **2015**, *5*, 11551. [CrossRef]
48. Reimann, D.; Nidadavolu, K.; ul Hassan, H.; Vajragupta, N.; Glasmachers, T.; Junker, P.; Hartmaier, A. Modeling Macroscopic Material Behavior With Machine Learning Algorithms Trained by Micromechanical Simulations. *Front. Mater.* **2019**, *6*, 181. [CrossRef]
49. Bag, S.; Mandal, R. Interaction from structure using machine learning: In and out of equilibrium. *Soft Matter* **2021**, *17*, 8322–8330. [CrossRef] [PubMed]
50. Swaddiwudhipong, S.; Hua, J.; Harsono, E.; Liu, Z.S.; Ooi, N.S.B. Improved algorithm for material characterization by simulated indentation tests. *Model. Simul. Mater. Sci. Eng.* **2006**, *14*, 1347–1362. [CrossRef]
51. Benitez, J.M.; Castro, J.L.; Requena, I. Are artificial neural networks black boxes? *IEEE Trans. Neural Netw.* **1997**, *8*, 1156–1164. [CrossRef] [PubMed]
52. Hornik, K.; Stinchcombe, M.; White, H. Multilayer feedforward networks are universal approximators. *Neural Netw.* **1989**, *2*, 359–366. [CrossRef]
53. Bergstra, J.; Bengio, Y. Random Search for Hyper-Parameter Optimization. *J. Mach. Learn. Res.* **2012**, *13*, 281–305.
54. Santurkar, S.; Tsipras, D.; Ilyas, A.; Madry, A. How Does Batch Normalization Help Optimization? In Proceedings of the 32nd International Conference on Advances in Neural Information Processing Systems 31 (NIPS 2018), Montreal, QC, Canada, 3–8 December 2018.

Article

A Smart Helmet-Based PLS-BPNN Error Compensation Model for Infrared Body Temperature Measurement of Construction Workers during COVID-19

Li Li [1], Jiahui Yu [1], Hang Cheng [2] and Miaojuan Peng [1,*]

[1] School of Mechanics and Engineering Science, Shanghai University, Shanghai 200044, China; lilishu@shu.edu.cn (L.L.); 19723402@shu.edu.cn (J.Y.)
[2] School of Communication & Information Engineering, Shanghai University, Shanghai 200044, China; ch20721335@shu.edu.cn
* Correspondence: mjpeng@shu.edu.cn

Abstract: In the context of the long-term coexistence between COVID-19 and human society, the implementation of personnel health monitoring in construction sites has become one of the urgent needs of current construction management. The installation of infrared temperature sensors on the helmets required to be worn by construction personnel to track and monitor their body temperature has become a relatively inexpensive and reliable means of epidemic prevention and control, but the accuracy of measuring body temperature has always been a problem. This study developed a smart helmet equipped with an infrared temperature sensor and conducted a simulated construction experiment to collect data of temperature and its influencing factors in indoor and outdoor construction operation environments. Then, a Partial Least Square–Back Propagation Neural Network (PLS-BPNN) temperature error compensation model was established to correct the temperature measurement results of the smart helmet. The temperature compensation effects of different models were also compared, including PLS-BPNN with Least Square Regression (LSR), Partial Least Square Regression (PLSR), and single Back Propagation Neural Network (BPNN) models. The results showed that the PLS-BPNN model had higher accuracy and reliability, and the determination coefficient of the model was 0.99377. After using PLS-BPNN model for compensation, the relative average error of infrared body temperature was reduced by 2.745 °C and RMSE was reduced by 0.9849. The relative error range of infrared body temperature detection was only 0.005~0.143 °C.

Keywords: personnel health monitoring; construction site management; smart helmet; infrared temperature measurement; temperature error compensation; BP neural network; COVID-19

1. Introduction

The emergence and spread of "COVID-19" around the world has brought new challenges to construction site management. Building construction sites are usually areas where people gather and are highly mobile. Under the strict epidemic prevention and control policy, once an infected person appears in the workplace, if not detected in time, it will not only affect the construction progress of the whole project, but also cause serious social hazards. COVID-19 is an acute respiratory infectious disease caused by SARS-COV-2 virus infection. Among the ascertained symptoms related to SARS-Cov-2 infection, there is an alteration of body temperature [1]. Initial screening of febrile individuals can be effective in preventing the spread of the virus [2–4]. Therefore, the real-time monitoring of the temperature of construction personnel has become one of the necessary options in current construction site management. At present, the body temperature monitoring of construction personnel mostly utilizes handheld temperature guns or fixed infrared thermometers [5], but these methods cannot achieve real-time monitoring and the tracking of body temperature. The use of wearable devices with temperature measurement function in construction personnel management is a feasible solution for real-time body temperature monitoring, and smart helmets equipped with infrared temperature sensors are an ideal carrier. A smart helmet is a head-mounted intelligent device that combines Internet of things technology with an ordinary helmet to realize corresponding intelligent functions. Smart helmets are often used in industries such as counter-terrorism, fire protection, and mining [6–8]. In recent years, smart helmets used by construction workers have also emerged. Altamura [9] developed a smart helmet named SAFE that can be applied to construction sites. The smart helmet is equipped with a temperature sensor, heart rate sensor, and smoke detector, which can monitor the wearer's physical condition and surrounding environment in real time and transmit data to the server through Wi-Fi. The intelligent HeadgearX helmet developed by Aliyev [10] is equipped with ten kinds of sensors, including a smoke sensor, environmental light sensor, and atmospheric sensor, and can communicate with mobile phone through Bluetooth. The matching Android application is also developed to add more functions, including those configurable air functions. Building project managers can monitor the real-time status of all site personnel from a central Web server. Such research provides direction and reference for the application of smart helmets in construction sites. Safety helmets are necessary protective equipment for construction workers. If safety helmet is used as the carrier of infrared temperature measurement module, it will not add additional burden to workers while monitoring their temperature in real-time. However, the goal of applying smart helmets for epidemic prevention and control in construction sites also puts forward more requirements for the accuracy of temperature monitoring.

In recent years, non-contact infrared temperature-sensing technology has developed rapidly, which has the characteristics of fast measurement speeds and high sensitivity. However, in the actual measurement, the accuracy of infrared temperature measurement is easily affected by the measurement distance, ambient temperature, emissivity of the measured object surface, and other factors. Therefore, there may be a large error between the temperature of the human epidermis (forehead, arm, etc.,) obtained by infrared thermometry and the basal body temperature in a general monitoring environment [11,12]. This leads to the common problems of low measurement accuracy and large measurement errors in body temperature measurement using infrared thermometry sensors. A number of studies have been carried out to improve the accuracy of infrared thermometry in measuring human body temperature. Overall, these studies can be divided into two categories:

The first category involves empirical regression models by studying the error relationship between body temperature measurements and true values. Xu, K. [13] proposed a multiple linear regression method to establish an infrared temperature measurement error compensation model to improve the measurement accuracy, but the physical meaning of the model was not clear enough, and the factors affecting the accuracy were not sufficiently considered. When the temperature measurement environment changed, the model could not accurately predict the actual temperature of the human body. Guo, Z. [14] proposed a nonlinear cubic polynomial fitting temperature compensation algorithm to address the shortcomings of the linear compensation model. The accuracy of this algorithm was improved by about 2.25 times compared to the linear model, but the error was still too large for the accuracy requirements of body temperature measurement.

The second category established theoretical models between body temperature measurements and influencing factors through theoretical analysis and experiments. Wei, S. L. [15] established an infrared incidence angle compensation algorithm based on Stefan's law to reduce the temperature measurement error caused by the variation of infrared incidence angle through the study and analysis of the measured data. However, this model did not consider the influence of other factors and was difficult to apply practically. Shajkofeci, A. [16] collected 19,392 sets of measurement data sets, and used the same precision infrared sensors at different locations while tracking outside temperature, room temperature, and time of measurement. On this basis, the relationship between outside, ambient temperatures, hours in the day, and the measured forehead temperature's first and second degrees of polynomials were established. Using these models, the influence of external disturbance on temperature measurement accuracy can be reduced. Although this method can greatly reduce the collinearity between these influence factors, the method of modeling separately may ignore the relationship between each influence factor.

In comparison, the first type of method is more practical, but a large amount of experimental data is required for model building. The experimental process of the second type of method is easy to control, but it is difficult to comprehensively consider various factors that affect the temperature measurement accuracy. Therefore, there were also studies that fused the two ideas and proposed a calibration algorithm that combines theory and experience. Based on the blackbody thermal radiation principle, AI, H. [17] converted the infrared signal into Celsius temperature signal through the correction look-up table method and applied the twice linear regression algorithm to establish an error compensation model for in-ear cavity infrared thermometry, considering the effect of ambient temperature, and obtained the model parameters through the blackbody standard experiment. The results showed that the temperature error in the range of 35~42 °C remains within ± 0.2 after using the model. Pan [18] proposed a nonlinear polynomial regression model to compensate for the measurement error caused by dust and measurement distance. The results showed that the model can significantly reduce the measurement error caused by these two factors, but did not help with the other influencing factors.

In general, a lot of progress has been made in the research of error compensation for infrared temperature measurement, which has created a good foundation for practical engineering applications. However, in different application scenarios, the causes of infrared temperature measurement error are not the same. When infrared temperature measurement technology is used in a smart helmet, the possible causes of measurement error include: (i) The influence of the wearer's environment on skin temperature; (ii) The influence of the sensor's environment on measurement accuracy; (iii) The influence of the wearer's sweat on skin reflectivity; (iv) The vaporization of the wearer's sweat leads to the reduction of skin temperature. These influences are related to a variety of factors. Therefore, in order to improve the measurement accuracy, the compensation calculation of the measurement error needs to fully consider the helmet-wearing environment and its contact with the human body.

The aim of this study is to comprehensively analyze the factors affecting the accuracy of the measured personnel's forehead epidermal temperature measurement and to establish a high-precision temperature measurement model, so as to reduce the misjudgment of the construction personnel's physical condition. Therefore, a smart helmet is developed in this study, which can not only monitor the wearer's temperature, but also obtain the temperature and humidity data inside the helmet. During the experiment, the wearer's real body temperature, ambient temperature and humidity, and ambient wind speed were collected. By analyzing the relationship between these environmental variables and temperature measurement error, the influence of the above factors on the temperature measurement accuracy of the smart helmet was quantified. Considering the multicollinearity of environmental variables and the nonlinear relationship between environmental variables and temperature measurement error, a modeling method combining multivariate statistical analysis theory and a neural network is proposed in this study, which can effectively improve the accuracy of the temperature measurement error compensation model.

Since the use of smart helmets for project management and personnel health monitoring in the actual construction environment is still an emerging technical tool, and its measurement precision largely affects the application and popularization of the smart helmet, the research in this study has important social significance and practical value in the context of a current human society that will coexist with the "COVID-19" epidemic for a long time.

2. Smart Helmet Development and Data Collection

2.1. Smart Helmet Temperature Measurement System

This study utilizes a smart helmet equipped with an infrared temperature sensor to continuously monitor and track the body temperature of personnel to obtain actual temperature data. The smart helmet is self-developed. In order to guarantee continuous data acquisition and communication, and to consider the subsequent temperature data correction needs, the smart helmet measurement system also includes a Temperature/Humidity (T/H) sensor for collecting the temperature and humidity inside the helmet, a 4G communication module for data transmission, a microprocessor for the control system, a digital display for data reading, and a rechargeable power supply module. The system is arranged as shown in Figure 1.

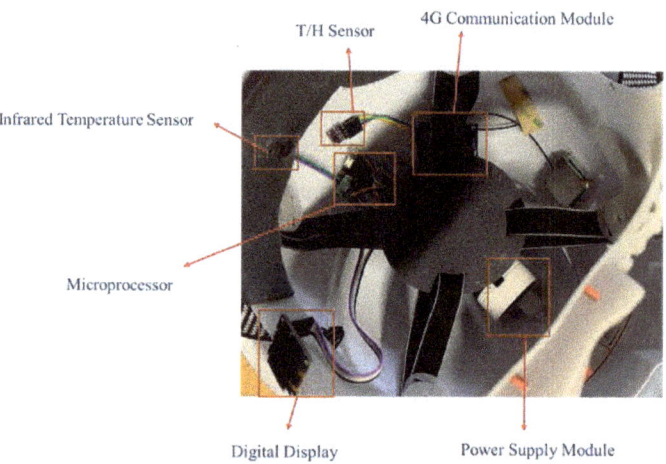

Figure 1. Structure of smart helmet system.

The T/H sensor is placed inside the helmet to collect real-time temperature and humidity data during the wearing process to support the subsequent temperature data correction. The infrared temperature sensor is placed on the contact point between the helmet liner and the human forehead to collect the infrared signal from the human forehead skin. Although in practical applications a temperature measurement accuracy of 0.1 °C is enough, higher measurement accuracy and resolution can bring more information, which helps to improve the application effect of the model. The infrared temperature sensor model used in this study is MLX90614ESF, and the measurement resolution of the sensor is 0.01 °C (measurement accuracy is 0.05 °C). The infrared signal collected by the infrared temperature sensor is transmitted to the microprocessor for processing after a series of amplification and filtering, and the temperature data of the human forehead skin is outputted. The smart helmet measurement process is shown in Figure 2.

Endurance capability is an issue that must be considered for Internet of things equipment. In order to reduce power consumption, the helmet adopts an STM32F411 microprocessor and carries out a low power consumption design. The average operating current of the microprocessor is 5.4 mA. The wireless communication module adopts a Quectel EC20 communication module, with an average operating current of 6.1 mA (data transmission every 10,000 ms). The total operating current of the smart helmet is 26.8 mA, and it is powered by a rechargeable lithium battery with a capacity of 3200 mAh, which can last up to 120 h.

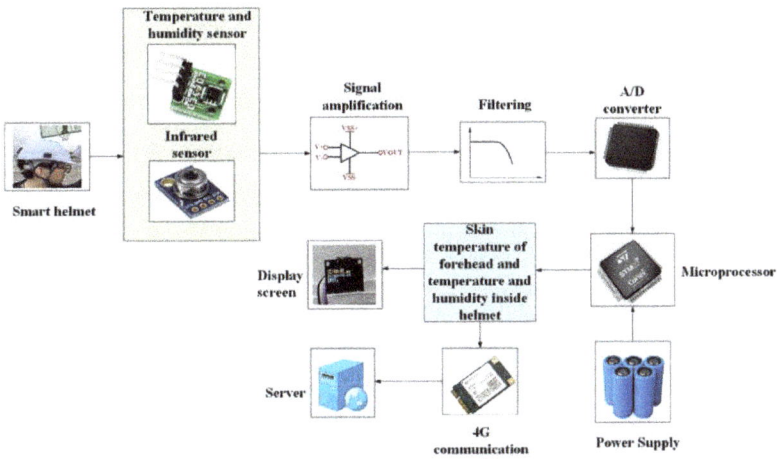

Figure 2. The smart helmet measurement process.

2.2. Influence Factors of Temperature Measurement Error

According to Kirchhoff's Law and Stefan–Boltzmann Law, the relation between the radiation energy, density, and temperature on the surface of an object complies with Equation (1):

$$M = \varepsilon \sigma T^4 \tag{1}$$

where, M is the radiation emission (J/(s·m²)), that is, the radiation power emitted per unit area, ε is the emissivity of the object, σ is Stephan–Boltzmann constant, T is the thermodynamic temperature of the body (K). It can be seen from Equation (1) that, if the radiation emission of an object is measured, the temperature of the object can be determined, which is the theoretical basis for infrared temperature measurement [19]. Therefore, the factors affecting the accuracy of infrared temperature measurement can be determined by analyzing the factors affecting the radiation emissivity.

The radiation received by the infrared sensor is mainly divided into three parts: radiation from the target, reflected radiation from the environment, and radiation from the atmosphere [20]. In other words, the temperature measured by the infrared temperature sensor includes the interference of various kinds of radiation in the measurement environment. The environment reflection radiation mainly related to the temperature and humidity of the environment in which the infrared sensor is located.

As the smart helmet is worn on the head, the temperature sensor location is close to the forehead, so that the effect of atmospheric transmittance is almost negligible. At the same time, since the construction workers may sweat a lot during the construction operation, and the sweat will interfere with the measurement accuracy of the infrared sensor, this study quantifies this factor by measuring the humidity inside the helmet. Besides, there is convective heat exchange between the human forehead surface and the outside air, and when the heat dissipation is high, the forehead temperature will drop, thus deviating from the true body temperature. The convective heat transfer coefficient is related to the wind speed in the environment, which means that the wind speed affects the measurement error of the infrared temperature sensor [21].

In order to quantify the degree of influence of the environmental factors on the infrared temperature measurement of smart helmets, the indicators selected for measurement and analysis in this study include ambient temperature (AT), ambient humidity (AH), temperature inside helmet (TI), humidity inside helmet (HI), and wind speed (WP).

2.3. Smart Helmet Temperature Measurement Experiment

In order to explore the degree of influence of environmental factors on the infrared temperature measurement of the smart helmet, and to establish a temperature error compensation model, this study conducted several groups of indoor and outdoor experiments to simulate the scenes of construction workers in indoor and outdoor construction operations, respectively. During the experiments, the temperature of the human forehead epidermis and the temperature and humidity inside the helmet were collected using the smart helmet, and the temperature inside the ear was measured using an ear temperature gun as the true value of body temperature [22]. Meanwhile, a thermometer, hygrometer, and anemometer were used to measure the external ambient temperature, humidity, and wind speed.

In order to simulate the working hours of a construction site, the experiment was conducted from 8:00 to 12:00 and 14:00 to 18:00. The experiment was carried out in groups of two persons each. One person wore a helmet to simulate the general labor intensity of construction and performed simple movements in the defined site, while the other person was responsible for reading and recording data from the display (Figure 3) on the helmet on time and was called the recorder.

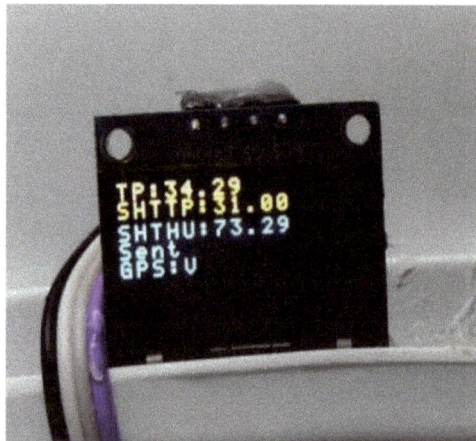

Figure 3. Display on smart helmet.

There were three key datasets on the display. TP represented the body temperature value collected by the infrared sensor on the smart helmet. SHTTP and SHTHU were the temperature and humidity inside the helmet, respectively. The specific experimental steps were as follows:

1. The experimenter wore a smart helmet and held a digital anemometer. The experimenter pressed the storage function of the digital anemometer to save the real-time ambient wind speed (Figure 4).
2. The experimenter used the ear temperature gun to measure his or her ear canal temperature, and then the recorder took a reading and recorded the value.
3. At the same time, the recorder quickly recorded the measured temperature displayed on the helmet, the temperature and humidity inside helmet, the wind speed displayed on the anemometer, and the ambient temperature and humidity displayed on the ambient thermometer and hygrometer.
4. In each recording, the true body temperature was recorded once. The helmet-measured temperature was recorded three times as measured temperature 1, measured temperature 2, and measured temperature 3. The average value was taken as the final measured temperature (MT) of the infrared temperature sensor to reduce the

random error. The difference between the measured temperature and the true body temperature was recorded as the temperature error.

5. The above steps were repeated, and data were recorded every 5 min. Each experiment lasted for 4 h. During the experiment, the experimenter was required to continuously walk around appropriately and wear the smart helmet continuously without removing the helmet until the end of the experiment. In order to simulate the different environments of indoor and outdoor construction, the experiment was divided into indoor and outdoor parts. The data categories and experiment durations were the same in both indoor and outdoor experiments for comparison purposes. The number of samples in each part was 245 sets, with a total of 490 sets. Figure 5 shows the distribution of the measured temperature and the true value of body temperature.

Figure 4. Experimenters measuring wind speed.

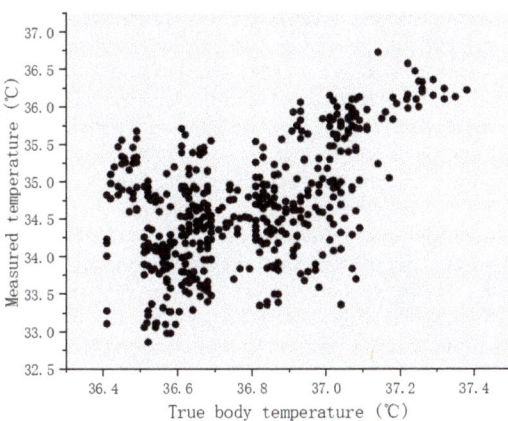

Figure 5. Scatter diagram of true body temperature and measured temperature.

As can be seen from Figure 5, the real body temperature is distributed between 36.4 °C and 37.5 °C, while the measured temperature is generally lower than the real temperature. The temperature data in this experiment can be considered to be in the normal range, as long-term physical activity leads to the rise of human body temperature, which may even exceed 38 °C [23–25].

3. Modeling and Data Analysis

3.1. Modeling Method

The purpose of this study is to analyze the influence of various influencing factors on the error of infrared temperature measurement according to the experimental data, and to establish the error compensation model of infrared temperature measurement. In previous studies, regression analysis (such as multivariate linear regression [26–30], ridge regression [31,32], and logistic regression [33,34]) is usually used to analyze the relationship between multiple factors and the establishment of a mathematical model. Moreover, the ordinary least square (OLS) method is the most widely-used parameter estimation method in regression analysis. Due to the multicollinearity problem among the factors influencing the temperature measurement error discussed in this study, this problem would have a great impact on the analysis results and even lead to model failure if the ordinary least square method was used for regression analysis [35]. In addition, since the infrared temperature measurement error was nonlinear, a simple linear processing cannot properly correct such errors [36].

To solve the above problems, it is necessary to find an analytical method that can overcome the problem of multicollinearity among the influencing factors. In previous studies, ridge regression, principal component regression, and partial least squares regression have achieved good results in overcoming the problem of multicollinearity [37–40]. Ridge regression is essentially an improved least squares estimation method. It is more practical to obtain the regression coefficient at the cost of losing some information and reducing accuracy by abandoning the unbiased nature of the least squares method. Therefore, compared with principal component regression and partial least squares regression, the regression coefficient of ridge regression model is higher, but the accuracy is lower [40]. Both partial least squares regression and principal component regression achieve the purpose of data dimensionality reduction by extracting principal components, and then overcome the influence of multicollinearity. Compared with the partial least square (PLS) method, although the principal component analysis (PCA) method can effectively simplify a high-dimensional variable system into a low-dimensional variable system, and all variables in the new variable system are linearly independent, it cannot avoid the influence of overlapping information in the original variables [41]. This overlapping information may sometimes not have much explanatory significance for the dependent variable and thus become noise. As the PCA completely leaves out the dependent variables when extracting the principal components, the principal component may have a strong generalization ability to the independent variable system, but its explanatory ability to the dependent variables may become very weak. PLS absorbs the idea of extracting components from PCA and simplifies the data structure on the one hand, and is able to correlate the set of independent variables and the set of dependent variables on the other. That is, PLS considers both the generalization of the components to the independent variables and pays more attention to the explanatory significance of dependent variables [42]. Therefore, using PLS method to extract the principal components of data can overcome the problem of multicollinearity among influencing factors and effectively eliminate noise in the data. Therefore, in this study, PLS method was used to extract the principal components.

To solve the problem of low accuracy regarding the prediction results of fitting multidimensional, nonlinear function by conventional methods, an artificial neural network is widely used in fitting nonlinear function [43–45]. An artificial neural network has the ability to approximate any nonlinear continuous function with arbitrary accuracy, and back propagation (BP) neural networks have strong self-learning behavior, self-organization, and a nonlinear approximation function [46,47]. As long as the number of neurons is sufficient, a BP neural network can fit complex nonlinear functions with only a three-layer structure, which greatly reduces the complexity of the network [48]. It not only reduces the calculation time, but also ensures the accuracy of the model.

Therefore, in this study the principal components extracted by the PLS method were used as input variables and the temperature errors were used as output variables for BP neural network training, and, finally, the temperature error compensation model coupled with PLS and BP neural networks (PLS-BPNN) was established. This model can effectively reduce the prediction error brought by linear processing and solve the nonlinear problem of the temperature compensation model. Figure 6 shows the structure diagram of the PLS-BPNN coupling model.

Input layer
Hidden layer
Output layer
x_1
x_2
x_k
Principal component extraction using PLS
t_1
t_2
t_n
h_1
h_2
h_m
y_1
y_2
y_j

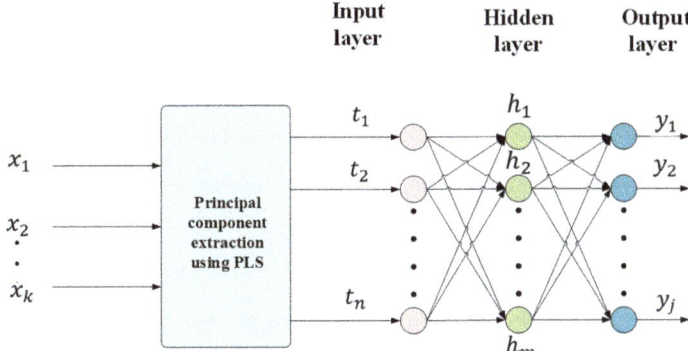

Figure 6. Structure diagram of the PLS-BPNN coupling model.

3.2. *Multicollinearity Analysis*

Multicollinearity is a statistical phenomenon in which predictor variables in a regression model are highly correlated [49]. It is a data problem which may cause serious difficulty with the reliability of the estimates of the model parameters [50]. Therefore, the influence of multicollinearity should be overcome. The influencing factors considered in this study may have multicollinearity, because there is a theoretical correlation between ambient temperature and ambient humidity, inside temperature and humidity, and ambient temperature and wind speed.

To verify this view, and to explore the correlation between ambient temperature (AT), ambient humidity (AH), temperature inside helmet (TI), humidity inside helmet (HI), and wind speed (WP) and temperature error (TE), the correlation coefficient between them is calculated, and the results are shown in Figure 7.

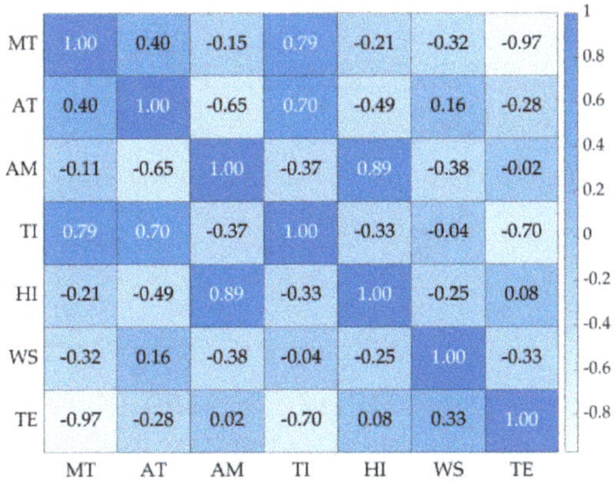

MT 1.00 0.40 -0.15 0.79 -0.21 -0.32 -0.97
AT 0.40 1.00 -0.65 0.70 -0.49 0.16 -0.28
AM -0.11 -0.65 1.00 -0.37 0.89 -0.38 -0.02
TI 0.79 0.70 -0.37 1.00 -0.33 -0.04 -0.70
HI -0.21 -0.49 0.89 -0.33 1.00 -0.25 0.08
WS -0.32 0.16 -0.38 -0.04 -0.25 1.00 -0.33
TE -0.97 -0.28 0.02 -0.70 0.08 0.33 1.00
MT AT AM TI HI WS TE
1
0.8
0.6
0.4
0.2
0
-0.2
-0.4
-0.6
-0.8

Figure 7. Correlation thermodynamic diagram.

The correlation thermodynamic diagram can clearly show the correlation between each variable. The scale on the right side of the thermodynamic diagram shows the color depth corresponding to different correlation coefficients. The color and corresponding number of each box represent the correlation coefficient between the two variables' corresponding to the box.

The correlation coefficient is the quantity of linear correlation between variables. There are many ways to define the correlation coefficient. The correlation coefficient used in this study is the most widely used Pearson correlation coefficient [51]. The Pearson correlation coefficients are between −1 and 1, where a result close to 1 indicates that the two variables are positively correlated, a result close to −1 indicates that they are negatively correlated, and one closer to 0 indicates that they are not correlated.

As can be seen in Figure 7, there are multiple correlations between independent variables affecting the infrared temperature measurement of the helmet. For example, the correlation coefficient between the infrared measured temperature and temperature inside the helmet is 0.79, and the correlation coefficient between the ambient temperature and the ambient humidity is −0.65. To further verify and quantify the multicollinearity between independent variables, the variance inflation factor (VIF) diagnostic method and tolerance value were used in this study to determine the degree of multicollinearity [52]. The VIF and tolerance are both widely-used measures of the degree of multicollinearity of the ith independent variable with the other independent variables in a regression model. Not uncommonly, a VIF of 10 or even one as low as 4 (equivalent to a tolerance level of 0.10 or 0.25) have been used as a rule of thumb to indicate excessive or serious multicollinearity [53].

The expression of variance inflation factor is: $VIF_i = (1 - R_i^2)^{-1}$. Where R_i is t the complex correlation coefficient of the ith independent variable (x_i) and other independent variables. The largest $(VIF)_k$ of all independent variables is often used to determine the degree of multicollinearity. As can be seen from Table 1, the variance inflation factors of three variables are greater than the critical value of 4, among which the VIF value of ambient humidity is about 8.468, which is the largest among the six variables.

Table 1. Results of covariance test for the influencing factors of infrared temperature measurement of smart helmets.

Variable	Tolerance	VIF
Measured temperature	0.271	3.684
Ambient temperature	0.280	3.577
Ambient humidity	0.118	8.468
Temperature inside helmet	0.191	5.234
Humidity inside helmet	0.171	5.845
Wind speed	0.663	1.509

3.3. Extraction of Principal Components

Therefore, this study next extracts the principal components of the independent and dependent variables using PLS. The analysis of the influencing factors shows that there are six possible factors affecting the infrared temperature measurement error, thus there are six independent variables, which are measured temperature (x_1), ambient temperature (x_2), ambient humidity (x_3), temperature inside helmet (x_4), humidity inside helmet (x_5), and wind speed (x_6), and the temperature error (y) to be compensated is the dependent variable. Thus, the 490 sets of experimental data were divided into two sets $X = [x_1, x_2, x_3, x_4, x_5, x_6]_{490 \times 6}$ and $Y = [y]_{490 \times 1}$. In order to eliminate the influence of data dimensions, X and Y are normalized as $E_0 = [E_{01}, E_{02}, E_{03}, E_4, E_{05}, E_{06}]_{490 \times 6}$ and $F_0 = [F_0]_{490 \times 1}$, respectively. Then, the first pair of principal components t_1 and u_1 of the two sets of variables can be extracted. According to the standardized observation data matrices E_0 and F_0 of the two sets of variable sets, the score vector of the first pair of components can be calculated and recorded as $\hat{t}_1$ and $\hat{u}_1$, as shown in Formula (2) and (3).

$$\hat{t}_1 = E_0 w_1 = \begin{bmatrix} x_{11} & \cdots & x_{16} \\ \vdots & \ddots & \vdots \\ x_{4901} & \cdots & x_{4906} \end{bmatrix} \begin{bmatrix} w_{11} \\ \vdots \\ w_{16} \end{bmatrix} = \begin{bmatrix} t_{11} \\ \vdots \\ t_{4901} \end{bmatrix} \quad (2)$$

$$\hat{u}_1 = E_0 v_1 = \begin{bmatrix} y_1 \\ \vdots \\ y_{490} \end{bmatrix} [v_1] = \begin{bmatrix} u_{11} \\ \vdots \\ u_{4901} \end{bmatrix} \quad (3)$$

where w_1 and v_1 are the transformation matrices of the first pair of principal components. According to the principle of principal component analysis in PLS, in order to maximize the correlation between t and u, that is, to maximize the covariance of t and u, the covariance cov (t_1, u_1) of the first pair of components t_1 and u_1 can be calculated by the inner product of the sum of the score vectors of the first pair of components. Therefore, the above requirements can be transformed into a mathematical conditional extreme value problem, as shown in Formula (4).

$$\begin{cases} \langle \hat{t}_1, \hat{u}_1 \rangle = w_1^T E_0^T F_0 v_1 \Rightarrow max \\ w_1^T w = ||w_1||^2 = 1, v_1^T v = ||v_1||^2 = 1 \end{cases} \quad (4)$$

Using the Lagrange Multiplier method, the above problem can be transformed into finding the unit vectors w_1 and v_1, so that $\theta_1 = w_1^T E_0^T F_0 v_1 \Rightarrow max$. Just by calculating the eigenvalues and eigenvectors of the m order matrix $M = E_0^T F_0 F_0^T E_0$, the maximum eigenvalue of M is θ_1^2, the corresponding unit eigenvector is w_1, and the corresponding $v_1 = \frac{w_1^T E_0^T F_0}{\theta_1}$. The following results were obtained after calculation:

$$w_1 = [-0.76526\ -0.2092\ -0.0361\ -0.5499\ 0.0199\ 0.2579]$$

$$v_1 = 1$$

Then, substitute w_1 and v_1 into Formula (2) and (3) to calculate t_1 and u_1. The regression equations of E_0 about t_1 and F_0 about u_1 are established respectively, $E_0 = \hat{t}_1 \alpha_1^T + E_1$, $F_0 = \hat{u}_1 \beta_1^T + F_1$, where E_1 and F_1 are residual matrix. After, replace the E_0 and F_0 with E_1 and F_1 respectively, repeat the above calculation, $t_2, t_3 \cdots t_r$, and $u_2, u_3 \cdots u_r$ can be calculated.

In general, PLS does not need to select all the existing components; however, like principal component analysis, only the first few components are selected. For the number of principal components to be extracted for modeling, the value can be determined by a cross validity test. Each time the ith sample is discarded, the remaining data samples are regressed by PLS method, and the regression equation fitted after extracting h (h is the number of principal components extracted) principal components is established. Then, the ith sample discarded previously is substituted into this regression equation to obtain the predicted value of y at the ith sample, which is denoted as $\hat{y}_i(h)$. Then, repeat the above steps for i = 1 to 490 to obtain the Prediction Residual Error Sum of Squares (PRESS) of the dependent variable y when h principal components are extracted, as shown in Formula (5). After that, all sample points are used to fit the regression equation with h principal components, and the predicted value of ith sample is thus obtained, which is denoted as $\hat{y}_{-i}(h)$. Then, the SS (Error Sum of Squares) of y can be calculated, as shown in Formula (6).

$$PRESS(h) = \sum_{i=1}^{490} y_i - \hat{y}_i(h) \quad (5)$$

$$SS(h) = \sum_{i=1}^{490} y_{-i} - \hat{y}_{-i}(h) \tag{6}$$

Generally, when $Q_h = 1 - \frac{PRESS(h)}{SS(h-1)} < 0.0975$, it indicates that the insertion of the hth new component has no significant improvement on the prediction ability of the model [54]. It is calculated that $Q_h < 0.0975$ when $h = 4$, therefore only three principal components need to be extracted in this study, and the expression is shown in Formula (7).

$$\begin{bmatrix} t_1 \\ t_2 \\ t_3 \end{bmatrix} = \begin{bmatrix} -0.7653 & -0.2092 & -0.0361 & -0.5499 & 0.0199 & 0.2579 \\ -0.5475 & 0.5350 & -0.5133 & 0.0961 & -0.3589 & 0.1119 \\ -0.6450 & 0.4394 & 0.0354 & 0.2354 & 0.2023 & -0.5416 \end{bmatrix} E_0^T \tag{7}$$

3.4. Fitting by BP Neural Network Model

Compared with the general neural network, a BP neural network can adjust the weights layer by layer, starting from the last layer, and the loss function is reduced to an acceptable range through multiple epochs [46]. The general form of weight adjustment in a neural network is $\Delta W = \eta(X)^T \delta$. Where, η is the learning rate, that is, the step size of weight adjustment, X is the input matrix, δ is the learning signal, that is, the direction of each weight adjustment, which is actually a gradient vector [55].

Suppose an N-layer BP neural network, its last layer of learning signal can be described as $\delta^n = (t-y) f'(X^n W^n)$, where t is the expected output, y is the model output, $f'(x)$ is the derivative of the activation function, X^n and W^n are the input matrix and weight matrix of the nth layer, respectively. Moreover, the learning signal of other layers other than the last layer is $\delta^{i+1} = \delta^i W^i f'(X^i W^i)$, where $i+1$ represents the layer after the ith layer.

This study adopts a three-layer BP neural network model, including input layer, hidden layer and output layer. The input layer of the model is $X = [t_1, t_2, t_3]$, the output layer is $Z = [Z]$, and the expected output is $Y = F_0$. Assuming that the hidden layer has m neurons, then the output matrix of the hidden layer is $H = [h_1, h_2, h_3 \cdots h_m]$. The weight matrix from the input layer to the hidden layer is $V = [v_1, v_2, v_3 \cdots v_j \cdots v_m]$, where v_j represents the weight vector of the jth neuron of the hidden layer. The weight matrix from the hidden layer to the output layer is $W = [w]$.

Due to the superposition of linear functions, no matter how many hidden layers are calculated, the final output results are linearly varied, that is, the whole model is linear. In order to remove the linearization of the whole neural network output and make the whole neural network model non-linear, the sigmoid function is adopted as the activation function in this study, as shown in Formula (8). Moreover, its derivative function is given in Formula (9). Sigmoid function is a bounded differentiable real function that is defined for all real input values and has a positive derivative at each point. It is often used as the activation function of neural network [56–58].

$$f(x) = \frac{1}{1 - e^x} \tag{8}$$

$$f'(x) = \frac{e^{-x}}{(1 + e^{-x})^2} \tag{9}$$

Then, the output function of the output layer is $Z = f(S)$, where $S = \sum_{j=0}^{m} w_j h_j$, and the output function of the hidden layer is $h_j = f(S_j)$, where $S_j = \sum_{i=1}^{3} v_{ij} x_i$. Formula (10) gives the means to calculate the loss function used in this study. Where n is the total number of training samples, $d(k)$ is the expected output of the corresponding input $x(i)$, and $z(k)$ is the actual output of the corresponding input $x(i)$. By substituting the output function of the output layer and the output function of the hidden layer into the loss function, it can be found that the loss function is a function of two weight matrices. In order to reduce the value of the loss function, the weight should be adjusted in the direction of negative gradient, as shown in Formula (11) and (12).

$$E = \frac{\sum_{k=1}^{n}(d(k) - z(k))^2}{n} \tag{10}$$

$$\Delta W_j = -\eta \frac{\partial E}{\partial w_j} \tag{11}$$

$$\Delta V_{ij} = -\eta \frac{\partial E}{\partial v_{ij}} \tag{12}$$

where ΔW_j is the weight adjustment value from the jth neuron in the hidden layer to the output layer, and ΔV_{ij} is the weight adjustment value from the ith neuron in the input layer to the jth neuron in the hidden layer, after taking the derivative of the above formulae, the learning signals of the output layer and the hidden layer are defined as $\delta^Z = -\frac{\partial E}{\partial S}$ and $\delta_j^H = -\frac{\partial E}{\partial S_j}$. Then, the expression for ΔW_j and ΔV_{ij} is $\Delta W_j = -\eta \delta^Z h_j$ and $\Delta V_{ij} = -\eta \delta_j^H x_i$, respectively. In the process of gradient descent optimization, if the learning rate is set too large, it will easily lead to model overfitting. However, if the learning rate is set too small, it will reduce the model optimization speed. Therefore, this study adopts adaptive learning rate to solve this contradiction. The adaptive rule of learning rate is given in Formula (13).

$$\Delta \eta(k) = \begin{cases} +a & \Delta E(k-1) < 0 \\ -b\eta(k-1) & \Delta E(k-1) > 0 \\ 0 & else \end{cases} \tag{13}$$

where, a and b are step constants, $a > 0$, $b > 0$, k represents the kth epoch. $\Delta E(k-1)$ represents the gradient value of the squared error function for the $k-1$ epochs of the BP neural network.

In this study, the initial learning rate is $\eta = 0.015$, a = 1.05, b = 0.7, the number of hidden layer neurons is 10. Seventy percent of the 490 groups of sample data are used as training set: 15% as a test set, and the other 15% as a verification set. Mean Square Error (MSE) is used to determine the fitting accuracy of the model. Figure 8 shows the MSE change curve of the model. It can be seen from the figure that the MSE of the data fitting results of the training set, test set, and verification set changes with an increase in the number of model epochs. The training stopped after 25 epochs of the model, and the model accuracy reached the requirements. The MES of the validation set was minimized at the 19th epoch, with a value of 0.007289.

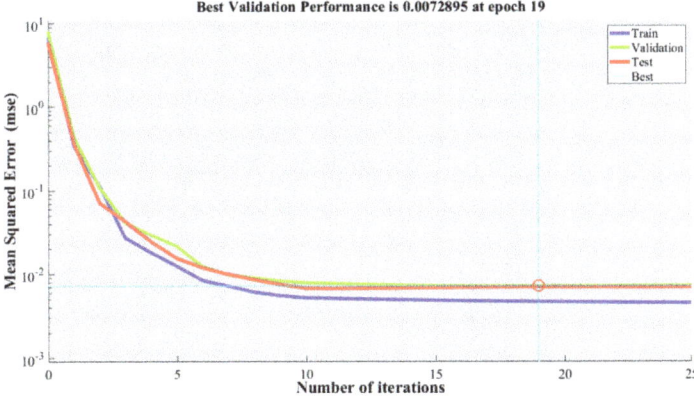

Figure 8. The MSE change curve of the model.

4. Modeling and Data Analysis

4.1. Multicollinearity Analysis

In order to test whether the modeling method of coupling a PLS and BP neural network has an improvement for the accuracy of the model compared with the single modeling method, this study used Least Square Regression (LSR), Partial Least Square Regression (PLSR), and BP neural network (BPNN) for modeling based on the same data, respectively. The fitting scatter plots and residual histograms of four temperature error compensation models are shown in Figures 9 and 10.

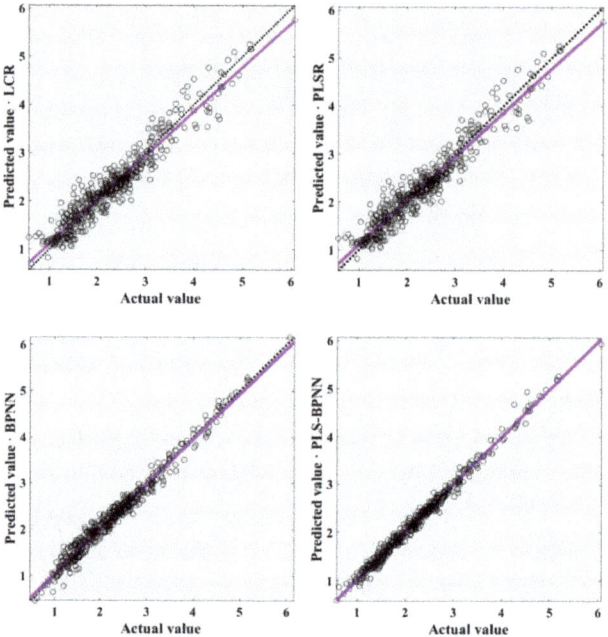

Figure 9. Scatter plot of fitting results of each model.

Figure 9 shows that the PLS-BPNN temperature error compensation model has the smallest relative error between the fitted values and the actual values, with most points falling on a straight line. The fits of the other models behave similarly, with more scattered points falling around the line. Besides, as shown in Figure 10, PLS-BPNN model also has the smallest residual distribution of −0.5 to 0.3, while the LSR model has the largest residual range of −1.0 to 1.0. This indicates that the PLS-BPNN model does significantly improve the temperature compensation accuracy.

In order to more clearly compare the fitting effects of the four models, the relative error, Root Mean Square Error (RMSE), and the temperature measurement results after applying the models were statistically analyzed, as shown in Table 2.

Table 2. Statistical table of fitting effect of each model.

Model	Number of Components	R^2	RMSE	Relative Error/Count		
				<0.1 °C	0.1 °C~0.3 °C	>0.3 °C
LSR	6	0.96079	0.242418341	162	221	107
PLSR	3	0.97542	0.192571607	180	264	46
BPNN	6	0.98915	0.129683998	272	208	10
PLS-BPNN	3	0.99377	0.092084235	372	116	2

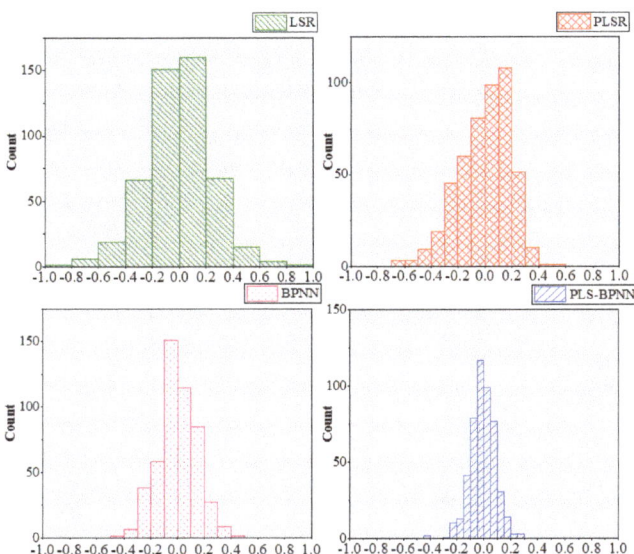

Figure 10. The residual histogram of each model.

Table 2 shows that the number of relative errors greater than 0.3 °C in the fitted data results of the LSR, PLSR, and BPNN models are 107, 46, and 16, respectively, while only two of the fitted results of the PLS-BPNN model have such a large error, and more than 75% of the fitted data have an error less than 0.1 °C. The R^2 of PLS-BPNN model is 0.99377, and the RMSE is about 0.092, indicating that more than 99% of the total error of the smart helmet temperature measurement system can be explained by the dependence between temperature error and various influencing factors. Less than 1% is influenced by random factors. The R^2 of the LCR, PLSR, and BPNN models are all lower than that of the PLS-BPNN model, and the RMSE of all three models is also higher than that of the PLS-BPNN model, indicating that the PLS-BPNN temperature error compensation model is a better fit than the other three models.

4.2. Infrared Temperature Measurement Compensation Test

In order to further verify the effectiveness of PLS-BPNN temperature error compensation model in practical engineering applications, 24 groups (as shown in Table 3) of test data were obtained using self-developed smart helmets in this study. The data was obtained in the same manner as the data used for modeling.

As can be seen from Table 3, the accuracy of the temperature data collected directly by the smart helmet can hardly meet the needs for body temperature detection, and the relative average error reaches 2.80 °C, and the RMSE is 1.052. Then, the temperature error compensation was calculated using the PLS-BPNN model. After using the PLS-BPNN model to compensate the calculation, the relative average error is reduced to 0.055 °C, and the RMSE is also reduced to 0.0671. Figure 11 shows the relative temperature errors before and after compensation.

From Figure 11, it can be seen that, after using the PLS-BPNN model, the relative error range of the infrared temperature measurement results is 0.005~0.143 °C, and the measurement accuracy has been significantly improved to meet the actual management needs of the construction site.

Table 3. Test data used to validate the model.

Measured Temperature (°C)	Ambient Temperature (°C)	Ambient Humidity (%)	Temperature Inside Helmet (°C)	Humidity Inside Helmet (%)	Wind Speed (m/s)	Temperature Error (°C)
33.05	26.41	71.75	28.79	70.86	3.65	3.44
33.12	26.35	42.95	24.04	49.26	1.45	3.49
32.47	27.70	47.09	24.22	44.09	1.99	4.32
33.51	29.07	46.55	28.79	48.14	0.38	3.10
32.32	28.14	40.6	24.81	48.55	1.34	4.30
32.71	26.98	42.69	24.20	50.00	1.01	3.86
32.74	27.55	42.69	24.58	50.00	2.71	3.86
32.75	27.03	46.78	24.39	46.3	2.75	4.05
32.77	27.46	46.94	24.44	47.16	3.11	4.02
34.92	23.56	60.39	28.97	53.82	0	1.96
33.66	25.80	71.26	29.05	71.56	2.99	2.82
33.73	26.46	68.73	27.52	68.64	0	3.04
34.65	24.76	78.36	27.83	70.49	0	1.76
34.66	32.94	56.11	30.69	67.29	1.46	2.14
33.67	26.46	48.72	27.36	46.05	2.83	3.13
34.66	24.49	58.48	29.79	57.46	1.39	2.04
34.63	23.71	60.16	28.22	53.56	0	2.24
34.65	32.01	56.23	30.63	63.02	0.19	2.34
34.67	24.67	74.39	27.87	73.96	0	1.83
35.12	24.35	81.18	28.35	70.19	0	1.49
35.54	24.56	59.59	29.50	56.59	0	1.42
36.24	34.79	40.16	32.48	36.00	1.90	0.96
31.88	27.49	44.32	24.58	51.26	2.88	4.62
33.80	25.27	81.39	27.40	73.73	0	2.70

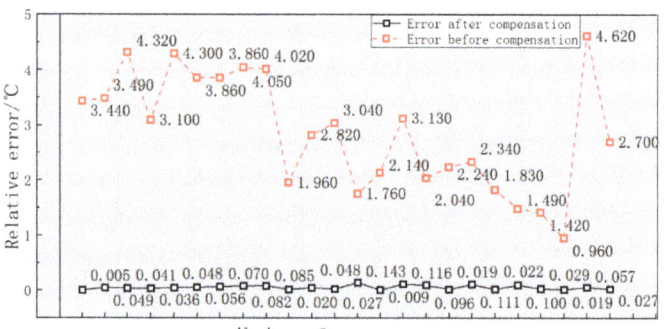

Figure 11. Temperature error before and after compensation of PLS-BPNN model.

The above test results show that the PLS-BPNN temperature error compensation model can better compensate the error between the measured value of the infrared temperature measurement system of the smart helmet and the actual body temperature, which further reflects the advantages of the coupled model in dealing with the multiple correlation and nonlinearity between the independent variables. At the same time, with the help of the PLS-BPNN model, the smart helmet equipped with an infrared temperature sensor can also play the role of human body temperature tracking and monitoring, assisting in epidemic prevention and control in the actual construction management.

5. Conclusions

For the problem that there may be a large difference between the temperature measured by the infrared temperature measurement system and the actual body temperature of the smart helmet, this study developed a smart helmet equipped with an infrared temperature sensor and designed a simulated construction experiment to collect temperature data and data of various influencing factors that may affect the accuracy of temperature measurement in indoor and outdoor operating environments, including ambient temperature, ambient humidity, temperature inside the helmet, humidity inside the helmet, and ambient wind speed. After that, a PLS-BPNN temperature error compensation model was established based on the experimental data to correct the temperature measurement results of the smart helmet. The model uses the PLS method to extract the principal components of the temperature influencing factors and uses them as input variables to effectively eliminate the effect of multicollinearity between input variables. Meanwhile, the advantage of a BP neural network in nonlinear approximation was used to solve the nonlinear problem of the coupled model.

In addition, this study also compared the temperature compensation effect of PLS-BPNN model with LSR, PLSR, and BPNN models, and the results showed that the PLS-BPNN model had a higher accuracy and reliability. For the experimental data collected in this study, the relative error range of infrared body temperature detection was only 0.005–0.143 °C after the compensation calculation of the PLS-BPNN model, which fully meets the requirements of personnel temperature monitoring in construction site management. That is, with the assistance of the PLS-BPNN temperature compensation model, the smart helmet equipped with infrared temperature sensor has good application prospects in construction personnel health management.

In the research process, it was found that, if the multivariate statistical analysis theory and neural network are well connected, the accuracy and efficiency of the model can be greatly improved. Therefore, this provides a new horizon for future research to solve similar problems.

In addition to this, the proposed research method has several limitations. Most of the temperature data used for modeling by this model are in the normal range, and there is a lack of data of people with fever, which may lead to the poor compensation effect of the model for the partial error of hyperthermia (temperature greater than 37.5 °C). Collecting more data can result in more accurate results. In future research, experimental data of febrile patients can be collected to improve the accuracy and generalizability of the model. Since neural network algorithms play a crucial role in the performance of the model, using other neural network algorithms or using different activation functions in the same neural network algorithm may help improve the accuracy and efficiency of our proposed method, and future research can try to use different neural network algorithms to improve the performance of the model.

Author Contributions: Funding acquisition, conceptualization and methodology, L.L.; device development, H.C.; experiments, data analysis and writing—original draft preparation, J.Y.; writing—review and editing, L.L. and M.P. All authors have read and agreed to the published version of the manuscript.

Funding: This research was supported by the National Natural Science Foundation of Shanghai, China (Funding Agency Project No. 19ZR1418800). The authors are grateful for their financial support.

Institutional Review Board Statement: Not applicable.

Informed Consent Statement: Not applicable.

Data Availability Statement: Data is contained within the article.

Acknowledgments: The authors would like to acknowledge the support and facilities provided by the Department of Civil Engineering, School of Mechanics and Engineering Science at Shanghai University to carry out the research. The assistance provided by Shuying Luo, Runzhi Yang, Yu Lu and Baihao Fang in conducting the simulated construction experiment is gratefully acknowledged by the authors.

Conflicts of Interest: The authors declare no conflict of interest.

References

1. Paules, C.I.; Marston, H.D.; Fauci, A.S. Coronavirus Infections—More Than Just the Common Cold. *J. Am. Med Assoc.* **2020**, *323*, 707–708. [CrossRef]
2. Lippi, G.; Sanchis-Gomar, F.; Henry, B.M. COVID-19: Unravelling the clinical progression of nature's virtually perfect biological weapon. *Ann. Transl. Med.* **2020**, *8*, 693. [CrossRef] [PubMed]
3. Viswanathan, M.; Kahwati, L.; Jahn, B.; Giger, K.; Gartlehner, G. Universal screening for SARS-CoV-2 infection: A rapid review. *Cochrane Database Syst. Rev. Online* **2020**, *9*. [CrossRef]
4. Zhang, J.; Liu, S.; Zhu, B. Fever screening methods in public places during the COVID-19 pandemic. *J. Hosp. Infect.* **2021**, *109*, 123–124. [CrossRef] [PubMed]
5. Lippi, G.; Mattiuzzi, C.; Henry, B. Is Body Temperature Mass Screening a Reliable and Safe Option for Preventing COVID-19 Spread? *SSRN Electron. J.* **2021**. [CrossRef]
6. Kodam, S.; Bharathgoud, N.; Ramachandran, H. A review on smart wearable devices for soldier safety during battlefield using WSN technology. *Mater. Today Proc.* **2020**, *33*, 4578–4585. [CrossRef]
7. Sawant, P.; Godse, S.; Thigale, V.; Kasar, K. Arduino Based Smart Helmet for Coal Mine Safety. In Proceedings of the 2nd International Conference on Communication & Information Processing (ICCIP) 2020, Pune, India, 8 July 2020.
8. Yong, J.A.; Kang, M.; Lee, T.G. Study on Remedies of Convergence Design for Personalized Fire Helmets. *J. Korean Soc. Precis. Eng.* **2016**, *33*, 371–376.
9. Altamura, A.; Inchingolo, F.; Mevoli, G.; Boccadoro, P. SAFE: Smart helmet for Advanced Factory Environment. *Internet Technol. Lett.* **2019**, *2*, e86. [CrossRef]
10. Aliyev, A.; Zhou, B.P. HeadgearX: A connected smart helmet for construction sites. In Proceedings of the 2020 ACM International Joint Conference on Pervasive and Ubiquitous Computing and Proceedings of the 2020 ACM International Symposium on Wearable Computers, New York, NY, USA, 14 September 2020.
11. Dell'Isola, G.B.; Cosentini, E.; Canale, L.; Ficco, G.; Dell'Isola, M. Noncontact Body Temperature Measurement: Uncertainty Evaluation and Screening Decision Rule to Prevent the Spread of COVID-19. *Sensors* **2021**, *21*, 346. [CrossRef] [PubMed]
12. Tanaka, Y.; Matsunaga, D.; Tajima, T.; Seyama, M. Skin-attachable Sensor for Core Body Temperature Monitoring. *IEEE Sens. J.* **2021**, *14*, 1.
13. Xu, K.; Zhao, L.; Yuan, Y. Measurement error analysis and compensation experiment research for medicinal infrared thermometer. *Electron. Meas. Technol.* **2014**, *37*, 104–118.
14. Guo, Z.; Dai, S.; Liu, Z.; You, C.; Cheng, Y.; Yu, L. Research on application of polynomial fitting technique in rotary kiln infrared temperature measurement system. *Infrared Phys. Technol.* **2016**, *79*, 160–164. [CrossRef]
15. Wei, S.; Qin, W.; Han, L.; Cheng, F. The research on compensation algorithm of infrared temperature measurement based on intelligent sensors. *Clust. Comput.* **2019**, *22*, 6091–6100. [CrossRef]
16. Shajkofci, A. Correction of human forehead temperature variations measured by non-contact infrared thermometer. *IEEE Sens. J.* **2021**, *99*, 1. [CrossRef]
17. Ai, H.; Hu, M.; Liu, H.; Yu, H.; Wang, G.; Wang, W. Development of ear cavity infrared thermometer based on thermal radiation. *Sens. Microsyst.* **2020**, *39*, 94–96.
18. Pan, D.; Jiang, Z.; Maldague, X.; Gui, W. Research on the Influence of Multiple Interference Factors on Infrared Temperature Measurement. *IEEE Sens. J.* **2021**, *21*, 10546–10555.
19. Ning, B.; Wu, Y. Research on Non-Contact Infrared Temperature Measurement. In Proceedings of the 2010 International Conference on Computational Intelligence and Software Engineering, Wuhan, China, 10–12 December 2010.
20. Shu, Q.; Dai, S.; Nie, H.; Yi, W. Dynamic temperature compensation model based on nonuniform temperature field change. *Infrared Phys. Technol.* **2019**, *101*, 25–31. [CrossRef]
21. Church, J.S.; Hegadoren, P.R.; Paetkau, M.J.; Miller, C.C.; Regev-Shoshani, G.; Schaefer, A.L.; Schwartzkopf-Genswein, K.S. Influence of environmental factors on infrared eye temperature measurements in cattle. *Res. Vet. Sci.* **2014**, *96*, 220–226. [CrossRef] [PubMed]
22. Kamada, Y.; Miyamoto, N.; Yamakage, M.; Tsujiguchi, N.; Namiki, A. Utility of an infrared ear thermometer as an intraoperative core temperature monitor. *Masui Jpn. J. Anesthesiol.* **1999**, *48*, 1121.
23. Gonzalez, A.J.; Teller, C.; Andersen, S.L.; Jensen, F.B. Influence of body temperature on the development of fatigue during prolonged exercise in the heat. *J. Appl. Physiol.* **1999**, *86*, 1032–1039. [CrossRef]
24. Campa, F.; Gatterer, H.; Lukaski, H.; Toselli, S. Stabilizing Bioimpedance-Vector-Analysis Measures With a 10-Minute Cold Shower After Running Exercise to Enable Assessment of Body Hydration. *Int. J. Sports Physiol. Perform.* **2019**, *14*, 1006–1009. [CrossRef]
25. Emerson, D.M.; Chen, S.C.; Kelly, M.R.; Parnell, B. Non-steroidal anti-inflammatory drugs on core body temperature during exercise: A systematic review. *J. Exerc. Sci. Fit. JESF* **2021**, *19*, 127–133. [CrossRef]
26. Werth, J.; Sigman, M.S. Linear Regression Model Development for Analysis of Asymmetric Copper Bisoxazoline Catalysis. *ACS Catal.* **2021**, *11*, 3916–3922. [CrossRef] [PubMed]
27. Cheng, J. Residential land leasing and price under public land ownership. *J. Urban Plan. Dev.* **2021**, *147*, 05021009. [CrossRef]
28. Cheng, J. Analysis of commercial land leasing of the district governments of Beijing in China. *Land Use Policy* **2021**, *100*, 104881. [CrossRef]

29. Cheng, J. Data analysis of the factors influencing the industrial land leasing in Shanghai based on mathematical models. *Math. Probl. Eng.* **2020**, *2020*, 9346863. [CrossRef]
30. Cheng, J. Mathematical Models and Data Analysis of Residential Land Leasing Behavior of District Governments of Beijing in China. *Mathematics* **2021**, *9*, 2314. [CrossRef]
31. Mancini, M.; Taavitsainen, V.; Toscano, G. Comparative study between Partial Least Squares and Rational function Ridge Regression models for the prediction of moisture content of woodchip samples using a handheld spectrophotometer. *J. Chemom.* **2021**, *35*, e3337. [CrossRef]
32. Panzone, L.; Ulph, A.; Areal, F.; Grippo, V. A ridge regression approach to estimate the relationship between landfill taxation and waste collection and disposal in England. *Waste Manag.* **2021**, *129*, 95–110. [CrossRef] [PubMed]
33. Ataman, M.G.; Sarıyer, G. Predicting waiting and treatment times in emergency departments using ordinal logistic regression models. *Am. J. Emerg. Med.* **2021**, *46*, 45–50. [CrossRef] [PubMed]
34. Cheng, J. Analyzing the factors influencing the choice of the government on leasing different types of land uses: Evidence from Shanghai of China. *Land Use Policy* **2020**, *90*, 104303. [CrossRef]
35. He, S.; Wang, Y. A Modified APLS for Key Performance Indicator-Related Diagnosis in Case of Outliers. In Proceedings of the Chinese Automation Congress (CAC), Jinan, China, 20–22 October 2017.
36. Zhang, J.; Lou, Y. Water Level Prediction Based on Improved Grey RBF Neural Network Model. In Proceedings of the 2016 IEEE Advanced Information Management, Communicates, Electronic and Automation Control Conference (IMCEC), Xi'an, China, 3–5 October 2016.
37. Herawati, N.; Nisa, K.; Setiawan, E. Regularized Multiple Regression Methods to Deal with Severe Multicollinearity. *Int. J. Stat. Appl.* **2018**, *8*, 167–172.
38. Evans, M. A partial least squares solution to the problem of multicollinearity when predicting the high temperature properties of 1Cr–1Mo–0.25V steel using parametric models. *J. Mater. Sci.* **2012**, *47*, 2712–2724. [CrossRef]
39. Cai, T.; Ju, C.; Yang, X. Comparison of Ridge Regression and Partial Least Squares Regression for Estimating Above-Ground Biomass with Landsat Images and Terrain Data in Mu Us Sandy Land, China. *Arid. Land Res. Manag.* **2009**, *23*, 248–261. [CrossRef]
40. Polat, E.; Gunay, S. The comparison of partial least squares regression, principal component regression and ridge regression with multiple linear regression for predicting pm10 concentration level based on meteorological parameters. *J. Data Ence* **2015**, *13*, 663–692.
41. Fita, K.; Arief, W. Principal Component Analysis (PCA) untuk Mengatasi Multikolinieritas terhadap Faktor Angka Kejadian Pneumonia Balita di Jawa Timur Tahun 2014. *J. Biom. Dan Kependud.* **2018**, *6*, 89.
42. Khedhe, L.; Ramirez, J.; Gorriz, J.M.; Brahim, A.; Segovia, F. Early diagnosis of Alzheimers disease based on partialleast squares, principal component analysis and support vector machine using segmented MRI images. *Neurocomputing* **2015**, *151*, 139–150. [CrossRef]
43. Li, M.; Verma, B. An Improved RBF Neural Network Approach to Nonlinear Curve Fitting. *Adv. Comput. Intell.* **2015**, *9095*, 262–275.
44. Wang, G.; Wu, J.; Yin, S.; Yu, L.; Wang, J. Comparison between BP Neural Network and Multiple Linear Regression Method. In Proceedings of the Information Computing and Applications—First International Conference, ICICA 2010, Tangshan, China, 15–18 October 2010.
45. An, Y.; Wang, X.; Qu, Z.; Liao, T.; Wu, L.; Nan, Z. Stable temperature calibration method of fiber Bragg grating based on radial basis function neural network. *Opt. Eng.* **2019**, *58*, 1. [CrossRef]
46. Wu, W.; Wang, J.; Cheng, M.; Li, Z. Convergence analysis of online gradient method for BP neural networks. *Neural Netw.* **2019**, *24*, 91–98. [CrossRef]
47. Sun, Y.; Yang, H. The Forecasting Method for the Furnace Bottom Temperature and Carbon Content of Submerged Arc Furnace Based on Improved BP Neural Network. In Proceedings of the International Conference on Computer, Mechatronics, Control and Electronic Engineering, Changchun, China, 24–26 August 2010.
48. Qiu, J.W.; Liu, Z.G.; Zhou, L.; Qin, R.X. Prediction Model of Gas Quantity Emitted from Coal Face Based on PCA-GA-BP Neural Network and Its Application. *J. Power Technol.* **2017**, *97*, 169–178.
49. Habshah, M.; Saroje, S.; Sohel, R. Collinearity diagnostics of binary logistic regression model. *J. Interdiscip. Math.* **2010**, *13*, 253–267.
50. Aylin, A. Multicollinearity. *Wiley Interdiscip. Rev. Comput. Stat.* **2010**, *2*, 370–374. [CrossRef]
51. Adler, J.; Parmryd, I. Quantifying colocalization by correlation: The Pearson correlation coefficient is superior to the Mander's overlap coefficient. *Cytom. Part A* **2010**, *77*, 33–42. [CrossRef]
52. Gilbert, C.L. The Diagnosis of Multicollinearity. *Oxf. Bull. Econ. Stat.* **2010**, *40*, 87–91. [CrossRef]
53. O'brien, R.M. A Caution Regarding Rules of Thumb for Variance Inflation Factors. *Qual. Quant.* **2007**, *41*, 673–690. [CrossRef]
54. Wold, S.; Sjöström, M. Lennart Eriksson, PLS-regression: A basic tool of chemometrics. *Chemom. Intell. Lab. Syst.* **2001**, *58*, 109–130. [CrossRef]
55. Buscema, M. Back Propagation Neural Networks. *Subst. Use Misuse* **1998**, *33*, 233–270. [CrossRef]
56. Torrontegui, E.; Garcia-Ripoll, J. Universal quantum perceptron as efficient unitary approximators. *Europhys. Lett.* **2018**, *125*, 30004. [CrossRef]

57. Ilunga, M.; Stephenson, D. Infilling streamflow data using feed-forward back-propagation (BP) artificial neural networks: Application of standard BP and pseudo Mac Laurin power series BP techniques. *Water SA* **2005**, *31*, 171–176. [CrossRef]
58. Langer, S. Approximating smooth functions by deep neural networks with sigmoid activation function. *J. Multivar. Anal.* **2021**, *182*, 104696. [CrossRef]

Article

Numerical Modeling on Crack Propagation Based on a Multi-Grid Bond-Based Dual-Horizon Peridynamics

Zili Dai [1], Jinwei Xie [1], Zhitang Lu [2], Shiwei Qin [1] and Lin Wang [3,4,*]

1. Department of Civil Engineering, Shanghai University, 99 Shangda Road, Shanghai 200444, China; zilidai@shu.edu.cn (Z.D.); xiejinwei@shu.edu.cn (J.X.); 10002358qsw@shu.edu.cn (S.Q.)
2. School of Resources and Environmental Engineering, Hefei University of Technology, Hefei 230009, China; zhitang.lu@hfut.edu.cn
3. SGIDI Engineering Consulting (Group) Co., Ltd., Shanghai 200093, China
4. Department of Geotechnical Engineering, College of Civil Engineering, Tongji University, Shanghai 200092, China
* Correspondence: 1410024@tongji.edu.cn; Tel.: +86-188-1787-9593

Citation: Dai, Z.; Xie, J.; Lu, Z.; Qin, S.; Wang, L. Numerical Modeling on Crack Propagation Based on a Multi-Grid Bond-Based Dual-Horizon Peridynamics. *Mathematics* **2021**, *9*, 2848. https://doi.org/10.3390/math9222848

Academic Editor: Efstratios Tzirtzilakis

Received: 15 September 2021
Accepted: 8 November 2021
Published: 10 November 2021

Publisher's Note: MDPI stays neutral with regard to jurisdictional claims in published maps and institutional affiliations.

Copyright: © 2021 by the authors. Licensee MDPI, Basel, Switzerland. This article is an open access article distributed under the terms and conditions of the Creative Commons Attribution (CC BY) license (https://creativecommons.org/licenses/by/4.0/).

Abstract: Peridynamics (PD) is a novel nonlocal theory of continuum mechanics capable of describing crack formation and propagation without defining any fracture rules in advance. In this study, a multi-grid bond-based dual-horizon peridynamics (DH-PD) model is presented, which includes varying horizon sizes and can avoid spurious wave reflections. This model incorporates the volume correction, surface correction, and a technique of nonuniformity discretization to improve calculation accuracy and efficiency. Two benchmark problems are simulated to verify the reliability of the proposed model with the effect of the volume correction and surface correction on the computational accuracy confirmed. Two numerical examples, the fracture of an L-shaped concrete specimen and the mixed damage of a double-edged notched specimen, are simulated and analyzed. The simulation results are compared against experimental data, the numerical solution of a traditional PD model, and the output from a finite element model. The comparisons verify the calculation accuracy of the corrected DH-PD model and its advantages over some other models like the traditional PD model.

Keywords: peridynamics; dual-horizon; crack propagation; variable horizon; multi-grid

1. Introduction

Material fracture is a classical problem in solid mechanics [1]. In contrast to experimental research, numerical simulations provide a more efficient approach to understanding material fractures since they eliminate the limitations of complex specimen preparation, test environment conditions, and loading systems. The finite element method (FEM) is one of the commonly used numerical methods for solving fracture problems [2,3]. However, the crack-induced spatial discontinuities are not compatible with the partial differential equations in classical FEM models [4]. To deal with this problem, some remeshing techniques were incorporated into FEM models, which were usually cumbersome and time consuming [5,6]. Recently, the extended finite element method (XFEM) was proposed to solve the intermittent problems of cracks, holes, and inclusions by introducing additional nodal degrees of freedom and local strengthening functions [7,8]. Besides, the element erosion technique [9,10] and the phase field method [11,12] were proposed to simulate the problems of crack propagation with different levels of success. However, these methods are not applicable to simulate complex multi-crack extended penetration problems in three dimensions [13].

In recent years, meshless methods have been developed and applied in various engineering fields. They can simulate complex discontinuity without the remeshing process. For example, Cheng and Li [14] proposed a complex variable meshless method for fracture problems. Gao and Cheng [15] developed a meshless manifold method based on the complex variable moving least-squares approximation and the finite cover theory for fracture problems. Khazal et al. [16] presented an extended element free Galerkin method (XEFGM) for fracture analysis of functionally graded materials. In addition, the discrete element method (DEM) is suitable for simulating crack formation and propagation based on the discontinuity assumption. For instance, Kou et al. [17] adopted the DEM to investigate the dynamic crack propagation and branching in brittle solids. Owayo et al. [18] investigated the formation and propagation of cracks in cement-based materials via DEM simulations. Although some promising achievements have been obtained through the above researches, DEM has limitations when describing the mechanical behavior of the continuous material.

More recently, Silling et al. [19,20] proposed a new nonlocal theory of continuum mechanics called peridynamics (PD) for solving material fracture problems. It describes such a phenomenon by means of the failure of bonds linking material points. This method replaces the differential form of traditional balance equations with an integral form to avoid the singularity problem arising from the derivations at discontinuities. Therefore, PD is appropriate to describe the crack propagation in a unified framework. Owing to these advantages, it has been successfully applied to crack propagation problems [21,22], composite material damage [23,24], fluid mechanics and acoustics [25], and heat conduction analysis [26,27] etc. There are several kinds of peridynamics, such as bond-based PD [19], state-based PD [28], and element-based PD [29] etc., and they can be easily coupled with other numerical methods to deal with the interaction between different materials, such as PD-FEM [30], PD-SPH [31], and PD-DEM [32].

In traditional PD, the problem domain should be discretized into a series of particles with the same size and uniform distribution, thus limiting its application to complex problems such as multiscale analysis, multi-material problems, and adaptive analysis. Dipasquale et al. [33] proposed an adaptive refinement-coarsening method and applied it to a one-dimensional elastic wave propagation simulation. However, the problem of spurious stress waves was not completely solved in this model. Bobaru et al. [34] introduced adaptive refinement algorithms for peridynamics to deal with static and dynamic elasticity problems in 1D. Shojaei et al. [35] proposed an adaptive refinement strategy to use a variable grid size in a peridynamic model, which was verified to be effective and efficient. This approach was then successfully applied to simulate the fracture of a ceramic disk under central thermal shock [36]. Ren et al. [37,38] proposed a dual-horizon peridynamics (DH-PD) model incorporating non-uniform particle distribution and variable horizons to completely solve the problem of spurious stress waves. Wang et al. [39] derived state-based DH-PD governing equations using the Euler-Lagrange description, and they analyzed the dispersion characteristics of the model.

In this study, a particle volume correction and a surface correction are introduced in the DH-PD model to improve the calculation accuracy. In addition, the computational efficiency of this model is increased by incorporating a multi-grid technique. Two benchmark problems are simulated to verify the calculation accuracy of this model. Finally, this model is applied to analyze two numerical examples to validate the model's reliability and applicability.

2. Peridynamics Theory
2.1. Traditional Peridynamics Theory

In traditional PD, the object occupying the spatial domain R is discretized into a series of closely arranged material points, as shown in Figure 1. The circular (spherical) region around the material point, $\mathbf{x}$, with itself as the center point and δ as the radius is called the horizon, H_δ. The interaction force between the material point, $\mathbf{x}$, with any other neighboring point, $\mathbf{x}'$, in the horizon ($\mathbf{x}' \in H_\delta$) is called a pairwise force (bond). At any moment, t, the governing equation for any material point, $\mathbf{x}$, is as follows [19]:

$$\rho \frac{\partial^2 \mathbf{u}(\mathbf{x},t)}{\partial t^2} = \int_{H_\mathbf{x}} \mathbf{f}(\boldsymbol{\eta}, \boldsymbol{\xi}) dV_{\mathbf{x}'} + b(\mathbf{x},t) \, \forall \boldsymbol{\eta}, \boldsymbol{\xi}. \tag{1}$$

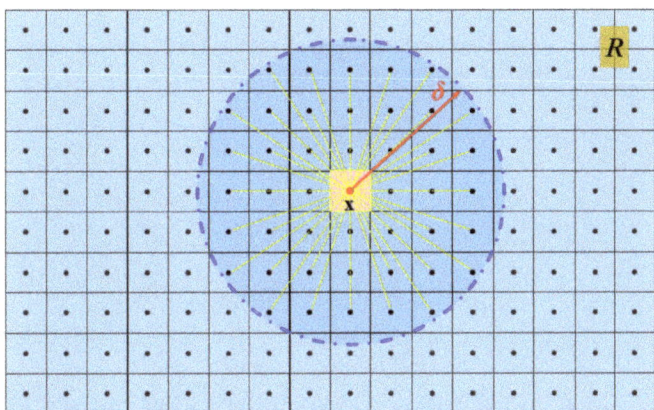

Figure 1. Peridynamics model.

In Equation (1), **f** is the pairwise bond force between the material point **x** and its neighboring point **x′**, ρ is the density of the material, **b** is the body force vector, and **u** is the displacement vector. The integration domain, H_x, is the horizon of material point, **x**, in the reference configuration, mathematically, as $H_x = \{x' \in R|\ \|x' - x\| \leq \delta\}$. Additionally, δ is the radius of the nonlocal horizon of the material point, which is constant for each material point in the traditional PD theory. Finally, $\xi = x' - x$ and $\eta = u' - u$ denote the relative position vector and the relative displacement vector with neighboring particles in the reference configuration, respectively.

The key to building a PD model is to find an appropriate pairwise force function, **f**. Theoretically, any function that satisfies the linear admissibility condition and the angular admissibility condition can be a pairwise force function. In a bond-based PD model, the direction of the pairwise force vector is parallel to the displacement vector, $\xi + \eta$. For microelastic materials, the pairwise force function in PD model is given by

$$\mathbf{f}(\eta, \xi) = \mu c(\delta) s(\eta, \xi) \frac{\eta + \xi}{\|\eta + \xi\|}. \tag{2}$$

In Equation (2), $c(\delta)$ denotes the microelastic modulus, which can be derived from the strain energy equivalence principle, and expressed in terms of E and ν:

$$c(\delta) = \begin{cases} \frac{2E}{A\delta^2} & \text{1D,} \\ \frac{3E}{\pi\delta^3(1-\nu)} & \text{planestress,} \\ \frac{3E}{\pi\delta^3(1+\nu)(1-2\nu)} & \text{planestrain,} \\ \frac{3E}{\pi\delta^4(1-2\nu)} & \text{3D.} \end{cases} \tag{3}$$

Additionally, s represents the bond stretch ratio between two material points, as defined by:

$$s(\eta, \xi) = \frac{\|\eta + \xi\| - \|\xi\|}{\|\xi\|}. \tag{4}$$

When s is greater than the critical elongation ratio, s_0, of the material, the bond between these two points is considered to be broken, and the corresponding pairwise force disappears. The critical elongation ratio, s_0, can be determined by the relationship given by Ren et al. [37]:

$$s_0(\delta) = \begin{cases} \sqrt{4\pi G_c/(9E\delta)} & \text{planestress,} \\ \sqrt{5\pi G_c/(12E\delta)} & \text{planestrain,} \\ \sqrt{5G_c/(6E\delta)} & \text{3D,} \end{cases} \tag{5}$$

where G_c is the critical energy release rate of the material.

The variable μ in Equation (2) is a historical parameter describing whether the bond is broken. In this case, μ is defined as:

$$\mu(t,\eta,\xi) = \begin{cases} 1, & s < s_0, \\ 0, & \text{other}. \end{cases} \quad (6)$$

According to the above criterion for bond breakage, the degree of damage at the local material point, x, can be expressed as:

$$\varphi(\mathbf{x},t) = 1 - \frac{\int_{H_x} \mu(t,\eta,\xi) dV_{x'}}{\int_{H_x} dV_{x'}}. \quad (7)$$

2.2. Dual-Horizon Peridynamics Theory

In traditional PD theory, the force acting on the particle x is the sum of the pairwise forces from all the neighboring particles in the horizon. Therefore, the horizon must be constant for all particles to ensure that the force always appears in pairs. If the horizons are variable, as shown in Figure 2, particle x is subjected to the force $\mathbf{f}(\eta,\xi)$ from the particle $\mathbf{x}'$ in its horizon. However, $\mathbf{x}'$ is not subjected to the force from x because its horizon does not include particle x. In this case, the existence of such an unbalanced force destroys the balance of linear momentum and angular momentum and results in ghost forces and spurious wave reflections during the simulation.

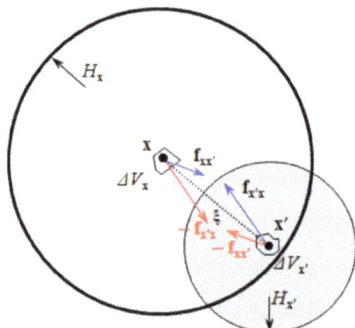

Figure 2. Force vector in peridynamics with varying horizons.

Recently, Ren et al. [37] proposed the concept of dual-horizon, which can solve the spurious wave reflection problem. The dual-horizon is a union of points, the horizons of which include x. It is expressed, mathematically, as $H'_x = \{\mathbf{x}' \| \mathbf{x} \in H_{x'}, \mathbf{x}' \in R\}$. The superscript prime of H'_x denotes a dual-horizon, and the subscript x denotes the object particle. Therefore, dual-horizon can be interpreted as a set of horizons that belong to particles that can include x in their horizons. In the DH-PD theory, a particle is subjected to two types of forces. The first one is the force from a neighboring particle in the horizon. The other one is the force from the particle in the dual-horizon. Furthermore, these two different types of forces are independent of each other, and the bond and dual bond can break independently in the fracture models.

In Figure 2, H_x is the horizon of particle x, where the bond $\mathbf{xx}'$ will exert a direct force $\mathbf{f}_{xx'}$ on x, and $\mathbf{x}'$ will be subjected to the reaction force $-\mathbf{f}_{xx'}$ according to Newton's third law. Likewise, the dual bond $\mathbf{x}'\mathbf{x}$ will exert a direct force $\mathbf{f}_{x'x}$ on $\mathbf{x}'$, and x will be subject to the reaction force $-\mathbf{f}_{\mathbf{x}'\mathbf{x}}$. The time-dependent governing equations of DH-PD [40] are given as follows:

$$\rho\frac{\partial^2 \mathbf{u}(\mathbf{x},t)}{\partial t^2} = \int_{H_\mathbf{x}} \mathbf{f}_{\mathbf{x}\mathbf{x}'}(\boldsymbol{\eta},\boldsymbol{\xi})\mathrm{d}V_{\mathbf{x}'} - \int_{H'_\mathbf{x}} \mathbf{f}_{\mathbf{x}'\mathbf{x}}(-\boldsymbol{\eta},-\boldsymbol{\xi})\mathrm{d}V_{\mathbf{x}'} + b(\mathbf{x},t), \qquad (8)$$

$$\begin{cases} \mathbf{f}_{\mathbf{x}\mathbf{x}'} = \mu c(\mathbf{x}',\delta_{\mathbf{x}'})s\frac{\boldsymbol{\eta}+\boldsymbol{\xi}}{\|\boldsymbol{\eta}+\boldsymbol{\xi}\|}, \\ \mathbf{f}_{\mathbf{x}'\mathbf{x}} = -\mu c(\mathbf{x},\delta_{\mathbf{x}})s\frac{\boldsymbol{\eta}+\boldsymbol{\xi}}{\|\boldsymbol{\eta}+\boldsymbol{\xi}\|}. \end{cases} \qquad (9)$$

The micromodulus, c, in Equation (9) depends on the particle spacing of the material point $\mathbf{x}$ and is half of the corresponding micromodulus in traditional PD, see Equation (3).

3. DH-PD Numerical Method

Figure 3 shows the program flowchart of the DH-PD model, which contains the pre-processing module, particle generation module, boundary treatment module, and damage degree calculation module. The C++ programming language is used to write the program code in this study.

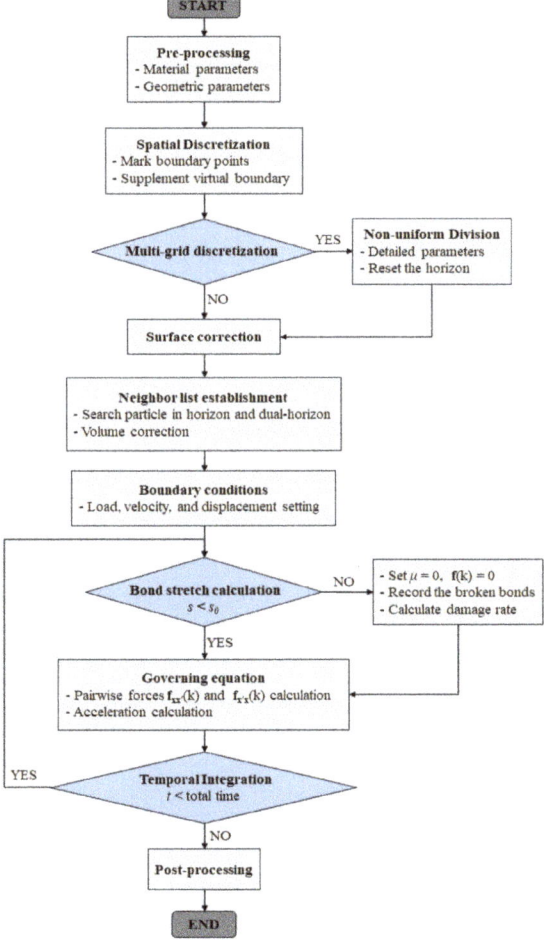

Figure 3. Program flowchart of the DH-PD model.

3.1. Non-Uniform Discretization

The problem domain in the PD model is discretized into a series of particles with the material information in the reference configuration. There are no elements or other geometrical connections between the particles. The size of each particle is uniformly arranged and contains a certain volume. The spatial information of each particle is characterized by the geometric center. Horizons of the particles in the DH-PD model are variable, so, finer discretization with smaller horizons is always used in the concerning region, such as the damage area. Additionally, the variability of the horizons requires coarser particles for the unimportant areas.

The discretization is carried out layer by layer. First, the domain is discretized into a series of coarse particles with the same spacing. Then, the second-level discretization is carried out in the area with high stress concentration. The coordinates of the second-level particles can be determined based on their geometric relationship with the first-level particles. For example, a two-dimensional plane consists of four particles (P_0, P_1, P_2, P_3) with a volume of V and a spacing of Δx, as shown in Figure 4. For the second-level discretization, a coarse particle (P_1) with the coordinates (x_1, y_1) can be divided into four fine particles (P_{10}, P_{11}, P_{12}, P_{13}), with a volume of 0.25 V and a spacing of 0.5 Δx. Therefore, the coordinates of the fine particle P_{11} are ($x_1 + \Delta x/4$, $y_1 + \Delta x/4$). In the same way, the second-level particle (P_{11}) can be divided into four third-level particles (P_{110}, P_{111}, P_{112}, P_{113}). The volume of the third-level particle is $V/16$, and the particle spacing is $\Delta x/4$. Based on this discretization, the coordinates of these finer particles can be easily determined by their geometrical relationships.

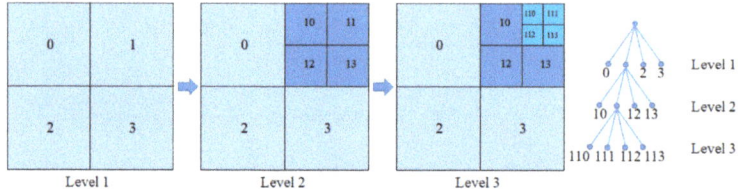

Figure 4. Layer-by-layer discretization in DH-PD model.

It is worth noting that, when the size difference between adjacent particles is too big, the finer particles cannot include any coarse particles in their horizons, which may result in bond deficiency and lead to unexpected failure near the interface. Therefore, in the presented model, the size difference between adjacent particles is suggested to be smaller than the radius of the finer particle's horizon.

3.2. Volume Correction and Surface Correction

In PD theory, the problem domain is discretized into a series of particles, and each particle interacts with the neighboring particles in its horizon. However, some particles are located on the boundary and are not completely included in the horizon, as shown in Figure 5. Therefore, the model requires corrections with regards to the volumes of these particles when calculating the pairwise forces. For the multilevel discretization in DH-PD, the horizons of different particles vary with particle size, the particle volume can be corrected as:

$$V_j = \begin{cases} \Delta x^3 & (\|\xi\| \leq \delta - 0.5\Delta x), \\ [(\delta + 0.5\Delta x - \|\xi\|)/\Delta x]\Delta x^3 & (\delta - 0.5\Delta x < \|\xi\| \leq \delta), \\ 0 & \text{otherwise.} \end{cases} \quad (10)$$

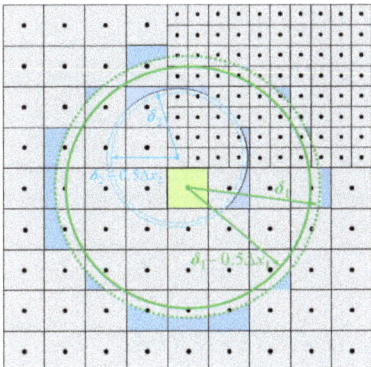

Figure 5. Volume correction for the collocation points inside the horizon.

For the particles near the boundary of the problem domain, the number of neighboring particles in the horizon is lower than other particles, as shown in Figure 6. Therefore, the stiffness of the particles near the boundary is falsely reduced [41]. To deal with this problem, Scabbia et al. [42] presented an effective approach to mitigate the surface effect in state-based Peridynamics. Madenci and Oterkus [43] reconstructed the strain energy density near the boundary through the force density method and energy method to obtain the corresponding correction coefficients. The surface correction factor can be obtained by exerting a simple fictitious load to the object along the direction of the reference coordinate system. Based on this, the ratio of the strain energy densities calculated through the classical continuum mechanics theory and PD theory can be used as a valid surface correction factor.

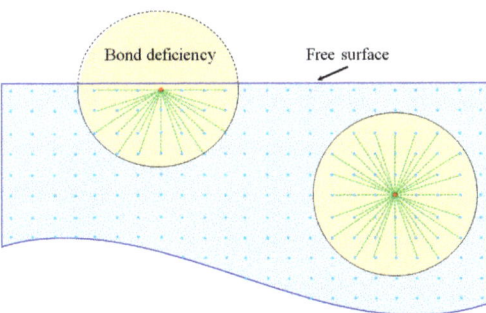

Figure 6. Bond deficiency for the material points close to the free surfaces.

3.3. Explicit Time Integration

Explicit time integration is the simplest solution for the PD equations in dynamics simulations. In this method, acceleration and velocity are approximatively determined by the finite difference form of the displacement [44]:

$$\ddot{\mathbf{u}}_{(k)}^{n} = \frac{\dot{\mathbf{u}}_{(k)}^{n+1} - \dot{\mathbf{u}}_{(k)}^{n}}{\Delta t}, \tag{11}$$

$$\dot{\mathbf{u}}_{(k)}^{n+1} = \ddot{\mathbf{u}}_{(k)}^{n}\Delta t + \dot{\mathbf{u}}_{(k)}^{n}. \tag{12}$$

In Equations (11) and (12), **u**, **u̇**, **ü** define the displacement, velocity, and acceleration vector, respectively. In addition, Δt represents the time increment, k denotes the particle number, and n equals the time step number. With this, displacement can be updated as:

$$\mathbf{u}_{(k)}^{n+1} = \dot{\mathbf{u}}_{(k)}^{n} \Delta t + \mathbf{u}_{(k)}^{n}. \tag{13}$$

Restricting the time step increment ensures the stability of the time integration, because the computational stability decreases as the time step increases. Silling and Askari [20] proposed a relationship,

$$\Delta t = \sqrt{\frac{2\rho}{\sum_p \Delta V_p C_p}}, \tag{14}$$

to determine the critical time step in a PD model, where p is the number of the neighboring particles in the horizon, ΔV_p is the volume of the neighboring particle, and C_p is the microelastic modulus of the material.

4. Numerical Examples and Discussions

In this section, two benchmark tests are simulated to verify the accuracy and stability of the corrected DH-PD model: longitudinal vibration of a bar and wave reflection in a rectangular plate. The numerical results are compared with the analytical solutions and the finite difference method (FDM) results to validate the computational accuracy and the feasibility of the non-uniform discretization. Then, the corrected DH-PD model simulates two numerical examples: fracture of an L-shaped concrete specimen and mixed damage of a double-edged notched (DEN) specimen. The applicability and unique advantages of this model in crack propagation modeling are discussed.

4.1. Benchmark Problem 1: Longitudinal Vibration of a Bar

Figure 7 shows a bar with a fixed end on the left. The set parameters for the bar include the length of the bar, L = 1 m, the elastic modulus, E = 200 GPa, its Poisson's ratio, ν = 0.33, and the density, ρ = 7850 kg/m³. The initial velocity of each material point is $v_x(x, t) = 0$, and the initial displacement gradient is defined as:

$$\frac{\partial u_x}{\partial x} = \varepsilon H(\Delta t - t), \tag{15}$$

where H is a step function, and ε = 0.001 is the initial strain.

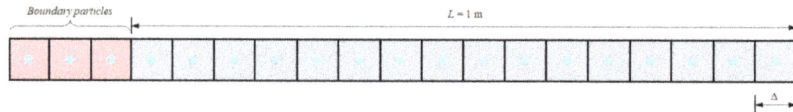

Figure 7. Geometry of a bar and its discretization.

The bar is discretized into 1000 particles with a particle size of Δx = 0.001 m. Three fictitious boundary particles are fixed at the left side of the bar for the enforcement of displacement constraints. "No-fail zone" is commonly used for some applications under extreme loading conditions to avoid unexpected failure between the particles close to the external boundaries. For the loading conditions in the numerical examples presented in this paper, no-fail zone is not used. The computational time step is set as Δt = 0.2 µs, and the horizon associated with each particle is set as $3\Delta x$. The particle with the initial position of x_0 = 0.5 m is selected as the analysis object. Its displacement time history is compared with the analytical solution [44], as shown in Figure 8. The expected longitudinal vibration is successfully captured by the DH-PD model after the volume correction and surface correction. Overall, the numerical results are consistent with the analytical solution, thus verifying the accuracy of the presented DH-PD model.

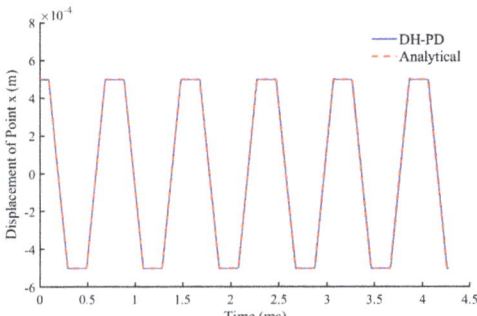

Figure 8. Variation of the displacement of the particle numbered 500 with time.

An error analysis is conducted, below, to assess the effect of the volume correction and surface correction on the calculation accuracy. The parameters are set $\|Error\| = \|u - u_{analytic}\|$ (shown in Figure 9), and the analysis shows that the introduction of the volume correction and surface correction reduces the error to 0.01 mm.

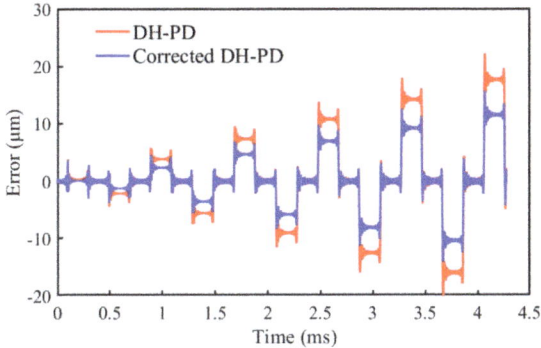

Figure 9. Errors of the DH-PD model with and without correction.

Figure 10 shows the convergence curves of DH-PD and corrected DH-PD models at $t = 4.0$ ms. It indicates that the L_2 error in the displacement of the corrected DH-PD model is smaller than that of the DH-PD model, thus verifying that the volume correction and surface correction can improve the computational accuracy to some extent. Figure 10b shows that horizon size has little effect on the computational accuracy for the corrected DH-PH model in this case study. According to Silling and Askari [20], the horizon radius slightly greater than $3\Delta x$ usually works well. Therefore, the horizon radius is fixed at 3.015 times the particle size in this work.

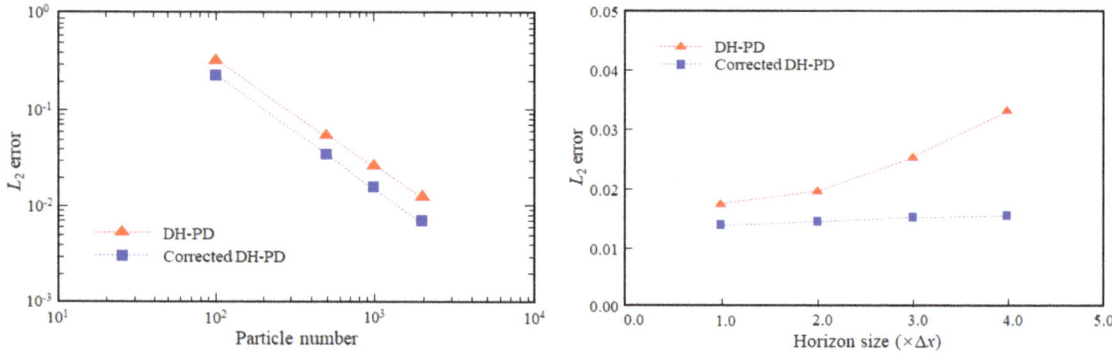

(a) Convergence curve with different discretization.

(b) Convergence curve with different horizon sizes.

Figure 10. Convergence curves in L_2 error norm of DH-PD and corrected DH-PD models.

4.2. Benchmark Problem 2: Wave Reflection in a Rectangular Plate

Figure 11 shows the geometric size of a rectangular plate in the initial state of: length, $L = 10$ m, width, $W = 1$ m, elastic modulus, $E = 10$ GPa, density, $\rho = 2500$ kg/m^3, and Poisson's ratio, $\nu = 0.33$. The left end of the plate is fixed, and the right end is assigned a velocity boundary, $v(t)$, based on Equation (16). In Equation (16), $H(t_0 - t)$ is the Heaviside function, and $t_0 = 2$ ms is the duration of the velocity boundary. The plate is dispersed into 1600 particles, and there is a dense area in the middle section of the plate with the following PD parameters: matter point dispersion spacing ($\Delta x = 0.1$ m), particle spacing in the encrypted region ($0.5\Delta x$), and the time step ($\Delta t = 1$ μs).

$$v(t) = (1 - \cos \frac{2\pi}{t_0} t) H(t_0 - t). \tag{16}$$

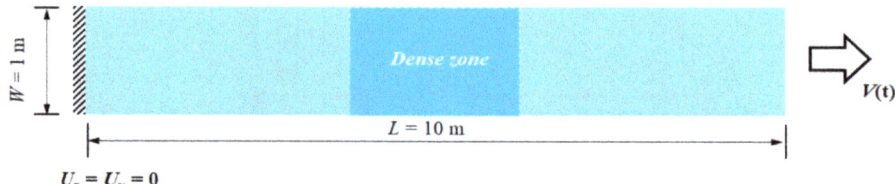

Figure 11. Geometry of the plate in the initial state.

The numerical results of the velocity wave propagation through the dense zone are shown in Figure 12 (DH-PD above, PD below). When the time is 2.4 ms, the velocity waveform transmitted is about to enter the dense area. Figure 12a shows that both PD and DH-PD simulate this stage accurately. When the time is 3.4 ms, the velocity of the center point in the dense area reaches the theoretical maximum of 2 m/s when using the DH-PD algorithm. When the traditional PD algorithm is used, the phenomenon of false wave reflection to the right will be found, weakening the wave peak of the velocity waveform in the dense area (Figure 12b). This violates the wave propagation theory in the same material and cannot completely simulate the wave propagation process. When the time reaches 4.6 ms, the velocity wave leaves the dense area and enters the non-dense area (Figure 12c).

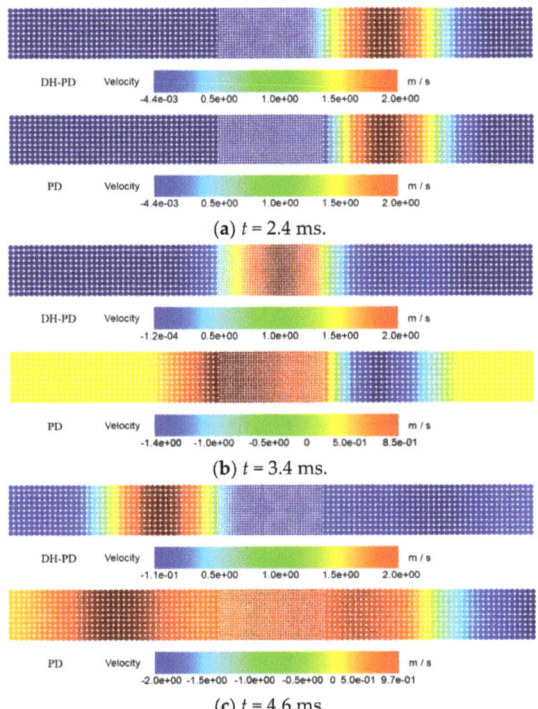

(a) t = 2.4 ms.

(b) t = 3.4 ms.

(c) t = 4.6 ms.

Figure 12. Velocity contour of wave passing through dense area.

The material points at the free end of the plate and the middle-end of the plate are monitored and their velocity characteristics are extracted and shown in Figure 13. The FDM simulation curves are almost identical to the analytical solutions, both of which can be used as a reference group. The conventional PD simulation is used to show anomalous spurious reflected waves. At a time of 3.5 ms, the velocity in the dense region is less than 1 m/s, which is half of the real value, and the spurious velocity wave is also received at the free end. DH-PD can simulate the complete propagation process of the wave, and it matches both the analytical solution and the FDM solution.

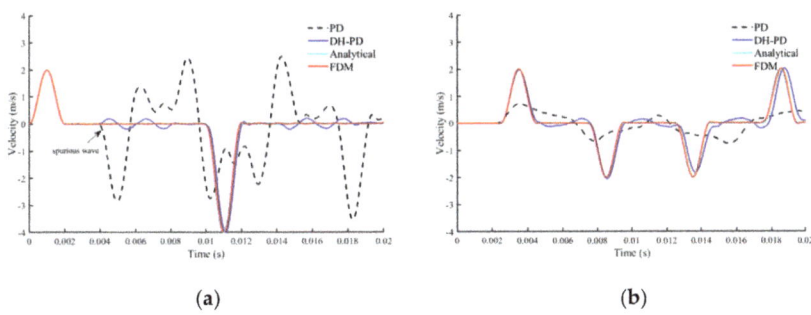

Figure 13. Time-velocity curves of analytical solution and numerical solution. (a) Velocity history at the free end of the bar. (b) Velocity history at the middle of the bar.

4.3. Numerical Application 1: Fracture of L-Shaped Concrete Specimen

Figure 14 shows the geometry of an L-shaped concrete specimen [45,46]. A total of 22,728 particles with different particle sizes and varying horizons are used in this case. Specifically, 7504 finer particles ($\Delta x = \Delta y = 1.25$ mm) are used near the corner of the L-shaped specimen, where the stress is relatively concentrated, 4300 coarser particles ($\Delta x = \Delta y = 5$ mm) are distributed at the periphery of the specimen, and 10,924 particles of size $\Delta x = \Delta y = 2.5$ mm are distributed between finer particles and coarser particles. The horizon size is set as 3.015 times the particle spacing. The information of the particles is shown in Table 1 and Figure 14. The other physical parameters include the modulus of elasticity, $E = 25.85$ GPa, the Poisson's ratio, $\nu = 0.18$, the energy release rate, $G_c = 65$ J/m^2, and the time increment, $\Delta t = 0.1$ µs. A displacement boundary, u, is exerted at the left side of the specimen, as shown in Figure 14.

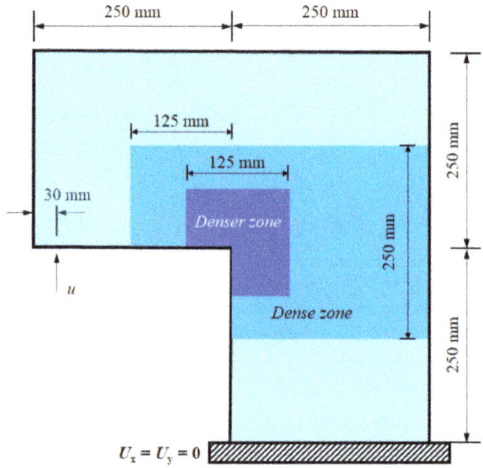

Figure 14. L-shaped plate geometry and three-level discretization.

Table 1. Values of peridynamics parameters for the DH-PD model.

Level	$\Delta x = \Delta y$	Horizon δ	Particle Numbers
I	5 mm	3.015 Δx	4300
II	2.5 mm	3.015 Δx	10,924
III	1.25 mm	3.015 Δx	7504
Total			22,728

Figure 15 shows the simulated crack propagation in the L-shaped plate. At $t = 0.65$ ms, a crack appears at the corner point of the L-shaped plate and propagates in the direction of 26° on the horizontal. Then, the direction of crack propagation changes to horizontal at a time close to $t = 1$ ms. The transverse crack expands to the right boundary of the specimen and cuts across the plate when $t = 2.5$ ms.

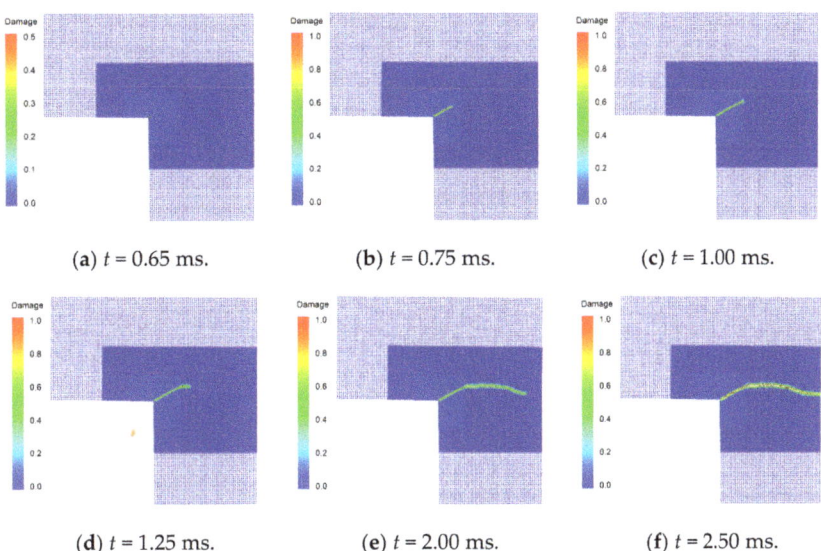

(a) t = 0.65 ms. (b) t = 0.75 ms. (c) t = 1.00 ms.

(d) t = 1.25 ms. (e) t = 2.00 ms. (f) t = 2.50 ms.

Figure 15. Snapshots of simulated crack propagation in the L-shaped plate.

Figure 16 shows the numerical and experimental crack propagation paths. The simulated results essentially coincide with the experimental data recorded in the literature [45]. To quantitatively compare the results, the Pearson correlation coefficient of the experimental and numerical crack paths in Figure 16 is calculated. In this case, 52 points on the crack paths with an equal horizontal distance from the corner point are selected as the analysis objects. Assuming the vector X $(x_1, x_2, x_3, \ldots \ldots, x_{52})$ represents the calculated vertical coordinates of these points, and Y $(y_1, y_2, y_3, \ldots \ldots, y_{52})$ represents the measured ones in the experiment, the Pearson correlation coefficient of the two vectors can be calculated as:

$$Corr(X, Y) = \frac{\sum\limits_{i=1}^{n}(x_i - \bar{x})(y_i - \bar{y})}{\sqrt{\sum\limits_{i=1}^{n}(x_i - \bar{x})^2 \times \sum\limits_{i=1}^{n}(y_i - \bar{y})^2}}. \tag{17}$$

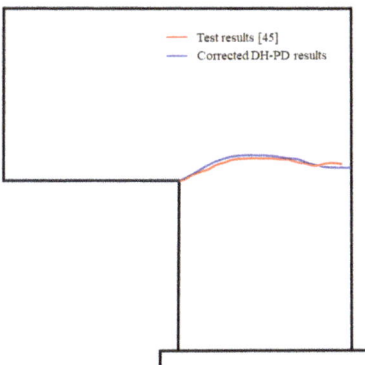

Figure 16. Comparison of the numerical and experimental crack propagation paths [45].

In Equation (17), $\bar{x}$ and $\bar{y}$ are the average values of the two data sets, respectively.

According to Equation (17), the correlation coefficient between the experimental and numerical results is calculated to be 0.988, suggesting that the numerical results have a strong correlation with the experimental data. Therefore, the calculation accuracy of the presented DH-PD model is verified.

To quantitatively compare the numerical and experimental results, the load-displacement curves are obtained based on the numerical results, and are compared with the experimental data in Figure 17. The comparison shows that the varying tendencies of the simulated curves match the experimental data well, and the calculated peak values of the load are close to the test value, thus verifying the validity and applicability of the presented model. In addition, the figure also shows that the corrected DH-PD model has a relatively higher simulation accuracy than DH-PD model.

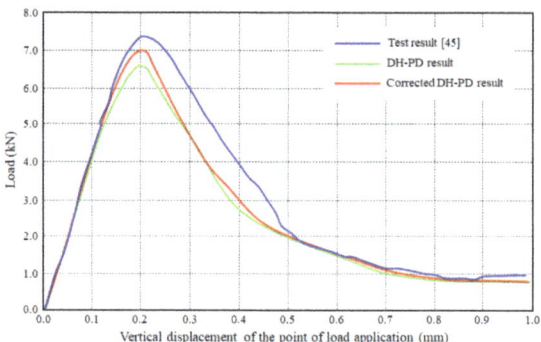

Figure 17. Comparison of the numerical and experimental displacement–load curves [45].

4.4. Numerical Application 2: Mixed Damage of a DEN Specimen

Figure 18 shows a square thin plate with a length of 200 mm on each side, an elastic modulus of E = 30 GPa, a density of ρ = 2265 kg/m^3, a Poisson's ratio of v = 0.33, and energy release rates of G_{Ic} = 110 J/m^2 and G_{IIc} = 1100 J/m^2. There is a prefabricated crack 25 mm in length and 5 mm in width on both sides of the specimen [46,47]. A uniform load, p, with a resultant force of 5 kN is applied in the horizontal direction on the left upper half and the right lower part of the plate. Meanwhile, a velocity load, v = 10 mm/s, is applied at the upper and lower boundaries of the plate, as shown in Figure 18.

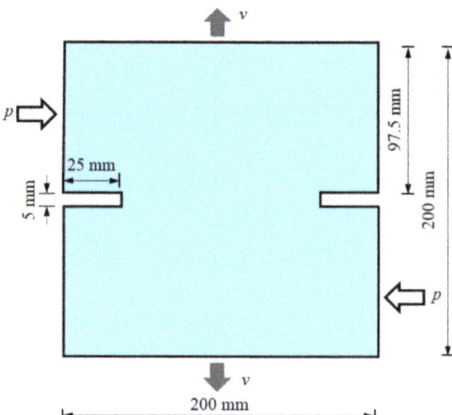

Figure 18. Geometric dimensions of a double-edged notched specimen.

The PD and DH-PD models are separately used to simulate this problem with the model parameters shown in Table 2. In the PD model, the square specimen is discretized into 25,440 particles with a spacing of $\Delta x = \Delta y = 1.25$ mm. In the DH-PD model, the specimen is discretized into two kinds of particles: 5280 finer particles with a spacing of $\Delta x = \Delta y = 1.25$ mm in the middle part of the specimen, and 5040 coarser particles with a spacing of $\Delta x = \Delta y = 2.5$ mm near the boundary of the specimen. The uniform force, p, on both sides is transformed into a physical load, $p/\Delta y$, which is applied to the particles at the outermost layer of the plate. The velocity load, v, is exerted on the three layers of particles at the upper and lower boundaries of the specimen. Finally, the step length is set to $\Delta t = 0.1$ μs.

Table 2. Values of peridynamics parameters for the PD and DH-PD models.

Model	$\Delta x = \Delta y$	Horizon δ	Particle Numbers
PD	1.25 mm	3.015 Δx	25,440
DH-PD	2.5 mm, 1.25 mm	3.015 Δx	5040 + 5280 = 10,320

Figure 19 shows the simulated crack propagation in the DEN specimen based on both the traditional PD model and the DH-PD model proposed in this work. The crack paths and the propagation velocities obtained from these two models match each other. To compare the computational efficiency of the two models, Table 3 shows the calculation times of the same simulation using both models. The DH-PD model drastically improves the use of computational resources largely by increasing efficiency by 119.4% under the same operation mode.

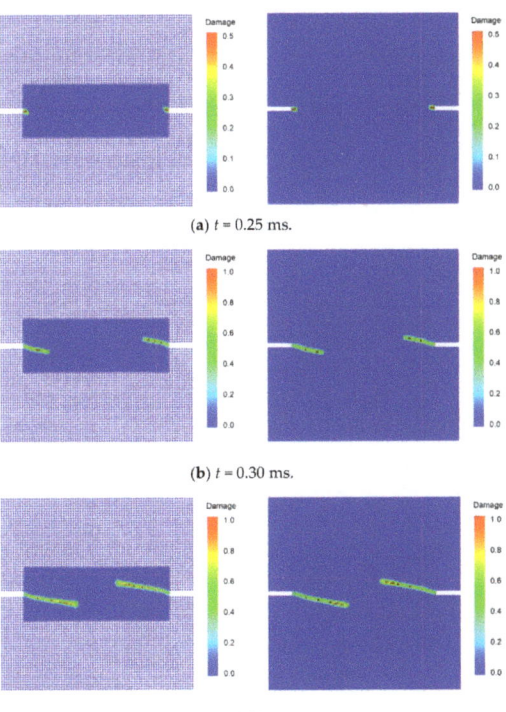

(a) $t = 0.25$ ms.

(b) $t = 0.30$ ms.

(c) $t = 0.35$ ms.

Figure 19. *Cont.*

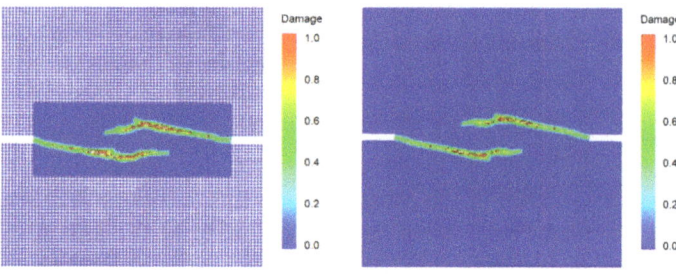

(**d**) t = 0.40 ms.

Figure 19. Snapshots of simulated crack propagation in the double-edged notched specimen using the DH-PD model (**left**) and traditional PD model (**right**).

Table 3. Calculation time and efficiency of the two models.

Model	Particle Numbers	Calculation Time
PD	25,440	390.172 s
DH-PD	10,320	177.866 s
Efficiency Increased		119.4%

Figure 20 compares the simulated crack paths with experimental data obtained by Nooru-Mohamed et al. [47], those calculated by the FEM model proposed in [48], and the traditional PD model. All the simulated crack paths coincide with the experimental results. To quantitatively analyze the computational accuracy of the corrected DH-PD model, Table 4 lists the Pearson correlation coefficients of the numerical and experimental crack paths shown in Figure 20. The comparison demonstrates that the simulation results obtained by the corrected DH-PD model proposed in this study match the experimental results better than those obtained by other numerical models.

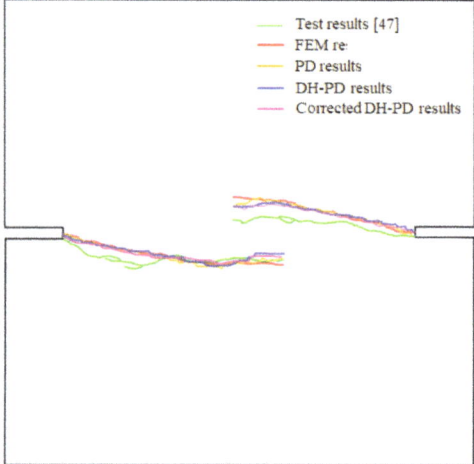

Figure 20. Comparison of the experimental and numerical (from the models of current study and other numerical studies) crack paths [47,48].

Table 4. Correlation coefficients between the test and numerical results on the crack paths.

Numerical Models	Corrected DH-PD	DH-PD	PD	FEM
Correlation Coefficients	0.957	0.952	0.952	0.929

5. Conclusions

In this study, an efficient DH-PD model was developed based on the PD theory and the concept of dual-horizon. In this model, a technique of nonuniformity discretization with variable horizons was incorporated, which significantly improved the computational efficiency. Moreover, volume correction and surface correction were introduced to improve computational accuracy of the model. Finally, the DH-PD model was verified and applied to simulate crack propagation problems, producing valuable results.

The presented DH-PD model was verified through the simulation of benchmark problems. After comparing the numerical results against the analytical solution and FDM results, high goodness of fit was obtained to verify the accuracy of the corrected DH-PD model. No spurious wave reflection was found during the simulation, confirming the advantage of the corrected DH-PD model over the traditional PD method. Additionally, the surface correction and particle volume correction could substantially reduce the calculation error.

In the simulation of the fracture of an L-shaped concrete specimen, the specimen was discretized into particles with three different sizes and varying horizons. The simulated crack propagation produced a crack path consistent with the experimental results. Based on the Pearson correlation coefficient for quantitatively comparing the results, the coefficient value of 0.988 verified the calculation accuracy of the presented DH-PD model.

The corrected DH-PD model simulates the mixed damage of a DEN specimen. The simulated crack paths were compared against the experimental data and the results obtained by the traditional PD model and the FEM model. The comparison showed that the corrected DP-PD model has a higher simulation accuracy than the FEM model and is computationally more efficient than the traditional PD method.

Author Contributions: Conceptualization, Z.D., L.W. and Z.L.; methodology, Z.D. and J.X.; writing—original draft preparation, Z.D. and J.X.; writing—review and editing, S.Q. and L.W.; visualization, J.X. and Z.L.; supervision, S.Q.; funding acquisition, Z.D., Z.L. and L.W. All authors have read and agreed to the published version of the manuscript.

Funding: This research was funded by the National Natural Science Foundation of China (Grant No. 42102318, 42002272, 41807266), the Program for Professor of Special Appointment (Eastern Scholar) at Shanghai Institutions of Higher Learning, and the Shanghai Science and Technology Innovation Action Plan (21DZ1204202).

Institutional Review Board Statement: Not applicable.

Informed Consent Statement: Not applicable.

Data Availability Statement: The data presented in this study are available on request from the corresponding author.

Acknowledgments: The authors are grateful for the support from the Department of Civil Engineering, Shanghai University.

Conflicts of Interest: The authors declare no conflict of interest.

References

1. Ravi-Chandar, K. Dynamic Fracture of Nominally Brittle Materials. *Int. J. Fract.* **1998**, *90*, 83–102. [CrossRef]
2. Ma, X.; Wang, F. The Fracture Analysis of Instop Gasket Using FEM Simulations. *Adv. Sci. Lett.* **2011**, *4*, 2573–2577. [CrossRef]
3. Ramaswamy, K.; Babu, P.R. Fracture analysis of composite pressure vessel using FEM. *Int. J. Comput. Mater. Sci. Eng.* **2021**, *10*, 2150003. [CrossRef]
4. Warren, T.L.; Silling, S.A.; Askari, A.; Weckner, O.; Epton, M.A.; Xu, J. A non-ordinary state-based peridynamic method to model solid material deformation and fracture. *Int. J. Solids Struct.* **2009**, *46*, 1186–1195. [CrossRef]

5. Hou, C.-Y. Various remeshing arrangements for two-dimensional finite element crack closure analysis. *Eng. Fract. Mech.* **2017**, *170*, 59–76. [CrossRef]
6. Bouchard, P.; Bay, F.; Chastel, Y.; Tovena, I. Crack propagation modelling using an advanced remeshing technique. *Comput. Methods Appl. Mech. Eng.* **2000**, *189*, 723–742. [CrossRef]
7. Moës, N.; Dolbow, J.; Belytschko, T. A finite element method for crack growth without remeshing. *Int. J. Numer. Methods Eng.* **1999**, *46*, 131–150. [CrossRef]
8. Chen, J.-W.; Zhou, X.-P. The enhanced extended finite element method for the propagation of complex branched cracks. *Eng. Anal. Bound. Elem.* **2019**, *104*, 46–62. [CrossRef]
9. Unosson, M.; Olovsson, L.; Simonsson, K. Failure modelling in finite element analyses: Element erosion with crack-tip enhancement. *Finite Elem. Anal. Des.* **2006**, *42*, 283–297. [CrossRef]
10. Alter, C.; Kolling, S.; Schneider, J. An enhanced non–local failure criterion for laminated glass under low velocity impact. *Int. J. Impact Eng.* **2017**, *109*, 342–353. [CrossRef]
11. Wang, L.; Zhou, X. Phase field model for simulating the fracture behaviors of some disc-type specimens. *Eng. Fract. Mech.* **2020**, *226*, 106870. [CrossRef]
12. Msekh, M.A.; Sargado, J.M.; Jamshidian, M.; Areias, P.M.; Rabczuk, T. Abaqus implementation of phase-field model for brittle fracture. *Comput. Mater. Sci.* **2015**, *96*, 472–484. [CrossRef]
13. Zhu, Q.Z.; Ni, T.; Zhao, L.Y. Simulations of crack propagation in rock-like materials using peridynamic method. *Chin. J. Rock Mech. Eng.* **2016**, *34*, 3507–3515. (in Chinese).
14. Cheng, Y.; Li, J. A complex variable meshless method for fracture problems. *Sci. China Ser. G Phys. Mech. Astron.* **2006**, *49*, 46–59. [CrossRef]
15. Gao, H.; Cheng, Y. A Complex Variable Meshless Manifold Method for Fracture Problems. *Int. J. Comput. Methods* **2010**, *7*, 55–81. [CrossRef]
16. Khazal, H.; Bayesteh, H.; Mohammadi, S.; Ghorashi, S.S.; Ahmed, A. An extended element free Galerkin method for fracture analysis of functionally graded materials. *Mech. Adv. Mater. Struct.* **2015**, *23*, 513–528. [CrossRef]
17. Kou, M.M.; Han, D.C.; Xiao, C.C.; Wang, Y.T. Dynamic fracture instability in brittle materials: Insights from DEM simulations. *Struct. Eng. Mech.* **2019**, *71*, 65–75.
18. Owayo, A.A.; Teng, F.C.; Chen, W.C. DEM simulation of crack evolution in cement-based materials under inclined shear test. *Constr. Build. Mater.* **2021**, *301*, 124087. [CrossRef]
19. Silling, S. Reformulation of elasticity theory for discontinuities and long-range forces. *J. Mech. Phys. Solids* **2000**, *48*, 175–209. [CrossRef]
20. Silling, S.; Askari, E. A meshfree method based on the peridynamic model of solid mechanics. *Comput. Struct.* **2005**, *83*, 1526–1535. [CrossRef]
21. Oh, M.; Koo, B.; Kim, J.-H.; Cho, S. Shape design optimization of dynamic crack propagation using peridynamics. *Eng. Fract. Mech.* **2021**, *252*, 107837. [CrossRef]
22. Ni, T.; Zaccariotto, M.; Zhu, Q.-Z.; Galvanetto, U. Static solution of crack propagation problems in Peridynamics. *Comput. Methods Appl. Mech. Eng.* **2019**, *346*, 126–151. [CrossRef]
23. Hu, Y.; Madenci, E. Peridynamics for fatigue life and residual strength prediction of composite laminates. *Compos. Struct.* **2017**, *160*, 169–184. [CrossRef]
24. Postek, E.; Sadowski, T. Impact model of the Al_2O_3/ZrO_2 composite by peridynamics. *Compos. Struct.* **2021**, *271*, 114071. [CrossRef]
25. Mikata, Y. Peridynamics for fluid mechanics and acoustics. *Acta Mech.* **2021**, *232*, 3011–3032. [CrossRef]
26. Mikata, Y. Peridynamics for Heat Conduction. *J. Heat Transf.* **2020**, *142*, 081402. [CrossRef]
27. Shou, Y.; Zhou, X. A coupled thermomechanical nonordinary state-based peridynamics for thermally induced cracking of rocks. *Fatigue Fract. Eng. Mater. Struct.* **2020**, *43*, 371–386. [CrossRef]
28. Silling, S.A.; Lehoucq, R.B. Convergence of Peridynamics to Classical Elasticity Theory. *J. Elast.* **2008**, *93*, 13–37. [CrossRef]
29. Liu, S.; Fang, G.; Liang, J.; Fu, M.; Wang, B. A new type of peridynamics: Element-based peridynamics. *Comput. Methods Appl. Mech. Eng.* **2020**, *366*, 113098. [CrossRef]
30. Sun, W.; Fish, J. Coupling of non-ordinary state-based peridynamics and finite element method for fracture propagation in saturated porous media. *Int. J. Numer. Anal. Methods Géoméch.* **2021**, *45*, 1260–1281. [CrossRef]
31. Ren, B.; Fan, H.; Bergel, G.L.; Regueiro, R.; Lai, X.; Li, S. A peridynamics–SPH coupling approach to simulate soil fragmentation induced by shock waves. *Comput. Mech.* **2015**, *55*, 287–302. [CrossRef]
32. Zhang, Y.; Pan, G.; Zhang, Y.H.; Haeri, S. A multi-physics peridynamics-DEM-IB-CLBM framework for the prediction of erosive impact of solid particles in viscous fluids. *Comput. Methods Appl. Mech. Eng.* **2019**, *352*, 675–690. [CrossRef]
33. DiPasquale, D.; Zaccariotto, M.; Galvanetto, U. Crack propagation with adaptive grid refinement in 2D peridynamics. *Int. J. Fract.* **2014**, *190*, 1–22. [CrossRef]
34. Bobaru, F.; Yang, M.; Alves, L.F.; Silling, S.A.; Askari, E.; Xu, J. Convergence, adaptive refinement, and scaling in 1D peridynaics. *Int. J. Numer. Methods Eng.* **2009**, *77*, 852–877. [CrossRef]
35. Shojaei, A.; Mossaiby, F.; Zaccariotto, M.; Galvanetto, U. An adaptive multi-grid peridynamic method for dynamic fracture analysis. *Int. J. Mech. Sci.* **2018**, *144*, 600–617. [CrossRef]

36. Bazazzadeh, S.; Mossaiby, F.; Shojaei, A. An adaptive thermo-mechanical peridynamic model for fracture analysis in ceramics. *Eng. Fract. Mech.* **2020**, *223*, 106708. [CrossRef]
37. Ren, H.; Zhuang, X.; Cai, Y.; Rabczuk, T. Dual-horizon peridynamics. *Int. J. Numer. Methods Eng.* **2016**, *108*, 1451–1476. [CrossRef]
38. Rabczuk, T.; Ren, H. A peridynamics formulation for quasi-static fracture and contact in rock. *Eng. Geol.* **2017**, *225*, 42–48. [CrossRef]
39. Wang, B.; Oterkus, S.; Oterkus, E. Derivation of dual-horizon state-based peridynamics formulation based on Euler–Lagrange equation. *Contin. Mech. Thermodyn.* **2020**, 1–21. [CrossRef]
40. Ren, H.; Zhuang, X.; Rabczuk, T. Dual-horizon peridynamics: A stable solution to varying horizons. *Comput. Methods Appl. Mech. Eng.* **2017**, *318*, 762–782. [CrossRef]
41. Le, Q.V.; Bobaru, F. Surface corrections for peridynamic models in elasticity and fracture. *Comput. Mech.* **2018**, *61*, 499–518. [CrossRef]
42. Scabbia, F.; Zaccariotto, M.; Galvanetto, U. A novel and effective way to impose boundary conditions and to mitigate the surface effect in state-based Peridynamics. *Int. J. Numer. Methods Eng.* **2021**, *122*, 5773–5811. [CrossRef]
43. Madenci, E.; Oterkus, E. Peridynamic Theory and Its Applications. In *Peridynamic Theory and Its Applications*; Springer: Berlin/Heidelberg, Germany, 2014.
44. Speronello, M. *Study of Computational Peridynamics, Explicit and Implicit Time Integration, Viscoelastic Material*; University of Padua: Padua, Italy, 2015.
45. Winkler, B.; Hofstetter, G.; Niederwanger, G. Experimental verification of a constitutive model for concrete cracking. *Proc. Inst. Mech. Eng. Part L J. Mater. Des. Appl.* **2001**, *215*, 75–86. [CrossRef]
46. Naderi, M.; Jung, J.; Yang, Q.D. A three dimensional augmented finite element for modeling arbitrary cracking in solids. *Int. J. Fract.* **2016**, *197*, 147–168. [CrossRef]
47. Nooru-Mohamed, M.B.; Schlangen, E.; van Mier, J.G. Experimental and numerical study on the behavior of concrete subjected to biaxial tension and shear. *Adv. Cem. Based Mater.* **1993**, *1*, 22–37. [CrossRef]
48. Ožbolt, J.; Reinhardt, H. Numerical study of mixed-mode fracture in concrete. *Int. J. Fract.* **2002**, *118*, 145–162. [CrossRef]

Article

An Extended Car-Following Model Based on Visual Angle and Electronic Throttle Effect

Hongxia Ge [1,2,3,*], Siteng Li [1,2,3] and Chunyue Yan [1,2,3]

[1] Faculty of Maritime and Transportation, Ningbo University, Ningbo 315211, China; 2011084006@nbu.edu.cn (S.L.); yan.chunyue@scientechmed.com (C.Y.)
[2] Jiangsu Province Collaborative Innovation Center for Modern Urban Traffic Technologies, Nanjing 210096, China
[3] National Traffic Management Engineering and Technology Research Centre, Ningbo University Sub-Centre, Ningbo 315211, China
* Correspondence: gehongxia@nbu.edu.cn

Abstract: With the continuous advancement of electronic technology, auto parts manufacturing institutions are gradually applying electronic throttles to automobiles for precise control. Based on the visual angle model (VAM), a car-following model considering the electronic throttle angle of the preceding vehicle is proposed. The stability conditions are obtained through linear stability analysis. By means of nonlinear analysis, the time-dependent Ginzburg–Landau (TDGL) equation is derived first, and then the modified Korteweg-de-Vries (mKdV) equation is derived. The relationship between the two is thus obtained. Finally, in the process of numerical simulations and exploration, it is shown how the visual angle and electronic throttle affect the stability of traffic flow. The simulation results in MATLAB software verify the validity of the model, indicating that the visual angle and electronic throttle can improve traffic stability.

Keywords: car-following model; visual angle model; electronic throttle angle; stability analysis

1. Introduction

Urban roads are an important link between the city's economy and development, and the stable operation of road traffic has an important impact on the city's construction. Nowadays, the increasing number of motor vehicles has seriously affected the driving environment, and traffic phenomena (such as traffic congestion, road overload, average speed drop, etc.) cannot be ignored. It requires a systematic view to guide the operation of traffic flow in order to integrate vehicles, road facilities and users into a whole and facilitate collaboration. The application of traffic flow theory can better analyze the traffic phenomenon and its essence, so that the road can maximize its effectiveness. The macroscopic model, mesoscopic model, and microscopic model are the general classification of the traffic flow model, including cellular automation models [1–4], car-following models [5–16], hydrodynamic lattice models [17–25], continuum models [26–32] and route optimization models [33–35]. Usually, the actual traffic flow is affected by the stimulation of time and space, and its change process is a dynamic and very complicated process. Therefore, in combination with practice, the basic idea of the generalized car-following theory is "response = sensitivity × stimulus".

According to the stimulation framework, the driver's response comes from the stimulus given by the environment. Different variants of the car following models that provide different stimuli for the driver in the traffic flow model are shown below. The Gazis–Herman–Rothery (GHR) model [36] is based on the "response = sensitivity × stimulus" framework, which is set under the assumption that the current driver is stimulated and the acceleration of the responsively controlled vehicle is affected by the current velocity, headway and velocity difference from the previous vehicle. Its formulation is as follows:

$$\frac{dv_n(t)}{dt} = \lambda \Delta v_n(t-\tau) \tag{1}$$

where the velocity of the n-th car at time t is represented by $v_n(t)$, the reaction time of the driver is expressed as τ, the sensitivity of the relative speed is expressed as λ, and the relative speed of time $t - \tau$ is expressed as $\Delta v_n(t-\tau)$.

The optimal velocity model (OVM for short) is proposed by Bando et al. [37]. They took the optimal velocity of driver into account. The OVM model formula is as follows:

$$\frac{dv_n(t)}{dt} = \alpha[V(\Delta x_n(t)) - v_n(t)] \tag{2}$$

where the sensitivity of a driver is represented by α, the optimal velocity function is represented by $V(\Delta x_n(t))$, and the difference in headway of two successive vehicles is represented by $\Delta x_n(t) = x_{n+1}(t) - x_n(t)$.

The acceleration in OVM is too high and the deceleration is impractical; therefore, Helbing et al. [38] put forward the generalized force model (GFM). GFM has two drawbacks under blocking density, one of which is that it cannot account for the delay time of the vehicle motion, and the other is that it cannot describe the velocity of kinematic wave speed. Jiang et al. [39,40] believed that only considering the impact of negative velocity difference on cars is still inadequate, so they developed the full velocity difference model (FVD). Its formula is as follows:

$$\frac{dv_n(t)}{dt} = \alpha[V(\Delta x_n(t)) - v_n(t)] + \lambda \Delta v_n(t) \tag{3}$$

where the speed difference coefficient is expressed as λ, and the difference in velocity of two successive vehicles is expressed as $\Delta v_n(t) = v_{n+1}(t) - v_n(t)$. All previously proposed models are based on the assumption that the driver's behavior is perfectly reasonable, and has the ability to accurately sense distance, speed and acceleration. It does not take into account the psychological characteristics of the driver who will change during the follow-up process. Based on the FVD, Jin [41] proposed a visual angle model (VAM), which introduces the follower driver's perspective into the car-following model by considering the perspective and its rate of change, as shown in Figure 1.

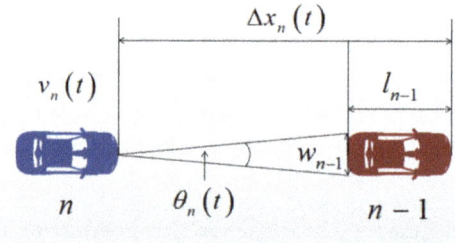

Figure 1. Car-following stimulated by the driver's perspective.

The model formula is as follows:

$$\frac{dv_n(t)}{dt} = \alpha[V(\theta_n(t)) - v_n(t)] - \lambda \frac{d}{dt}\theta_n(t) \tag{4}$$

where the driver's sensitivity to the difference between the optimal velocity and the current velocity is represented by α; the driver's optimal velocity based on the follower's perspective is represented by $V(\theta_n(t))$; the angle of view observed by the driver of the n-th car at time t is represented by $\theta_n(t)$; the velocity of n-th car at time t is represented by $v_n(t)$; and the sensitivity of the stimulus $d\theta_n(t)/dt$ is represented by λ.

The driver's visual angle can be approximated as follows:

$$\theta_n(t) = \frac{w_{n-1}}{\Delta x_n(t) - l_{n-1}} \tag{5}$$

where w_{n-1} and l_{n-1} are the width and the length of the $(n-1)$-th car, and $\Delta x_n(t)$ is the headway between the n-th car and $(n-1)$-th car.

The car-following process is generally limited to a single lane. If the driver sees that the vehicle in front is close to them, the possibility of rear-end collision increases. The stimulus of the preceding vehicle to the driver of the following car prompts the driver of the following car to increase the distance between the two cars. The width and length of the preceding vehicle will also affect the driver's perspective of judging the traffic situation ahead. If the driver is unable to take precautions against the traffic ahead, out of the psychological stimulus to protect their own safety, the driver of the following vehicle will increase the distance between the two vehicles at this time.

In order to obtain an accurate expression of the driver's visual angle, assuming that the definition of uniform traffic flow is that all vehicles are moving at the optimal velocity $V(\theta_0)$ and the same distance from the preceding vehicle h, we use the following formula:

$$x_n^0(t) = hn + V(\theta_0)t \tag{6}$$

where the optimal velocity is denoted as $V(\theta_0)$, the distance headway is expressed as h, the position of the n-th car is expressed as $x_n^0(t)$, and the visual angle of the driver of the rear vehicle is expressed as $\theta_0(t) = w_{n-1}/h - l_{n-1}$. Each parameter in the equation is in a stable state. Adding a small disturbance $x_n(t) = x_n^0(t) + y_n(t)$, $\theta_n(t)$ can be rewritten as follows:

$$\theta_n(t) = \frac{w_{n-1}}{h + \Delta y_n(t) - l_{n-1}} = \frac{w_{n-1}[(h - l_{n-1}) - \Delta y_n(t)]}{(h - l_{n-1})^2 - (\Delta y_n(t))^2} \tag{7}$$

Equation (8) can be derived by eliminating the second-order term of $\Delta y_n(t)$:

$$\theta_n(t) = \frac{w_{n-1}}{(h - l_{n-1})} - \frac{w_{n-1} \cdot \Delta y_n(t)}{(h - l_{n-1})^2} \tag{8}$$

The follower's visual angle and its rate of change can be obtained by deriving the derivation of t on both sides of the Equation (8):

$$\frac{d}{dt}\theta_n(t) = -\frac{w_{n-1}}{(h - l_{n-1})^2}\Delta y'_n(t) \tag{9}$$

Substituting Equation (9) into Equation (4), we can obtain a more intuitive expression of VAM:

$$\frac{dv_n(t)}{dt} = \alpha[V(\theta_n(t)) - v_n(t)] + \lambda \frac{w_{n-1}}{(h - l_{n-1})^2}\Delta v_n(t) \tag{10}$$

When the vehicle is driving on the road, the visual system is the most important channel for the driver to perceive external information. If the driver observes that the distance between their vehicle and the preceding vehicle gradually becomes smaller, the driver will immediately make adjustments to the current driving behavior.

In addition, the electronic throttle angle is the core variable of the traffic flow stability control system, which is related to the velocity and acceleration of the vehicle. It mainly transmits the operation information of the vehicle in front to the rear, thereby affecting the stability of road traffic. Therefore, considering the above two factors comprehensively, it is closer to the actual traffic situation and provides a reference for road traffic management.

This paper comprehensively considers the two factors of visual angle and electronic throttle effect to make the model closer to the actual traffic situation in the simulation process. Section 2 introduces the influence of the external factor of the angle of view and the internal factor of the electronic throttle on the car-following behavior of the vehicle. Both are taken into account in the car-following model, and its linear stability conditions are provided through calculation and analysis. Section 3 performs a nonlinear analysis near the critical point to derive the TDGL equation. In Section 4, the mKdV equation is provided through calculation and analysis. In Section 5, the factors considered in this paper are numerically simulated by using MATLAB to analyze the impact of information transfer in the actual transportation system. In Section 6, the conclusions are summarized finally.

2. The Extended Model and Linear Stability Analysis

From the driver's perspective, consider the driver's attention to the surrounding environment and the psychological pressure caused by the surrounding objects on the driver, and use mathematical models to abstractly express the influence of external objects on the driver's driving behavior. From the perspective of the automobile structure, the electronic throttle is the core component of the automobile engine operation, and its working performance directly affects the performance of the vehicle.

An electronic throttle system consists of a DC drive (powered by the chopper), a gearbox, a valve plate, a dual return spring, and a position sensor. The driver can control the velocity and acceleration of the vehicle by controlling the angle of the electronic throttle. When the driver steps on the accelerator pedal, it does not directly drive the throttle, but first collects the pedal information and inputs it to the control unit. The control unit drives the throttle valve plate to open and performs precise control of the opening angle according to the input information and the control algorithm pre-stored in it. The proposed model in this paper takes the electronic throttle angle difference of the preceding vehicle into account, which is shown below:

$$\frac{dv_n(t)}{dt} = \alpha \left[V(\theta_n) \left(-\frac{w_{n-1}}{(h-l_{n-1})^2} \Delta x_n(t) \right) - v_n(t) \right] + \lambda \frac{w_{n-1}}{(h-l_{n-1})^2} \Delta v_{n-1}(t) \\ + k(\beta_n(t) - \beta_{n-1}(t)) \tag{11}$$

The electronic throttle angle difference was quoted by Qin et al. [42]. The mathematical relation between the speed and acceleration and electronic throttle angle is as follows:

$$\beta_n(t) = \frac{1}{q}\left[\frac{dv_n(t)}{dt} + p(v_n(t) - v_e)\right] + \beta_e \tag{12}$$

where the current balance speed is represented by v_e, the current balance electronic throttle angle is represented by β_e, which corresponds to the current balance speed, and p and q both represent constants and are greater than zero.

Calculate the difference between the electronic throttle angle of the n-th car and the $(n-1)$-th car by Equation (12):

$$\beta_n(t) - \beta_{n-1}(t) = \frac{1}{q}\left[\frac{dv_n(t)}{dt} - \frac{dv_{n-1}(t)}{dt} + p(v_n(t) - v_{n-1}(t))\right] \tag{13}$$

Substituting Equation (13) into Equation (11), the new expression of Equation (11) is calculated as follows:

$$\frac{dv_n(t)}{dt} = \alpha \left[V(\theta_n) \left(-\frac{w_{n-1}}{(h-l_{n-1})^2} \Delta x_n(t) \right) - v_n(t) \right] + \lambda \frac{w_{n-1}}{(h-l_{n-1})^2} \Delta v_{n-1}(t) \\ + \frac{k}{q}\left[\frac{dv_n(t)}{dt} - \frac{dv_{n-1}(t)}{dt} + p(v_n(t) - v_{n-1}(t))\right] \tag{14}$$

where the headway distance between the $(n+1)$-th car (the preceding car) and the n-th car (the rear car) is denoted by $\Delta x_n(t) = x_{n+1}(t) - x_n(t)$, the different sensitivity of each driver is denoted by α, and the electronic throttle angle difference coefficient is denoted by k.

The optimal velocity function adopts the following formula:

$$V(\theta_n(t)) = V_1 + V_2\tanh[C_1(w_{n-1}/\theta_n(t)) - C_2] \tag{15}$$

where the various parameters are calibrated as follows: $V_1 = 6.75$ m/s, $V_2 = 7.91$ m/s, $C_1 = 0.13$ m^{-1}, $C_2 = 1.57$. $\Delta x_n = h_c : V''(h_c) = 0$ is the turning point of the increasing function $V(\cdot)$, which has an upper limit.

The TDGL equation can be derived from Equation (14). In order to reduce the difficulty of subsequent nonlinear analysis and improve comprehensibility, Equation (14) is rewritten into a new form:

$$\begin{aligned}\frac{d^2x_n(t)}{dt^2} =& \alpha\left[V(\theta_n)\left(-\frac{w_{n-1}}{(h-l_{n-1})^2}\Delta x_n(t)\right) - \frac{dx_n(t)}{dt}\right] \\ &+ \lambda\frac{w_{n-1}}{(h-l_{n-1})^2}\left(\frac{dx_n(t)}{dt} - \frac{dx_{n-1}(t)}{dt}\right) \\ &+ \frac{k}{q}\left[\frac{d^2x_n(t)}{dt^2} - \frac{d^2x_{n-1}(t)}{dt^2} + p\left(\frac{dx_n(t)}{dt} - \frac{dx_{n-1}(t)}{dt}\right)\right]\end{aligned} \tag{16}$$

In addition, Equation (16) can be rewritten as a formula with headway as follows:

$$\begin{aligned}\frac{d^2\Delta x_n(t)}{dt^2} =& \alpha\left[V(\theta_n)\left(-\frac{w_{n-1}}{(h-l_{n-1})^2}\Delta x_{n+1}(t)\right) - V(\theta_n)\left(-\frac{w_{n-1}}{(h-l_{n-1})^2}\Delta x_n(t)\right)\right. \\ &\left. - \frac{d\Delta x_n(t)}{dt}\right] + \lambda\frac{w_{n-1}}{(h-l_{n-1})^2}\left(\frac{d\Delta x_n(t)}{dt} - \frac{d\Delta x_{n-1}(t)}{dt}\right) \\ &+ \frac{k}{q}\left[\frac{d^2\Delta x_n(t)}{dt^2} - \frac{d^2\Delta x_{n-1}(t)}{dt^2} + p\left(\frac{d\Delta x_n(t)}{dt} - \frac{d\Delta x_{n-1}(t)}{dt}\right)\right]\end{aligned} \tag{17}$$

The traffic flow is assumed to reach a steady state. Under this assumption, all vehicles drive forward with a constant headway h and a constant speed $V(\theta_0)$. Thus, we will analyze the following equation based on the steady-state solution as follows:

$$x_n^0(t) = hn + V(\theta_0)t, \ h = L/N \tag{18}$$

where the total number of vehicles is represented by N, and the road length is represented by L. Assume that $y_n(t)$ causes a small disturbance to the steady state $x_n(t) = x_n^0(t) + y_n(t)$, and linearizes the equation as follows:

$$\begin{aligned}\frac{d^2y_n(t)}{dt^2} =& \alpha\left[V'(\theta_0)\left(-\frac{w_{n-1}}{(h-l_{n-1})^2}\Delta y_n(t)\right) - \frac{dy_n(t)}{dt}\right] \\ &+ \lambda\frac{w_{n-1}}{(h-l_{n-1})^2}\left(\frac{dy_n(t)}{dt} - \frac{dy_{n-1}(t)}{dt}\right) \\ &+ \frac{k}{q}\left[\frac{d^2y_n(t)}{dt^2} - \frac{d^2y_{n-1}(t)}{dt^2} + p\left(\frac{dy_n(t)}{dt} - \frac{dy_{n-1}(t)}{dt}\right)\right]\end{aligned} \tag{19}$$

where the specific items in the formula are the following: $\Delta y_n(t) = y_{n+1}(t) - y_n(t)$, $V'(\theta_0) = dV(\theta)/d\theta|_{\theta=\theta_0}$. Expanding $y_n(t)$ with the form of $y_n(t) = e^{ikn+zt}$, we have the following:

$$z^2 = \alpha \left[V'(\theta_0) \left(-\frac{w_{n-1}}{(h-l_{n-1})^2} \right) \left(e^{ik} - 1 \right) - z \right] + \lambda z \frac{w_{n-1}}{(h-l_{n-1})^2} \left(1 - e^{-ik}\right)$$
$$+ \frac{k}{q} \left(z^2 \left(1 - e^{-ik}\right) + pz\left(1 - e^{-ik}\right) \right) \tag{20}$$

If we set $z = z_1(ik) + z_2(ik)^2 + \cdots$ and only retain the first and second order terms of ik, then we can obtain the following:

$$z_1 = -\frac{w_{n-1}}{(h-l_{n-1})^2} V'(\theta_0) \tag{21}$$

$$z_2 = -\frac{V'(\theta_0)w_{n-1}}{\alpha(h-l_{n-1})^2} \left(\frac{\alpha}{2} + \frac{w_{n-1}(\lambda - V'(\theta_0))}{(h-l_{n-1})^2} + \frac{\alpha pk}{q} \right) \tag{22}$$

where $z_2 > 0$ is the premise of the stability of the initial uniform traffic flow, from which the stability conditions of the new model are calculated as follows:

$$\alpha > \frac{2w_{n-1}(\lambda - V'(\theta_0))}{(h-l_{n-1})^2} - \frac{2pk}{q} \tag{23}$$

The neutral stability condition is as follows:

$$\alpha = \frac{2w_{n-1}(\lambda - V'(\theta_0))}{(h-l_{n-1})^2} - \frac{2pk}{q} \tag{24}$$

When λ and k are fixed, the neutral stability curves with different values of $w = 1.8, 2.0, 2.2$ are as plotted in Figure 2. It considers the potential impact of the vehicle width of the vehicle in front on the transportation system. In the case of the same value, with the width of the vehicle increases, the neutral stability curve moves upward, and the stable area is gradually compressed. It indicates that the increase in vehicle width has caused disturbance to the driver's visual angle, and visual obstruction increases the psychological pressure of the driver and affects the control of the vehicle. It shows that considering the driver's angle of view has a negative impact on the steady state operation of the transportation system.

As shown in Figure 3a–c, when λ and w are fixed, the stable and unstable regions represented by neutral curves with different $k = 0.3, 0.5, 0.8$ values will change. As the value of the coefficient of the electronic throttle angle k increases, the neutral stability curve moves downward, and the stability area gradually expands, indicating that a new factor has a positive impact on the stability of traffic flow. Therefore, considering the electronic throttle angle, the reliability of the system is greatly increased, and the safety of driving is ensured.

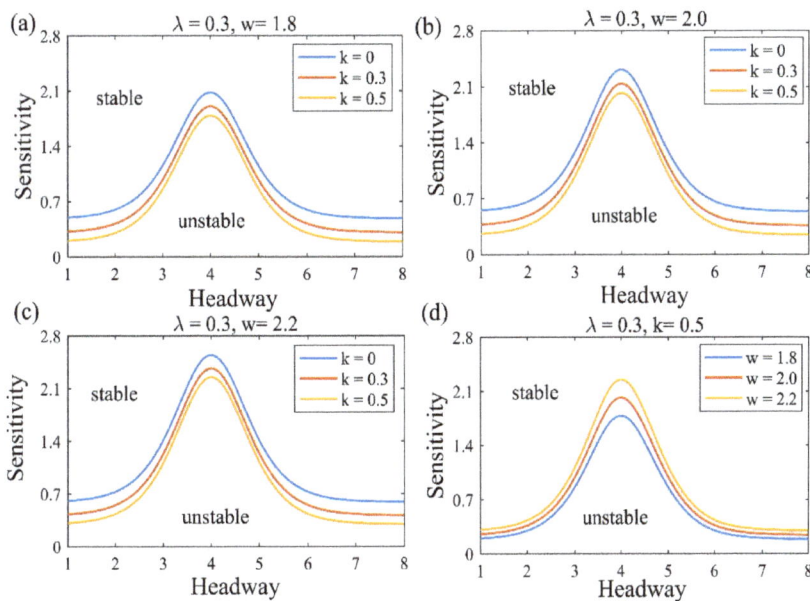

Figure 2. The phase diagram in the headway sensitivity for different values of λ and w.

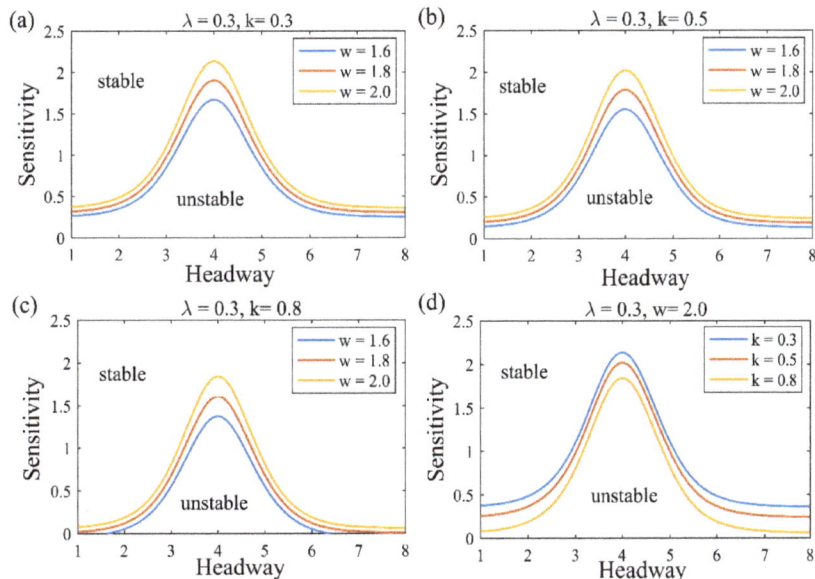

Figure 3. The phase diagram in the headway sensitivity for different values of λ and k.

Obviously, considering the combined effects of electronic throttle angle and driver's visual angle, it can effectively alleviate traffic congestion, avoid the occurrence of traffic jams and strengthen the stability of traffic flow, which is in good agreement with the actual road conditions.

3. The TDGL Equation

It is necessary to construct the traffic flow models by which one can derive the TDGL equation since the thermodynamic theory of jamming transition can be formulated by the TDGL equation [43]. In this section, we perform a nonlinear analysis of Equation (17) near the critical point (h_c, α_c) to obtain the TDGL equation describing the traffic behaviors in this extended model. By introducing the slow scale of time variable t, space variable n and constant b, the following definitions of slow variables X and T are obtained:

$$X = \varepsilon(n + bt), \quad T = \varepsilon^3 t, \quad 0 < \varepsilon \ll 1 \tag{25}$$

The headway $\Delta x_n(t)$ is as follows:

$$\Delta x_n(t) = h_c + \varepsilon R(X, T) \tag{26}$$

where h_c stands for safety distance.

By inserting Equations (25) and (26) to Equation (17), as the Taylor expanding to the fifth-order of ε, we can obtain the nonlinear partial differential equation as follows:

$$\begin{aligned}
&\varepsilon^2 \left(-\frac{w_{n-1}}{(h-l_{n-1})^2} V' - b \right) \partial_X R + \varepsilon^3 \left(-\frac{w_{n-1}}{(h-l_{n-1})^2} \left(\tfrac{1}{2} V' + \lambda \tau b \right) + bp\tau \left(\tfrac{k}{q} - 1 \right) \right) \partial_X^2 R \\
&+ \varepsilon^4 \left[\left(-\frac{w_{n-1}}{(h-l_{n-1})^2} \left(\tfrac{1}{6} V' + \tfrac{\lambda \tau b}{2} \right) + \tfrac{bpk\tau}{2q} \right) \partial_X^3 R + \left(-\frac{w_{n-1}}{(h-l_{n-1})^2} \right) \tfrac{1}{2} V''' \partial_X R^3 - \partial_T R \right] \\
&+ \varepsilon^5 \left\{ \left(-\frac{w_{n-1}}{(h-l_{n-1})^2} \left(\tfrac{1}{24} V' - \tfrac{\lambda \tau b}{6} \right) - \tfrac{bp\lambda \tau}{3q} \right) \partial_X^4 R \right. \\
&\left. + \left(-\frac{w_{n-1}}{(h-l_{n-1})^2} \right) \tfrac{3}{4} V''' \partial_X^2 R^3 + \left(\frac{w_{n-1}\lambda \tau}{(h-l_{n-1})^2} - 2\tau b + \tfrac{k\tau p}{q} \right) \partial_X \partial_T R \right\} = 0
\end{aligned} \tag{27}$$

Traffic behavior is considered to be near the tipping point $\tau = (1 + \varepsilon^2)\tau_c$. Eliminating the second-order and third-order terms of ε from Equation (27) by taking $b = \left(-\frac{w_{n-1}}{(h-l_{n-1})^2} \right) V'$, finally the equation is as follows:

$$\begin{aligned}
\varepsilon^4 \partial_T R &= \varepsilon^4 \left(-\frac{w_{n-1}}{(h-l_{n-1})^2} \left(\tfrac{1}{6} V' + \tfrac{\lambda \tau b}{2} \right) + \tfrac{bpk\tau}{2q} \right) \partial_X^3 R + \left(-\frac{w_{n-1}}{(h-l_{n-1})^2} \right) \tfrac{1}{2} V''' \varepsilon^4 \partial_X R^3 \\
&+ \varepsilon^3 \left(-\frac{w_{n-1}}{(h-l_{n-1})^2} \left(\tfrac{1}{2} V' + \lambda \tau b \right) + bp\tau \left(\tfrac{k}{q} - 1 \right) \right) \partial_X^2 R \\
&+ \varepsilon^5 \left(-\frac{w_{n-1}}{(h-l_{n-1})^2} \left(\tfrac{1}{24} V' - \tfrac{\lambda \tau b}{6} \right) - \tfrac{bp\lambda \tau}{3q} \right) \partial_X^4 R \\
&+ \varepsilon^5 \left(-\frac{w_{n-1}}{(h-l_{n-1})^2} \right) \tfrac{3}{4} V''' \partial_X^2 R^3 \\
&+ \varepsilon^5 \left\{ \left(\frac{w_{n-1}\lambda}{(h-l_{n-1})^2} - 2b + \tfrac{kp}{q} \right) \left(-\frac{w_{n-1}}{(h-l_{n-1})^2} \left(\tfrac{1}{6} V' + \tfrac{\lambda \tau b}{2} \right) + \tfrac{bpk\tau}{2q} \right) \right\} \partial_X^4 R
\end{aligned} \tag{28}$$

The variables $x = \varepsilon^{-1} X$ and $t = \varepsilon^{-3} T$ are converted by variables X and T, and equation $S(x, t) = \varepsilon R(X, T)$ is established. Equation (28) is finally transformed into the following form:

$$\begin{aligned}
\partial_t S &= \left(-\frac{w_{n-1}}{(h-l_{n-1})^2} \left(\tfrac{1}{6} V' + \tfrac{\lambda \tau b}{2} \right) + \tfrac{bpk\tau}{2q} \right) \partial_x^3 S + \left(-\frac{w_{n-1}}{(h-l_{n-1})^2} \right) \tfrac{1}{2} V''' \partial_x S^3 \\
&+ \left(-\frac{w_{n-1}}{(h-l_{n-1})^2} \left(\tfrac{1}{2} V' + \lambda \tau b \right) + bp\tau \left(\tfrac{k}{q} - 1 \right) \right) \partial_x^2 S \\
&+ \left(-\frac{w_{n-1}}{(h-l_{n-1})^2} \left(\tfrac{1}{24} V' - \tfrac{\lambda \tau b}{6} \right) - \tfrac{bp\lambda \tau}{3q} \right) \partial_x^4 S \\
&+ \left(-\frac{w_{n-1}}{(h-l_{n-1})^2} \right) \tfrac{3}{4} V''' \partial_x^2 S^3 \\
&+ \left[\left(\frac{w_{n-1}\lambda}{(h-l_{n-1})^2} - 2b + \tfrac{kp}{q} \right) \left(-\frac{w_{n-1}}{(h-l_{n-1})^2} \left(\tfrac{1}{6} V' + \tfrac{\lambda \tau b}{2} \right) + \tfrac{bpk\tau}{2q} \right) \right] \partial_x^4 S
\end{aligned} \tag{29}$$

By adding term $\left(-\frac{w_{n-1}}{(h-l_{n-1})^2}\right)\left(-\frac{w_{n-1}}{(h-l_{n-1})^2}\left(\frac{1}{2}V' + \lambda\tau b\right) + bp\tau\left(\frac{k}{q} - 1\right)\right)\partial_x S$ on two sides of Equation (29) and performing variable conversion $t = t_1$, $x_1 = x - \left(-\frac{w_{n-1}}{(h-l_{n-1})^2}\right)$. $\left(\frac{w_{n-1}(V'(\theta_0) - \lambda)}{(h-l_{n-1})^2} \cdot \frac{2q}{2pk+q}\right)\partial_x S$ for Equation (29), we obtain the following:

$$\partial_{t_1} S = \left(\partial_{x_1} + \left(\frac{1}{2}V' + \lambda\tau b\right)\partial_{x_1}^2\right)$$
$$\times \left\{\left(-\frac{w_{n-1}}{(h-l_{n-1})^2}\left(\frac{1}{6}V' + \frac{\lambda\tau b}{2}\right) + \frac{bpk\tau}{2q}\right)\partial_{x_1}^2 S \right.$$
$$\times \left(\left(-\frac{w_{n-1}}{(h-l_{n-1})^2}\left(\frac{1}{2}V' + \lambda\tau b\right) + bp\tau\left(\frac{k}{q} - 1\right)\right)S\right) + \frac{w_{n-1}}{(h-l_{n-1})^2}\frac{1}{2}V'''S^3\right\} \quad (30)$$

The thermodynamic potential is defined as follows:

$$\phi(S) \equiv -\left(-\frac{w_{n-1}}{(h-l_{n-1})^2}\right)\left(-\frac{w_{n-1}}{(h-l_{n-1})^2}\left(\frac{1}{2}V' + \lambda\tau b\right) + bp\tau\left(\frac{k}{q} - 1\right)\right)S^2 - \frac{1}{24}V'''S^4 \quad (31)$$

By rewriting Equation (30) with Equation (31), the following TDGL equation is obtained:

$$\partial_{t_1} S = -\left(\partial_{x_1} + \left(\frac{1}{2}V' + \lambda\tau b\right)\partial_{x_1}^2\right)\frac{\partial\Phi(S)}{\partial S} \quad (32)$$

$$\Phi(S) \equiv \int dx_1 \left[\frac{1}{2}\left(-\frac{w_{n-1}}{(h-l_{n-1})^2}\left(\frac{1}{6}V' + \frac{\lambda\tau b}{2}\right) + \frac{bpk\tau}{2q}\right)(\partial_{x_1}S)^2 + \phi(S)\right] \quad (33)$$

where the function derivative is denoted by $\partial\Phi(S)/\partial S$. TDGL Equation (32) can obtain a uniform solution, such as Equation (34), and a kink solution, such as Equation (35), when only non-trivial solutions $S \neq 0$ are considered. Both of them are stable solutions:

$$S(x_1, t_1) = \pm\left(\frac{\frac{3}{4}\left(-\frac{(h-l_{n-1})^2}{w_{n-1}}\right)\left(-\frac{w_{n-1}}{(h-l_{n-1})^2}\left(\frac{1}{2}V' + \lambda\tau b\right) + bp\tau\left(\frac{k}{q} - 1\right)\right)}{V'''}\right)^{1/2} \quad (34)$$

$$S(x_1, t_1) = \pm\left(\frac{\frac{3}{4}\left(-\frac{(h-l_{n-1})^2}{w_{n-1}}\right)\left(-\frac{w_{n-1}}{(h-l_{n-1})^2}\left(\frac{1}{2}V' + \lambda\tau b\right) + bp\tau\left(\frac{k}{q} - 1\right)\right)}{V'''}\right)^{1/2}$$
$$\times \tanh\left\{\left[\left(\frac{w_{n-1}}{(h-l_{n-1})^2}\left(\frac{1}{24}V' - \frac{\lambda\tau b}{6}\right) + \frac{bp\lambda\tau}{3q}\right)\left(-\frac{w_{n-1}}{(h-l_{n-1})^2}\left(\frac{1}{2}V' + \lambda\tau b\right)\right) \times (x_1 - x_0)\right]^{1/2}\right\} \quad (35)$$

where x_0 is a constant. According to Equation (35), we obtain the coexistence curve under the following conditions:

$$\partial\phi/\partial S = 0, \quad \partial^2\phi/\partial S^2 > 0 \quad (36)$$

Equation (31) is substituted into Equation (36) to calculate the coexistence curve, which has the original parameters:

$$(\Delta s)_{co} = s_c \pm \left(\frac{\frac{3}{4}\left(-\frac{(h-l_{n-1})^2}{w_{n-1}}\right)\left(-\frac{w_{n-1}}{(h-l_{n-1})^2}\left(\frac{1}{2}V' + \lambda\tau b\right) + bp\tau\left(\frac{k}{q} - 1\right)\right)}{V'''}\right)^{1/2} \quad (37)$$

The spinodal line is given by the following condition:

$$\partial^2 \phi / \partial S^2 = 0 \qquad (38)$$

The spinodal line calculated by substituting Equation (31) into Equation (38) is described by the following:

$$(\Delta s)_{sp} = s_c \pm \left(\frac{\frac{1}{4}\left(-\frac{(h-l_{n-1})^2}{w_{n-1}}\right)\left(-\frac{w_{n-1}}{(h-l_{n-1})^2}\left(\frac{1}{2}V' + \lambda\tau b\right) + bp\tau\left(\frac{k}{q}-1\right)\right)}{V'''} \right)^{1/2} \qquad (39)$$

The critical point with the original parameters can be obtained by Equation (39) and condition $\partial \phi / \partial S = 0$ as follows:

$$(\Delta s)_{co} = h_c, \quad \alpha = \frac{2w_{n-1}(\lambda - V'(\theta_0))}{(h-l_{n-1})^2} - \frac{2pk}{q} \qquad (40)$$

4. The mKdV Equation

The slow-changing behavior at the long wavelength near the critical point is also worthy of our consideration. In a similar way, we consider the change in traffic behavior near the critical point. The slow scales of the space variable n and the time variable t are extracted with the derivation of the TDGL equation. Eliminating the second and third order terms of ε through taking $\alpha_c = \frac{2w_{n-1}(\lambda - V'(\theta_0))}{(h-l_{n-1})^2} - \frac{2bk}{c}$, $\alpha_c = (1+\varepsilon^2)\alpha$ into Equation (17), we then obtain the following:

$$\varepsilon^4 \left(\partial_T R - g_1 \partial_X^3 R - g_2 \partial_X R^3 \right) - \varepsilon^5 \left(g_3 \partial_X^2 R + g_4 \partial_X^4 R + g_5 \partial_X^2 R^3 \right) = 0 \qquad (41)$$

where the five coefficients g_i are shown in Table 1 below.

Table 1. The coefficients g_i in Equation (41).

g_1	g_2
$\left(-\frac{w_{n-1}}{(h-l_{n-1})^2}\left(\frac{1}{6}V' + \frac{\lambda\tau b}{2}\right) + \frac{bpk\tau}{2q}\right)$	$\left(-\frac{w_{n-1}}{(h-l_{n-1})^2}\right)\frac{1}{2}V'''$
g_3	g_5
$\left(-\frac{w_{n-1}}{(h-l_{n-1})^2}\left(\frac{1}{2}V' + \lambda\tau b\right) + bp\tau\left(\frac{k}{q}-1\right)\right)$	$\left(-\frac{w_{n-1}}{(h-l_{n-1})^2}\right)\frac{3}{4}V'''$
g_4	
$\left(\frac{w_{n-1}\cdot\lambda}{(h-l_{n-1})^2} - 2b + \frac{kp}{q}\right)\left(-\frac{w_{n-1}}{(h-l_{n-1})^2}\left(\frac{1}{6}V' + \frac{\lambda\tau b}{2}\right) + \frac{bpk\tau_c}{2q}\right) - \frac{3}{4}V'''\left(-\frac{w_{n-1}}{(h-l_{n-1})^2}\right)\left(-\frac{w_{n-1}}{(h-l_{n-1})^2}\left(\frac{1}{6}V' + \frac{\lambda\tau b}{2}\right) + \frac{bpk\tau}{2q}\right)$	

In the table $V' = dV(\Delta x_n)/d\Delta x_n |_{\Delta x_n = h_c}$ and $V''' = d^3V(\Delta x_n)/d\Delta x_n^3 |_{\Delta x_n = h_c}$. So as to derive the regularized equation, we can perform simple variable conversion:

$$T = \frac{1}{g_1}T', \quad R = \sqrt{\frac{g_1}{g_2}}R' \qquad (42)$$

So, the standard mKdV equation with $o(\varepsilon)$ correction term is as follows:

$$\partial_{T'}R' = \partial_X^3 R' - \partial_X R'^3 - \varepsilon \left[\frac{g_3}{g_1}\partial_X^2 R' + \frac{g_4}{g_1}\partial_X^4 R' + \frac{g_5}{g_2}\partial_X^2 R'^3 \right] \qquad (43)$$

Without considering the $o(\varepsilon)$ term, they only take the kink solution as the mKdV equation of the required solution:

$$R_0'(X, T') = \sqrt{c}\tanh\sqrt{\frac{c}{2}}(X - cT') \tag{44}$$

Presuming $R'(X, T') = R_0'(X, T') + \varepsilon R_1'(X, T')$, the $o(\varepsilon)$ correction is considered. So as to define the propagation velocity c for the kink solution, it can be based on the solvability condition. The solvability clause is as follows:

$$(R_0', M[R']) \equiv \int_{-\infty}^{+\infty} dX R_0' M[R_0'] = 0 \tag{45}$$

where $M[R_0'] = \frac{g_3}{g_1}\partial_X^2 R' + \frac{g_4}{g_1}\partial_X^4 R' + \frac{g_5}{g_2}\partial_X^2 R'^3$, we obtain the details of the total velocity c as follows:

$$c = \frac{5g_2 g_3}{2g_2 g_4 - 3g_1 g_5} \tag{46}$$

Therefore, the mKdV equation is obtained as the general kink–antikink solution of the headway:

$$\Delta x_n(t) = h_c \pm \sqrt{\frac{g_1 c}{g_2}\left(\frac{\tau}{\tau_c} - 1\right)} \times \tanh\sqrt{\frac{c}{2}\left(\frac{\tau}{\tau_c} - 1\right)} \times \left[n + (1 - cg_1)\left(\frac{\tau}{\tau_c} - 1\right)t\right] \tag{47}$$

when $V''' < 0$, the reciprocal of the driver's sensitivity coefficient is τ.

The coexisting phase is also represented by a kink solution whose Equation (47) is consistent with that obtained from the TDGL Equation (35). This result indicates that the interference is depicted either by the solution description of the TDGL equation or by the propagation solution of the mKdV equation.

5. Numerical Simulation

Through previous research and the conclusions drawn above, discrete equations can be used in the process of modeling and numerical simulation. We conducted numerical simulations through the computer mathematics software MATLAB. The equation used is as follows:

$$\Delta t^2 \left[V(\theta_0)\left(\frac{-w_{n-1}}{(h-l_{n-1})^2}\Delta x_{n+1}(t)\right) - V(\theta_0)\left(\frac{-w_{n-1}}{(h-l_{n-1})^2}\Delta x_n(t)\right)\right] - \Delta t \cdot \frac{-w_{n-1}\lambda\tau}{(h-l_{n-1})^2}$$
$$\cdot [\Delta x_n(t + \Delta t) - \Delta x_n(t) - (\Delta x_{n-1}(t + \Delta t) - \Delta x_{n-1}(t))] + \frac{k\tau}{q}[\Delta x_n(t + 2\Delta t) - 2\Delta x_n(t + \Delta t) \tag{48}$$
$$+ \Delta x_n(t) - (\Delta x_{n-1}(t + 2\Delta t) - 2\Delta x_{n-1}(t + \Delta t) + \Delta x_{n-1}(t))]$$
$$+ \Delta t \cdot \frac{k\tau p}{q}[\Delta x_n(t + \Delta t) - \Delta x_n(t) - (\Delta x_{n-1}(t + \Delta t) - \Delta x_{n-1}(t))] = 0$$

The initial conditions are the following:

$$\begin{cases} \Delta x_j(0) = \Delta x_0 = 5.0, \ x_j(1) = \Delta x_0 = 5.0, \ j \neq 50, 51. \\ \Delta x_j(1) = 5.0 - 0.5, \ j = 50. \\ \Delta x_j(1) = 5.0 + 0.5, \ j = 51. \end{cases} \tag{49}$$

$N = 100$ is the total number of vehicles and $\alpha = 2$ is the driver's sensitivity coefficient.

Under the condition of setting different parameters, simulations were performed on the extended model. In Figure 4, under the conditions of different values of $w(w = 1.6, 1.8, 2.0, 2.2)$, the evolution results of vehicle flow correspond to the subgraphs in Figure 4a–d, respectively. Especially when $w = 1.6$, the traffic flow is in the most stable state that explains the width of the preceding car having a certain influence on the follower's visual angle. It can be observed and analyzed that with the addition of small disturbances, the initial stable traffic flow transforms into a non-uniform density wave, and the form of this unstable density wave is just the kink–antikink solution of the mKdV equation. It is obvious from the four subgraphs in in Figure 4a–d that the amplitude of the kink–antikink solution gradually decreases with the increase in the parameter w. The results show that considering the vehicle width of the preceding vehicle will interfere with the follower's perspective, which will inevitably affect the stability of the traffic flow. The wider the vehicle width, the more it can interfere with the driver's perspective and have a negative impact on traffic flow stability.

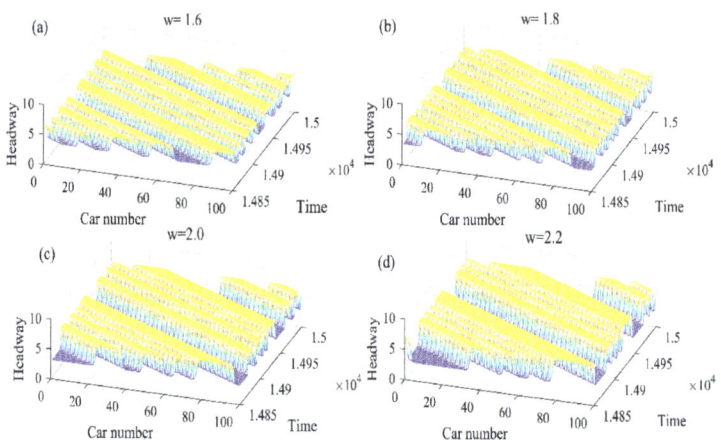

Figure 4. Spatiotemporal evolution patterns of the headway from $t = 14,800$ to $15,000$ with different values of w.

The four sub-pictures in Figure 5a–d correspond to the four sub-pictures in Figure 4a–d, respectively. They are cross-sectional views taken at the same time, representing the headway time-distance distribution and density wave of the preceding vehicle width w at time $t = 15,000$. Gradually, as the parameters decrease w, the amplitude of the traffic flow becomes smaller. It means that the stability of traffic flow can be positively influenced by considering the information of the width of the preceding vehicle.

The extended model performed a series of simulations under different electronic throttle angle coefficient coefficients $k(k = 0, 0.1, 0.3, 0.5)$, as shown in Figure 6. Electronic throttle can improve the safety, dynamics, stability and economy of car driving, and can effectively alleviate traffic congestion. From the four sub-graphs in Figure 6, the traffic flow is in the most stable state when the electronic throttle angle coefficient is $k = 0.5$. It is evident from the subgraphs in Figure 6a–d that the amplitude of the kink-antikink solution decreases with the increase in the angle coefficient of the electronic throttle k. It can be observed from the figure that as the fluctuation distance of the traffic flow extends backward, the fluctuation amplitude gradually weakens. The overall trend of traffic flow fluctuations is to reduce to disappear, which shows that considering the handling performance of the vehicle ahead (electronic throttle angle coefficient), the traffic flow can be effectively stabilized. Because the improved model considers the car-following state, it provides a reference for the driver and can adjust the car-following behavior more comprehensively. Therefore, considering the factor of the electronic throttle angle, it is better to provide a reference for the driver, and more fully adjust the current driving state.

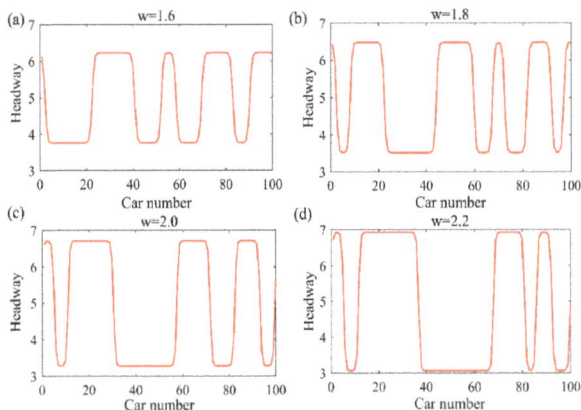

Figure 5. Profiles of the density wave at $t = 15,000$ corresponding to Figure 4, respectively.

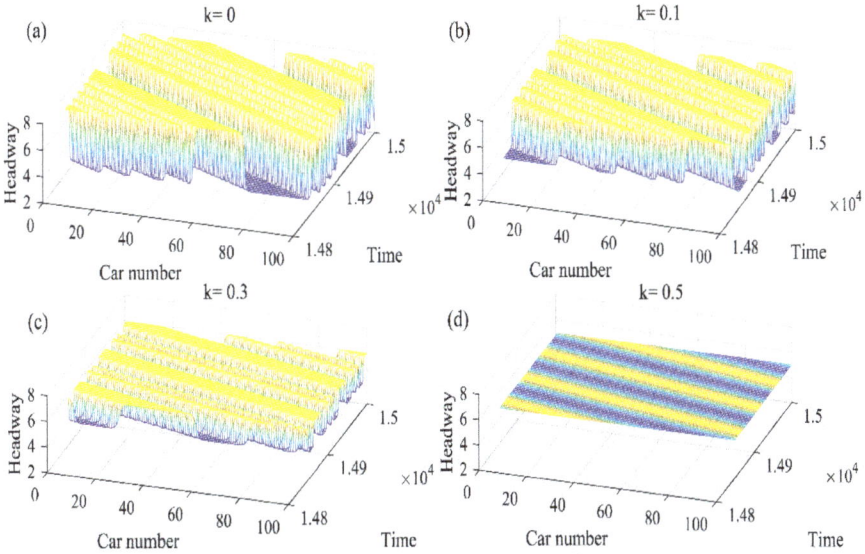

Figure 6. Spatiotemporal evolution patterns of the headway from $t = 14,800$ to $15,000$ with different values of k.

The sub-pictures in Figure 7a–d correspond to the sub-pictures in Figure 6a–d, respectively. They show a cross-sectional view of the fluctuation of traffic flow at a selected moment $t = 15,000$, indicating the headway profiles and density wave curve of the electronic throttle angle of the preceding vehicle. From Figure 7a–d, considering the electronic throttle feedback coefficient of the preceding vehicle, the traffic jam can be effectively alleviated, and the traffic interference can be effectively reduced. As the feedback coefficient of the electronic throttle increases, the amplitude of the density wave gradually decreases, and the traffic flow tends to be stable. From the Figure 7, with the adjustment of the parameters, the transportation system can have obvious positive effects.

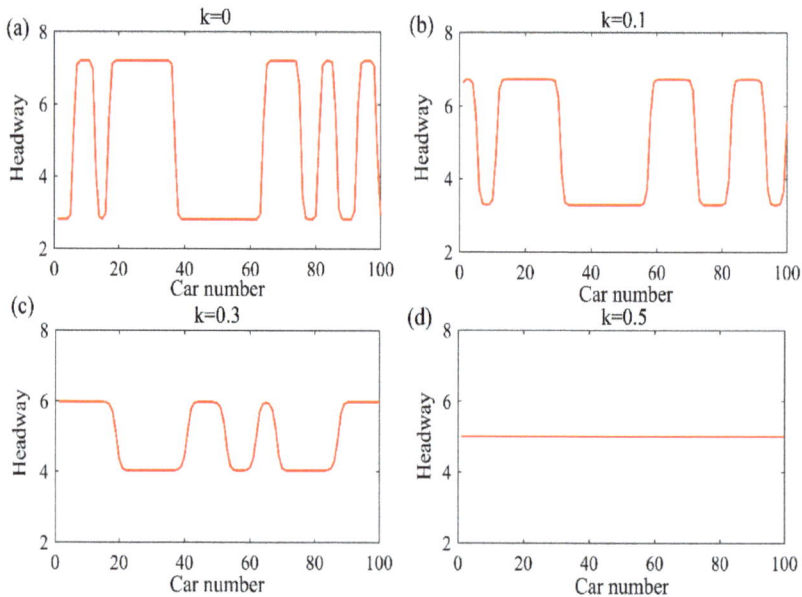

Figure 7. Profiles of the density wave at $t = 15,000$ corresponding to Figure 6, respectively.

The relationship between the headway distance and the traffic flow, the velocity and the density hysteresis loop relationships are shown in Figure 8, respectively. It shows that as the value increases λ, the size of the loop decreases. This also indicates that considering the speed difference between the current vehicle and the front vehicle can effectively alleviate urban road traffic congestion, reduce the incidence of accidents, and reduce traffic losses.

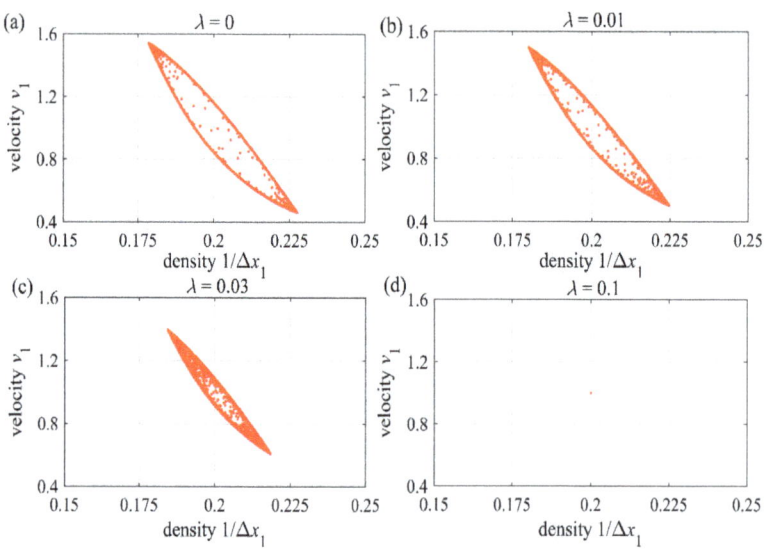

Figure 8. Hysteresis loops obtained from the velocities $v_1(t)$ and the densities $\rho_1(t) = 1/\Delta x_1(t)$ respectively.

6. Conclusions

The model in this paper is based on VAM to describe changes in traffic conditions. From the perspective of the driver, it better combines human factors and achieves a more ideal simulation result. The influence of the electronic throttle angle feedback of the preceding vehicle is taken into consideration. By carrying out linear analysis, neutral stability curves and critical points are obtained. The TDGL equation is obtained by nonlinear analysis, and then the coexistence curve, metastable curve and critical point are described according to the obtained thermodynamic potential. The mKdV equation of the model is obtained by the same method.

Numerical simulation through MATLAB shows that the driver will perceive objects around the vehicle, such as other vehicles, infrastructures and so on, during the driving process. These environmental objects will form a stimulus for the driver (for example, the stimulus of the front vehicle to the driver's perspective) with varying degrees of intensity. Analyzing and modeling this stimulus will help understand the behavior of the driver during driving. Numerical simulation also shows that the electronic throttle is the core component of automobile engine operation, and its working performance directly affects the performance of the vehicle. Therefore, it is necessary to consider the impact of the electronic throttle angle difference between the preceding vehicle and the current vehicle on the traffic. In the past few decades, the intelligent transportation system (ITS) has achieved rapid development, and the number of cars has also shown a rapid upward trend. Our research helps people better understand the characteristics of traffic flow from the aspects of vehicle external environment and internal structure. This can effectively alleviate traffic congestion, which is of great significance for intelligent highway construction and improving driver's driving environment. Finally, by comparing the theoretical analysis with numerical simulation, the conclusions are highly consistent.

Author Contributions: H.G.: Conceptualization, Methodology, Software; S.L.: Numerical simulation, Writing-Original draft preparation.; C.Y.: Supervision, Writing-Reviewing and Editing. All authors have read and agreed to the published version of the manuscript.

Funding: This work is supported by the National Key Research and Development Program of China-Traffic Modeling, Surveillance and Control with Connected & Automated Vehicles (Grant No. 2017YFE9134700) and the K.C. Wong Magna Fund in Ningbo University, China.

Institutional Review Board Statement: Not applicable.

Informed Consent Statement: Not applicable.

Data Availability Statement: The data used to support the findings of this study are available from the corresponding author upon request.

Conflicts of Interest: The authors declare no conflict of interest.

References

1. Tang, T.Q.; Rui, Y.X.; Zhang, J.; Shang, H.Y. A cellular automation model accounting for bicycle's group behavior. *Phys. A* **2018**, *492*, 1782–1797. [CrossRef]
2. Tian, H.H.; Xue, Y.; Kan, S.J.; Jiang, Y.J. Study on the energy consumption using the cellular automaton mixed traffic model. *Acta Phys. Sin.* **2009**, *58*, 4506–4513. [CrossRef]
3. Zhou, X.M.; Hu, J.J.; Jing, X.F.; Xiao, Z.Y. Cellular automaton simulation of pedestrian flow considering vision and multi-velocity. *Phys. A* **2019**, *514*, 982–992. [CrossRef]
4. Xue, S.Q.; Jia, B.; Jiang, R. A behavior based cellular automaton model for pedestrian counter flow. *J. Stat. Mech. Theory Exp.* **2016**, *2016*, 113204. [CrossRef]
5. Peng, G.H.; Lu, W.Z.; He, H.D.; Gu, Z.H. Nonlinear analysis of a new car-following model accounting for the optimal velocity changes with memory. *Commun. Nonlinear Sci. Numer. Simul.* **2016**, *40*, 197–205. [CrossRef]
6. Ge, H.X.; Dai, S.Q.; Dong, L.Y.; Xue, Y. Stabilization effect of traffic flow in an extended car-following model based on an intelligent transportation system application. *Phys. Rev. E* **2004**, *70*, 066134. [CrossRef]
7. Yu, S.W.; Tang, J.J.; Xin, Q. Relative velocity difference model for the car-following theory. *Nonlinear Dyn.* **2018**, *91*, 1415–1428. [CrossRef]

8. Zhu, W.X.; Li, D.Z. A new car-following model for autonomous vehicles flow with mean expected velocity field. *Phys. A* **2018**, *492*, 2154–2165.
9. Zhu, W.X.; Zhang, H.M. Analysis of mixed traffic flow with human-driving and autonomous cars based on car-following model. *Phys. A* **2018**, *496*, 274–285. [CrossRef]
10. Zhu, W.X.; Jun, D.; Zhang, L.D. A compound compensation method for car-following model. *Commun. Nonlinear Sci. Numer. Simul.* **2016**, *39*, 427–441. [CrossRef]
11. Ou, H.; Tang, T.Q. An extended two-lane car-following model accounting for inter-vehicle communication. *Phys. A* **2018**, *495*, 260–268. [CrossRef]
12. Wang, Y.; Li, X.P.; Tian, J.F.; Jiang, R. Stability Analysis of Stochastic Linear Car-Following Models. *Transp. Sci.* **2020**, *54*, 274–297. [CrossRef]
13. Xin, Q.; Yang, N.Y.; Fu, R.; Yu, S.W.; Shi, Z.K. Impacts analysis of car following model considering variable vehicular gap policies. *Phys. A* **2018**, *501*, 338–355. [CrossRef]
14. Yu, W.; Huang, M.X.; Ren, J.; Shi, Z.K. An improved car-following model considering velocity fluctuation of the immediately ahead car. *Phys. A* **2016**, *449*, 1–17. [CrossRef]
15. Yu, S.W.; Shi, Z.K. An improved car-following model considering headway changes with memory. *Phys. A Stat. Mech. Appl.* **2015**, *421*, 1–14. [CrossRef]
16. Jin, Z.Z.; Cheng, R.J.; Ge, H.X. Nonlinear density wave investigation for an extended car-following model considering driver's memory and jerk. *Mod. Phys. Lett. B* **2018**, *32*, 1750366. [CrossRef]
17. Du, W.J.; Li, Y.Z.; Zhang, J.G.; Yu, J.N. Stability analysis of a general nonlinear car-following model. *Int. J. Control.* **2020**, *93*, 1461–1469. [CrossRef]
18. Sun, D.H.; Liu, H.; Zhang, G. A new lattice hydrodynamic model with the consideration of flux change rate effect. *Nonlinear Dyn.* **2018**, *92*, 351–358. [CrossRef]
19. Redhu, P.; Gupta, A.K. Delayed-feedback control in a lattice hydrodynamic model. *Commun. Nonlinear Sci. Numer. Simul.* **2015**, *27*, 263–270. [CrossRef]
20. Peng, G.H.; Yang, S.H.; Qing, L. Feedback control pattern for a new lattice hydrodynamic model accounting for historic evolution information. *Int. J. Control.* **2020**, *93*, 2370–2377. [CrossRef]
21. Zhou, J.; Shi, Z.K. A new lattice hydrodynamic model for bidirectional pedestrian flow with the consideration of lateral discomfort. *Nonlinear Dyn.* **2015**, *81*, 1113–1131. [CrossRef]
22. Cheng, R.J.; Wang, Y.N. An extended lattice hydrodynamic model considering the delayed feedback control on a curved road. *Phys. A* **2019**, *513*, 510–517. [CrossRef]
23. Liu, Y.; Wong, C.K. A two-dimensional lattice hydrodynamic model considering shared lane marking. *Phys. Lett. A* **2020**, *384*, 126668. [CrossRef]
24. Cen, B.L.; Xue, Y.; Zhang, Y.C.; Wang, X.; He, H.D. A feedback control method with consideration of the next-nearest-neighbor interactions in a lattice hydrodynamic model. *Phys. A Stat. Mech. Appl.* **2020**, *559*, 125055. [CrossRef]
25. Chang, Y.Y.; He, Z.T.; Cheng, R.J. An extended lattice hydrodynamic model considering the driver's sensory memory and delayed-feedback control. *Phys. A* **2019**, *514*, 522–532. [CrossRef]
26. Yu, L. A new continuum traffic flow model with two delays. *Phys. A Stat. Mech. Appl.* **2020**, *545*, 123757. [CrossRef]
27. Zhai, C.; Wu, W.T. A new continuum model with driver's continuous sensory memory and preceding vehicle's taillight. *Commun. Theor. Phys.* **2020**, *72*, 105004. [CrossRef]
28. Sun, L.; Jafaripournimchahi, A.; Kornhauser, A.; Hu, W.S. A new higher-order viscous continuum traffic flow model considering driver memory in the era of autonomous and connected vehicles. *Phys. A Stat. Mech. Its Appl.* **2020**, *547*, 123829. [CrossRef]
29. Cheng, R.J.; Ge, H.X.; Wang, J.F. An extended continuum model accounting for the driver's timid and aggressive attributions. *Phys. Lett. A* **2017**, *381*, 1302–1312. [CrossRef]
30. Cheng, R.J.; Ge, H.X.; Wang, J.F. KdV-Burgers equation in a new continuum model based on full velocity difference model considering anticipation effect. *Phys. A* **2017**, *481*, 52–59. [CrossRef]
31. Tang, T.Q.; Luo, X.F.; Zhang, J.; Chen, L. Modeling electric bicycle's lane-changing and retrograde behaviors. *Phys. A* **2018**, *490*, 1377–1386. [CrossRef]
32. Zhai, C.; Wu, W.T. Analysis of drivers' characteristics on continuum model with traffic jerk effect. *Phys. Lett. A* **2018**, *382*, 3381–3392. [CrossRef]
33. Ma, C.X.; Hao, W.; Wang, A.B.; Zhao, H.X. Developing a coordinated signal control system for urban ring road under the vehicle-infrastructure connected environment. *IEEE Access* **2018**, *6*, 52471–52478. [CrossRef]
34. Ma, C.X.; Hao, W.; He, R.C.; Jia, X.Y.; Pan, F.Q.; Fan, J.; Xiong, R.Q. Distribution path robust optimization of electric vehicle with multiple distribution centers. *PLoS ONE* **2018**, *13*, e0193789. [CrossRef] [PubMed]
35. Ma, C.X.; Hao, W.; Pan, F.Q.; Xiang, W. Road screening and distribution route multi-objective robust optimization for hazardous materials based on neural network and genetic algorithm. *PLoS ONE* **2018**, *13*, e0198931. [CrossRef]
36. Gazis, D.C.; Herman, R.; Rothery, R.W. Nonlinear follow-the-leader models of traffic flow. *Oper. Res.* **1961**, *9*, 545–567. [CrossRef]
37. Bando, M.; Haseba, K.; Nakayama, A.; Shibata, A.; Sugiyama, Y. Dynamical model of traffic congestion and numerical simulation. *Phys. Rev.* **1995**, *51*, 1035–1042. [CrossRef]
38. Helbing, D.; Tilch, B. Generalized force model of traffic dynamics. *Phys. Rev. E* **1998**, *58*, 133–138. [CrossRef]

39. Jiang, R.; Wu, Q.S.; Zhu, Z.J. Full velocity difference model for a car-following theory. *Phys. Rev. E* **2001**, *64*, 017101. [CrossRef]
40. Jiang, R.; Wu, Q.S. Two-lane totally asymmetric exclusion processes with particle creation and annihilation. *Phys. A* **2007**, *375*, 247–256. [CrossRef]
41. Jin, S.; Wang, D.H.; Huang, Z.Y.; Tao, P.F. Visual angle model for car-following theory. *Phys. A* **2011**, *390*, 1931–1940. [CrossRef]
42. Qin, Y.Y.; Wang, H.; Ran, B. Car-following model of connected and autonomous vehicles considering multiple feedbacks. *Transp. Syst. Eng. Inf.* **2018**, *18*, 48–54.
43. Nagatani, T. TDGL and MKDV equations for jamming transiton in the lattice models of traffic. *Phys. A* **1999**, *264*, 581–592. [CrossRef]

Article

Research on Dynamic Response Characteristics for Basement Structure of Heavy Haul Railway Tunnel with Defects

Jinfei Chai [1,2,3]

[1] Railway Engineering Research Institute, China Academy of Railway Sciences Corporation Limited, Beijing 100081, China; chaijinfei@rails.cn; Tel.: +86-18-810-640-475
[2] State Key Laboratory for Track Technology of High-Speed Railway, Beijing 100081, China; tkytjs00@sina.com
[3] Beijing Tieke Special Engineering Technology Corporation Limited, Beijing 100081, China; tktzgs00@163.com

Abstract: Based on the basic principle of thermodynamics, an elastoplastic damage constitutive model of concrete is constructed in this paper. The model is realized and verified in FLAC3D, which provides a solid foundation for the study of dynamic response and fatigue damage to the base structure of a heavy haul railway tunnel. The dynamic response and damage distribution of the base structure of a heavy-duty railway tunnel with defects were numerically simulated by the concrete elastic-plastic damage constitutive model. Then, by analyzing the response characteristics of the tunnel basement structure under different surrounding rock softening degrees, different foundation suspension range and different foundation structure damage degree are determined. The results show the following: (1) The elastoplastic damage constitutive model of concrete can well describe the stress–strain relationship of materials, especially with the simulation results of post peak softening being in good agreement with the test results, and the simulation effect of the unloading–reloading process of the cyclic loading and unloading test also meet the requirements. (2) The initial stress field and dynamic response of the tunnel basement structure under the action of train vibration load are very different from the ideal state of the structure design when the surrounding rock of the base is softened, the base is suspended, or the basement structure is damaged. With the surrounding rock softening, basement hanging, or basement structure damage developing to a certain extent, the basement structure will be damaged. (3) The horizontal dynamic stress amplitude increases with the increase in the softening degree of the basement surrounding rock. The horizontal dynamic stress of the measuring point increases with the increase in the width of the hanging out area when the hanging out area is located directly below the loading line. When the degree of damage to the basement structure is aggravated, the horizontal dynamic tensile stress of each measuring point gradually decreases. (4) The maximum principal stress increment increases with the increase in the fracture degree of the basement structure, while the minimum principal stress increment decreases with the increase in the fracture degree of the basement structure, but the variation range of the large and minimum principal stress increments is small. The research results have important theoretical and practical significance for further analysis of the damage mechanism and control technology of the foundation structure of a heavy haul railway tunnel with defects.

Keywords: heavy haul; railway tunnel; basement structure; dynamic response characteristics; defects

1. Introduction

Through the analysis of the field investigation results of tunnel defects at home and abroad, it was found that the basement structure of the tunnel is the most common site of tunnel structure defects. After long operation periods, many tunnel basement structures will show damage, subsidence, and other defects, and the track irregularity will be aggravated, even leading to rail fracture in serious cases, which poses a threat to the safety of train operation. At present, the academic understanding of the causes of the defects in the tunnel basement structure is as follows: under the coupling effect of train vibration and groundwater and other external environmental factors, the bedrock at the bottom of the tunnel softens and breaks into fine particles, which are carried away by groundwater erosion. The bedrock gradually forms cavities, and the contact state between the tunnel basement structure and the bedrock gradually deteriorates, which eventually leads to the deterioration of the tunnel basement structure. The defect is now present. It can be seen that the condition of the tunnel basement is one of the key factors affecting the service condition of its structure [1–14].

In the analysis of the impact of train load on dangerous roads, subgrades, and the surrounding environment, field test technology is the most direct, obvious, and reliable research method. The early vibration prediction is based on a large number of field test results, and an empirical formula is devised to analyze it. Koch et al. [15] carried out a field test and analysis of the vibration and noise caused by subway operation in view of its influence on surface buildings and obtained a mathematical expression of the variation of noise wave velocity in a tunnel with the thickness of lining shed at a driving speed of 60 km/h. The research team of Zach and Rutishauser analyzed the vibration frequency and acceleration characteristics of the tunnel structure through field tests [16]. Based on the European Union scientific research project, Degrende conducted a series of field tests on the vibration of 35 test trains during operation of the London Metro at a speed of 20–50 km/h [17]. The test objects included train, rail, tunnel side wall, team invert, surrounding soil layer, surface, and two buildings 70 m away from the tunnel, and the time history curve of speed or acceleration at each measuring point was recorded. The test results showed that the dynamic responses of the rail, tunnel side wall, and invert increased with the increase in driving speed.

The field testing of tunnel vibration under train load was started late by domestic scholars. Pan and Xie obtained the dynamic response characteristics of several points on the tunnel lining gun structure through field tests of the Beijing Metro. Combined with the track acceleration data and the vibration of the vehicle system, the mathematical expression of train load was obtained [18]. Zhang and Bai obtained the train vibration signals through a field test and analyzed them. It was found that these signals could be regarded as a kind of periodic vibration combination [19]. Furthermore, the mathematical expression of track vibration acceleration caused by a train passing was obtained through Fourier transform spectrum analysis. Li and Gao obtained the acceleration of the concrete bottom layer 0.55 m below the rail surface through a field test of train vibration in the Jinjiayan Tunnel and pointed out that the vibration caused by the train load occurred on the lining, which can cause defects in the bottom structure [20]. Wang and Yang conducted a field test on the vibration of the Zhuting Tunnel structure on the Beijing to Guangzhou Railway and analyzed the measured data by power spectral density [21]. On this basis, the wheel rail vibration analysis model was established, and the mathematical expression of train vibration load was obtained. Xue et al. obtained the vertical vibration velocity of the tunnel invert and foundation soil as well as the attenuation law of soil pressure along the depth by simulating the cyclic dynamic load test of high-speed train vibration in a loess tunnel and further analyzed the variation law of foundation soil pressure and excess hydrostatic pressure with vibration frequency [22]. Peng et al. analyzed the dynamic response of the bottom structure of the Wushiling Tunnel under train load through a field test of vertical static and dynamic stress and acceleration [23]. Shi et al. conducted a long-term test and analysis of the dangerous deformation of a bottom structure and the stress of invert concrete and reinforcement of the Xichongzi Tunnel of the Wuhan Guangzhou high-speed railway and concluded that the tunnel bottom structure experienced the repeated change process of uplift subsidence, and the stress of invert concrete and reinforcement experienced the repeated change process of tension compression. In the process of tunnel construction, the invert is in an unfavorable stress state, so it should be closed as soon as possible to ensure operation safety [24]. Fu et al., through a field test of the Sanjiacun Tunnel on the Shuozhou to Huanghua Railway, statistically analyzed the dynamic stress of the filling layer in different surrounding rock sections, converted the dynamic force into static value using the soil column method, and obtained the impact coefficient of the base structure. Based on this, the dynamic response and impact coefficient of the basement structure of the dangerous track under the action of a heavy-duty train were analyzed by establishing a comprehensive analysis model of train tunnel track structure [25]. Yu et al. studied the virtual hybrid simulation method for underground structures subjected to seismic loadings [26,27]. Based on the Least Square Method, some scholars have analyzed different cases [28–41].

Based on the above research, the theoretical analysis of the vibration response of tunnel structure under train load can only analyze some simplified problems, and there are many assumptions, which is difficult to reflect the real state of the analysis object.

The reasonable description of concrete damage evolution process under the static and dynamic coupling of surrounding rock pressure and train load is the key to effectively evaluate the base condition of heavy haul railway tunnel, and it is the basis to reasonably and accurately reflect the health state of base structure of heavy haul railway tunnel. In order to reasonably and accurately reflect the dynamic response characteristics of the base structure of the defective heavy haul railway tunnel, the following studies are carried out in this paper: Section 1 introduces the previous research results; Section 2 establishes the elastic-plastic damage model based on the previous research; Section 3 verifies the rationality, correctness, and effectiveness of the elastic-plastic damage model by numerical tests; Section 4 carries out the dynamic response simulation test of the foundation structure of a heavy-duty railway tunnel by using the elastic-plastic damage model; Section 5 analyzes the test data of dynamic response simulation test of foundation structure of a heavy haul railway tunnel; Section 6 draws the research conclusions and further observations.

2. Establishment of Elastoplastic Damage Model

The tensile damage variable and shear damage variable are used to phenomenally reflect the influence of micro damage on the degradation of macro strength and stiffness of concrete. The elastic Helmholtz free energy of material is defined in the effective stress space; the development and evolution processes of material damage and plastic deformation are determined, and the elastic-plastic damage constitutive model in accordance with the basic principle of thermodynamics is constructed based on the non-associated flow law.

2.1. Lastoplastic Damage Constitutive Relation

(1) Stress–strain relationship

According to the plastic increment theory, the total strain tensor of materials can generally be divided into elastic strain tensor ε^e and plastic strain tensor ε^p.

$$\varepsilon = \varepsilon^e + \varepsilon^p \tag{1}$$

The elastic part can be obtained by Hooke's law.

$$\sigma = C\varepsilon^e \tag{2}$$

where σ is Cauchy stress tensor;
C is the elastic stiffness tensor.

According to Lemaitre's equivalent stress assumption, the elastoplastic constitutive relationship of nondestructive materials in effective stress space can be defined.

$$\bar{\sigma} = C_0(\varepsilon - \varepsilon^p) \tag{3}$$

where $\bar{\sigma}$ is the effective stress tensor; C_0 is the initial elastic stiffness tensor.

In order to clearly distinguish the different effects of tensile and compressive stress on materials, the effective stress tensor $\bar{\sigma}$ is decomposed into positive stress $\bar{\sigma}^+$ and negative stress $\bar{\sigma}^-$.

$$\bar{\sigma} = \bar{\sigma}^+ + \bar{\sigma}^- \tag{4}$$

$$\bar{\sigma}^+ = \sum_i \langle \bar{\sigma}_i \rangle (p_i \otimes p_i) \tag{5}$$

where $\langle x \rangle = \begin{cases} 0 & x < 0 \\ x & x \geq 0 \end{cases}$ is the Macaulay Function;

p_i is the Eigenvector of the $\bar{\sigma}$.

(2) Elastic Helmholtz free energy

Faria et al. proposed the elastic Helmholtz free energy function based on the positive and negative decomposition of effective stress in the effective stress space.

$$\psi = (1 - D^+)\psi_0^+ + (1 - D^-)\psi_0^- = \frac{1}{2}(1 - D^+)\bar{\sigma}^+ : C_0^{-1} : \bar{\sigma}^+ + \frac{1}{2}(1 - D^-)\bar{\sigma}^- : C_0^{-1} : \bar{\sigma}^- \tag{6}$$

Inside:

$$C_0^{-1} = \frac{1}{E}\left[\frac{1+v}{2}(\delta_{ik}\delta_{jl} + \delta_{il}\delta_{jk}) - v\delta_{ij}\delta_{kl}\right] \tag{7}$$

where E is the elastic modulus;
v is the Poisson's ratio;
δ_{ij} is the Kronecker symbol.
Then, it is deduced that

$$\sigma = \frac{\partial \psi}{\partial \varepsilon} = (1 - D^+)\bar{\sigma}^+ + (1 - D^-)\bar{\sigma}^- \tag{8}$$

(3) Damage criterion

The tensile damage energy release rate Z^+ and shear damage energy release rate Z^- corresponding to the tensile e damage variable D^+ and compressive damage variable D^- can be expressed as

$$Z^+ = -\frac{\partial \psi^+}{\partial D^+} = \psi_0^+ \tag{9}$$

$$Z^- = -\frac{\partial \psi^-}{\partial D^-} = \psi_0^- \tag{10}$$

According to the assumption of damage energy release rate by Li et al. [42], this paper adopts a similar definition of damage energy release rate.

$$\bar{\tau}^+ = g(Z^+) = \sqrt{E_0\left(\bar{\sigma}^+ : C_0^{-1} : \bar{\sigma}^+\right)} \tag{11}$$

$$\bar{\tau}^- = \alpha \bar{I}_1 + \sqrt{\bar{J}_2} \tag{12}$$

where $\bar{\tau}^+$ and $\bar{\tau}^-$ are tensile and compressive forces, respectively;
E_0 is the initial Young's modulus of the material.
Based on the above definition of damage energy release rate, the following damage criteria are established

$$\bar{\tau}^+ - r^+ \leq 0 \tag{13}$$

$$\bar{\tau}^- - r^- \leq 0 \tag{14}$$

where r^+ and r^- are the threshold values of tensile and compressive forces, respectively, and the initial values are r_0^+ and r_0^-, respectively, controlling the range of linear elastic region, and the relationship between tensile and compressive strength is

$$r_0^+ = f_0^+ \tag{15}$$

$$r_0^- = \left(\frac{\sqrt{3}}{3} - \alpha\right) f_0^- \tag{16}$$

where f_0^+ and f_0^- are the linear upper limit strength under uniaxial tension and compression, which are generally taken according to the following two formulas

$$f_0^+ = (0.6 \sim 0.8) f_t \tag{17}$$

$$f_0^- = (0.3 \sim 0.5) f_c \tag{18}$$

where f_t and f_c are uniaxial tensile strength and uniaxial compressive strength, respectively.

2.2. Internal Variable Evolution Process

(1) Damage variable

Based on the above damage criteria and according to the orthogonal flow law, the damage change rate can be obtained by the following formula

$$\dot{D}^{\pm} = \dot{r}^{\pm} \frac{\partial G^{\pm}(r^{\pm})}{\partial r^{\pm}} \tag{19}$$

The damage loading and unloading can be judged by Kuhn–Tucker Relationship

$$\dot{r}^{\pm} \geq 0 \qquad G^{\pm} \leq 0 \qquad \dot{r}^{\pm} G^{\pm} = 0 \tag{20}$$

When $G^{\pm} \leq 0$, $\dot{r}^{\pm} = 0$ then $\dot{D}^{\pm} = 0$, it is in the stage of damage unloading or neutral load change, and the material damage will no longer increase. When $\dot{r}^{\pm} \geq 0$, $G^{\pm} = 0$, $\dot{r}^{\pm} = \bar{\tau}^{\pm} \geq 0$, get Formula (21).

$$\dot{D}^{\pm} = \dot{G}^{\pm}(r^{\pm}) \geq 0 \tag{21}$$

According to the following constraints of tensile and shear damage variables, both tensile and shear damage variables adopt the expressions proposed by Mazars et al.

$$0 \leq G^{\pm}(r^{\pm}) \leq 1 \qquad \dot{G}^{\pm}(r^{\pm}) \geq 0 \qquad G^{\pm}(r_0^{\pm}) = 0 \tag{22}$$

$$D^+ = 1 - \frac{r_0^+(1 - A^+)}{r^+} - A^+ \exp\left[B^+\left(1 - \frac{r^+}{r_0^+}\right)\right] \tag{23}$$

$$D^- = 1 - \frac{r_0^-(1 - A^-)}{r^-} - A^- \exp\left[B^-\left(1 - \frac{r^-}{r_0^-}\right)\right] \tag{24}$$

where A^+, B^+, A^- and B^- are constitutive model parameters, A^+ and B^+ can be calibrated by uniaxial tensile test, A^- and B^- can be calibrated by uniaxial compression test.

(2) Plastic deformation

The evolution process of material plastic deformation is described by the Empirical Formula [43] proposed by Wu.

$$\dot{\varepsilon}^p = \xi^p E_0 H(\dot{D}^-) \frac{\langle \varepsilon^e : \dot{\varepsilon} \rangle}{\bar{\sigma} : \bar{\sigma}} : \bar{\sigma} \tag{25}$$

where ξ^p is the empirical parameter of the model, which can be roughly calibrated by uniaxial compression test. $H(\bullet)$ is the Heaviside step function.

3. Numerical Test Verification of Elastoplastic Damage Model

The reasonable description of the damage evolution process in concrete under the static and dynamic coupling of surrounding rock pressure and train load was the core issue in the establishment of the concrete elastic–plastic damage model in this chapter. It was the key to effectively evaluating the base condition of the heavy haul railway tunnel and the basis for reasonably and accurately reflecting the health state of the base structure of the heavy haul railway tunnel.

Using the elastic-plastic damage model established in Section 2, the monotonic loading and cyclic loading and unloading tests were numerically simulated in FLAC3D. The loading mode was consistent with the prototype test. The numerical simulation results and test results were compared to verify the correctness of the constitutive model and the effectiveness of the model program. However, because the path dependence of unloading stiffness is not considered in this model, the hysteretic characteristics after unloading and reloading cannot be reproduced.

3.1. Uniaxial Tensile Test

The uniaxial tensile test simulated the Gopalarantam–Shah test [42]. The initial Young's modulus E_0 measured in the literature was 3.1×10^4 MPa, and the tensile strength f_0^+ was 3.48 MPa. The numerical simulation parameters are shown in Table 1. The comparison between the numerical simulation results and test results is shown in Figure 1. It can be seen that the model in this paper better described the whole process curve of stress–strain in concrete materials under a uniaxial tensile stress state, including the softening section.

Table 1. Simulation parameters of the uniaxial tensile test.

E_0/MPa	f_0^+/MPa	A^+	B^+	ξ^p
3.1×10^4	3.48	1.0	0.518	0.52

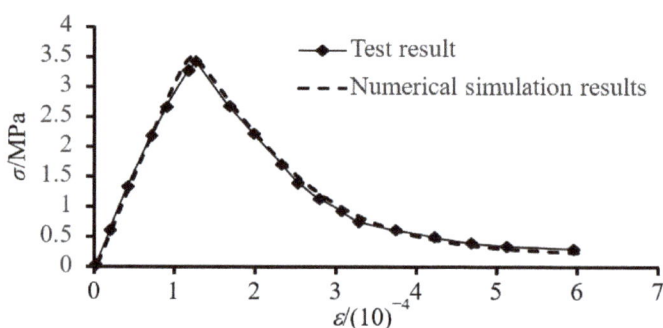

Figure 1. Comparison of numerical simulation result and experimental result (uniaxial tensile test).

3.2. Uniaxial Compression Test

The uniaxial compression test simulated the uniaxial compression test of Karsan and Jirsa [43]. The initial Young's modulus E_0 measured was 3.17×10^4 MPa, and the compressive strength f_0^- was 27.6 MPa. The numerical simulation parameters are shown in Table 2. The comparison between the numerical simulation results and test results is shown in Figure 2. The model in this paper also well simulated the stress–strain curve, including the softening section under a uniaxial compression stress state, and the program operation results were satisfactory.

Table 2. Simulation parameters of uniaxial compression test.

E_0/MPa	f_0^-/MPa	A^-	B^-	ζ^p
3.17×10^4	10.2	1.0	0.16	0.42

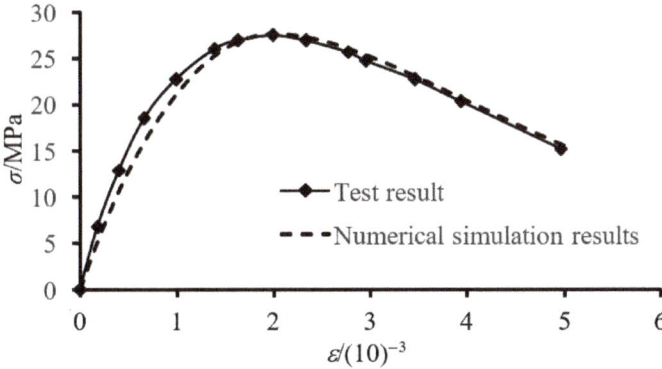

Figure 2. Comparison of numerical simulation result and experimental result (uniaxial compression test).

3.3. Biaxial Stress Test

The biaxial stress test simulated the test done by Kurfer et al. [44]. In their biaxial stress test, the measured Young's modulus was 3.10×10^4 MPa and the compressive strength was 32.0 MPa. The numerical simulation parameters are shown in Table 3. The working conditions where the stress ratios of σ_1/σ_2 comprised $-1:0$ and $-1:-1$ were simulated, respectively. The comparison between the numerical calculation results and the test results is shown in Figure 3. It can be seen that the simulation effect of the model for the material stress–strain relationship under biaxial stress also met the requirements.

Table 3. Simulation parameters of biaxial stress test.

E_0/MPa	f_0^-/MPa	A^-	B^-	ζ^p
3.10×10^4	15.0	1.0	0.19	0.37

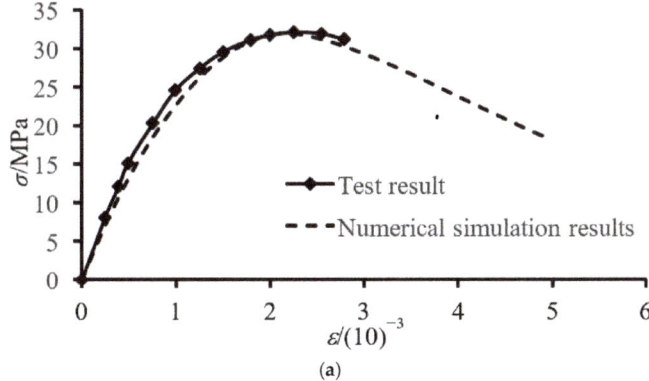

(a)

Figure 3. Cont.

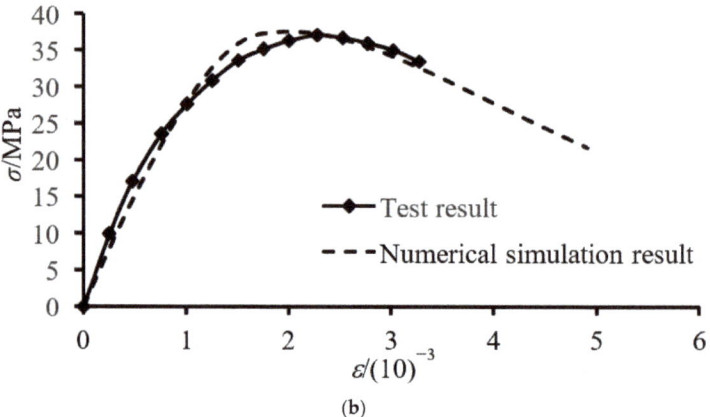

(b)

Figure 3. Comparison of numerical simulation result and experimental result (biaxial stress test). (a) $\sigma_1/\sigma_2 = -1:0$; (b) $\sigma_1/\sigma_2 = -1:-1$.

3.4. Cyclic Tensile Test

The cyclic tensile test simulated Taylor's test [45]. In Taylor's uniaxial repeated tensile test, the measured Young's modulus was 3.17×10^4 MPa and the tensile strength was 3.47 MPa. The numerical simulation parameters are shown in Table 4. The comparison between the numerical calculation results and test results is shown in Figure 4. It can be seen that the model not only well described the post peak strength softening stage, but also effectively simulated the elastic unloading–reloading process.

Table 4. Simulation parameters of the cyclic tensile test.

E_0/MPa	f_0^+/MPa	A^+	B^+	ξ^p
3.17×10^4	3.47	1.0	0.518	0.52

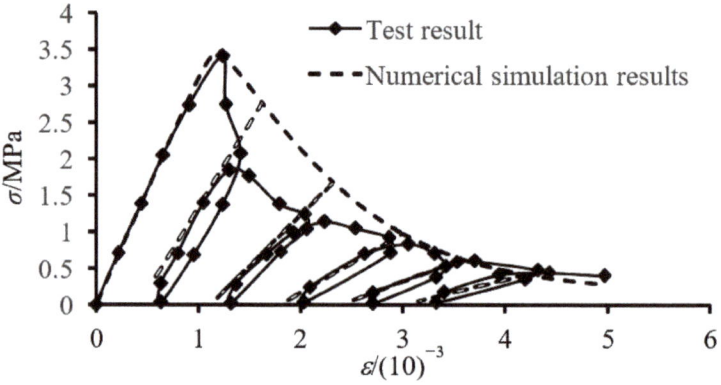

Figure 4. Comparison of numerical simulation result and experimental result (cyclic tensile test).

3.5. Cyclic Compression Test

The cyclic tensile test simulated the cyclic compression test conducted by Karsan and Jirsa [43]. The measured elastic modulus was 3.0×10^4 MPa, and the compressive strength was 27.6 MPa. The numerical simulation parameters are shown in Table 5. The comparison between numerical calculation results and test results is shown in Figure 5. The model had a good simulation effect on the loading process of cyclic compression test.

The elastic unloading–reloading process shown by the numerical calculation was slightly different from the test results and could not describe the hysteretic phenomenon in the unloading–reloading process in the test.

Table 5. Simulation parameters of cyclic compression test.

E_0/MPa	f_0^-/MPa	A^-	B^-	ζ^p
3.0×10^4	13.8	1.0	0.16	0.42

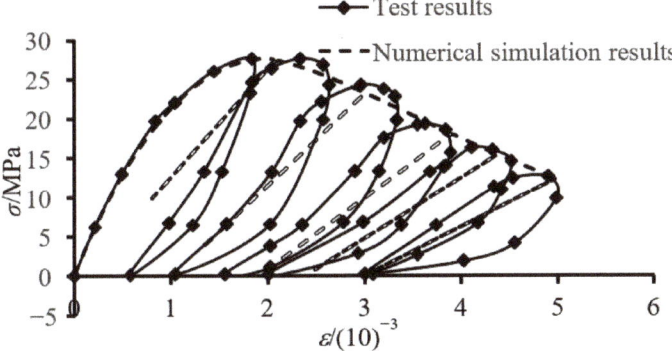

Figure 5. Comparison of numerical simulation result and experimental result (cyclic compression test).

4. Simulation Experiment on Dynamic Response of the Foundation Structure of a Heavy Haul Railway Tunnel

4.1. Introduction of Finite Element Calculation Model

The three-dimensional dynamic numerical analysis model was established to simulate the response characteristics of the tunnel basement structure under dynamic load and to analyze the dynamic stress and damage distribution of each part of the tunnel basement structure.

4.1.1. Numerical Model

As shown in Figure 6, the model size is 80 m × 1 m × 80 m, and the unit thickness is taken along the tunnel axis. The tunnel axis is located in the center of the model, and the length and width of the model are both 80 m. The developed elastoplastic damage model is used for the surrounding rock, invert, filling layer, primary support, secondary lining, and other tunnel structures.

Figure 6. Numerical simulation model.

4.1.2. Calculation Condition

The standard cross-section of railway double line composite lining tunnel is taken as the typical calculation cross-section. As the measured field data revealed that the running speed of a heavy train has little influence on the dynamic stress of the tunnel foundation structure, the numerical analysis mainly focused on the influence of different design parameters of foundation structure and different conditions of the tunnel foundation on the dynamic response and damage characteristics of the tunnel foundation structure. The calculation conditions under different design parameters of the tunnel basement structure are shown in Table 6.

Table 6. Calculation cases with different design parameters of the tunnel base structure.

Influence Factor	Grade of Surrounding Rock	Thickness Invert	Rise Span Ratio of Invert
Specific parameters	III	30 cm	1/15
	IV	40 cm	1/12
	V	50 cm	1/10
	VI	60 cm	1/8

The benchmark calculation example of the above conditions was as follows: the axle load of the train is 30 t, the surrounding rock grade is grade V, the invert thickness is 50 cm, the rise span ratio is 1/12, and the train load acts on the side of the heavy train line. Other conditions only need to change the corresponding parameters.

4.1.3. Calculation Parameters

The basic physical and mechanical parameters of surrounding rock were adopted as shown in Table 7. The mechanical damage parameters of concrete are shown in Table 8.

Table 7. Basic mechanical parameters of concrete and surrounding rock.

Structure	Elasticity Modulus/GPa	Poisson's Ratio	Weight/(kN·m^{-3})	Cohesion/kPa	Friction Angle/°
Ballast	32.0	0.18	25.0	/	/
Filling layer	29.0	0.18	25.0	/	/
Invert	30.0	0.18	25.0	/	/
Second lining	30.0	0.18	25.0	/	/
First branch	27.5	0.18	25.0	/	/
Surrounding rock	1.5	0.36	19.5	200	42

Table 8. Mechanical damage parameters of concrete.

Structure	f_0^-/MPa	f_0^+/MPa	A^-	B^-	A^+	B^+	ζ^p
Ballast	8.44	1.26	1.15	0.23	1.0	0.58	0.35
Filling layer	4.76	0.89	0.98	0.16	1.0	0.51	0.41
Invert	6.68	1.10	1.05	0.18	1.0	0.54	0.39
Second lining	6.68	1.10	1.05	0.18	1.0	0.54	0.39
First branch	3.84	0.77	0.94	0.14	1.0	0.46	0.43

4.1.4. Simulation Method of Train Dynamic Load

Under the condition of a 30 t axle load and 80 km/h running speed, the Single Side Static Wheel Weight P_0 = 150 kn and the Unsprung Mass M_0 = 1200 kg were adopted. The time history curve of the artificial excitation force as shown in Figure 7 was obtained by Formula (26). The load acts on the rail simulated by Beam element.

$$F(t) = k_1 k_2 (P_0 + P_1 \sin \omega_1 t + P_2 \sin \omega_2 t + P_3 \sin \omega_3 t) \tag{26}$$

where P_0 is the static load of the wheel. P_1, P_2, P_3 are typical vibration load values related to ride irregularity, dynamic additional load, and wave abrasion, respectively, corresponding to a typical value of control condition ①–③ in Table 4. k_1 is the wheel rail force superposition coefficient. k_2 is the rail dispersion transfer coefficient.

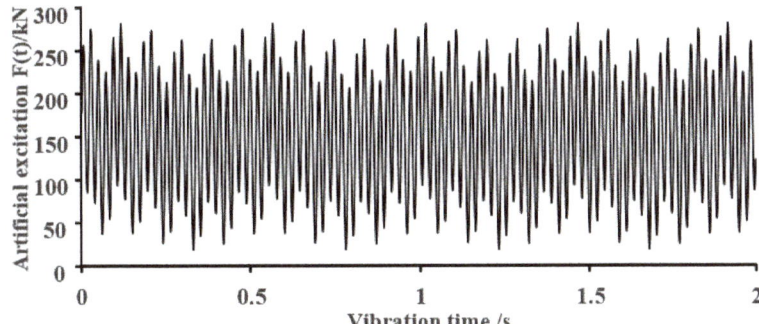

Figure 7. Simulative train load time history curve.

The wavelength management values of track geometric irregularity correspond to ①, ②, and ③ in Table 9.

Table 9. Track geometry irregularity management value in the UK.

Control Conditions	Wavelength/m	Normal Vector/mm
According to ride comfort ①	50.00	16.00
	20.00	9.00
	10.00	5.00
According to the dynamic additional load acting on the line ②	5.00	2.50
	2.00	0.60
	1.00	0.30
Wave abrasion ③	0.50	0.10
	0.05	0.005

4.1.5. Boundary Conditions

The setting of artificial boundary conditions and vibration wave input are the key links to realize dynamic numerical analysis, which directly affect the accuracy and credibility of the calculation results. In the engineering rock mass in semi-infinite space, when the vibration wave propagates around, it will transmit and refract when it meets the structure or rock mass structural plane and interfere with the incident wave to form a complex wave field. In the near-field dynamic numerical analysis, in order to effectively simulate the stray scattered wave passing through the truncated boundary of the model and make the vibration wave energy escape to infinity, it is necessary to introduce artificial boundary conditions to eliminate the reflection and oscillation of vibration wave on the artificial cutting boundary of the calculation area. In the FLAC3D dynamic analysis of this chapter, the free field boundary is used as the boundary condition of dynamic analysis.

In the numerical simulation of the vibration response of near surface structures such as slopes and shallow buried underground structures, the free field motion without structures must be considered at the lateral boundary of the numerical model. In the numerical simulation, the free field motion is applied to the model boundary, so that the artificial boundary remains non reflective. The lateral boundary of the discrete model simulates the viscous boundary through the coupling of damper and free field, and the unbalanced force on the free field node is applied to the boundary node of the discrete model. The unbalanced force on a plane parallel to the axis in the normal direction can be expressed as

$$\begin{cases} F_x = -\rho C_p \left(v_x^m - v_x^{ff} \right) A + F_x^{ff} \\ F_y = -\rho C_s \left(v_y^m - v_y^{ff} \right) A + F_y^{ff} \\ F_z = -\rho C_s \left(v_z^m - v_z^{ff} \right) A + F_z^{ff} \end{cases} \tag{27}$$

where ρ is the material medium density. C_p and C_s represent the wave velocities of P-wave and S-wave in material medium, respectively; A is the influence area of free field nodes. $v_x^m, v_y^m, v_z^m, v_x^{ff}, v_y^{ff}, v_z^{ff}$ represent the three components along the coordinate axis of the particle vibration velocity caused by fluctuation on the main node on the artificial boundary and the corresponding free field node respectively. $F_x^{ff}, F_y^{ff}, F_z^{ff}$ represent the contribution of normal stress and tangential stress of free field node influence element to node force, respectively.

If the calculation model is a homogeneous medium without near surface structures, the calculation area is consistent with the motion law of free field, and the lateral damper does not work. When the two move relatively, the damper absorbs the energy of the external traveling wave. In FLAC3D, the free field boundary condition requires that the bottom surface of the model be a horizontal plane and the normal direction be an axial direction. The side must be vertical and the normal direction axis or axis direction.

4.1.6. Layout of Measuring Points

The arrangement of measuring points is shown in Figure 8. Measuring points 1 and 5 are respectively located at the joint of side invert and side wall of the loaded line and the empty line, and measuring points 2, 3, and 4 are respectively located at the right rail of the loaded line, the center of the tunnel, and just below the center of the empty line.

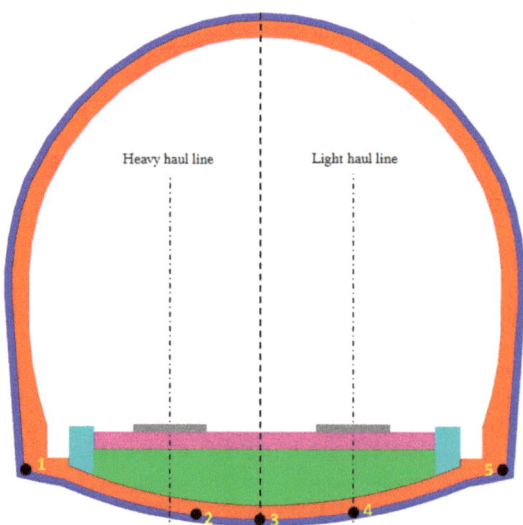

Figure 8. Measuring point layout.

5. Analysis of Simulation Experiment Test Data

5.1. Horizontal Dynamic Stress

5.1.1. Influence of Rock Softening on Basement

The amplitude of the horizontal dynamic stress at measuring points 2, 3, and 4 under different softening degrees of the basement surrounding rock is shown in Table 10 and Figure 9.

Table 10. Horizontal dynamic stress amplitudes of measuring points 2, 3, and 4 under different softening degrees of the basement surrounding rock.

Measuring Point	Horizontal Dynamic Stress Amplitude/kPa under Different Softening Degrees of the Basement Surrounding Rock			
	30% Reduction	50% Reduction	80% Reduction	90% Reduction
2	−177.9	−186.6	−214.6	−240.8
3	−93.6	−101.7	−117.4	−139.1
4	−37.6	−38.7	−47.9	−58.8

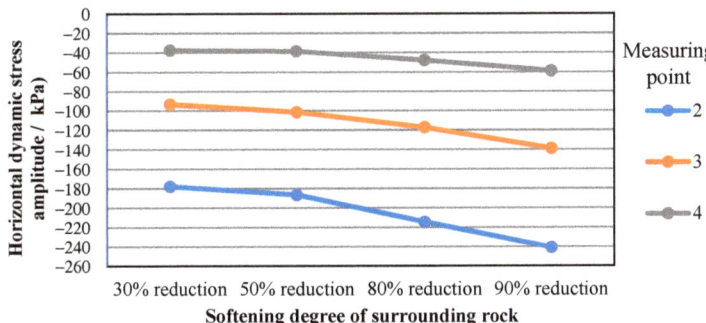

Figure 9. Horizontal dynamic stress amplitudes of measuring points 2, 3, and 4 under different softening degrees of the basement surrounding rock.

Under different softening degrees of the basement surrounding rock, the horizontal dynamic stress of measuring points 2, 3, and 4 was tensile stress. The results showed that the horizontal dynamic stress of the measuring point under the heavy vehicle line (measuring point 2) was the largest, the measuring point under the tunnel center (measuring point 3) was the second largest, and the measuring point under the empty vehicle line (measuring point 4) was the smallest; the horizontal dynamic stress amplitude increased with the increase in the softening degree of the basement surrounding rock, and the horizontal dynamic stress amplitudes of the measuring points 2, 3, and 4 were −240.5, −138.4, and −59.3 kPa, respectively, when the mechanical parameters of the basement surrounding rock were reduced by 90%.

5.1.2. The Influence of Base Hanging

The time history curves of the horizontal dynamic stress of measuring points 2, 3, and 4 under different basement hanging ranges are shown in Figure 3, and the amplitudes of horizontal dynamic stress at measuring points 2, 3, and 4 under different basement hanging ranges are shown in Table 11 and Figure 10.

The results showed that the horizontal dynamic stress of the measuring point increased with the increase in the width of the hanging out area when the hanging out area was located directly below the loading line; when the hanging out area was located at different positions on the base but with the same width, the horizontal dynamic stress of the measuring point was quite different.

Table 11. Horizontal dynamic stress amplitudes of measuring points 2, 3, and 4 under different basement hanging ranges.

Measuring Point	Horizontal Dynamic Stress Amplitude/kPa under Different Basement Hanging Ranges			
	1/4 Width Loading Line	1/2 Width Empty Line	1/2 Width Loading Line	3/4 Width Loading Line
2	−211.8	−184.9	−264.3	−332.2
3	−93.7	−123.3	−119.8	−216.5
4	−37.6	−82.5	−31.6	−55.3

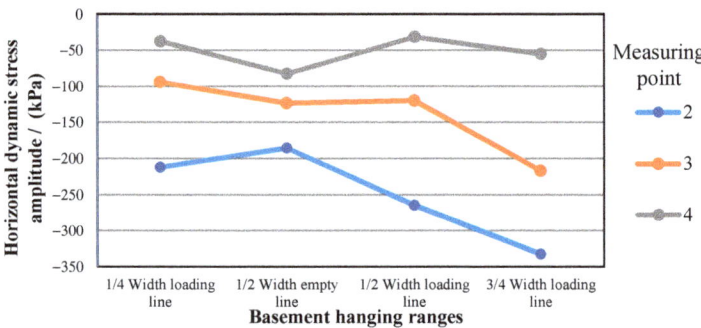

Figure 10. Horizontal dynamic stress amplitudes diagram of measuring points 2, 3, and 4 under different basement hanging ranges.

5.1.3. Influence of Basement Structure Damage

The amplitudes of horizontal dynamic stress at measuring points 2, 3, and 4 under different degrees of damage to the basement structure are shown in Table 12 and Figure 11.

Table 12. Horizontal dynamic stress amplitudes of measuring points 2, 3, and 4 under different degrees of damage to the foundation structure.

Measuring Point	Horizontal Dynamic Stress Amplitude/kPa under Different Degrees of Damage to the Basement Structure			
	10% Reduction	20% Reduction	50% Reduction	80% Reduction
2	−147.8	−138.3	−106.8	−51.2
3	−76.4	−71.9	−47.9	−16.7
4	−31.2	−27.5	−17.7	−6.2

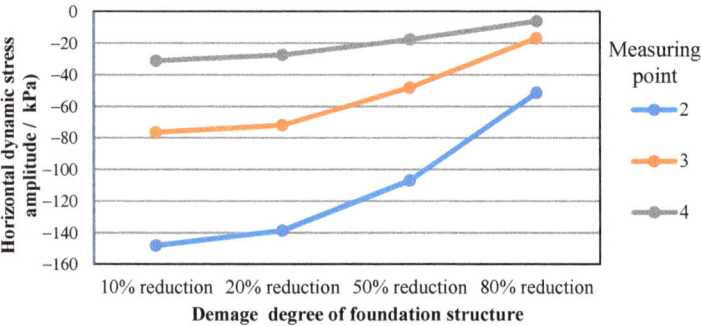

Figure 11. Horizontal dynamic stress amplitudes diagram of measuring points 2, 3, and 4 under different degrees of damage to the foundation structure.

The results showed that the horizontal dynamic tensile stress of measuring points 2, 3, and 4 was also the tensile stress under different degrees of damage to the basement structure. When the degree of damage to the basement structure was aggravated, the horizontal dynamic tensile stress of each measuring point gradually decreased.

5.2. Principal Stress

5.2.1. Influence of Rock Softening on Basement

The maximum amplitudes of principal stress at measuring points 1, 2, 3, and 5 under different softening degrees of the basement surrounding rock are shown in Table 13, Figures 12 and 13.

Table 13. Maximum principal stress amplitude of measuring points 1, 2, 3, and 5 under different softening degrees of basement surrounding rock.

Measuring Point	Maximum Principal Stress Amplitude/kPa under Different Softening Degrees of Basement Surrounding Rock							
	Maximum Principal Stress				Maximum Principal Stress Increment			
	30%	50%	80%	90%	30%	50%	80%	90%
1	421	387	346	329	−2.7	−1.9	1.4	2.1
2	109	138	162	168	35.8	31.8	28.5	24.9
3	111	96	98	103	21.6	20.2	18.8	16.9
5	437	386	341	321	0.5	−1.2	−1.1	−0.6

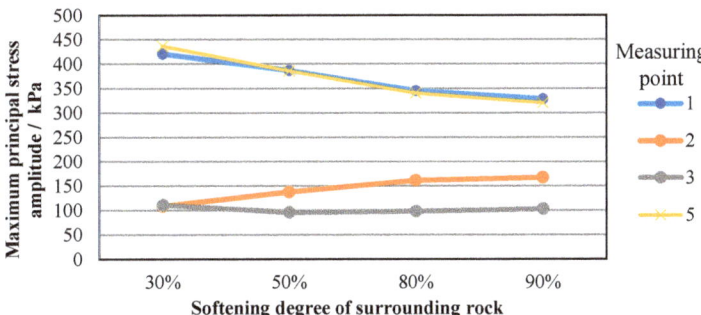

Figure 12. Maximum principal stress amplitude diagram of measuring points 1, 2, 3, and 5 under different softening degrees of basement surrounding rock.

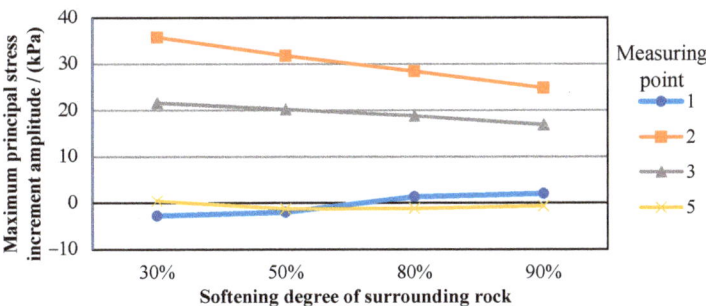

Figure 13. Maximum principal stress increment amplitude of measuring points 1, 2, 3, and 5 under different softening degrees of basement surrounding rock.

The minimum amplitudes of principal stress at measuring points 1, 2, 3, and 5 under different softening degrees of the basement surrounding rock are shown in Table 14, Figures 14 and 15.

Table 14. Minimum principal stress amplitude of measuring points 1, 2, 3, and 5 under different softening degrees of basement surrounding rock.

Measuring Point	Minimum Principal Stress Amplitude/kPa under Different Softening Degrees of Basement Surrounding Rock							
	Minimum Principal Stress				Minimum Principal Stress Increment			
	30%	50%	80%	90%	30%	50%	80%	90%
1	1706	1615	1471	1407	−55.5	−52.3	−49.2	−53.6
2	1478	1748	2206	2342	−171.2	−187.6	−215.8	−240.1
3	1382	1576	2047	2226	−95.3	−98.4	−117.9	−136.2
5	1727	1639	1498	1425	−11.5	−10.1	−8.4	−6.5

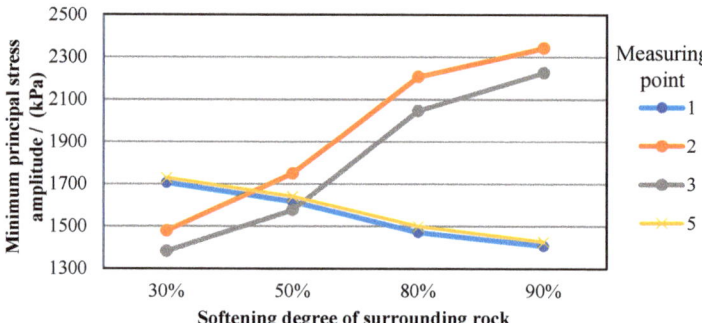

Figure 14. Minimum principal stress amplitude diagram of measuring points 1, 2, 3, and 5 under different softening degrees of basement surrounding rock.

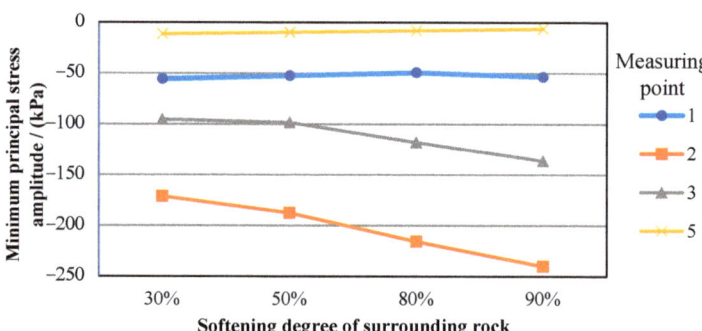

Figure 15. Minimum principal stress increment amplitude diagram of measuring points 1, 2, 3, and 5 under different softening degrees of basement surrounding rock.

The results showed that when the mechanical parameters of bedrock were reduced by 30, 50, 80, and 90%, the maximum principal stress and minimum principal stress of each measuring point were compressive stress, that is, after the train load, the position of each measuring point was still in a compression state; the increment of principal stress, especially the increment of minimum principal stress, was smaller than the initial value of principal stress; the maximum principal stress and minimum principal stress of measuring points 2 and 3 increased with the increase in softening degree of the basement surrounding rock. The large and minimum principal stresses of measuring points 1 and 5 decreased with the increase in the softening degree of the surrounding rock. The influence of dynamic load on the stress of measuring points 2 (directly below the heavy vehicle line) and 3 (directly below the tunnel center) was greater than that of measuring points 1 and 5 at the junction of the side wall and invert.

5.2.2. Influence of Basement Hanging Ranges

The maximum amplitudes of principal stress measuring points 1, 2, 3, and 5 under different basement hanging ranges are shown in Table 15, Figures 16 and 17.

Table 15. Maximum principal stress amplitude of measuring points 1, 2, 3, and 5 under different basement hanging ranges.

Measuring Point	Maximum Principal Stress Amplitude/kPa under Different Basement Hanging Ranges							
	Maximum Principal Stress				Maximum Principal Stress Increment			
	1/4 Width Loading Line	1/2 Width Empty Line	1/2 Width Loading Line	3/4 Width Loading Line	1/4 Width Loading Line	1/2 Width Empty Line	1/2 Width Loading Line	3/4 Width Loading Line
1	415	436	357	346	−2.2	−6.4	4.6	3.9
2	11	212	−9	−16	8.7	40.3	8.9	−20.5
3	246	508	286	−17	35.2	−17.6	3.7	−1.3
5	437	353	435	287	−0.8	4.5	−7.4	−31.6

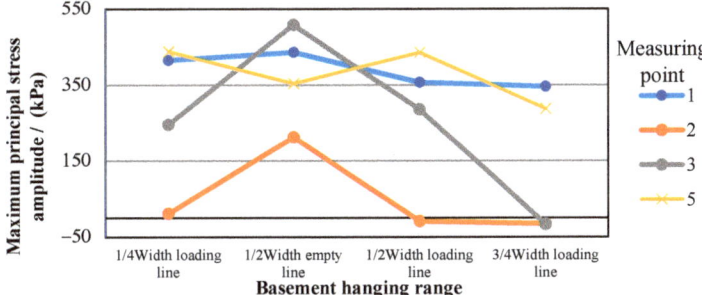

Figure 16. Maximum principal stress increment amplitude diagram of measuring points 1, 2, 3, and 5 under different basement hanging ranges.

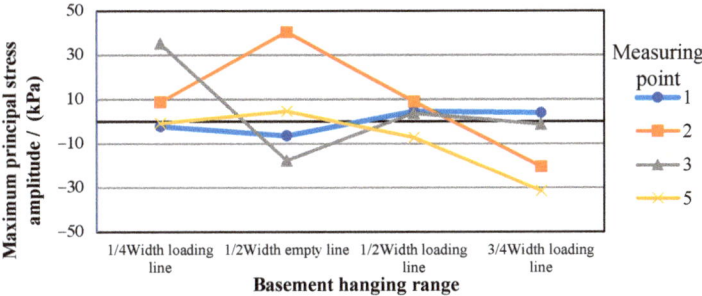

Figure 17. Maximum principal stress amplitude diagram of measuring points 1, 2, 3, and 5 under different basement hanging ranges.

The minimum amplitudes of principal stress measuring points 1, 2, 3, and 5 under different basement hanging ranges are shown in Table 16, Figures 18 and 19.

Table 16. Minimum principal stress amplitude of measuring points 1, 2, 3, and 5 under different basement hanging ranges.

Measuring Point	Minimum Principal Stress Amplitude/kPa under Different Basement Hanging Ranges							
	Minimum Principal Stress				Minimum Principal Stress Increment			
	1/4 Width Loading Line	1/2 Width Empty Line	1/2 Width Loading Line	3/4 Width Loading Line	1/4 Width Loading Line	1/2 Width Empty Line	1/2 Width Loading Line	3/4 Width Loading Line
1	1638	2009	1259	1279	−58.1	−57.2	14.6	19.2
2	1590	2106	1397	176	−206.3	−186.4	−265.8	−296.7
3	1547	1947	2332	492	−94.5	−135.3	−94.9	−198.4
5	1819	1235	2041	2154	−11.8	−18.2	−5.8	13.3

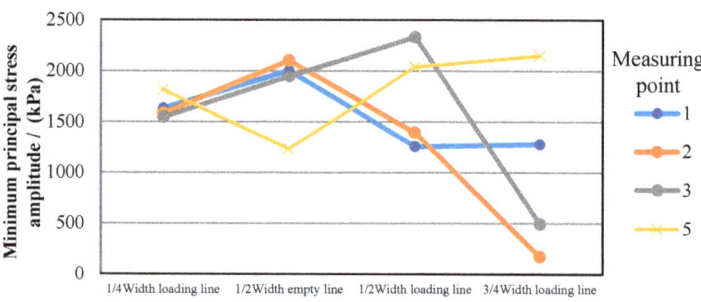

Figure 18. Minimum principal stress amplitude diagram of measuring points 1, 2, 3, and 5 under different basement hanging ranges.

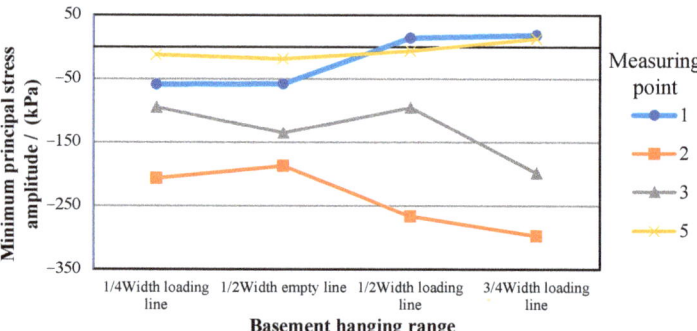

Figure 19. Minimum principal stress increment amplitude diagram of measuring points 1, 2, 3, and 5 under different basement hanging ranges.

The results showed that the main stress amplitude of each measuring point in the basement hanging empty range did not exceed the tensile strength and compressive strength of concrete material. When the hanging empty area was directly below the heavy vehicle line, the main stress amplitude of measuring point 2 changed from 12 to −11 kPa when the hanging empty area width increased from 1/4 to 1/2, and the main stress amplitude of measuring point 3 changed from 293 to −18 kPa when the hanging empty area width increased from 1/2 to 3/4. The results showed that the minimum principal stress amplitudes of measuring points 2 and 3 decreased sharply from 1408 and 2344 kPa to 182 and 500 kPa, respectively; when the hanging out area was located at different positions of the tunnel bottom and the hanging out width was the same, the stress of each measuring point was very different; when the hanging out area was located under the heavy vehicle line and the width was 1/2, the minimum principal stress amplitudes of measuring points

1 and 5 were 2020 and 1243 kPa, respectively, while the hanging out area was located under the empty vehicle line and the width was 1/2. The minimum principal stresses of measuring points 1 and 5 were 1276 and 2054 kPa, respectively.

5.2.3. Influence of Basement Structure Damage

The maximum principal stress amplitudes at measuring points 1, 2, 3, and 5 under different degrees of damage to the basement structure are shown in Table 17, Figures 20 and 21.

Table 17. Maximum principal stress amplitude of measuring points 1, 2, 3, and 5 under different degrees of damage to the basement structure.

Measuring Point	Maximum Principal Stress Amplitude/kPa under Different Degrees of Damage to the Basement Structure							
	Maximum Principal Stress				Maximum Principal Stress Increment			
	10%	20%	50%	80%	10%	20%	50%	80%
1	425	428	426	426	0.7	0.7	2.2	3.5
2	96	101	105	114	38.9	39.8	45.1	56.2
3	115	116	114	118	22.4	22.6	22.5	27.9
5	427	429	424	423	−2.1	−1.9	1.0	1.7

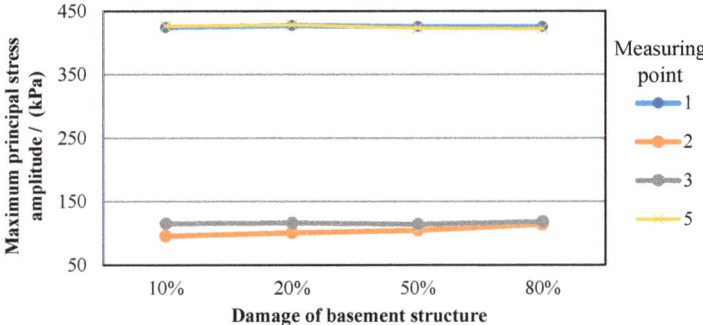

Figure 20. Maximum principal stress amplitude diagram of measuring points 1, 2, 3, and 5 under different degrees of damage to the basement structure.

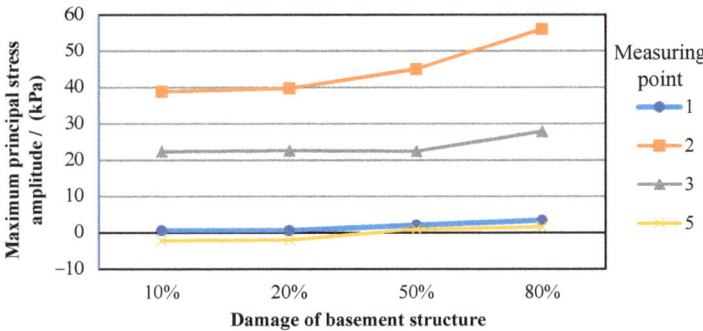

Figure 21. Maximum principal stress increment amplitude diagram of measuring points 1, 2, 3, and 5 under different degrees of damage to the basement structure.

The minimum principal stress amplitudes at measuring points 1, 2, 3, and 5 under different degrees of damage to the basement structure are shown in Table 18, Figures 22 and 23.

Table 18. Minimum principal stress amplitude of measuring points 1, 2, 3, and 5 under different degrees of damage to the basement structure.

Measuring Point	Minimum Principal Stress Amplitude/kPa under Different Degrees of Damage to the Basement Structure							
	Minimum Principal Stress				Minimum Principal Stress Increment			
	10%	20%	50%	80%	10%	20%	50%	80%
1	1766	1764	1765	1764	−44.5	−45.6	−47.5	−47.8
2	1317	1317	1332	1361	−151.3	−148.2	−107.1	−51.1
3	1279	1279	1298	1315	−77.6	−70.2	−51.3	−16.5
5	1782	1776	1780	1769	−14.3	−11.2	−13.6	−17.9

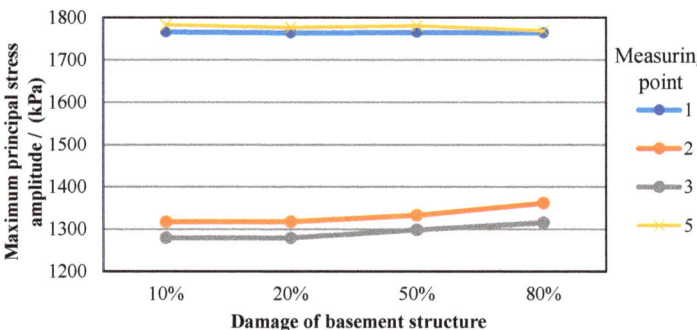

Figure 22. Minimum principal stress amplitude diagram of measuring points 1, 2, 3, and 5 under different degrees of damage to the basement structure.

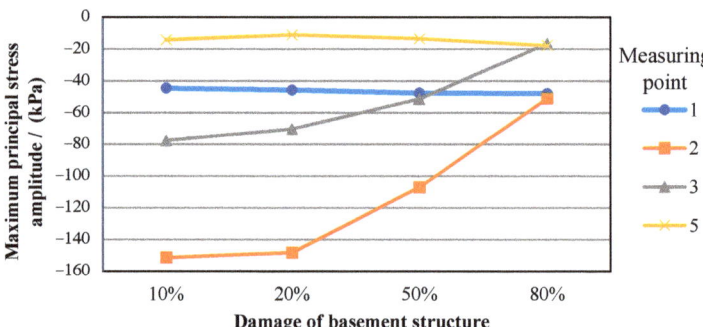

Figure 23. Minimum principal stress increment amplitude diagram of measuring points 1, 2, 3, and 5 under different degrees of damage to the basement structure.

The results showed that the maximum principal stress increment increased with the increase in the fracture degree of the basement structure, while the minimum principal stress increment decreased with the increase in the fracture degree of the basement structure, but the variation range of the large and minimum principal stress increments was small.

6. Conclusions and Further Observations

6.1. Conclusions

Based on the basic principle of thermodynamics, the elastoplastic damage constitutive model of concrete is constructed in this paper. The model is realized and verified in FLAC3D, which provides a solid foundation for the study of dynamic response and fatigue damage to the base structure of a heavy haul railway tunnel. The dynamic response and damage distribution of the base structure of a heavy-duty railway tunnel with defects were numerically simulated by the concrete elastic–plastic damage constitutive model. Then, by analyzing the response characteristics of tunnel basement structure under different surrounding rock softening degree, different foundation suspension range and different foundation structure damage degree are determined. The research results have reference value for analyzing the dynamic response characteristics of the basement structure of a heavy haul railway tunnel with different defects.

The following conclusions can be made.

(1) The elastoplastic damage constitutive model.

The elastoplastic damage constitutive model of concrete can well describe the stress–strain relationship of materials, especially the simulation results of post peak softening, which were in good agreement with the test results. Meanwhile, the simulation effect of the unloading–reloading process of the cyclic loading and unloading test also met the requirements, so as to verify the rationality of the model and the correctness of the model program.

(2) Health status of tunnel basement structure.

The initial stress field and dynamic response of the tunnel basement structure under the action of train vibration load are very different from the ideal state of the structure design when the surrounding rock of the base is softened, suspended, or damaged. When the surrounding rock softens, basement hanging or basement structure damage develops to a certain extent, and the basement structure suffers damage.

(3) Horizontal dynamic stress.

The horizontal dynamic stress amplitude increases with the increase in the softening degree of the basement surrounding rock. The horizontal dynamic stress of the measuring point increases with the increase in the width of the hanging out area when the hanging out area is located directly below the loading line. When the hanging out area is located at different positions of the base but has the same width, the horizontal dynamic stress of the measuring point is quite different. With the aggravation of the degree of damage to the basement structure, the horizontal dynamic tensile stress of each measuring point gradually decreases.

(4) Principal stress

When the mechanical parameters of bedrock are reduced by 30, 50, 80, and 90%, the maximum principal stress and minimum principal stress of each measuring point are compressive stress, that is, after the train load, the position of each measuring point is still in a compression state; the increment of principal stress, especially the increment of minimum principal stress, is smaller than the initial value of principal stress. The maximum principal stress increment increases with the increase in the fracture degree of the basement structure. The minimum principal stress increment decreases with the increase in the fracture degree of the basement structure. But the variation range of the large and minimum principal stress increments is small.

6.2. Further Observations

Through theoretical analysis and numerical simulation, this paper studied the dynamic response characteristics, vibration characteristics, and damage distribution characteristics of the basement structure of a heavy haul railway tunnel with defects. Although some conclusions were drawn, there are still some imperfections in the content of this paper due to the limitations of time and conditions, and there are many problems that need further study:

(1) This paper only performed a numerical analysis of the damage to the tunnel base structure and did not study the damage to the base surrounding rock. Mechanical properties such as strength and stiffness of the surrounding rock are weaker than that of the base structure and are more prone to damage. The elastic–plastic damage model of surrounding rock can be introduced into a later numerical analysis to study the damage to the surrounding rock.

(2) In this paper, the dynamic response and damage distribution of the basement structure of the heavy-duty railway tunnel were analyzed only through numerical calculation. It is hoped that in future research, the damage development and defect generation mechanism of the basement of the heavy-duty railway tunnel at the mesoscale level will be analyzed with the indoor test method.

Funding: This research was funded by the Research Project of the China Academy of Railway Sciences Corp. Ltd., grant number 2020YJ089.

Data Availability Statement: The data used to support the findings of this study are available within the article.

Acknowledgments: Thanks to Weibin Ma and Wenhao Zou of the Railway Engineering Research Institute of the China Academy of Railway Sciences Corp. Ltd. for their guidance in the research methods in this paper. Thanks to Yan Du of the Beijing University of Science and Technology for his support in the numerical calculations in this paper.

Conflicts of Interest: The author declares no conflict of interest.

References

1. Shi, W.B.; Miao, L.C.; Luo, J.L.; Zhang, H.L. The Influence of the Track Parameters on Vibration Characteristics of Subway Tunnel. *Shock. Vib.* **2018**, *2018*, 2506909. [CrossRef]
2. Qian, L.X. The World Latest Progress of Heavy Railway Transportation Technology. *Electr. Drive Locomot.* **2010**, *2010*, 3–7.
3. Zhai, W.J.; Gao, P.; Liu, P.; Wang, K. Reducing rail side wear on heavy-haul railway curves based on wheel-rail dynamic interaction. *Veh. Syst. Dyn.* **2014**, *52*, 440–454. [CrossRef]
4. Chen, C.K.; Kang, H. Numerical simulation of fire temperature field for heavy-haul railway tunnel with extremely abundant fuel. *Fire Saf. Sci.* **2013**, *22*, 24–30.
5. Tao, Z.G.; Zhu, C.; He, M.C.; Karakus, M. A physical modeling-based study on the control mechanisms of Negative Poisson's ratio anchor cable on the stratified toppling deformation of anti-inclined slopes. *Int. J. Rock Mech. Min. Sci.* **2021**, *138*, 104632. [CrossRef]
6. Tao, Z.G.; Shu, Y.; Yang, X.J.; Peng, Y.Y.; Chen, Q.H.; Zhang, H.J. Physical model test study on shear strength characteristics of slope sliding surface in Nanfen open-pit mine. *Int. J. Min. Sci. Technol.* **2020**, *30*, 421–429. [CrossRef]
7. Li, B.L.; Lan, J.Q.; Si, G.Y.; Lin, G.P.; Hu, L.Q. NMR-based damage characterisation of backfill material in host rock under dynamic loading. *Int. J. Min. Sci. Technol.* **2020**, *30*, 329–335. [CrossRef]
8. Mark, C. An updated empirical model for ground control in U.S. multiseam coal mines. *Int. J. Min. Sci. Technol.* **2021**, *31*, 163–174. [CrossRef]
9. Krawczyk, J. A preliminary study on selected methods of modeling the effect of shearer operation on methane propagation and ventilation at longwalls. *Int. J. Min. Sci. Technol.* **2020**, *30*, 675–682. [CrossRef]
10. Wang, Q.; Qin, Q.; Jiang, B.; Xu, S.; Zeng, Z.N.; Luan, Y.C.; Liu, B.H.; Zhang, H.J. Mechanized construction of fabricated arches for large-diameter tunnels. *Autom. Constr.* **2021**, *124*, 103583. [CrossRef]
11. Liu, F.B.; Cheng, Y.M. The improved element-free Galerkin method based on the nonsingular weight functions for inhomogeneous swelling of polymer gels. *Int. J. Appl. Mech.* **2018**, *10*, 1850047. [CrossRef]
12. Liu, F.B.; Wu, Q.; Cheng, Y.M. A meshless method based on the nonsingular weight functions for elastoplastic large deformation problems. *Int. J. Appl. Mech.* **2019**, *11*, 1950006. [CrossRef]
13. Wu, Q.; Liu, F.B.; Cheng, Y.M. The interpolating element-free Galerkin method for three-dimensional elastoplasticity problems. *Eng. Anal. Bound. Elem.* **2020**, *115*, 156–167. [CrossRef]
14. Yu, S.Y.; Peng, M.J.; Cheng, H.; Cheng, Y.M. The improved element-free Galerkin method for three-dimensional elastoplasticity problems. *Eng. Anal. Bound. Elem.* **2019**, *104*, 215–224. [CrossRef]
15. Koch, K.W. Comparative values of structure-borne sound levels in track tunnels. *J. Sound Vib.* **1979**, *66*, 355–362. [CrossRef]
16. Lei, X.Y.; Noda, N.A. Analyses of dynamic response of vehicle and track coupling system with random irregularity of track vertical Profile. *J. Sound Vib.* **2002**, *258*, 147–165. [CrossRef]
17. Degrandea, C.; Schevenelsa, M.; Chatterjeea, P.; Van de Velde, W.; Hölscher, P.; Hopman, V.; Wang, A.; Dadkah, N. Vibrations due to a test train at variable speeds in a deep bored tunnel embedded in London Clay. *J. Sound Vib.* **2006**, *293*, 626–644. [CrossRef]
18. Pan, C.; Li, D.; Xie, Z. Discussion on the influence of train vibration on environment in Beijing subway. *Vib. Shock.* **1995**, *14*, 29–34.
19. Zhang, Y.; Bai, B. Study on the vibration response of tunnel subjected to high speed train loading. *Vib. Shock.* **2001**, *20*, 91–93.
20. Li, D.; Gao, F. Field test and analysis of train vibration in Jinjiayan tunnel. *J. Lanzhou Railw. Univ.* **1997**, *16*, 7–11.
21. Wang, X.; Yang, D.; Gao, W. In-situ vibration measurement and load simulation of the raising speed train in railway tunnel. *Vib. Shock.* **2005**, *24*, 107.
22. Xue, F.; Ma, J.; Yan, L.; Liu, Z.; Cheng, Q.; Chen, C. Cyclic dynamic test of water-rich loess tunnel subgrade for high-speed railway. *Vib. Shock.* **2010**, *29*, 226–230.

23. Peng, L.; Tan, C.; Shi, C.; Huang, L. Field test study on the disease treatment of foundation base in railway tunnel. *China Railw. Sci.* **2005**, *26*, 39.
24. Shi, C.; Lei, M.; Yang, C.; Ding, Z. In-situ monitoring and analysis of mechanical characteristics and deformation of bottom structure of tunnels. *Chin. J. Geotech. Eng.* **2012**, *34*, 879–884.
25. Fu, B.; Ma, W.; Guo, X.; Niu, Y. Base load characteristics and dynamic response analysis of tunnel under heavy haul train. *Railw. Constr. Technol.* **2013**, *2013*, 1–5.
26. Yu, H.; Yuan, Y.; Bobet, A. Seismic analysis of long tunnels: A review of simplified and unified methods. *Undergr. Space* **2017**, *2*, 73–87. [CrossRef]
27. Yu, H.; Li, Y.; Shao, X.; Cai, X. Virtual hybrid simulation method for underground structures subjected to seismic loadings. *Tunn. Undergr. Space Technol.* **2021**, *110*, 103831. [CrossRef]
28. Cheng, J. Residential land leasing and price under public land ownership. *J. Urban Plan. Dev.* **2021**, *147*, 05021009. [CrossRef]
29. Cheng, J. Analysis of commercial land leasing of the district governments of Beijing in China. *Land Use Policy* **2021**, *100*, 104881. [CrossRef]
30. Cheng, J. Analyzing the factors influencing the choice of the government on leasing different types of land uses: Evidence from Shanghai of China. *Land Use Policy* **2020**, *90*, 104303. [CrossRef]
31. Cheng, J. Data analysis of the factors influencing the industrial land leasing in Shanghai based on mathematical models. *Math. Probl. Eng.* **2020**, *2020*, 9346863. [CrossRef]
32. Cheng, J. Mathematical models and data analysis of residential land leasing behavior of district governments of Beijing in China. *Mathematics* **2021**, *9*, 2314. [CrossRef]
33. Zheng, G.D.; Cheng, Y.M. The improved element-free Galerkin method for diffusional drug release problems. *Int. J. Appl. Mech.* **2020**, *12*, 2050096. [CrossRef]
34. Wu, Q.; Peng, P.P.; Cheng, Y.M. The interpolating element-free Galerkin method for elastic large deformation problems. *Sci. China Technol. Sci.* **2021**, *64*, 364–374. [CrossRef]
35. Cheng, H.; Peng, M.J.; Cheng, Y.M. The hybrid complex variable element-free Galerkin method for 3D elasticity problems. *Eng. Struct.* **2020**, *219*, 110835. [CrossRef]
36. Li, J.; Wu, J. Study on elastoplastic damage constitutive model of concrete I: Basic formula. *J. Civ. Eng.* **2005**, *38*, 14–20.
37. Wu, J. The Elastoplastic Damage Constitutive Model of Concrete based on the Damage Energy Release Rate and the Application in Structural Nonlinear Analysis. Ph.D. Thesis, Tongji University, Shanghai, China, 2004.
38. Ma, W.B.; Chai, J.F.; Li, Z.F.; Han, Z.L.; Ma, C.F.; Li, Y.J.; Zhu, Z.Y.; Liu, Z.Y.; Niu, Y.B.; Ma, Z.G.; et al. Research on vibration Law of railway tunnel substructure under different axle loads and health conditions. *Shock. Vib.* **2021**, *2021*, 9954098. [CrossRef]
39. Han, Z.L.; Ma, W.B.; Chai, J.F.; Zhu, Z.Y.; Lin, C.N.; An, Z.L.; Ma, C.F.; Xu, X.L.; Xu, T.Y. A Treatment Technology for Optimizing the Stress State of Railway Tunnel Bottom Structure. *Shock. Vib.* **2021**, *2021*, 9191232. [CrossRef]
40. Ma, W.B.; Chai, J.F.; Han, Z.L.; Ma, Z.G.; Guo, X.X.; Zou, W.H.; An, Z.L.; Li, T.F.; Niu, Y.B. Research on Design Parameters and Fatigue Life of Tunnel Bottom Structure of Single-Track Ballasted Heavy-Haul Railway Tunnel with 40-Ton Axle Load. *Math. Probl. Eng.* **2020**, *2020*, 3181480. [CrossRef]
41. Chai, J.F. Research on Multijoint Rock Failure Mechanism Based on Moment Tensor Theory. *Math. Probl. Eng.* **2020**, *2020*, 6816934. [CrossRef]
42. Gooalaratnam, V.S.; Shah, S.P. Softing response of plain concrete in direct tension. *ACI J.* **1985**, *82*, 310–323.
43. Karsan, I.D.; Jirsa, J.O. Behavior of concrete under compressive loading. *J. Struct. Div.* **1969**, *95*, 2535–2563. [CrossRef]
44. Kupfer, H.; Hilsdorf, H.K.; Rusch, H. Behavior of concrete under biaxial stresses. *ACI J.* **1969**, *66*, 656–666. [CrossRef]
45. Taylor, R.L. *FEAP: A Finite Element Analysis Program for Engineering Workstation*; Rep. No. UCB/SEMM-92 (Draft Version); Department of Civil Engineering, University of California: Berkeley, CA, USA, 1992.

Article

Impact of Strong Wind and Optimal Estimation of Flux Difference Integral in a Lattice Hydrodynamic Model

Huimin Liu and Yuhong Wang *

Faculty of Maritime and Transportation, Ningbo University, Ningbo 315211, China; 1911084015@nbu.edu.cn
* Correspondence: wangyuhong@nbu.edu.cn

Abstract: A modified lattice hydrodynamic model is proposed, in which the impact of strong wind and the optimal estimation of flux difference integral are simultaneously analyzed. Based on the control theory, the stability condition is acquired through linear analysis. The modified Korteweg-de Vries (mKdV) equation is derived via nonlinear analysis, in order to express a description of the evolution of density waves. Then, numerical simulation is conducted. From the simulation results, strong wind can largely influence the traffic flow stability. The stronger the wind becomes, the more stable the traffic flow is, to some extent. Similarly, the optimal estimation of flux difference integral also contributes to stabilizing traffic flow. The simulation results show no difference compared with the theoretical findings. In conclusion, the new model is able to make the traffic flow more stable.

Keywords: traffic flow; the lattice hydrodynamic model; control signal; strong wind; optimal estimation of flux difference integral

1. Introduction

As is known to us, traffic congestion is a very distressing problem, caused by the substantial increase in the number of vehicles. The bad traffic has seriously affected our travel and production activities. To better study and resolve the traffic problems, scholars put forward a number of traffic flow models [1–38] from diverse points of view, such as car-following models [9–20], cellular automation models [21–23], continuum models [24–27], and lattice hydrodynamic models [28–38]. These models provided reliable theoretical guidance for resolving traffic jams.

In 1998, Nagatani [39] gained a great deal of enlightenment from the car-following theory, and then proposed the earliest lattice hydrodynamic model. The model can depict the actual traffic flow appropriately. Afterwards, large numbers of traffic factors were combined into Nagatani's model. Tian [40] took the density difference into consideration. Zhao [41] developed a model accounting for historical current integration, and its effectiveness in enhancing traffic flow stability was tested. The model that takes into account the characteristics of drivers was brought forward by Sharma [42]. In fact, drivers also tend to have a strong desire of driving smoothly. For this reason, a modified model was proposed by Wang [43].

However, the models above are mostly from the perspectives of human factors. The effort is few and far between what has been made to research the influence of the ex-tremely bad weather, in particular, strong winds. In our daily life, we often hear the news that numerous traffic accidents have happened because of strong wind. As a result, the research of strong wind is of great necessity, and many experts have committed themselves to researching the influence of strong wind on traffic flow. Kwon [44] reported that traffic accidents may occur due to the wind force. The effect of strong wind was studied by Liu [45]. The research results of a study applying a car-following model suggest that strong wind is advantageous for the stability of traffic flow. Here, we study this factor in a lattice model.

What is more, lots of traffic information, which can be conducive to ease traffic jams, should be used as soon as possible, especially the information of the optimal estimation of flux difference. Yang [46] examined this information on a single lane. Then, this factor was incorporated into a two-lane system by Peng [47]. In reality, driving is a successive process. Therefore, in order to better reflect the real traffic, the continuous information of the optimal estimation of flux difference between time t and $t - \tau$ (named as the optimal estimation of flux difference integral) is considered in this paper. The control method was a good approach to maintain the traffic flow stability, which has been examined by many researchers. For instance, delayed-feedback control was exerted to significantly investigate the lattice model by Ge [48]. The control signal is of significant value to ease traffic congestion. Recently, Zhu [49] regarded the rate of optimal velocity change as a novel control strategy. Up until now, the optimal estimation of flux difference integral and strong wind have not been examined in any lattice models. Motivated by the mentioned viewpoints, the two factors are explored in an extended model, to reveal their impact on traffic flow. Within this model, the optimal estimation of flux difference integral is regarded as the new control signal.

The structure of the current paper is shown below. The first step is to propose the new model, which can be observed in Section 2. Then, the model's stability condition is explored via the control method in Section 3.1. The next two steps, shown in Sections 3.2 and 4, are about the detailed description of the nonlinear analysis and numerical simulations, respectively. The final section eventually presents the conclusions of the research.

2. Methods: The Modified Model

Hydrodynamics models are widely exerted to simulate phase change phenomena in traffic. The initial lattice model on a single lane is presented by Nagatani [24], and the scholars became accustomed to writing it in the following discretized form:

$$\partial_t \rho_j + \rho_0 (\rho_j v_j - \rho_{j-1} v_{j-1}) = 0, \tag{1}$$

$$\partial_t (\rho_j v_j) = a\rho_0 V(\rho_{j+1}) - a\rho_j v_j. \tag{2}$$

where ρ_j stands for the density of lattice j, v_j is the velocity of lattice j, ρ_0 signifies the local average density, a is the reciprocal of the driver's delay time, indicating the driver's sensitivity. Equation (1) is the continuity equation that is one of the three basic equations of hydrodynamics and is the concrete expression of the law of mass conservation in hydrodynamics. Similarly to the car-following model, Equation (2) utilizes the optimal velocity function $V(\cdot)$ to realize that drivers can adjust their speed according to the number of vehicles in front of them.

In fact, driving tends to be affected by strong wind. When the wind becomes great enough, drivers have to adjust the speed of their vehicles to avoid the impact of it. On the grounds of the analysis of the impact of strong wind in a car-following model [45], we further explore the impact of wind in a lattice model. Moreover, the effect of optimal estimation of flux difference integral [46] has not been researched in the wind. According to the opinions above, the modified model is demonstrated as below:

$$\partial_t \rho_j + \rho_0 (q_j - q_{j-1}) = 0, \tag{3}$$

$$\partial_t (q_j) = a\rho_0 (1 - \xi) V(\rho_{j+1}) - aq_j + ak \int_{t-\tau}^{t} [\rho_0 V(\rho_0) - q_j(t)] dt. \tag{4}$$

where ξ is the coefficient that varies with the change in wind force. When $\xi = 0$, vehicles are not under the influence of strong wind; k represents the control coefficient; $\int_{t-\tau}^{t} [\rho_0 V(\rho_0) - q_j(t)] dt$ stands for the optimal estimation of flux difference integral; $V(\cdot)$

reflects the optimal velocity function, and its formats exerted in this investigation is expressed as follows:

$$V(\rho) = \frac{v_{\max}}{2}\left[\tanh\left(\frac{1}{\rho} - \frac{1}{\rho_c}\right) + \tanh\left(\frac{1}{\rho_c}\right)\right]. \tag{5}$$

where ρ_c denotes safety density and $v_{\max}$ is maximum speed.

3. Discussion

3.1. Linear Stability Analysis

The control method is properly utilized to implement the linear analysis of the novel model, and the linear stability condition is deduced in this part. To start with, the steady state of the traffic flow is displayed as the following:

$$[\rho_n, q_n]^T = [\rho_n^*, q_n^*]^T, \tag{6}$$

where ρ_n^* and q_n^* are the expected density and flux, separately.

Subsequently, with the consideration of small disturbances around the steady state, the following equation is derived:

$$\partial_t \delta\rho_{j+1} + \rho_0(\delta q_{j+1} - \delta q_j) = 0, \tag{7}$$

$$\partial_t(\delta q_j) = a\rho_0(1-\xi)\Lambda\delta\rho_{j+1} - a\delta q_j + ak\tau[\rho_0 V(\rho_0) - \delta q_j(t - \gamma\tau)]. \tag{8}$$

where $\Lambda = \left.\frac{\partial V(\rho_{n+1})}{\partial \rho_{n+1}}\right|_{\rho_{n+1}=\rho^*}$, $\delta\rho_j = \rho_j - \rho^*$ and $\delta q_j = q_j - q^*$.

After the Laplace transform is applied, Equations (7) and (8) can be rewritten as below:

$$sP_{j+1}(s) - \rho_{j+1}(0) + \rho_0[Q_{j+1}(s) - Q_j(s)] = 0, \tag{9}$$

$$sQ_j(s) - q_j(0) = a\rho_0(1-\xi)\Lambda P_{j+1}(s) - aQ_j(s) + ak\tau\left[\frac{1}{s}\rho_0 V(\rho_0) - e^{-s\gamma\tau}Q_j(s)\right]. \tag{10}$$

where $L(\rho_{j+1}) = P_{j+1}(s)$, $L(q_j) = Q_j(s)$ and $L(q_j(t - \gamma\tau)) = e^{-s\gamma\tau}Q_j(s)$.

When $P_{j+1}(s)$ in Equations (9) and (10) is eliminated, the transfer relationship can be described in the following form:

$$Q_j(s) = \frac{-a\rho_0^2(1-\xi)\Lambda}{p(s)}Q_{j+1}(s) + \frac{a\rho_0(1-\xi)\Lambda}{p(s)}\rho_{j+1}(0) + ak\tau\rho_0 V(\rho_0) + \frac{1}{p(s)}q_j(0). \tag{11}$$

where $p(s) = (1 - ak\gamma\tau^2)s^2 + a(1 + k\tau)s - a\rho_0^2(1-\xi)\Lambda$ indicates the characteristic polynomial. Then, the transfer function $G(s)$ is acquired in accordance with Equation (11), and $G(s)$ represents the relationship between flux Q_j and Q_{j+1}. The expression of $G(s)$ is as follows:

$$G(s) = \frac{-a\rho_0^2(1-\xi)\Lambda}{(1 - ak\gamma\tau^2)s^2 + a(1 + k\tau)s - a\rho_0^2(1-\xi)\Lambda}. \tag{12}$$

In the control system, as long as $p(s)$ is steady and $\|G(s)\|_\infty \leq 1$, traffic congestion will not take place. Based on the Hurwitz stability criterion, if all the coefficients of the quadratic polynomial $p(s)$ are greater than zero, namely, $k \leq \frac{1}{a\gamma\tau^2}$ and $-a\rho_0^2(1-\xi)\Lambda > 0$, we can derive that $p(s)$ is stable. Next, the process of solving the inequality $\|G(s)\|_\infty \leq 1$ is given below:

$$\|G(s)\|_\infty = \sup_{\omega \in [0,\infty)} |G(j\omega)| \leq 1, \tag{13}$$

$$|G(j\omega)| = \sqrt{G(j\omega)G(-j\omega)} = \sqrt{\frac{(a\rho_0^2(1-\xi)\Lambda)^2}{((1-ak\gamma\tau^2)\omega^2 + a\rho_0^2(1-\xi)\Lambda)^2 + a^2(1+k\tau)^2\omega^2}} \leq 1. \tag{14}$$

The condition of $\|G(s)\|_\infty \leq 1$ is rewritten by further simplifying Equation (14), as follows:

$$2a\rho_0^2(1-\xi)\Lambda - 2a^2\rho_0^2(1-\xi)\Lambda k\gamma\tau^2 + a^2(1+k\tau)^2 \geq 0. \tag{15}$$

Finally, the sufficient condition of Equation (15) can be simplified in the following form:

$$a \leq \frac{-2\rho_0^2(1-\xi)\Lambda}{(1+k\tau)^2 - 2k\gamma\tau^2\rho_0^2(1-\xi)\Lambda}. \tag{16}$$

The neutral stability curves are illustrated in Figure 1, where the density–sensitivity space is separated into two parts by the curves; without satisfying the stability condition, the region below the solid line is an unstable area. Conversely, the other part, satisfying the stability condition, is the stability area. By observing Figure 1a, we could find that the stable region significantly expands when ξ increases. In Figure 1b, with the rise in k, the unstable region declines. This means that both the strong wind and optimal flux difference integral do help to boost the enhancement of traffic flow stability, thus reducing the occurrence of traffic congestion.

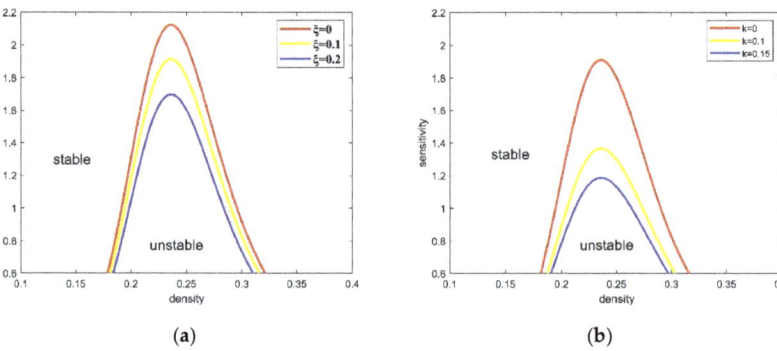

Figure 1. Phase diagram in parameter space (ρ, α). (**a**) $k = 0$, (**b**) $\xi = 0.1$.

3.2. Nonlinear Analysis

Aimed to acquire the mKdV equation describing the kink–antikink soliton wave, nonlinear analysis was conducted near the critical point (ρ_c, a_c). Firstly, we define the slow variables X and T with time t and lattice j in the following form:

$$X = \varepsilon(j + bt), T = \varepsilon t^3, 0 < \varepsilon \ll 1, \tag{17}$$

where b stands for an undetermined parameter. For $\rho_j(t)$, the following equation is satisfied:

$$\rho_j(t) = \rho_c + \varepsilon R(X, T), \tag{18}$$

Employing Equations (17) and (18) to replace Equation (4), and then expanding it to the fifth order of ε through Taylor's formula, we obtain the following nonlinear equation:

$$\begin{aligned}&\varepsilon^2 k_1 \partial_X R + \varepsilon^3 k_2 \partial_X^2 R \\ &+ \varepsilon^4 \left[k_8 \partial_T R + k_3 \partial_X^3 R + k_4 \partial_X R^3\right] + \varepsilon^5 \left[k_5 \partial_X \partial_T R + k_6 \partial_X^4 R + k_7 \partial_X^2 R^3\right] = 0\end{aligned} \tag{19}$$

where $k_i(i = 1, 2, \cdots, 8)$ is elaborated in Table 1, $V' = \frac{\partial V(\rho)}{\partial \rho}\big|_{\rho=\rho_c}$ and $V''' = \frac{\partial^3 V_0(\rho)}{\partial \rho^3}\big|_{\rho=\rho_c}$.

Table 1. The coefficients k_i of the new model.

k_1	$a(b + \rho_c^2(1-\xi)V'(\rho_c) + kb\tau)$
k_2	$b^2 + \frac{1}{2}a\rho_c^2(1-\xi)V'(\rho_c) - \frac{1}{2}akb^2\tau^2$
k_3	$\frac{1}{6}(a\rho_c^2(1-\xi)V'(\rho_c) + akb^3\tau^3)$
k_4	$\frac{1}{6}a\rho_c^2(1-\xi)V'''(\rho_c)$
k_5	$2b - akb\tau^2$
k_6	$\frac{1}{24}(\rho_c^2(1-\xi)V'(\rho_c) - b^4\tau^4)$
k_7	$\frac{1}{12}a\rho_c^2 V'''(\rho_c)$
k_8	$a(1+k\tau)$

Using $b = -\frac{\rho_c^2(1-\xi)V'(\rho_c)}{1+k\tau}$ and $a_c = a(1+\varepsilon^2)$, ε^2 and ε^3 are eliminated in Equation (19). Then, the formula can be simplified as follows:

$$\varepsilon^4 \left(g_1 \partial_X^3 R + g_2 \partial_X R^3 + \partial_T R \right) + \varepsilon^5 \left(g_4 \partial_X^4 R + g_5 \partial_X^2 R^3 + g_3 \partial_X^2 R \right) = 0, \tag{20}$$

where $g_i (i = 1, 2, \cdots, 8)$ is elaborated in Table 2.

Table 2. The coefficients g_i of the new model.

g_1	$\frac{1}{6}(a\rho_c^2(1-\xi)V'(\rho_c) + akb^3\tau^3)$
g_2	$\frac{1}{6}a\rho_c^2(1-\xi)V'''(\rho_c)$
g_3	$\frac{\rho_c^4(1-\xi)^2 V'^2(\rho_c)}{(1+k\tau)^2}$
g_4	$\frac{1}{24}(a\rho_c^2(1-\xi)V'(\rho_c) - b^4\tau^4)$
g_5	$\frac{1}{12}a\rho_c^2(1-\xi)V'''(\rho_c)$

After Equation (20) is transformed with $T = \frac{1}{g_1}T'$, $R = \sqrt{\frac{g_1}{g_2}}R'$, the regularized mKdV equation that has the correction term $O(\varepsilon)$, is obtained:

$$\partial_{T'} R' = \partial_X^3 R' - \partial_X R'^3 + \varepsilon \left[\frac{g_3}{g_1} \partial_X^2 R' + \frac{g_4}{g_1} \partial_X^4 R' + \frac{g_5}{g_2} \partial_X^2 R'^3 \right], \tag{21}$$

When the $O(\varepsilon)$ is ignored, the regularized mKdV equation can be obtained, and its soliton solution is as follows:

$$R'_0(X, T') = \sqrt{c} \tanh \sqrt{\frac{c}{2}} (X - cT'). \tag{22}$$

To derive the propagation velocity c in Equation (22), the equation $R'(X, T') = R'_0(X, T') + \varepsilon R'_1(X, T')$ is presumed, and the solvability condition given below must be satisfied:

$$(R'_0, M[R'_0]) \equiv \int_{-\infty}^{+\infty} dX' R'_0 M[R'_0] = 0, \tag{23}$$

where $M[R'_0] = \frac{g_3}{g_1} \partial_X^2 R' + \frac{g_4}{g_1} \partial_X^4 R' + \frac{g_5}{g_2} \partial_X^2 R'^3$. Consequently, we acquire the general speed c, shown as follows:

$$c = \frac{5 g_2 g_3}{2 g_2 g_4 - 3 g_1 g_5}. \tag{24}$$

Then, utilizing $T = \frac{1}{g_1}T'$ and $R = \sqrt{\frac{g_1}{g_2}}R'$ for substitution in Equation (22), the expression of $R(X, T)$ is shown as follows:

$$R(X, T) = \sqrt{\frac{g_1 c}{g_2}} \tanh\left(\sqrt{\frac{c}{2}}(X - cg_1 T)\right). \tag{25}$$

Eventually, the general solution of the kink–antikink soliton of the density wave is deduced by inserting Equation (25) into Equation (18), as follows:

$$\rho_j(t) = \rho_c + \varepsilon\sqrt{\frac{g_1 c}{g_2}} \tanh\left(\sqrt{\frac{c}{2}}(X - cg_1 T)\right), \tag{26}$$

4. Results of Numerical Simulation

To investigate the effect of strong wind and optimal estimation of flux difference integral, numerical simulation is conducted on the proposed model. We choose $N = 100$, signifying the total number of sites, and the original conditions for the new model are given as follows:

$$\rho_j(1) = \rho_j(0) = \begin{cases} \rho_0, & j \neq \frac{N}{2}, \frac{N}{2}+1, \\ \rho_0 - 0.05, & j = \frac{N}{2}, \\ \rho_0 + 0.05, & j = \frac{N}{2}+1. \end{cases} \tag{27}$$

where $\rho_0 = \rho_c = 0.25$, $a = 1.3$, $t = 3000$, and $v_{\max} = 2$.

Figures 2 and 3 only consider the effect of strong wind, whereas Figure 2 illustrates the space-time evolution of the densities for $\zeta = 0, 0.1, 0.2, 0.3$, severally. With the rise in the value of ζ, the amplitude of the curve decreases. In Figure 3, the density profile at time $t = 3000s$, with different ζ, is demonstrated. Comparing the patterns from (a) to (d) in Figure 3, it could be discovered that the fluctuation amplitude of the curves obviously declines. Based on the figures above, when the wind force becomes stronger and stronger, the traffic flow tends to be more stable, to some extent. That is to say, the strong wind is conducive to stabilizing the traffic flow.

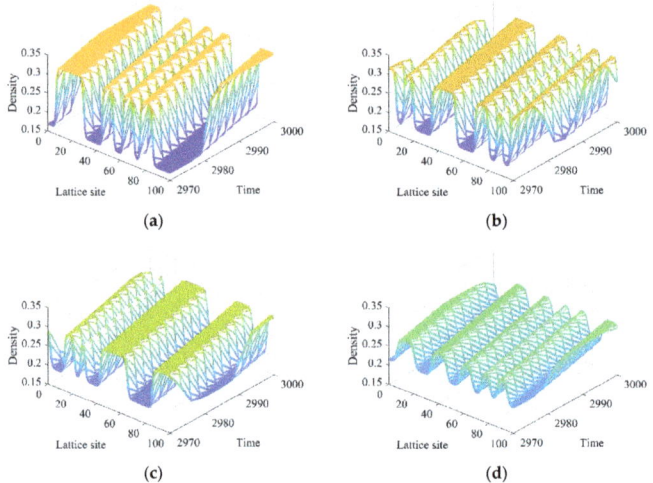

Figure 2. The evolution of the traffic densities for different values of parameter ζ. (a) $\zeta = 0$, (b) $\zeta = 0.1$, (c) $\zeta = 0.2$, (d) $\zeta = 0.3$.

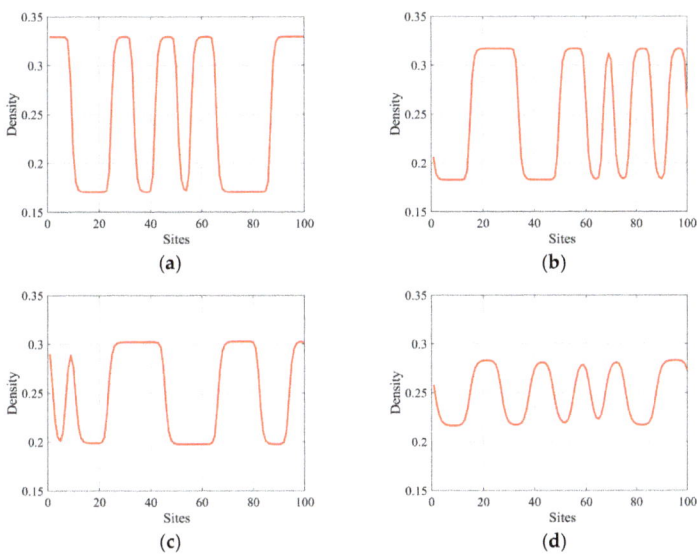

Figure 3. The density profile at $t = 3000s$ under the different values of ζ. (a) $\zeta = 0$, (b) $\zeta = 0.1$, (c) $\zeta = 0.2$, (d) $\zeta = 0.3$.

Then, we further consider the control signal on the grounds of accounting for the strong wind. The simulation result is given in Figures 4 and 5.

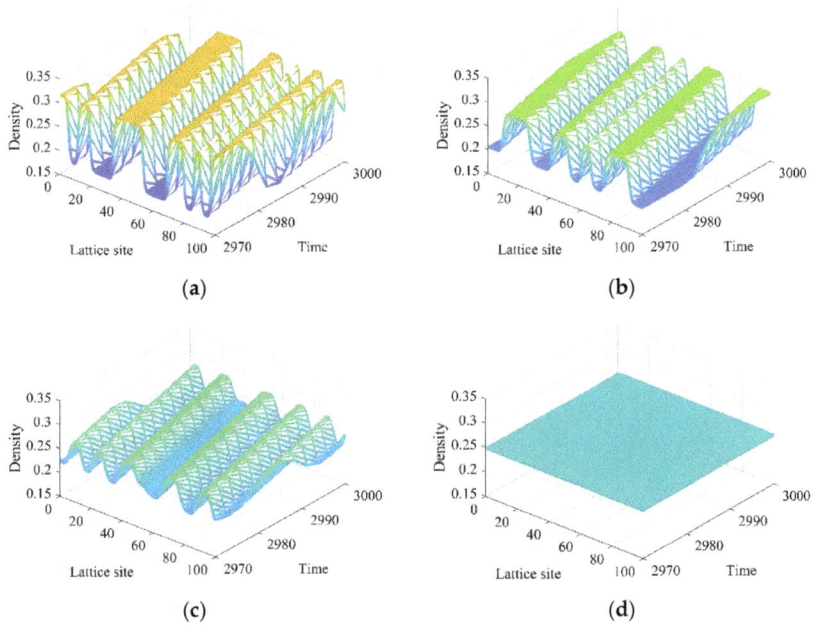

Figure 4. The evolution of the traffic flux for different values of parameter k. (a) $k = 0$, (b) $k = 0.1$, (c) $k = 0.15$, (d) $k = 0.2$.

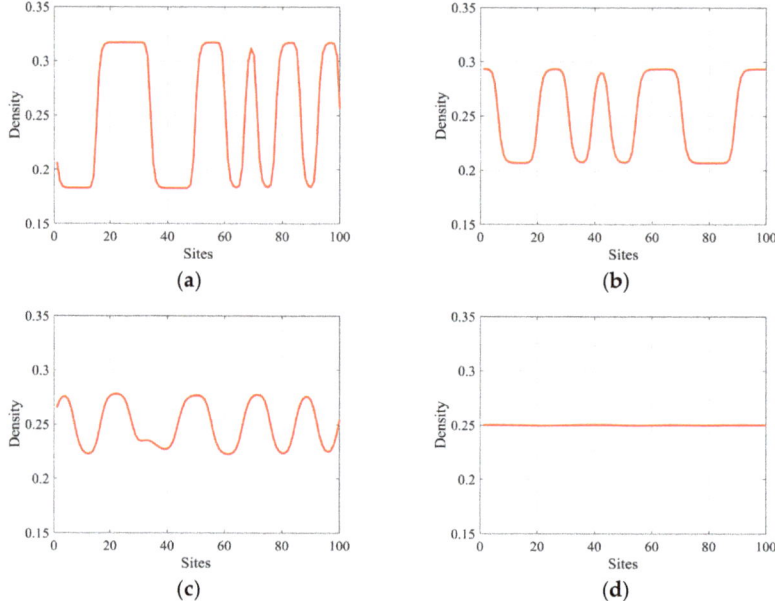

Figure 5. The flux profile at $t = 3000s$ under the different value of k. (**a**) $k = 0$, (**b**) $k = 0.1$, (**c**) $k = 0.15$, (**d**) $k = 0.2$.

Figure 4 represents the space-time evolution of the densities for different coefficients $k = 0$, 0.1, 0.15, 0.2, where $\xi = 0.1$. Figure 5 depicts the density profile at time $t = 3000s$, corresponding to Figure 4. From the two figures, we know that the oscillation amplitude of the density wave lessens with the rise in k. In view of the results, traffic flow becomes steadier when the control signal is taken into consideration.

In the congested areas, driving must become very difficult, and drivers have to accelerate or decelerate to alter the condition of the traffic. Diverse traffic flow state paths of acceleration or deceleration would result in the hysteresis phenomenon, which is demonstrated not only in the flux–density diagram, but also in the velocity–density diagram.

Figures 6 and 7 show the hysteresis loops of traffic flux and density, and the hysteresis loops of velocity and density, respectively, under the influence of strong wind. A similarity between the two figures is that the size of the hysteresis loop decreases with the rise in coefficient ξ. The above phenomenon reflects that the stability of traffic flow has been enhanced.

Then, we fix the coefficient ξ and further consider the feedback control. The corresponding hysteresis loops are shown in Figures 8 and 9. The hysteresis loop narrows to a point, indicating that traffic congestion was largely absent at the moment when the value k increased to 0.2.

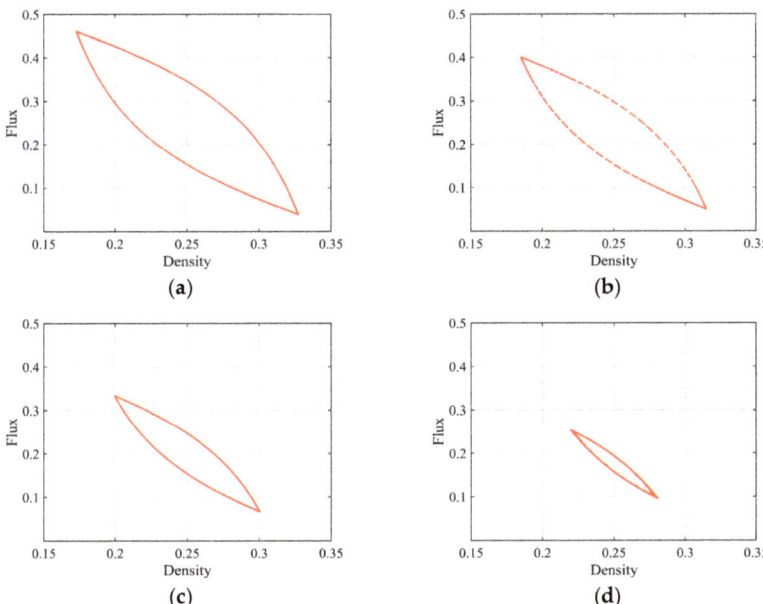

Figure 6. The hysteresis loops of traffic flux and density for different ζ. (**a**) $\zeta = 0$, (**b**) $\zeta = 0.1$, (**c**) $\zeta = 0.2$, (**d**) $\zeta = 0.3$.

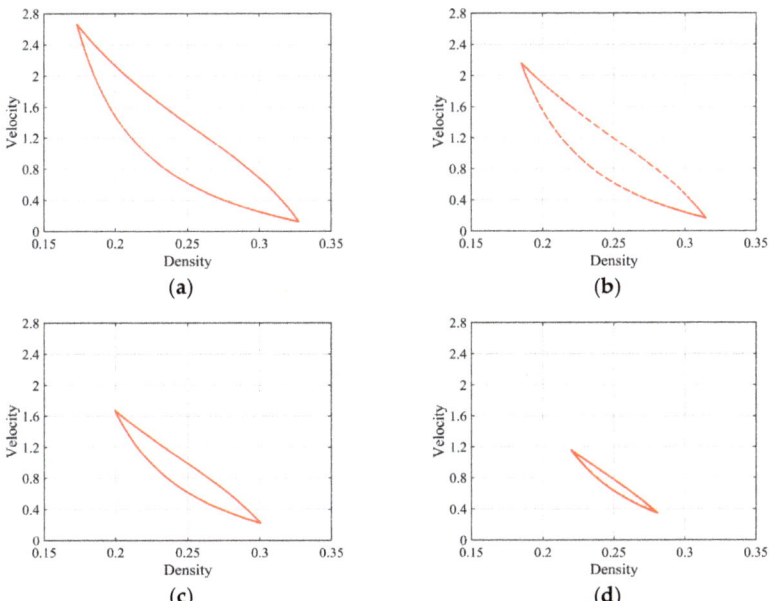

Figure 7. The hysteresis loops of velocity and density for different ζ. (**a**) $\zeta = 0$, (**b**) $\zeta = 0.1$, (**c**) $\zeta = 0.2$, (**d**) $\zeta = 0.3$.

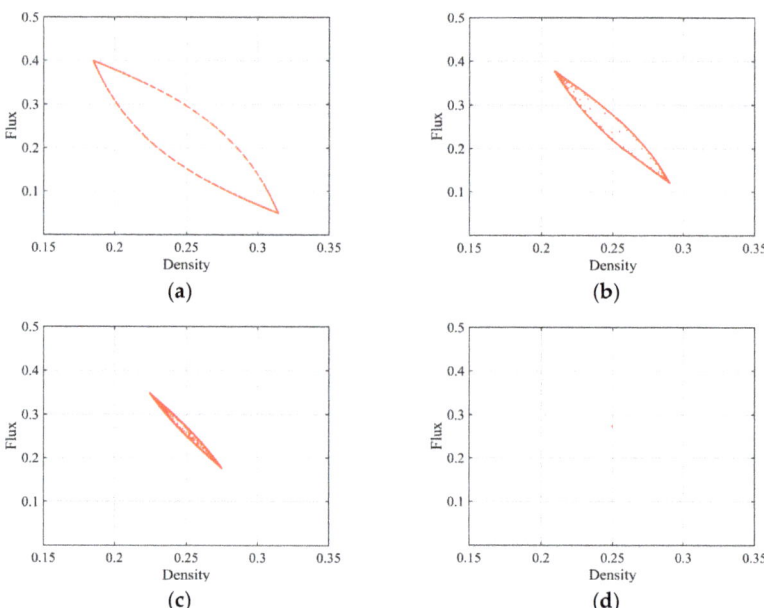

Figure 8. The hysteresis loops of traffic flux and density for different k. (**a**) $k = 0$, (**b**) $k = 0.1$, (**c**) $k = 0.15$, (**d**) $k = 0.2$.

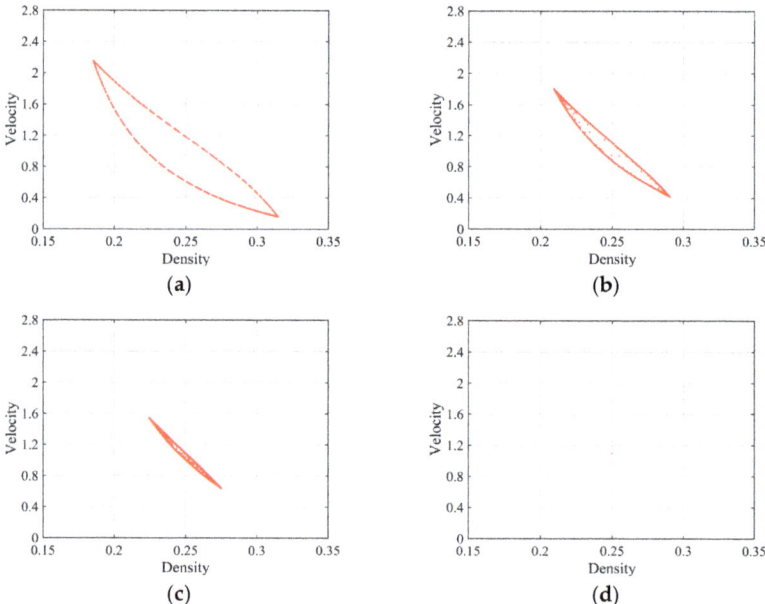

Figure 9. The hysteresis loops of velocity and density for different k. (**a**) $k = 0$, (**b**) $k = 0.1$, (**c**) $k = 0.15$, (**d**) $k = 0.2$.

5. Conclusions

The impact of strong wind and optimal flux difference integral are incorporated in a new model, and the influence of the two factors on traffic flow has been investigated through linear analysis, as well as nonlinear analysis, in this paper. In the linear analysis, the stability condition was obtained by utilization of the control method. The mKdV equation, which describes the propagating features of traffic density waves, is acquired via nonlinear analysis. Then, numerical simulation carried out on the new model revealed that the optimal flux difference integral avails to stabilize the traffic flow. Moreover, to a certain extent, the traffic flow becomes more stable with the increase in strong wind. The simulation presents the same results as the theoretical analysis. Hence, the model proposed in this study is conducive to understanding the underlying mechanism of traffic congestion, thus alleviating traffic jams.

Author Contributions: Methodology, H.L. and Y.W.; validation, Y.W.; formal analysis, H.L.; writing—original draft preparation, H.L.; writing—review and editing, Y.W.; supervision, Y.W.; funding acquisition, Y.W. All authors have read and agreed to the published version of the manuscript.

Funding: This work is supported by the National Natural Science Foundation of China (Grant No.71571107) and the K.C. Wong Magna Fund in Ningbo University, China.

Institutional Review Board Statement: Not applicable.

Informed Consent Statement: Not applicable.

Data Availability Statement: The data used to support the findings of this study are available from the corresponding author upon request.

Conflicts of Interest: The authors declare no conflict of interest.

References

1. Ma, C.; Wei, H.; He, R. Distribution path robust optimization of electric vehicle with multiple distribution centers. *PLoS ONE* **2018**, *13*, e0193789.
2. Ma, C.; Wei, H.; Pan, F. Road screening and distribution route multi-objective robust optimization for hazardous materials based on neural network and genetic algorithm. *PLoS ONE* **2018**, *13*, e0198931.
3. Ma, C.; He, R.; Zhang, W. Path optimization of taxi carpooling. *PLoS ONE* **2018**, *13*, e0203221.
4. Ma, C.; Wei, H.; Wang, A. Developing a coordinated signal control system for urban ring road under the vehicle-infrastructure connected environment. *IEEE Access* **2018**, *6*, 52471–52478. [CrossRef]
5. Tang, T.; Luo, X.; Zhang, J.; Chen, L. Modeling electric bicycle's lane-changing and retrograde behaviors. *Phys. A* **2018**, *490*, 1377–1386. [CrossRef]
6. Tang, T.; Zhang, J.; Liu, K. A speed guidance model accounting for the driver's bounded rationality at a signalized intersection. *Phys. A* **2017**, *473*, 45–52. [CrossRef]
7. Wu, X.; Zhao, X.; Song, H. Effects of the prevision relative velocity on traffic dynamics in the ACC strategy. *Phys. A* **2019**, *515*, 192–198. [CrossRef]
8. Tang, T.; Shi, W.; Huang, H. A route-based traffic flow model accounting for interruption factors. *Phys. A* **2019**, *514*, 767–785. [CrossRef]
9. Guo, Y.; Xue, Y.; Shi, Y. Mean-field velocity difference model considering the average effect of multi-vehicle interaction. *Commun. Nonlinear Sci. Numer. Simul.* **2018**, *59*, 553–564. [CrossRef]
10. Zhu, W.; Jun, D.; Zhang, L. A compound compensation method for car-following model. *Commun. Nonlinear Sci. Numer. Simul.* **2016**, *39*, 427–441. [CrossRef]
11. Bando, M.; Hasebe, K.; Nakayama, A. Dynamical model of traffic congestion and numerical simulation. *Phys. Rev. E* **1995**, *51*, 1035–1042. [CrossRef] [PubMed]
12. Zhu, W.; Zhang, L. Analysis of car-following model with cascade compensation strategy. *Phys. A* **2016**, *449*, 265–274. [CrossRef]
13. Zhu, W.; Zhang, H. Analysis of mixed traffic flow with human-driving and autonomous cars based on car-following model. *Phys. A* **2018**, *496*, 274–285. [CrossRef]
14. Wang, J.; Sun, F.; Ge, H. Effect of the driver's desire for smooth driving on the car-following model. *Phys. A* **2018**, *512*, 96–108. [CrossRef]
15. Zhu, W.; Zhang, L. A new car-following model for autonomous vehicles flow with mean expected velocity field. *Phys. A* **2018**, *492*, 2154–2165.
16. Sun, Y.; Ge, H.; Cheng, R. An extended car-following model under V2V communication environment and its delayed-feedback control. *Phys. A* **2018**, *508*, 349–358. [CrossRef]
17. Sun, Y.; Ge, H.; Cheng, R. An extended car-following model considering drivers memory and average speed of preceding vehicles with control strategy. *Phys. A* **2019**, *521*, 752–761. [CrossRef]
18. Wang, T.; Cheng, R.; Ge, H. An extended two-lane lattice hydrodynamic model for traffic flow on curved road with passing. *Phys. A* **2019**, *533*, 121915. [CrossRef]

19. Ou, H.; Tang, T. An extended two-lane car-following model accounting for inter-vehicle communication. *Phys. A* **2018**, *495*, 260–268. [CrossRef]
20. Xin, Q.; Yang, N.; Fu, R. Impacts analysis of car following models considering variable vehicular gap policies. *Phys. A* **2018**, *501*, 338–355. [CrossRef]
21. Tang, T.; Rui, Y.; Zhang, J.; Shang, H. A cellular automation model accounting for bicycle's group behavior. *Phys. A* **2018**, *492*, 1782–1797. [CrossRef]
22. Xue, Y.; Dong, L.; Dai, S. An improved one-dimensional cellular automaton model of traffic flow and the effect of deceleration probability. *Acta Phys. Sin.* **2001**, *50*, 445–449. [CrossRef]
23. Gao, K.; Jiang, R.; Hu, S.; Wang, B.; Wu, Q. Cellular-automaton model with velocity adaptation in the framework of Kerner's three-phase traffic theory. *Phys. Rev. E* **2007**, *76*, 026105. [CrossRef] [PubMed]
24. Cheng, R.; Ge, H.; Wang, J. The nonlinear analysis for a new continuum model considering anticipation and traffic jerk effect. *Appl. Math. Comput.* **2018**, *332*, 493–505.
25. Cheng, R.; Ge, H.; Wang, J. KdV-Burgers equation in a new continuum model based on full velocity difference model considering anticipation effect. *Phys. A* **2017**, *481*, 52–59. [CrossRef]
26. Cheng, R.; Ge, H.; Wang, J. An extended continuum model accounting for the driver's timid and aggressive attributions. *Phys. Lett. A* **2017**, *381*, 1302–1312. [CrossRef]
27. Zhai, Q.; Ge, H.; Cheng, R. An extended continuum model considering optimal velocity change with memory and numerical tests. *Phys. A* **2018**, *490*, 774–785.
28. Cheng, R.; Wang, Y. An extended lattice hydrodynamic model considering the delayed feedback control on a curved road. *Phys. A* **2019**, *513*, 510–517. [CrossRef]
29. Kaur, R.; Sharma, S. Modeling and simulation of driver's anticipation effect in a two lane system on curved road with slope. *Phys. A* **2018**, *499*, 110–120. [CrossRef]
30. Jiang, C.; Cheng, R.; Ge, H. Mean-field flow difference model with consideration of on-ramp and off-ramp. *Phys. A* **2019**, *513*, 465–476. [CrossRef]
31. Jiang, C.; Cheng, R.; Ge, H. An improved lattice hydrodynamic model considering the "backward looking" effect and the traffic interruption probability. *Nonlinear Dyn.* **2017**, *91*, 777–784. [CrossRef]
32. Kaur, R.; Sharma, S. Analyses of a heterogeneous lattice hydrodynamic model with low and high-sensitivity vehicles. *Phys. Lett. A* **2018**, *382*, 1449–1455. [CrossRef]
33. Peng, G.; Kuang, H.; Qing, L. A new lattice model of traffic flow considering driver's anticipation effect of the traffic interruption. *Phys. A* **2018**, *507*, 374–380. [CrossRef]
34. Wang, Q.; Ge, H. An improved lattice hydrodynamic model accounting for the effect of "backward looking" and flow integral. *Phys. A* **2019**, *513*, 438–446. [CrossRef]
35. Redhu, P.; Gupta, A. Delayed-feedback control in a lattice hydrodynamic model. *Commun. Nonlinear Sci. Numer. Simul.* **2015**, *27*, 263–270. [CrossRef]
36. Qin, S.; Ge, H.; Cheng, R. A new lattice hydrodynamic model based on control method considering the flux change rate and delay feedback signal. *Phys. Lett. A* **2018**, *382*, 482–488. [CrossRef]
37. Chang, Y.; He, Z.; Cheng, R. An extended lattice hydrodynamic model considering the driver's sensory memory and delayed-feedback control. *Phys. A* **2019**, *514*, 522–532. [CrossRef]
38. Peng, G.; Zhao, H.; Liu, X. The impact of self-stabilization on traffic stability considering the current lattice's historic flux for two-lane freeway. *Phys. A* **2019**, *515*, 31–37. [CrossRef]
39. Nagatani, T. Modified KdV equation for jamming transition in the continuum models of traffic. *Phys. A* **1998**, *261*, 599–607. [CrossRef]
40. Tian, J.; Yuan, Z.; Jia, B.; Li, M.; Jiang, G. The stabilization effect of the density difference in the modified lattice hydrodynamic model of traffic flow. *Phys. A* **2012**, *391*, 4476–4482. [CrossRef]
41. Zhao, H.; Zhang, G.; Li, W.; Gu, T.; Zhou, D. Lattice hydrodynamic modeling of traffic flow with consideration of historical current integration effect. *Phys. A* **2018**, *503*, 1204–1211. [CrossRef]
42. Sharma, S. Modeling and analyses of drivers characteristics in a traffic system with passing. *Nonlinear Dyn.* **2016**, *86*, 2093–2104. [CrossRef]
43. Wang, J.; Sun, F.; Ge, H. An improved lattice hydrodynamic model considering the driver's desire of driving smoothly. *Phys. A* **2019**, *515*, 119–129. [CrossRef]
44. Kwon, S.; Kim, D.; Lee, S. Deisgn criteria of wind barriers for traffic. part 1: Wind barrier performance. *Wind Struct.* **2011**, *14*, 55–70. [CrossRef]
45. Liu, Y.; Shi, Z.; Ai, W. An improved car-following model accounting for impact of strong wind. *Math. Probl. Eng.* **2017**, *2017*, 4936490. [CrossRef]
46. Yang, S.; Li, C.; Tang, X.; Tian, C. Effect of optimal estimation of flux difference information on the lattice traffic flow model. *Phys. A* **2016**, *463*, 394–399. [CrossRef]
47. Peng, G.; Yang, S.; Xia, D.; Li, X. A novel lattice hydrodynamic model considering the optimal estimation of flux difference effect on two-lane highway. *Phys. A* **2018**, *506*, 929–937. [CrossRef]

48. Ge, H.; Cui, Y.; Zhu, K.; Cheng, R. The control method for the lattice hydrodynamic model. *Commun. Nonlinear Sci. Numer. Simul.* **2015**, *22*, 903–908. [CrossRef]
49. Zhu, C.; Zhong, S.; Li, G.; Ma, S. New control strategy for the lattice hydrodynamic model of traffic flow. *Phys. A* **2017**, *468*, 445–453. [CrossRef]

Article

The Improved Element-Free Galerkin Method for 3D Helmholtz Equations

Heng Cheng [1,*] and Miaojuan Peng [2]

[1] School of Applied Science, Taiyuan University of Science and Technology, Taiyuan 030024, China
[2] Department of Civil Engineering, School of Mechanics and Engineering Science, Shanghai University, Shanghai 200444, China; mjpeng@shu.edu.cn
* Correspondence: chengheng@shu.edu.cn; Tel.: +86-178-3511-1258

Abstract: The improved element-free Galerkin (IEFG) method is proposed in this paper for solving 3D Helmholtz equations. The improved moving least-squares (IMLS) approximation is used to establish the trial function, and the penalty technique is used to enforce the essential boundary conditions. Thus, the final discretized equations of the IEFG method for 3D Helmholtz equations can be derived by using the corresponding Galerkin weak form. The influences of the node distribution, the weight functions, the scale parameters of the influence domain, and the penalty factors on the computational accuracy of the solutions are analyzed, and the numerical results of three examples show that the proposed method in this paper can not only enhance the computational speed of the element-free Galerkin (EFG) method but also eliminate the phenomenon of the singular matrix.

Keywords: improved element-free Galerkin method; Helmholtz equation; penalty method; improved moving least-squares approximation

1. Introduction

As an important elliptic differential equation, the Helmholtz equation has been widely applied in many different fields, such as mechanics, acoustics, physics, electromagnetics, engineering, and so on. It is well known that how to achieve the numerical solutions of Helmholtz equations effectively and accurately is one of the important directions in the scientific research.

Currently, many meshless methods have been used for researching Helmholtz equations, such as the element-free Galerkin (EFG) method [1], meshless Galerkin least-square method [2], meshless hybrid boundary-node method [3], boundary element-free method [4], and complex variable boundary element-free method [5,6]. Compared to the traditional finite difference method [7–10] and the finite element method, meshless methods [11–15] are based on scattered point approximation, which can avoid the mesh reconstruction, and thus a higher accuracy of the numerical solutions can be obtained.

As an important meshless method, the EFG method [16] was studied by Belytschko et al. In this method, a trial function is established by using the moving least-squares (MLS) approximation. Cheng et al. analyzed the error estimates of EFG method for potential problems [17]. Because the MLS approximation is based on the least-squares method [18–22], the disadvantages of the least-squares method also exist in the MLS approximation, in which sometimes ill-conditional or singular matrices occur.

In order to eliminate the singular matrices, the improved moving least-squares (IMLS) approximation [23] was proposed by Cheng et al., in which the orthogonal function system with a weight function is used as basis function, and thus can make up for the deficiency of the MLS approximation and has greater computational efficiency, using the IMLS approximation to establish the trial function. Thus, the improved element-free Galerkin (IEFG) method was applied for potential [24], transient heat conduction problems [25], the wave equation [26], the Schrödinger equation [27], advection–diffusion [28], elastodynamics [29],

elastoplasticity [30], viscoelasticity [31], and diffusional drug release [32] problems. From these studies, we can see that under similar computational accuracy, the IEFG method has higher computational speed than the EFG method. As we know, meshless methods are based on node approximation without mesh reconstruction. When solving large deformation problems and dynamic propagation of cracks, the meshless method can obtain greater precision than the finite element method. In order to take advantage of the IEFG method further, Zhang et al. [33] developed the enriched IEFG method to solve 2D fracture problems. In this method, the enriched basis function is used at the tip of the crack. As a result, the singularity of the stresses at the tip of the crack can be shown better than in the IEFG method. Cai et al. [34] used the IEFG method for solving large elastoplasticity deformation problems. Three numerical examples are given to show that the numerical solutions are in good agreement with the solutions of finite element method software ANASYS and can enhance the computational efficiency of the EFG method.

By introducing the singular weight function into the MLS approximation, Lancaster et al. presented an interpolating MLS method [35]. The boundary conditions could be enforced directly in the corresponding meshless method. Based on the concept of an inner production, Ren et al. improved the interpolating MLS method [36] by using the singular weight function in interpolating points and orthogonalizing some of the base functions. Thus, the corresponding interpolating EFG method was presented for potential [37], transient heat conduction [38], and some mechanics [39–41] problems. Compared with the traditional EFG method, the interpolating EFG method has higher computational efficiency. Additionally, the interpolating smoothed particle method was developed by Qin et al. [42].

Using the nonsingular weight function, Wang et al. developed the improved interpolating MLS method [43], which can overcome the difficulties caused by the singular weight function in the interpolating MLS method, and used this method to construct the trial function. The improved interpolating EFG method was presented for potential [43] and several large deformation problems [44–46].

Based on the approximation of the vector function, the complex variable moving least-squares (CVMLS) approximation was presented by Cheng et al. [47]. Based on the CVMLS approximation and Galerkin weak form, the complex variable element-free Galerkin (CVEFG) method [48] was presented. Moreover, based on the conjugate basis function, Bai et al. proposed the improved CVMLS approximation to construct the shape function, and the improved CVEFG method was presented for elasticity problems [49]. The improved CVEFG method has higher computational accuracy and efficiency than the EFG method, but it cannot be applied to 3D problems directly because the complex theory is used. Chen et al. [50,51] proposed the complex variable reproducing kernel particle method.

By combining meshless methods and the finite difference method, the hybrid CVEFG method [52–56], dimension-splitting EFG method [57–60], dimension-splitting reproducing kernel particle method [61–64], interpolating dimension-splitting EFG method [65] and hybrid generalized interpolated EFG method [66] were proposed. These methods can greatly improve the computational efficiency of the traditional meshless method for solving multi-dimensional problems.

The IEFG method has some advantages over the traditional EFG method, such as higher computational efficiency, avoiding matrix inversion, and eliminating singular matrix. Therefore, it has been applied to many science and engineering problems. However, 3D Helmholtz equations have not been studied by the IEFG method yet, and the corresponding parameters cannot be discussed; thus, the computational accuracy and efficiency of the IEFG method for 3D Helmholtz equations are also uncertain. In order to overcome the disadvantage of the lower efficiency of the EFG method, this paper presents the IEFG method for solving 3D Helmholtz equations. The trial function was established by using the IMLS approximation, using the penalty technique to enforce the essential boundary conditions. The final discretized equations could be derived by using the corresponding weak form. Thus, we obtained the final formulate of the IEFG method for 3D Helmholtz equations.

In Section 4, the influences of the node distribution, the weight functions, the scale parameters, and the penalty factors on the computational accuracy of the solutions are analyzed by giving examples. It is shown that the IEFG method for Helmholtz equations is convergent. Compared with the EFG method, the IEFG method has greater computational speed. Moreover, the singular matrix can be eliminated.

2. The IMLS Approximation

The approximation of a function $u(x)$ is

$$u^h(x) = \sum_{i=1}^{m} p_i(x) \cdot a_i(x) = \pmb{p}^{\mathrm{T}}(x) \cdot \pmb{a}(x), \ (x \in \Omega), \tag{1}$$

where $\pmb{p}^{\mathrm{T}}(x)$ is the basis function vector, m is the basis function number, and

$$\pmb{a}^{\mathrm{T}}(x) = (a_1(x), a_2(x), \cdots, a_m(x)) \tag{2}$$

is the coefficient vector of $\pmb{p}^{\mathrm{T}}(x)$.

In general,

$$\pmb{p}^{\mathrm{T}}(x) = (1, x_1, x_2, x_3), \tag{3}$$

$$\pmb{p}^{\mathrm{T}}(x) = (1, x_1, x_2, x_3, x_1^2, x_2^2, x_3^2, x_1 x_2, x_2 x_3, x_1 x_3). \tag{4}$$

The local approximation is

$$u^h(x, \hat{x}) = \sum_{i=1}^{m} p_i(\hat{x}) \cdot a_i(x) = \pmb{p}^{\mathrm{T}}(\hat{x}) \cdot \pmb{a}(x). \tag{5}$$

Define

$$J = \sum_{I=1}^{n} w(x - x_I)[u^h(x, x_I) - u_I]^2 = \sum_{I=1}^{n} w(x - x_I) \left[\sum_{i=1}^{m} p_i(x_I) \cdot a_i(x) - u_I \right]^2, \tag{6}$$

where $w(x - x_I)$ is a weighting function, and x_I ($I = 1, 2, \cdots, n$) are the nodes with influence domains covering point x.

Equation (6) can be written as

$$J = (\pmb{Pa} - \pmb{u})^{\mathrm{T}} \pmb{W}(x)(\pmb{Pa} - \pmb{u}), \tag{7}$$

where

$$\pmb{u}^{\mathrm{T}} = (u_1, u_2, \cdots, u_n), \tag{8}$$

$$\pmb{P} = \begin{bmatrix} p_1(x_1) & p_2(x_1) & \cdots & p_m(x_1) \\ p_1(x_2) & p_2(x_2) & \cdots & p_m(x_2) \\ \vdots & \vdots & \ddots & \vdots \\ p_1(x_n) & p_2(x_n) & \cdots & p_m(x_n) \end{bmatrix}, \tag{9}$$

and

$$\pmb{W}(x) = \begin{bmatrix} w(x - x_1) & 0 & \cdots & 0 \\ 0 & w(x - x_2) & \cdots & 0 \\ \vdots & \vdots & \ddots & \vdots \\ 0 & 0 & \cdots & w(x - x_n) \end{bmatrix}. \tag{10}$$

From

$$\frac{\partial J}{\partial \pmb{a}} = \pmb{A}(x)\pmb{a}(x) - \pmb{B}(x)\pmb{u} = 0, \tag{11}$$

we have

$$\pmb{A}(x)\pmb{a}(x) = \pmb{B}(x)\pmb{u}, \tag{12}$$

where
$$A(x) = P^T W(x) P, \tag{13}$$
$$B(x) = P^T W(x). \tag{14}$$

Equation (12) sometimes forms a singular or ill-conditional matrix. In order to make up for this deficiency, for basis functions
$$q = (q_i) = (1, x_1, x_2, x_3, x_1^2, x_2^2, x_3^2, x_1 x_2, x_2 x_3, x_3 x_1, \cdots), \tag{15}$$
using the Gram–Schmidt process, we can obtain
$$p_i = q_i - \sum_{k=1}^{i-1} \frac{(q_i, p_k)}{(p_k, p_k)} p_k, \ (i = 1, 2, 3, \cdots), \tag{16}$$
and
$$(p_i, p_j) = 0, \ (i \neq j). \tag{17}$$
Then, from Equation (12), $a(x)$ can be obtained as
$$a(x) = A^*(x) B(x) u, \tag{18}$$
where
$$A^*(x) = \begin{bmatrix} \frac{1}{(p_1, p_1)} & 0 & \cdots & 0 \\ 0 & \frac{1}{(p_2, p_2)} & 0 & 0 \\ \vdots & \vdots & \ddots & \vdots \\ 0 & 0 & \cdots & \frac{1}{(p_n, p_n)} \end{bmatrix}. \tag{19}$$

Substituting Equation (18) into Equation (5), we have
$$u^h(x) = \Phi^*(x) u = \sum_{I=1}^n \Phi_I^*(x) u_I, \tag{20}$$
where
$$\Phi^*(x) = (\Phi_1^*(x), \Phi_2^*(x), \cdots, \Phi_n^*(x)) = p^T(x) A^*(x) B(x) \tag{21}$$
is the shape function.

This is the IMLS approximation [23], in which the shape function can be obtained more easily than the MLS approximation. Moreover, the IMLS approximation can also avoid the singular matrix. Thus, it can enhance the computational efficiency of the MLS approximation.

3. The IEFG Method for 3D Helmholtz Equations

The governing equation is
$$\Delta u + k^2 u = f(x), \ (x = (x_1, x_2, x_3) \in \Omega) \tag{22}$$
and the boundary conditions are
$$u(x) = \bar{u}, \ (x \in \Gamma_u), \tag{23}$$
$$q(x) = \frac{\partial u(x)}{\partial x_1} n_1 + \frac{\partial u(x)}{\partial x_2} n_2 + \frac{\partial u(x)}{\partial x_3} n_3 = \bar{q}, \ (x \in \Gamma_q), \tag{24}$$
where k^2 is the wave number, $f(x)$ is the given function, $\bar{u}$ and $\bar{q}$ are the given values, and $\Gamma = \Gamma_u \cup \Gamma_q$, $\Gamma_u \cap \Gamma_q = \emptyset$, $n_i \ (i = 1, 2, 3)$ is the unit outward normal to the boundary Γ in direction x_i.

For 3D Helmholtz equations, the equivalent functional is

$$\Pi = \int_\Omega u(\frac{1}{2}k^2 u - f)\mathrm{d}\Omega - \int_\Omega \frac{1}{2}\left[\left(\frac{\partial u}{\partial x_1}\right)^2 + \left(\frac{\partial u}{\partial x_2}\right)^2 + \left(\frac{\partial u}{\partial x_3}\right)^2\right]\mathrm{d}\Omega - \int_{\Gamma_q} u\bar{q}\mathrm{d}\Gamma. \quad (25)$$

By introducing the penalty technique to apply the boundary conditions, we can obtain the modified functional

$$\Pi^* = \Pi + \frac{\alpha}{2}\int_{\Gamma_u}(u-\bar{u})(u-\bar{u})\mathrm{d}\Gamma, \quad (26)$$

where α is the penalty factor.

Let

$$\delta\Pi^* = 0. \quad (27)$$

We can obtain the following equivalent integral weak form

$$\begin{array}{c}\int_\Omega \delta u \cdot k^2 u \mathrm{d}\Omega - \int_\Omega \delta(Lu)^\mathrm{T} \cdot (Lu)\mathrm{d}\Omega - \int_\Omega \delta u \cdot f \mathrm{d}\Omega - \int_{\Gamma_q} \delta u \cdot \bar{q}\mathrm{d}\Gamma \\ +\alpha\int_{\Gamma_u} \delta u \cdot u \mathrm{d}\Gamma - \alpha\int_{\Gamma_u}\delta u \cdot \bar{u}\mathrm{d}\Gamma = 0,\end{array} \quad (28)$$

where

$$L(\cdot) = \begin{bmatrix}\frac{\partial}{\partial x_1} \\ \frac{\partial}{\partial x_2} \\ \frac{\partial}{\partial x_3}\end{bmatrix}(\cdot). \quad (29)$$

In the cubic domain Ω, we employ M nodes x_I ($I = 1, 2, \cdots, M$). Thus, we have

$$u_I = u(x_I). \quad (30)$$

From the IMLS approximation, we can obtain

$$u(x) = \mathbf{\Phi}^*(x)\mathbf{u} = \sum_{I=1}^n \Phi_I^*(x)u_I, \quad (31)$$

where

$$\mathbf{u} = (u_1, u_2, \cdots, u_n)^\mathrm{T}. \quad (32)$$

From Equations (29) and (31), we have

$$Lu(x) = \sum_{I=1}^n \begin{bmatrix}\frac{\partial}{\partial x_1} \\ \frac{\partial}{\partial x_2} \\ \frac{\partial}{\partial x_3}\end{bmatrix}\Phi_I^*(x)u_I = \sum_{I=1}^n B_I u_I = B(x)\mathbf{u}, \quad (33)$$

where

$$B(x) = (B_1, B_2, \cdots, B_n), \quad (34)$$

$$B_I = \begin{bmatrix}\Phi_{I,1}^*(x) \\ \Phi_{I,2}^*(x) \\ \Phi_{I,3}^*(x)\end{bmatrix}. \quad (35)$$

Substituting Equations (31) and (33) into Equation (28), we have

$$\begin{array}{c}\int_\Omega \delta[\mathbf{\Phi}^*(x)\mathbf{u}]^\mathrm{T} \cdot k^2 \cdot [\mathbf{\Phi}^*(x)\mathbf{u}]\mathrm{d}\Omega - \int_\Omega \delta[B(x)\mathbf{u}]^\mathrm{T}[B(x)\mathbf{u}]\mathrm{d}\Omega \\ -\int_{\Gamma_q}\delta[\mathbf{\Phi}^*(x)\mathbf{u}]^\mathrm{T} \cdot \bar{q}\mathrm{d}\Gamma - \int_\Omega \delta[\mathbf{\Phi}^*(x)\mathbf{u}]^\mathrm{T} \cdot f\mathrm{d}\Omega \\ \alpha\int_{\Gamma_u}\delta[\mathbf{\Phi}^*(x)\mathbf{u}]^\mathrm{T} \cdot [\mathbf{\Phi}^*(x)\mathbf{u}]\mathrm{d}\Gamma - \alpha\int_{\Gamma_u}\delta[\mathbf{\Phi}^*(x)\mathbf{u}]^\mathrm{T} \cdot \bar{u}\mathrm{d}\Gamma = 0.\end{array} \quad (36)$$

In Equation (36), the form of $\mathbf{u}$ is the same as Equation (32), and $n = M$.

All integral terms in Equation (36) are analyzed as follows:

$$\int_\Omega \delta[\mathbf{\Phi}^*(x)u]^\mathrm{T} \cdot k^2 \cdot [\mathbf{\Phi}^*(x)u] \mathrm{d}\Omega = \delta u^\mathrm{T} \cdot k^2 [\int_\Omega \mathbf{\Phi}^{*\mathrm{T}}(x)\mathbf{\Phi}^*(x)\mathrm{d}\Omega] \cdot u, \qquad (37)$$

$$\int_\Omega \delta[B(x)u]^\mathrm{T} \cdot [B(x)u]\mathrm{d}\Omega = \delta u^\mathrm{T} \cdot [\int_\Omega B^\mathrm{T}(x)B(x)\mathrm{d}\Omega] \cdot u, \qquad (38)$$

$$\int_\Omega \delta[\mathbf{\Phi}^*(x)u]^\mathrm{T} \cdot f \mathrm{d}\Omega = \delta u^\mathrm{T} \cdot [\int_\Omega \mathbf{\Phi}^{*\mathrm{T}}(x) f \mathrm{d}\Omega], \qquad (39)$$

$$\int_{\Gamma_q} \delta[\mathbf{\Phi}^*(x)u]^\mathrm{T} \cdot \bar{q}\mathrm{d}\Gamma = \delta u^\mathrm{T} \cdot [\int_{\Gamma_q} \mathbf{\Phi}^{*\mathrm{T}}(x)\bar{q}\mathrm{d}\Gamma], \qquad (40)$$

$$\alpha \int_{\Gamma_u} \delta[\mathbf{\Phi}^*(x)u]^\mathrm{T} \cdot [\mathbf{\Phi}^*(x)u]\mathrm{d}\Gamma = \delta u^\mathrm{T} \cdot [\alpha \int_{\Gamma_u} \mathbf{\Phi}^{*\mathrm{T}}(x)\mathbf{\Phi}^*(x)\mathrm{d}\Gamma] \cdot u, \qquad (41)$$

$$\alpha \int_{\Gamma_u} \delta[\mathbf{\Phi}^*(x)u]^\mathrm{T} \cdot \bar{u}\mathrm{d}\Gamma = \delta u^\mathrm{T} \cdot [\alpha \int_{\Gamma_u} \mathbf{\Phi}^{*\mathrm{T}}(x)\bar{u}\mathrm{d}\Gamma]. \qquad (42)$$

Let

$$C = k^2 \int_\Omega \mathbf{\Phi}^{*\mathrm{T}}(x)\mathbf{\Phi}^*(x)\mathrm{d}\Omega, \qquad (43)$$

$$K = \int_\Omega B^\mathrm{T}(x)B(x)\mathrm{d}\Omega, \qquad (44)$$

$$F_1 = \int_\Omega \mathbf{\Phi}^{*\mathrm{T}}(x) f \mathrm{d}\Omega, \qquad (45)$$

$$F_2 = \int_{\Gamma_q} \mathbf{\Phi}^{*\mathrm{T}}(x)\bar{q}\mathrm{d}\Gamma, \qquad (46)$$

$$K^\alpha = \alpha \int_{\Gamma_u} \mathbf{\Phi}^{*\mathrm{T}}(x)\mathbf{\Phi}^*(x)\mathrm{d}\Gamma, \qquad (47)$$

$$F^\alpha = \alpha \int_{\Gamma_u} \mathbf{\Phi}^{*\mathrm{T}}(x)\bar{u}\mathrm{d}\Gamma. \qquad (48)$$

Substituting Equations (37)–(42) into Equation (36), we can obtain

$$\delta u^\mathrm{T}(Cu - Ku - F_1 - F_2 - F^\alpha + K^\alpha u) = 0. \qquad (49)$$

The δu^T is arbitrary; thus we can obtain

$$\widetilde{K}u = \widetilde{F}, \qquad (50)$$

where

$$\widetilde{K} = C - K + K^\alpha, \qquad (51)$$

$$\widetilde{F} = F_1 + F_2 + F^\alpha. \qquad (52)$$

This is the IEFG method for 3D Helmholtz equations.

4. Numerical Examples

The formula of the relative error is

$$\left\| u - u^h \right\|_{L^2(\Omega)}^{rel} = \frac{\left\| u - u^h \right\|_{L^2(\Omega)}}{\|u\|_{L^2(\Omega)}}, \qquad (53)$$

where

$$\left\| u - u^h \right\|_{L^2(\Omega)} = \left(\int_\Omega (u - u^h)^2 \mathrm{d}\Omega \right)^{1/2}. \qquad (54)$$

In order to illustrate the advantages of the IFFG method, we chose three examples from other literature. The nodes distributed in the problem domains of these numerical examples were regular, the linear basis function was selected, and $3 \times 3 \times 3$ Gaussian points were selected in each integral cell. The IEFG and the EFG methods are used to solve these examples.

The following equation is considered in the first example:

$$\Delta u + u = (12x_1^2 - x_1^4) \sin x_2 \cos x_3. \tag{55}$$

The boundary conditions are

$$u(0, x_2, x_3) = 0, \tag{56}$$

$$u(\pi, x_2, x_3) = \pi^4 \sin x_2 \cos x_3, \tag{57}$$

$$u(x_1, 0, x_3) = u(x_1, \pi, x_3) = 0, \tag{58}$$

$$u(x_1, x_2, 0) = -u(x_1, x_2, \pi) = x_1^4 \sin x_2. \tag{59}$$

The problem domain is $\Omega = [0, \pi] \times [0, \pi] \times [0, \pi]$, and

$$u = x_1^4 \sin x_2 \cos x_3 \tag{60}$$

is the analytical solution.

In order to study the convergence of the EFG and the IEFG methods for Helmholtz equations, all parameters of both methods were kept the same. The cubic spline weight functions were used, $d_{max} = 1.35$, $\alpha = 2.0 \times 10^4$. Table 1 shows the relationship between relative errors and node distribution. It is shown that, with the increase in nodes, the precision of numerical solutions improves as well, but the computational efficiency is reduced gradually. Therefore, the two methods in this paper are convergent. Both the computational accuracy and efficiency are considered, and $15 \times 15 \times 15$ regularly distributed nodes are selected.

Table 1. Relative errors and CPU times of the improved element-free Galerkin (IEFG) and element-free Galerkin (EFG) methods with the increase in node distribution.

Nodes	Relative Error		Time (s)	
	IEFG	EFG	IEFG	EFG
$7 \times 7 \times 7$	4.3092%	4.3092%	5.5	5.8
$11 \times 11 \times 11$	1.3234%	1.3234%	26.7	28.5
$13 \times 13 \times 13$	0.8832%	0.8832%	49.9	53.1
$15 \times 15 \times 15$	0.6296%	0.6296%	92.1	98.0
$17 \times 17 \times 17$	0.4706%	0.4706%	152.0	161.9
$21 \times 21 \times 21$	0.2905%	0.2905%	384.5	398.6
$25 \times 25 \times 25$	0.1967%	0.1967%	903.3	940.2
$29 \times 29 \times 29$	0.1520%	0.1520%	1907.2	1937.1
$33 \times 33 \times 33$	0.1075%	0.1075%	4287.2	4408.3

The effects of the weight function, the scale parameter of the influence domain, and the penalty factor on solution of the IEFG method will be discussed.

(1) Weight function

When the cubic spline function is used, $15 \times 15 \times 15$ regularly distributed nodes and $14 \times 14 \times 14$ background integral cells are selected, $\alpha = 2.0 \times 10^4$, $d_{max} = 1.35$. Thus, the smaller relative error is 0.6296%. When the quartic spline function is used, and the same regularly distributed nodes and background integral grids are used, $\alpha = 2.2 \times 10^4$, $d_{max} = 1.28$, the smaller relative error is 0.6274%. It is shown that the similar relative errors can be obtained when using two weight functions.

In addition, the singular matrix can be avoided in the IEFG method when using the cubic spline function. If $d_{max} = 1.0$, the quartic spline function is selected. Unfortunately, the singular matrix occurs and the final result cannot be obtained. When the cubic spline function is used, the relative error is 0.6451%.

Thus, the cubic spline function is selected.

(2) Scale parameter

The same node distribution and background integral grids are selected, $\alpha = 2.0 \times 10^4$, and the cubic spline function is used. Figure 1 shows the relationship between d_{max} and relative errors. Because of the error of computer itself, the relative error become larger when $d_{max} = 1.2$. It is shown that when $d_{max} = 1.35$, the relative error is smaller.

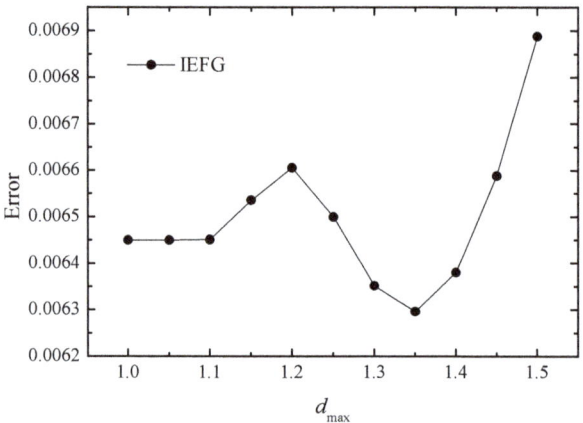

Figure 1. The error of the numerical solutions of the IEFG method with the increase in d_{max}.

(3) Penalty factor

The same node distribution, background integral grids, and weight function are selected, $d_{max} = 1.35$. Figure 2 shows the relationship between α and relative errors. It is shown that when $\alpha = 2.0 \times 10^4$, the relative error is smaller.

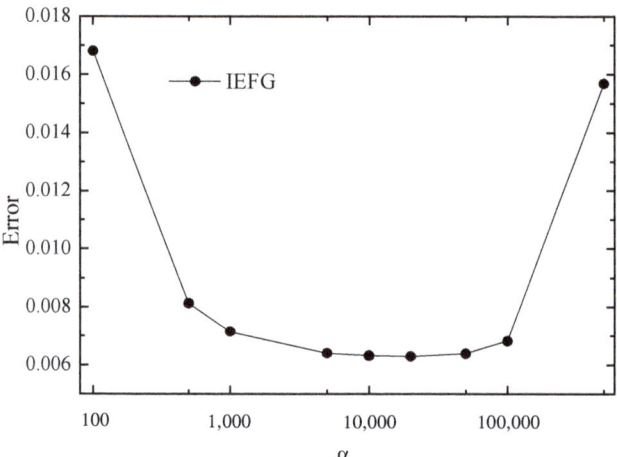

Figure 2. The error of the numerical solutions of the IEFG method with the increase in α.

The IEFG method is selected to solve it, 15 × 15 × 15 regularly distributed nodes and 14 × 14 × 14 background integral cells are selected, and the cubic spline function is used, $\alpha = 2.0 \times 10^4$, $d_{max} = 1.35$. When using the EFG method to solve it, the same parameters are selected, and thus the relative errors of two methods are equal to 0.6296%.

Figures 3–5 show the comparison between numerical solutions and analytical ones, and the CPU times of the IEFG method and the EFG method are 92.1 s and 98.0 s, respectively. Obviously, higher computational efficiency can be obtained when using the IEFG method.

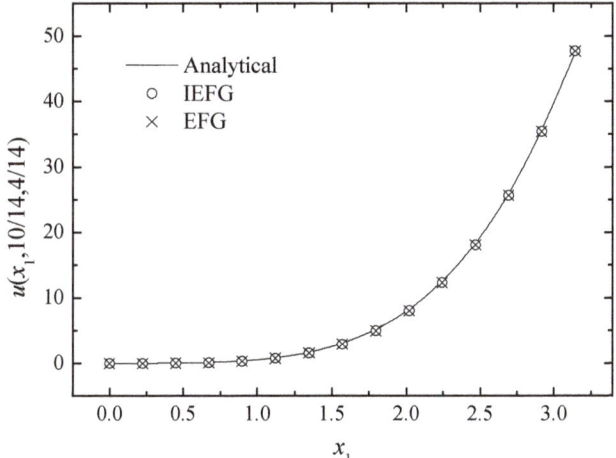

Figure 3. The comparison of the numerical and analytical solutions of the two methods along the x_1-axis.

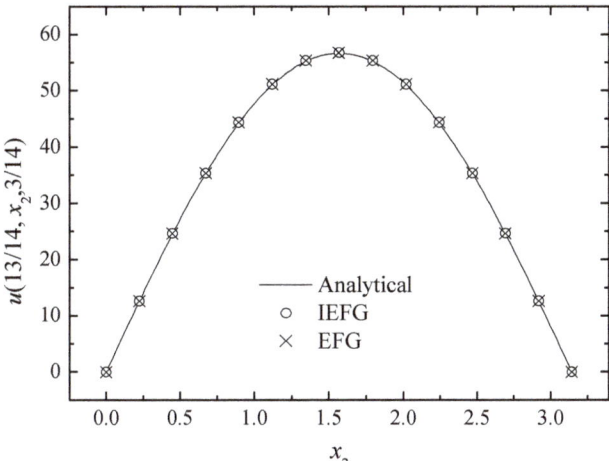

Figure 4. The comparison of the numerical and analytical solutions of the two methods along the x_2-axis.

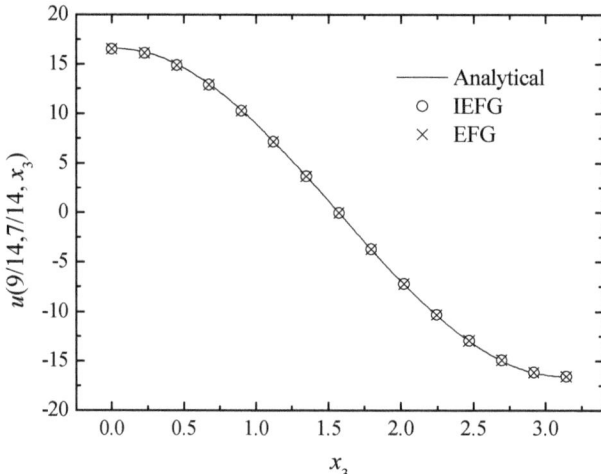

Figure 5. The comparison of the numerical and analytical solutions of the two methods along the x_3-axis.

Additionally, the singular matrix can be avoided when constructing the shape functions when the IEFG is used. If $d_{\max} = 1.0$ and other parameters are the same, two methods are used to solve it, and two different results are obtained. When the EFG method is used, the singular matrix occurs and the final result cannot be obtained. However, using the IEFG method to solve it, the relative error of the numerical solutions is 0.6451%. The numerical and analytical results are compared in Figure 6; it is shown that the numerical results are in good agreement with the analytical ones.

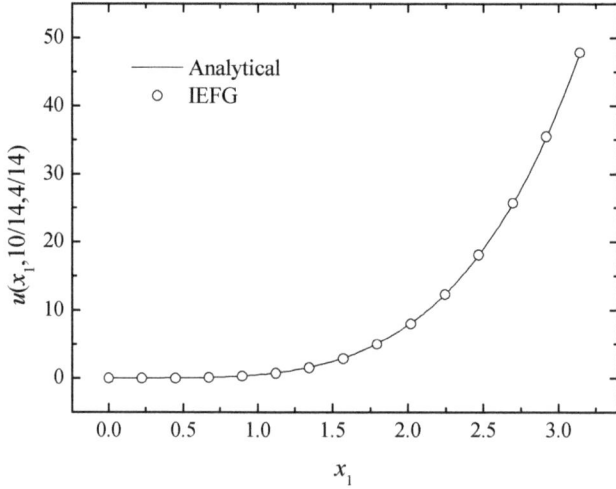

Figure 6. The numerical and analytical solutions of the IEFG method along the x_1-axis.

The second example [67] is
$$\Delta u - k^2 u = 0. \tag{61}$$
The boundary conditions are
$$u(0, x_2, x_3) = e^{(\xi_2 x_2 + \xi_3 x_3)}, \tag{62}$$
$$u(1, x_2, x_3) = e^{(\xi_1 + \xi_2 x_2 + \xi_3 x_3)}, \tag{63}$$
$$u(x_1, 0, x_3) = e^{(\xi_1 x_1 + \xi_3 x_3)}, \tag{64}$$
$$u(x_1, 1, x_3) = e^{(\xi_1 x_1 + \xi_2 + \xi_3 x_3)}, \tag{65}$$
$$u(x_1, x_2, 0) = e^{(\xi_1 x_1 + \xi_2 x_2)}, \tag{66}$$
$$u(x_1, x_2, 1) = e^{(\xi_1 x_1 + \xi_2 x_2 + \xi_3)}. \tag{67}$$
The problem domain is $\Omega = [0,1] \times [0,1] \times [0,1]$, and
$$u = e^{(\xi_1 x_1 + \xi_2 x_2 + \xi_3 x_3)} \tag{68}$$
is the analytical solution.

We set $k = 2$, $\xi_1 = 1$, and $\xi_2 = 0.5$. The IEFG method is used to solve it, $\alpha = 1.7 \times 10^3$, $d_{\max} = 1.21$. The $15 \times 15 \times 15$ regularly distributed nodes and $14 \times 14 \times 14$ background integral grids are used. When using the EFG method to solve it, the same parameters are selected, and thus the same computational accuracy can be obtained. The relative errors of both methods are equal to 0.0844%. Figures 7–9 show the comparison of the numerical solutions of the two methods and the analytical ones. The CPU times of the IEFG method and the EFG method are 92.1 s and 98.0 s, respectively. We can see that the computational results of both methods are in very good agreement with the analytical ones.

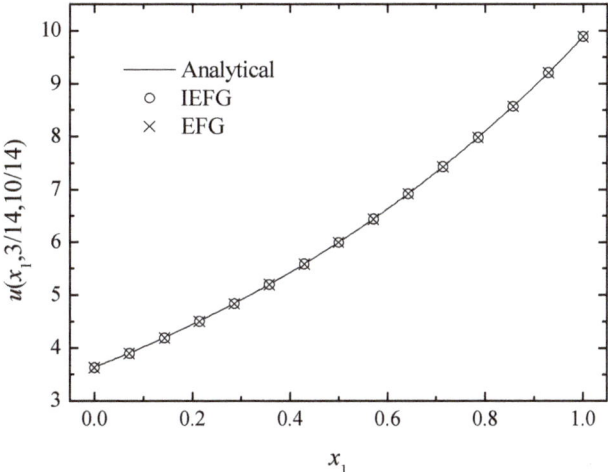

Figure 7. The comparison of the numerical and analytical solutions of the two methods along the x_1-axis.

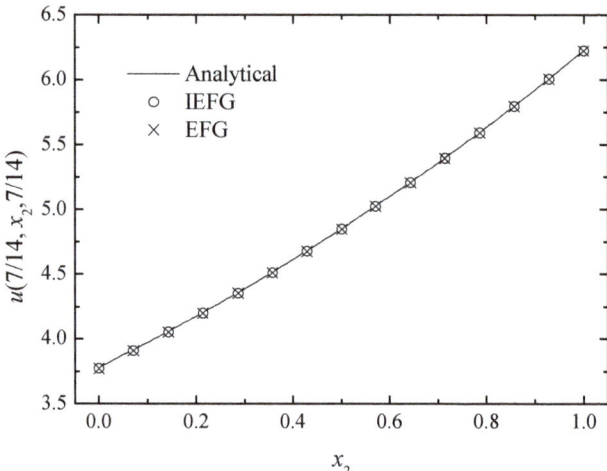

Figure 8. The comparison of the numerical and analytical solutions of the two methods along the x_2-axis.

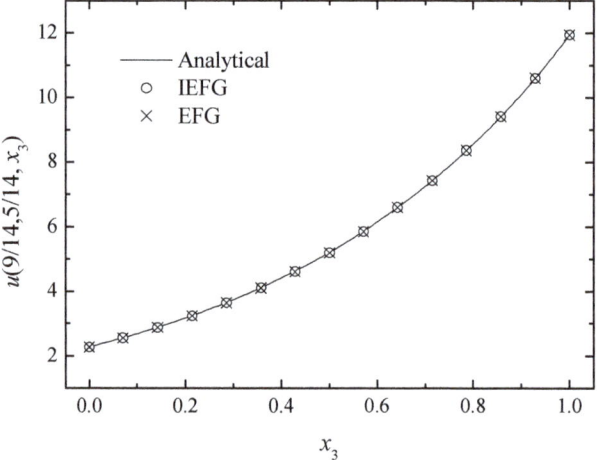

Figure 9. The comparison of the numerical and analytical solutions of the two methods along the x_3-axis.

When different parameters are selected, $k = 5$, $\zeta_1 = 3$, and $\zeta_2 = 2.7$. Using two methods to solve it, the same parameters are used. Thus, the relative errors of both methods are equal to 0.5295%. Figures 10–12 show the comparison of the numerical solutions of the two methods and the analytical ones, and the CPU times of the IEFG method and the EFG method are 92.1 s and 98.0 s, respectively. We can see that the computational results of both methods are in good agreement with the analytical ones.

We can select $k = 10$, $\zeta_1 = 5.8$, and $\zeta_2 = 6.2$. Using the two methods to solve it, the same parameters are used, and the relative errors of both methods are equal to 2.3884%. Figures 13–15 show the comparison of the numerical solutions of the two methods and the analytical ones. The computational results of both methods are in good agreement with the analytical ones.

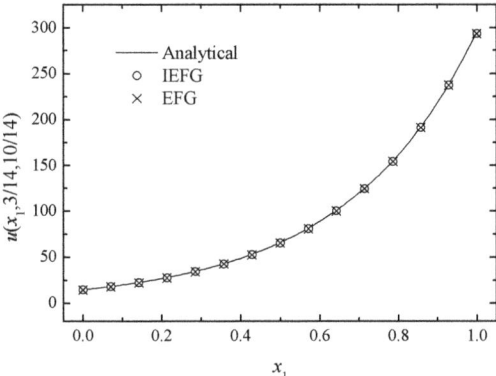

Figure 10. The comparison of the numerical and analytical solutions of the two methods along the x_1-axis.

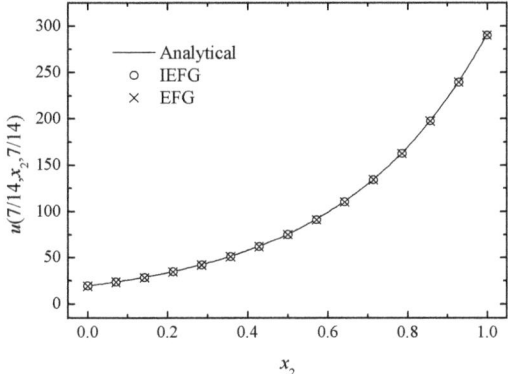

Figure 11. The comparison of the numerical and analytical solutions of the two methods along the x_2-axis.

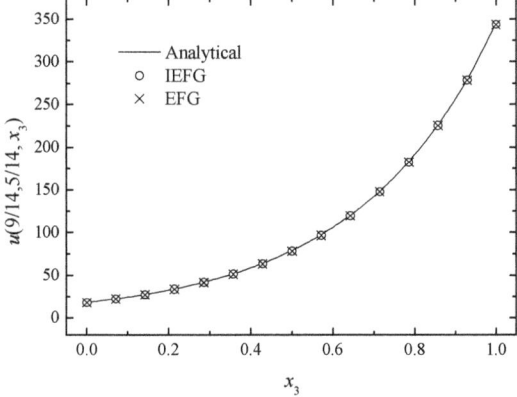

Figure 12. The comparison of the numerical and analytical solutions of the two methods along the x_3-axis.

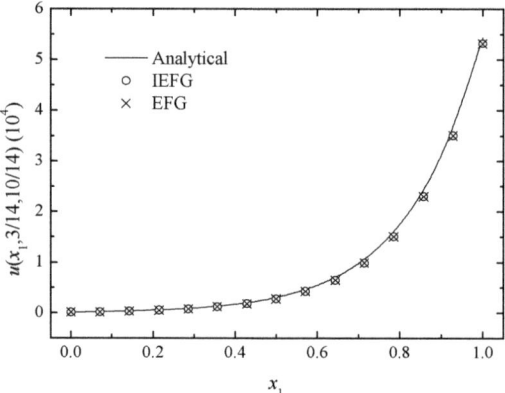

Figure 13. The comparison of the numerical and analytical solutions of the two methods along the x_1-axis.

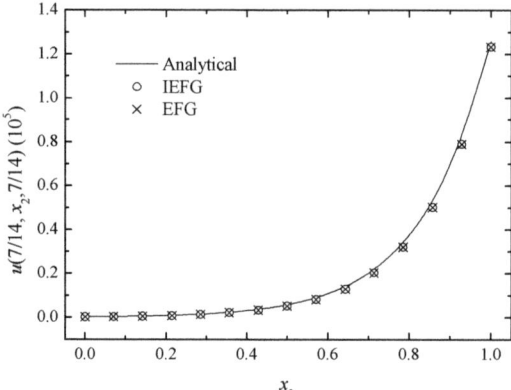

Figure 14. The comparison of the numerical and analytical solutions of the two methods along the x_2-axis.

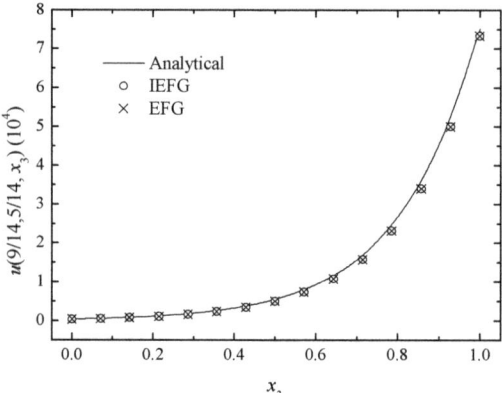

Figure 15. The comparison of the numerical and analytical solutions of the two methods along the x_3-axis.

From this example, we can draw two conclusions: On the one hand, the IEFG method has greater computational efficiency; on the other hand, the bigger the wave numbers are, the lower the computational accuracy.

Similarly, if $d_{\max} = 1.0$, we select $k = 10$, $\xi_1 = 5.8$, and $\xi_2 = 6.2$. When the EFG method is used, unfortunately, the singular matrix occurs. When the IEFG method is used, the relative error is 2.4229%. The numerical solutions and analytical ones are compared in Figure 16. It is shown that the numerical results are in good agreement with the analytical ones.

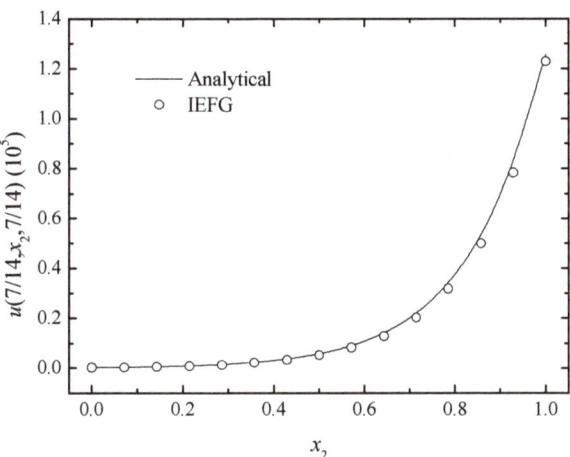

Figure 16. The numerical and analytical solutions of the IEFG method along the x_2-axis.

The third example [68] is

$$\Delta u + k^2 u = (k^2 - 3\pi^2)\cos(\pi x_1)\sin(\pi x_2)\sin(\pi x_3). \tag{69}$$

The boundary conditions are

$$\frac{\partial u(0, x_2, x_3)}{\partial x_1} = \frac{\partial u(1, x_2, x_3)}{\partial x_1} = 0, \tag{70}$$

$$u(x_1, 0, x_3) = u(x_1, 1, x_3) = 0, \tag{71}$$

$$u(x_1, x_2, 0) = u(x_1, x_2, 1) = 0. \tag{72}$$

The problem domain is $\Omega = [0,1] \times [0,1] \times [0,1]$, and

$$u = \cos(\pi x_1)\sin(\pi x_2)\sin(\pi x_3) \tag{73}$$

is the analytical solution.

The IEFG method is used to solved it. The wave number is selected as 100, and $19 \times 19 \times 19$ regularly distributed nodes and $18 \times 18 \times 18$ background integral cells are used, $\alpha = 1.9 \times 10^7$, $d_{\max} = 1.1$. When using the EFG method to solve it, the same parameters are selected, and the relative errors of both methods are equal to 0.8646%. Figures 17–19 show the comparison of the numerical solutions and the analytical ones. We can see that numerical solutions are in good agreement with the analytical ones. The CPU times of the IEFG method and the EFG method are 200.6 s and 208.1 s, respectively.

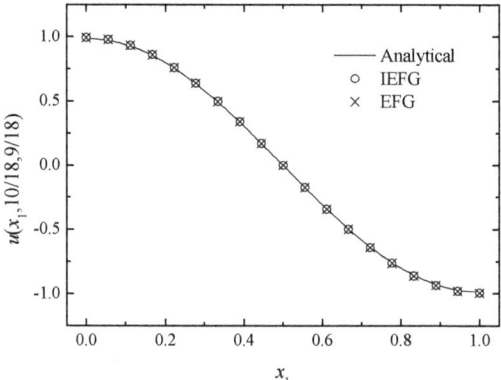

Figure 17. The comparison of the numerical and analytical solutions of the two methods along the x_1-axis.

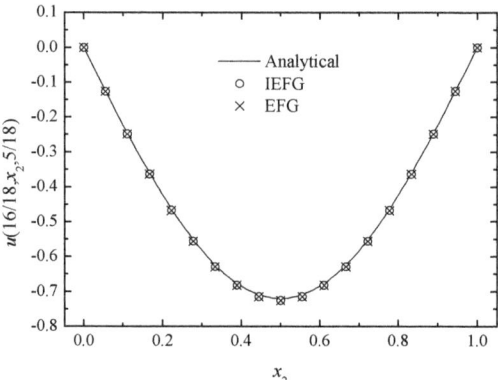

Figure 18. The comparison of the numerical and analytical solutions of the two methods along the x_2-axis.

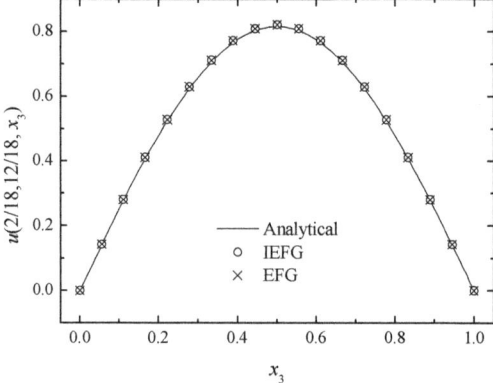

Figure 19. The comparison of the numerical and analytical solutions of the two methods along the x_3-axis.

A similar computational accuracy can be obtained when using the two methods, but the higher computational speed can be obtained when using the IEFG method.

Similarly, if $d_{max} = 1.0$, when the EFG method is used, the singular matrix occurs and the final result cannot be obtained. However, when the IEFG method is selected, the relative error is 0.8648%. The numerical solutions and the analytical one are compared in Figure 20, where it is shown that the numerical results are in good agreement with the analytical ones.

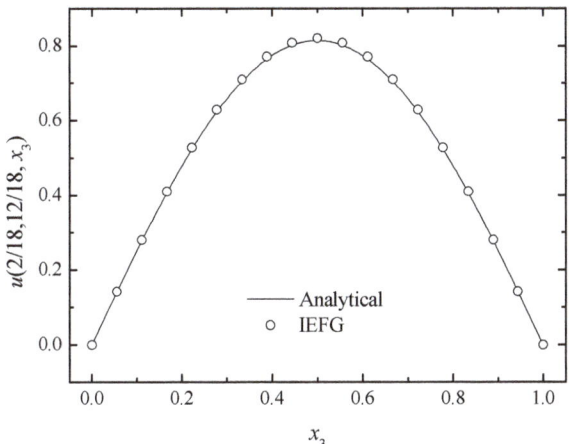

Figure 20. The numerical and analytical solutions of the IEFG method along the x_3-axis.

5. Conclusions

In order to solve 3D Helmholtz equations efficiently, the IEFG method is proposed in this paper.

Some numerical examples are given in Section 4, and the convergence of the IEFG method is proven numerically. From these examples, we can see that the IEFG method in this paper can not only enhance the computational speed of the traditional EFG method, but also eliminate the phenomenon of the singular matrix.

Author Contributions: Conceptualization, M.P.; methodology, M.P.; software, H.C.; writing—original draft preparation, H.C.; writing—review and editing, M.P.; visualization, H.C.; supervision, M.P.; funding acquisition, H.C. All authors have read and agreed to the published version of the manuscript.

Funding: This research was funded by the Science and Technology Innovation Project of Shanxi Colleges and Universities (grant number 2020L0344) and the Scientific Research Foundation of Taiyuan University of Science and Technology (grant number 20202065).

Institutional Review Board Statement: Not applicable.

Informed Consent Statement: Not applicable.

Data Availability Statement: Not applicable.

Conflicts of Interest: The authors declare no conflict of interest.

References

1. Bouillarda, P.H.; Suleaub, S. Element-Free Galerkin solutions for Helmholtz problems: Formulation and numerical assessment of the pollution effect. *Comput. Methods Appl. Mech. Eng.* **1998**, *162*, 317–335. [CrossRef]
2. Zeng, H.; Peng, L.; Zhao, G.; Han, C. A meshless Galerkin least-square method for the Helmholtz equation. *Eng. Anal. Bound. Elem.* **2011**, *35*, 868–878.
3. Miao, Y.; Wang, Y.; Wang, Y.H. A meshless hybrid boundary-node method for Helmholtz problems. *Eng. Anal. Bound. Elem.* **2009**, *33*, 120–127. [CrossRef]

4. Chen, L.C.; Liu, X.; Li, X.L. The boundary element-free method for 2D interior and exterior Helmholtz problems. *Comput. Math. Appl.* **2019**, *77*, 846–864.
5. Li, X.L.; Zhang, S.G.; Wang, Y.; Chen, H. A complex variable boundary element-free method for potential and Helmholtz problems in three dimensions. *Int. J. Comput. Methods* **2020**, *17*, 1850129. [CrossRef]
6. Chen, L.C.; Li, X.L. A complex variable boundary element-free method for the Helmholtz equation using regularized combined field integral equations. *Appl. Math. Lett.* **2020**, *101*, 106067. [CrossRef]
7. Savovic, S.; Djordjevich, A. Numerical solution of diffusion equation describing the flow of radon through concrete. *Appl. Radiat. Isot.* **2008**, *66*, 552–555. [CrossRef] [PubMed]
8. Ashyralyev, A.; Aggez, N. Finite Difference Method for Hyperbolic Equations with the Nonlocal Integral Condition. *Discret. Dyn. Nat. Soc.* **2011**, *2011*, 562385. [CrossRef]
9. Ivanovic, M.; Svicevic, M.; Savovic, S. Numerical solution of Stefan problem with variable space grid method based on mixed finite element/finite difference approach. *Int. J. Numer. Methods Heat Fluid Flow* **2017**, *27*, 2682–2695. [CrossRef]
10. Sowmiya, G.K.; Revathi, M. Numerical Method of Linear Hyperbolic Partial Differential Equation by Finite Difference Method with Conservation Law. *Int. J. Adv. Sci. Technol.* **2020**, *29*, 14–23.
11. Thounthong, P.; Khan, M.N.; Hussain, I.; Ahmad, I.; Kumam, P. Symmetric radial basis function method for simulation of elliptic partial differential equations. *Mathematics* **2018**, *6*, 327. [CrossRef]
12. Ahmad, I.; Ahsan, M.; Din, Z.U.; Ahmad, M.; Kumam, P. An efficient local formulation for time-dependent PDEs. *Mathematics* **2019**, *7*, 216. [CrossRef]
13. Ahmad, I.; Ahmad, H.; Thounthong, P.; Chu, Y.M.; Cesarano, C. Solution of multi-term time-fractional PDE models arising in mathematical biology and physics by local meshless method. *Symmetry* **2020**, *12*, 1195. [CrossRef]
14. Wang, F.Z.; Zheng, K.H.; Ahmad, I.; Ahmad, H. Gaussian radial basis functions method for linear and nonlinear convection-diffusion models in physical phenomena. *Open Phys.* **2021**, *19*, 69–76. [CrossRef]
15. Dai, B.D.; Cheng, Y.M. Local boundary integral equation method based on radial basis functions for potential problems. *Acta Phys. Sin.* **2007**, *56*, 597–603.
16. Belytschko, T.; Lu, Y.Y.; Gu, L. Element-free Galerkin Methods. *Int. J. Numer. Methods Eng.* **1994**, *37*, 229–256. [CrossRef]
17. Cheng, R.J.; Cheng, Y.M. Error estimates of element-free Galerkin method for potential problems. *Acta Phys. Sin.* **2008**, *57*, 6037–6046.
18. Cheng, J. Residential land leasing and price under public land ownership. *J. Urban Plan. Dev.* **2021**, *147*, 05021009. [CrossRef]
19. Cheng, J. Analysis of commercial land leasing of the district governments of Beijing in China. *Land Use Policy* **2021**, *100*, 104881. [CrossRef]
20. Cheng, J. Analyzing the factors influencing the choice of the government on leasing different types of land uses: Evidence from Shanghai of China. *Land Use Policy* **2020**, *90*, 104303. [CrossRef]
21. Cheng, J. Data analysis of the factors influencing the industrial land leasing in Shanghai based on mathematical models. *Math. Probl. Eng.* **2020**, *2020*, 9346863. [CrossRef]
22. Cheng, J. Mathematical models and data analysis of residential land leasing behavior of district governments of Beijing in China. *Mathematics* **2021**, *9*, 2314. [CrossRef]
23. Cheng, Y.M.; Chen, M.J. A boundary element-free method for linear elasticity. *Acta Mech. Sin.* **2003**, *35*, 181–186.
24. Zhang, Z.; Zhao, P.; Liew, K.M. Analyzing three-dimensional potential problems with the improved element-free Galerkin method. *Comput. Mech.* **2009**, *44*, 273–284. [CrossRef]
25. Zhang, Z.; Wang, J.F.; Cheng, Y.M.; Liew, K.M. The improved element-free Galerkin method for three-dimensional transient heat conduction problems. *Sci. China Phys. Mech. Astron.* **2013**, *56*, 1568–1580. [CrossRef]
26. Zhang, Z.; Li, D.M.; Cheng, Y.M.; Liew, K.M. The improved element-free Galerkin method for three-dimensional wave equation. *Acta Mech. Sin.* **2012**, *28*, 808–818. [CrossRef]
27. Cheng, R.J.; Cheng, Y.M. Solving unsteady Schrödinger equation using the improved element-free Galerkin method. *Chin. Phys. B* **2016**, *25*, 020203. [CrossRef]
28. Cheng, H.; Zheng, G.D. Analyzing 3D advection-diffusion problems by using the improved element-free Galerkin method. *Math. Probl. Eng.* **2020**, *2020*, 4317538. [CrossRef]
29. Zhang, Z.; Hao, S.Y.; Liew, K.M.; Cheng, Y.M. The improved element-free Galerkin method for two-dimensional elastodynamics problems. *Eng. Anal. Bound. Elem.* **2013**, *37*, 1576–1584. [CrossRef]
30. Yu, S.Y.; Peng, M.J.; Cheng, H.; Cheng, Y.M. The improved element-free Galerkin method for three-dimensional elastoplasticity problems. *Eng. Anal. Bound. Elem.* **2019**, *104*, 215–224. [CrossRef]
31. Peng, M.J.; Li, R.X.; Cheng, Y.M. Analyzing three-dimensional viscoelasticity problems via the improved element-free Galerkin (IEFG) method. *Eng. Anal. Bound. Elem.* **2014**, *40*, 104–113. [CrossRef]
32. Zheng, G.D.; Cheng, Y.M. The improved element-free Galerkin method for diffusional drug release problems. *Int. J. Appl. Mech.* **2020**, *12*, 2050096. [CrossRef]
33. Zhang, Z.; Liew, K.M.; Cheng, Y.M.; Lee, Y.Y. Analyzing 2D fracture problems with the improved element-free Galerkin method. *Eng. Anal. Bound. Elem.* **2008**, *32*, 241–250. [CrossRef]
34. Cai, X.J.; Peng, M.J.; Cheng, Y.M. The improved element-free Galerkin method for elastoplasticity large deformation problems. *Sci. Sin. Phys. Mech. Astron.* **2018**, *48*, 024701. [CrossRef]

35. Lancaster, P.; Salkauskas, K. Surfaces generated by moving least squares methods. *Math. Comput.* **1981**, *37*, 141–158. [CrossRef]
36. Ren, H.P.; Cheng, Y.M.; Zhang, W. Researches on the improved interpolating moving least-squares method. *Chin. J. Eng. Math.* **2010**, *27*, 1021–1029.
37. Ren, H.P.; Cheng, Y.M. The interpolating element-free Galerkin (IEFG) method for two-dimensional potential problems. *Eng. Anal. Bound. Elem.* **2012**, *36*, 873–880. [CrossRef]
38. Liu, D.; Cheng, Y.M. The interpolating element-free Galerkin method for three-dimensional transient heat conduction problems. *Results Phys.* **2020**, *19*, 103477. [CrossRef]
39. Wu, Q.; Liu, F.B.; Cheng, Y.M. The interpolating element-free Galerkin method for three-dimensional elastoplasticity problems. *Eng. Anal. Bound. Elem.* **2020**, *115*, 156–167. [CrossRef]
40. Wu, Q.; Peng, P.P.; Cheng, Y.M. The interpolating element-free Galerkin method for elastic large deformation problems. *Sci. China Technol. Sci.* **2021**, *64*, 364–374. [CrossRef]
41. Cheng, Y.M.; Bai, F.N.; Liu, C.; Peng, M.J. Analyzing nonlinear large deformation with an improved element-free Galerkin method via the interpolating moving least-squares method. *Int. J. Comput. Mater. Sci. Eng.* **2016**, *5*, 1650023.
42. Qin, Y.X.; Li, Q.Y.; Du, H.X. Interpolating smoothed particle method for elastic axisymmetrical problem. *Int. J. Appl. Mech.* **2017**, *9*, 1750022. [CrossRef]
43. Wang, J.F.; Sun, F.X.; Cheng, Y.M. An improved interpolating element-free Galerkin method with nonsingular weight function for two-dimensional potential problems. *Chin. Phys. B* **2012**, *21*, 090204. [CrossRef]
44. Liu, F.B.; Cheng, Y.M. The improved element-free Galerkin method based on the nonsingular weight functions for elastic large deformation problems. *Int. J. Comput. Mater. Sci. Eng.* **2018**, *7*, 1850023. [CrossRef]
45. Liu, F.B.; Wu, Q.; Cheng, Y.M. A meshless method based on the nonsingular weight functions for elastoplastic large deformation problems. *Int. J. Appl. Mech.* **2019**, *11*, 1950006. [CrossRef]
46. Liu, F.B.; Cheng, Y.M. The improved element-free Galerkin method based on the nonsingular weight functions for inhomogeneous swelling of polymer gels. *Int. J. Appl. Mech.* **2018**, *10*, 1850047. [CrossRef]
47. Cheng, Y.M.; Peng, M.J.; Li, J.H. The complex variable moving least-square approximation and its application. *Acta Mech. Sin.* **2005**, *37*, 719–723.
48. Peng, M.J.; Liu, P.; Cheng, Y.M. The complex variable element-free Galerkin (CVEFG) method for two-dimensional elasticity problems. *Int. J. Appl. Mech.* **2009**, *1*, 367–385. [CrossRef]
49. Bai, F.N.; Li, D.M.; Wang, J.F.; Cheng, Y.M. An improved complex variable element-free Galerkin method for two-dimensional elasticity problems. *Chin. Phys. B* **2012**, *21*, 020204. [CrossRef]
50. Chen, L.; Cheng, Y.M. Reproducing kernel particle method with complex variables for elasticity. *Acta Phys. Sin.* **2008**, *57*, 1–10. [CrossRef]
51. Chen, L.; Cheng, Y.M. The complex variable reproducing kernel particle method for elasto-plasticity problems. *Sci. China Phys. Mech. Astron.* **2010**, *53*, 954–965. [CrossRef]
52. Cheng, H.; Peng, M.J.; Cheng, Y.M. The dimension splitting and improved complex variable element-free Galerkin method for 3-dimensional transient heat conduction problems. *Int. J. Numer. Methods Eng.* **2018**, *114*, 321–345. [CrossRef]
53. Cheng, H.; Peng, M.J.; Cheng, Y.M. A hybrid improved complex variable element-free Galerkin method for three-dimensional potential problems. *Eng. Anal. Bound. Elem.* **2017**, *84*, 52–62. [CrossRef]
54. Cheng, H.; Peng, M.J.; Cheng, Y.M. A fast complex variable element-free Galerkin method for three-dimensional wave propagation problems. *Int. J. Appl. Mech.* **2017**, *9*, 1750090. [CrossRef]
55. Cheng, H.; Peng, M.J.; Cheng, Y.M. A hybrid improved complex variable element-free Galerkin method for three-dimensional advection-diffusion problems. *Eng. Anal. Bound. Elem.* **2018**, *97*, 39–54. [CrossRef]
56. Cheng, H.; Peng, M.J.; Cheng, Y.M.; Meng, Z.J. The hybrid complex variable element-free Galerkin method for 3D elasticity problems. *Eng. Struct.* **2020**, *219*, 110835. [CrossRef]
57. Meng, Z.J.; Cheng, H.; Ma, L.D.; Cheng, Y.M. The dimension split element-free Galerkin method for three-dimensional potential problems. *Acta Mech. Sin.* **2018**, *34*, 462–474. [CrossRef]
58. Meng, Z.J.; Cheng, H.; Ma, L.D.; Cheng, Y.M. The dimension splitting element-free Galerkin method for 3D transient heat conduction problems. *Sci. China Phys. Mech. Astron.* **2019**, *62*, 040711. [CrossRef]
59. Meng, Z.J.; Cheng, H.; Ma, L.D.; Cheng, Y.M. The hybrid element-free Galerkin method for three-dimensional wave propagation problems. *Int. J. Numer. Methods Eng.* **2019**, *117*, 15–37. [CrossRef]
60. Ma, L.D.; Meng, Z.J.; Chai, J.F.; Cheng, Y.M. Analyzing 3D advection-diffusion problems by using the dimension splitting element-free Galerkin method. *Eng. Anal. Bound. Elem.* **2020**, *111*, 167–177. [CrossRef]
61. Peng, P.P.; Wu, Q.; Cheng, Y.M. The dimension splitting reproducing kernel particle method for three-dimensional potential problems. *Int. J. Numer. Methods Eng.* **2020**, *121*, 146–164. [CrossRef]
62. Peng, P.P.; Cheng, Y.M. Analyzing three-dimensional transient heat conduction problems with the dimension splitting reproducing kernel particle method. *Eng. Anal. Bound. Elem.* **2020**, *121*, 180–191. [CrossRef]
63. Peng, P.P.; Cheng, Y.M. Analyzing three-dimensional wave propagation with the hybrid reproducing kernel particle method based on the dimension splitting method. *Eng. Comput.* **2021**, 1–17. [CrossRef]
64. Peng, P.P.; Cheng, Y.M. A hybrid reproducing kernel particle method for three-dimensional advection-diffusion problems. *Int. J. Appl. Mech.* **2021**, *13*, 2150085. [CrossRef]

65. Wu, Q.; Peng, M.J.; Cheng, Y.M. The interpolating dimension splitting element-free Galerkin method for 3D potential problems. *Eng. Comput.* **2021**, 1–15. [CrossRef]
66. Wang, J.F.; Sun, F.X. A hybrid generalized interpolated element-free Galerkin method for Stokes problems. *Eng. Anal. Bound. Elem.* **2020**, *111*, 88–100. [CrossRef]
67. Marin, L. A meshless method for the numerical solution of the Cauchy problem associated with three-dimensional Helmholtz-type equations. *Appl. Math. Comput.* **2005**, *165*, 274–355. [CrossRef]
68. Cheng, D.S.; Chen, B.W.; Chen, X.L. A robust optimal finite difference scheme for the three-dimensional Helmholtz equation. *Math. Probl. Eng.* **2019**, *2019*, 8532408. [CrossRef]

MDPI
St. Alban-Anlage 66
4052 Basel
Switzerland
Tel. +41 61 683 77 34
Fax +41 61 302 89 18
www.mdpi.com

Mathematics Editorial Office
E-mail: mathematics@mdpi.com
www.mdpi.com/journal/mathematics

www.ingramcontent.com/pod-product-compliance
Lightning Source LLC
LaVergne TN
LVHW070505100526
838202LV00014B/1793